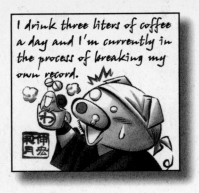

I drink three liters of coffee a day and I'm currently in the process of breaking my own record.

Concerning the four bonus pages in the comic book…
 "I can't believe you revealed the heroine's measurements. I'm disappointed." "Well done, Watsuki! Good job!" It's interesting to hear opinions that are the complete opposite. The bonus pages are my way of thanking the people who bought the manga. They sometimes contain spoilers, so after you've read the manga, please check them out when you have the time.
   —**Nobuhiro Watsuki**

Nobuhiro Watsuki earned international accolades for his first major manga series, **Rurouni Kenshin**, about a wandering swordsman in Meiji Era Japan. Serialized in Japan's *Weekly Shonen Jump* from 1994 to 1999, **Rurouni Kenshin**, available in North America from VIZ Media, quickly became a worldwide sensation, inspiring a spin-off short story ("Yahiko no Sakabatô"), an animated TV show and a series of novels. Watsuki's latest hit, **Buso Renkin**, began publication in *Weekly Shonen Jump* in June 2003.

BUSO RENKIN
VOL. 2
The SHONEN JUMP ADVANCED
Manga Edition

STORY AND ART BY
NOBUHIRO WATSUKI

Translation and English Adaptation/Mayumi Kobayashi
Touch-up Art & Lettering/James Gaubatz
Design/Yukiko Whitley
Editor/Urian Brown

Managing Editor/Frances E. Wall
Editorial Director/Elizabeth Kawasaki
VP & Editor in Chief/Yumi Hoashi
Sr. Director of Acquisitions/Rika Inouye
Sr. VP of Marketing/Liza Coppola
Exec. VP of Sales & Marketing/John Easum
Publisher/Hyoe Narita

Printed in the U.S.A.

Published by VIZ Media, LLC
P.O. Box 77010
San Francisco, CA 94107

SHONEN JUMP ADVANCED Manga Edition
10 9 8 7 6 5 4 3 2
First printing, October 2006
Second printing, October 2006

THE WORLD'S MOST
CUTTING-EDGE MANGA

SHONEN JUMP
ADVANCED
www.shonenjump.com

VIZ
MEDIA
www.viz.com

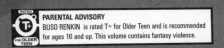

RATED
T+
FOR OLDER
TEEN

PARENTAL ADVISORY
BUSO RENKIN is rated T+ for Older Teen and is recommended
for ages 16 and up. This volume contains fantasy violence.

SHONEN JUMP ADVANCED MANGA EDITION

Buso Renkin™

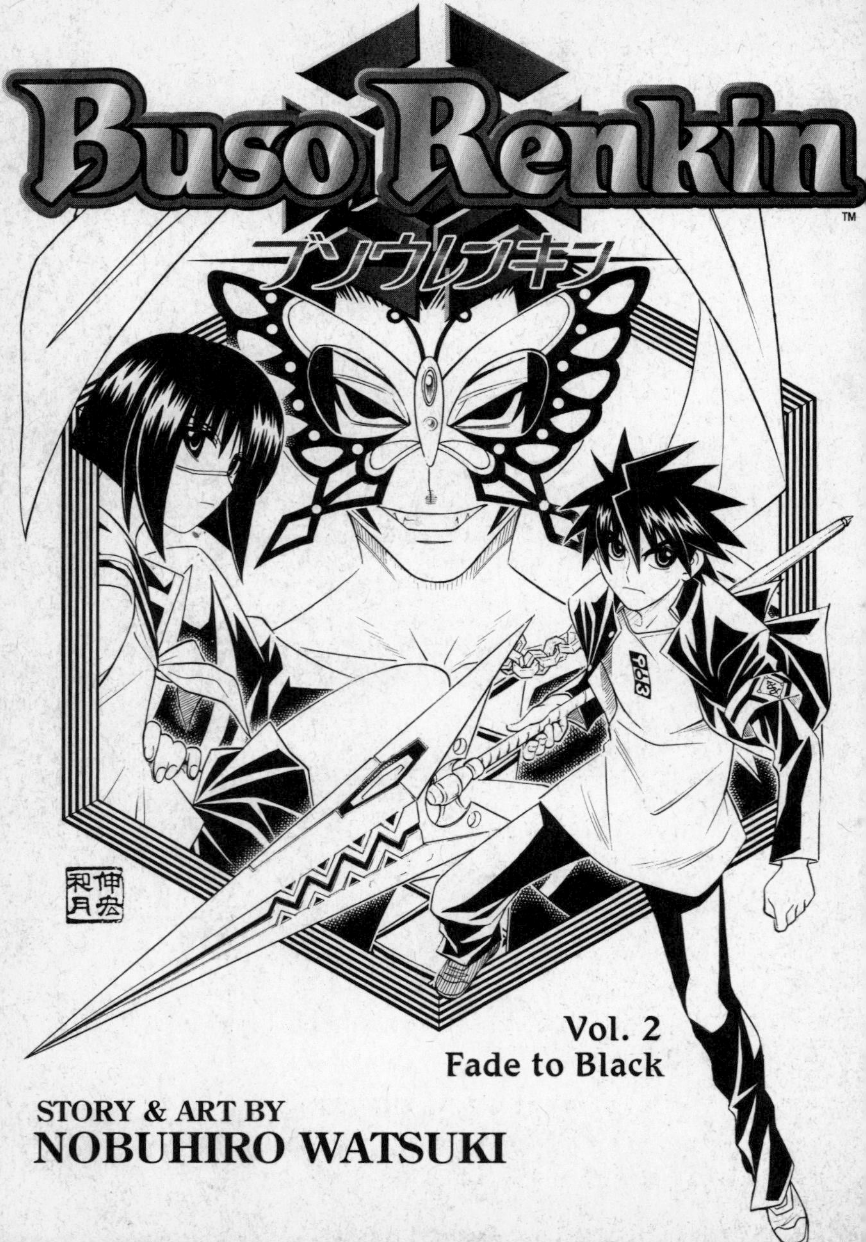
ブソウレンキン
伸宏
和月

Vol. 2
Fade to Black

STORY & ART BY
NOBUHIRO WATSUKI

Alchemy: An early scientific practice that that swept through all of Europe, and combines elements of various disciplines. Such studies were based on the transmutation of base metals into gold, and the preparation of the Elixir of Immortality, none of which succeeded. However, unknown to the public, two alchemic studies achieved success of super-paranormal proportions—the Homunculus and Kakugane.

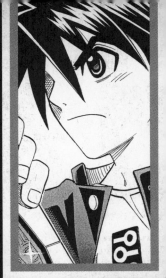

CHARACTE

Kakugane: A super-paranormal alloy that uses the most advanced alchemic technology. It is activated by one's survival instincts, the deepest part of the human psyche. It can heighten one's ability to heal, and can also become a one-of-a-kind weapon by materializing the wielder's fighting instincts. The weapon is called the Buso Renkin; each differs in shape and function.

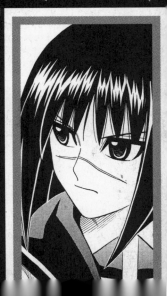

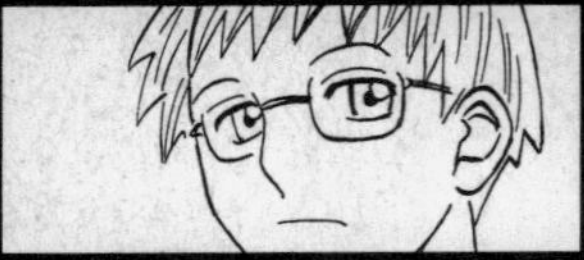
Kouji Rokumasu

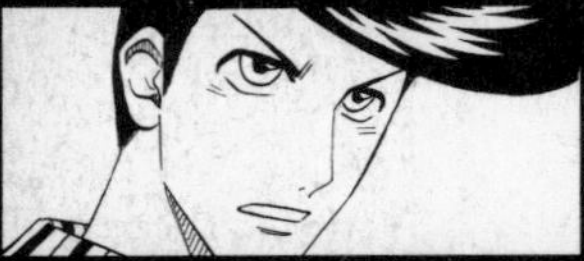
Hideyuki Okakura

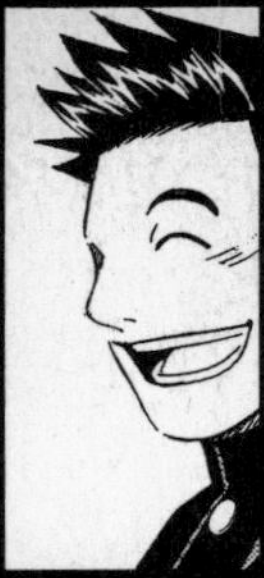
Masashi Daihama

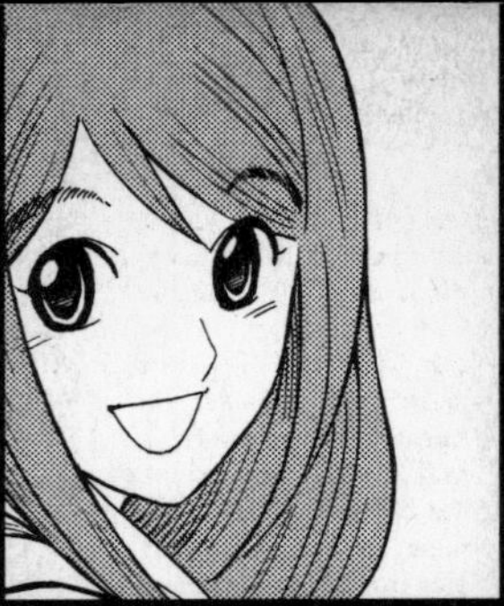
Mahiro Muto

S T O R Y

Alchemist Warrior Tokiko used herself as bait to lure out a man-eating Homunculus when Kazuki Muto, an unsuspecting high school student, tried to save her—and was killed. But Kazuki received a new lease on life when Tokiko gave him the "Kakugane," which was activated by his fighting instincts, and formed a new Buso Renkin, which he used to vanquish the Homunculus! Thus, a new Homunculus-busting team was formed...

A new threat emerges when Papillon Mask, the Creator of the Homunculus, attacks Tokiko with a Homunculus core that turns humans into Homunculi. Although Tokiko manages to prevent the core from entering her brain, it lodges itself within her stomach. The only way she can be saved is to capture the Creator, who can make an antidote, within a week. After discovering that the Creator is a third-year student at Kazuki's Ginsei Academy, the hunt is on! On the fourth day of their search, Kazuki is challenged by a Homunculus named Kawazui, and agrees to a one-on-one battle in order to protect a weakened Tokiko. During the battle, Kazuki realizes a new power of his Buso Renkin—the cloth on the end of it turns into energy when it resonates with his will to fight. Cornering Kawazui, Kazuki tries to find out where the Creator is, but just before getting the information, collapses from exhaustion. He awakens to find a concerned Tokiko by his side ...

The Papillon Mask Creator

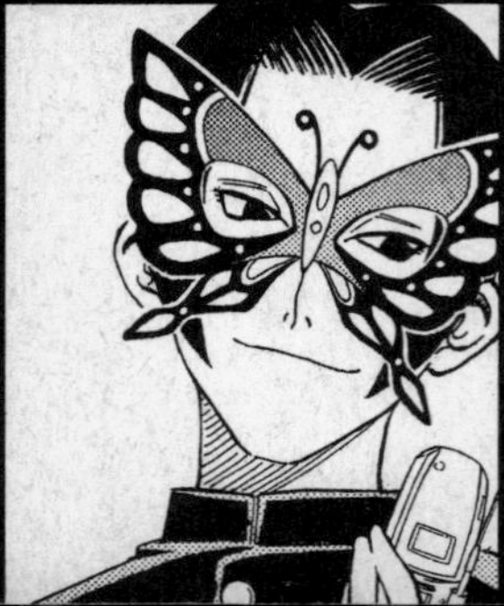

Homunculus

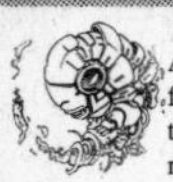
An artificial life form created though alchemic research. Once the Homunculus core created from an organism's cell lodges itself in the human brain, it will take control of the host's body. The core alters the compounds of the body, which takes on physical attributes of the original organism. A Homunculus can only be destroyed by the power of alchemy.

Homunculus Washio

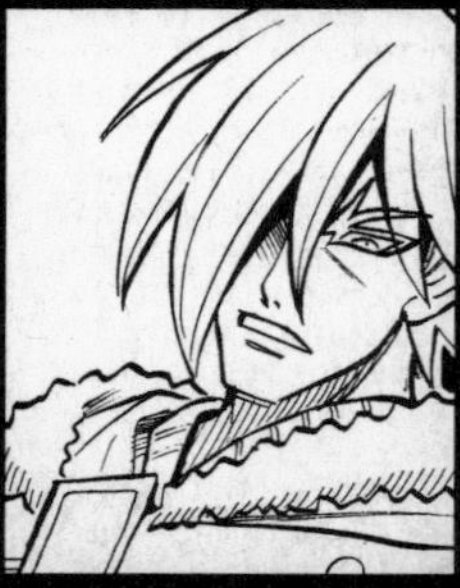

BUSO RENKIN
Volume 2: Fade to Black

CONTENTS

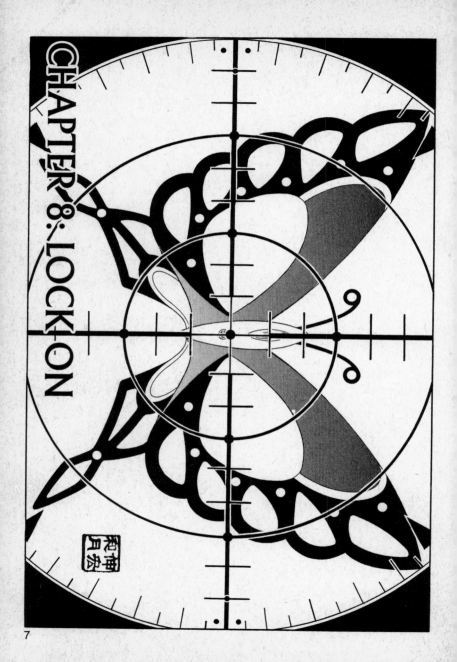

CHAPTER 8: LOCK-ON

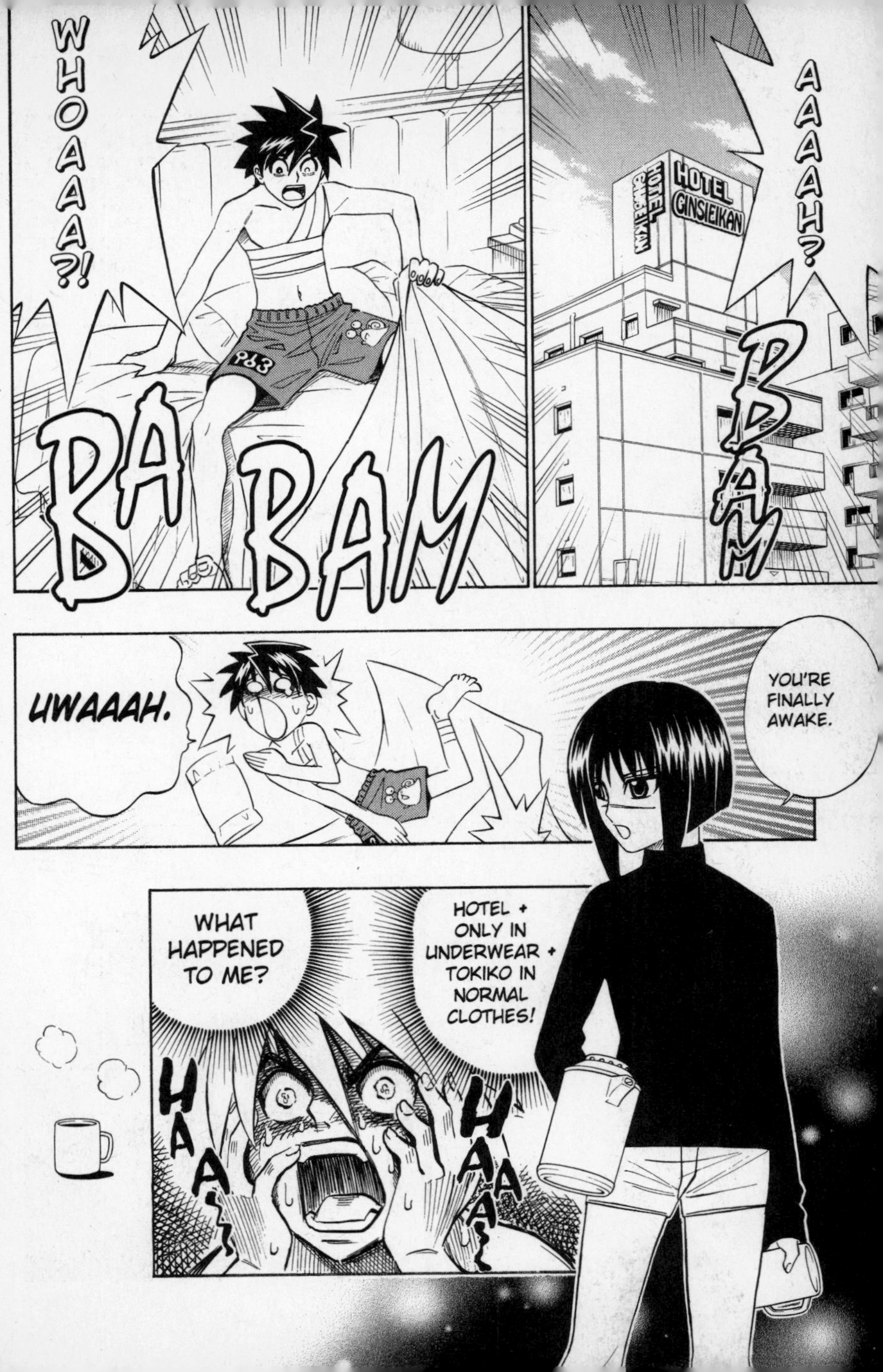

HOTEL GINSIEIKAN
AAAAAH?
BAM
WHOAAAA?!
BA BAM
YOU'RE FINALLY AWAKE.
UWAAAH.
HOTEL + ONLY IN UNDERWEAR + TOKIKO IN NORMAL CLOTHES!
WHAT HAPPENED TO ME?
HAAA
HAAA

READ THIS WAY

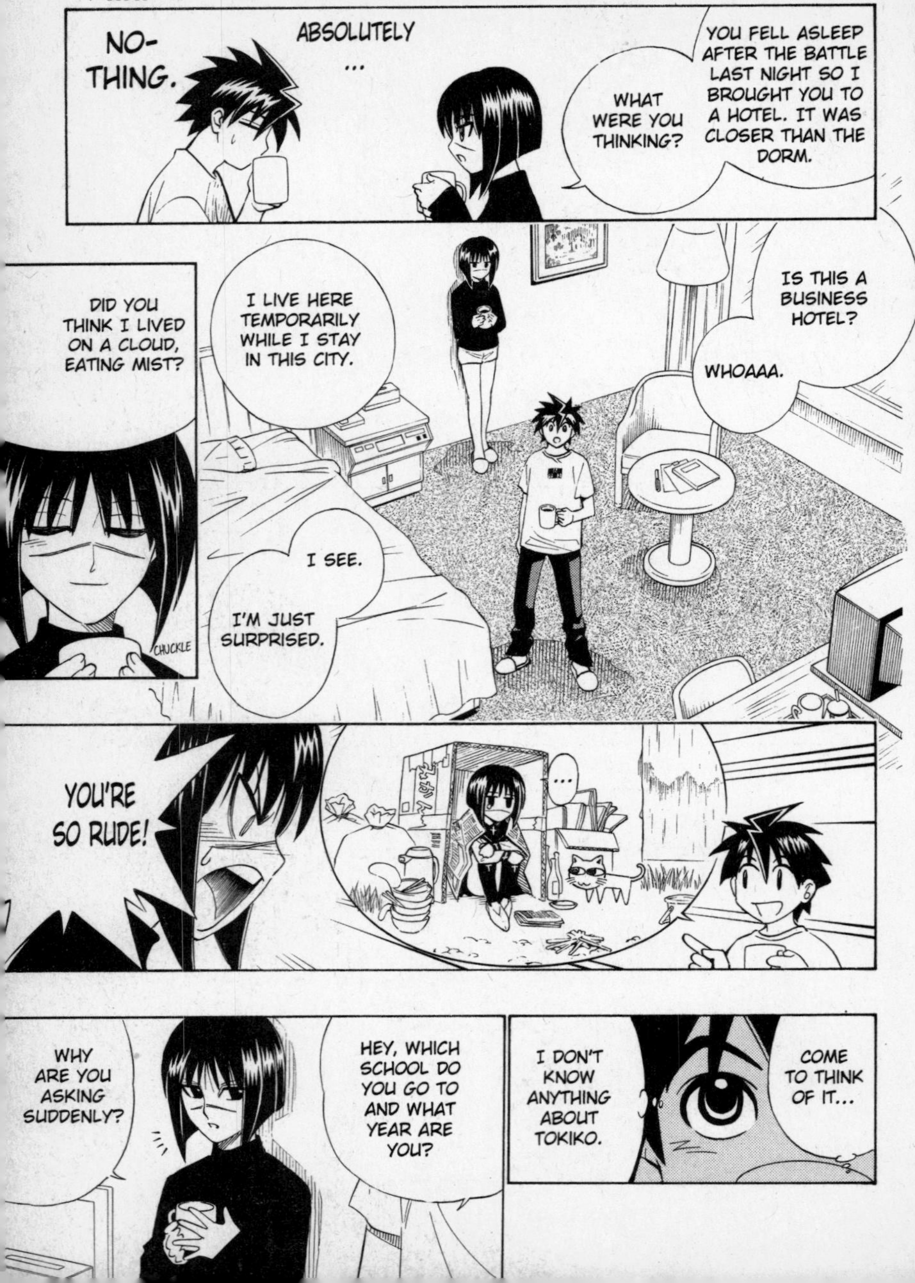
YOU FELL ASLEEP AFTER THE BATTLE LAST NIGHT SO I BROUGHT YOU TO A HOTEL. IT WAS CLOSER THAN THE DORM.
WHAT WERE YOU THINKING?
ABSOLUTELY ...
NO-THING.
IS THIS A BUSINESS HOTEL?
WHOAAA.
I LIVE HERE TEMPORARILY WHILE I STAY IN THIS CITY.
I SEE.
I'M JUST SURPRISED.
DID YOU THINK I LIVED ON A CLOUD, EATING MIST?
CHUCKLE
...
YOU'RE SO RUDE!
COME TO THINK OF IT...
I DON'T KNOW ANYTHING ABOUT TOKIKO.
HEY, WHICH SCHOOL DO YOU GO TO AND WHAT YEAR ARE YOU?
WHY ARE YOU ASKING SUDDENLY?

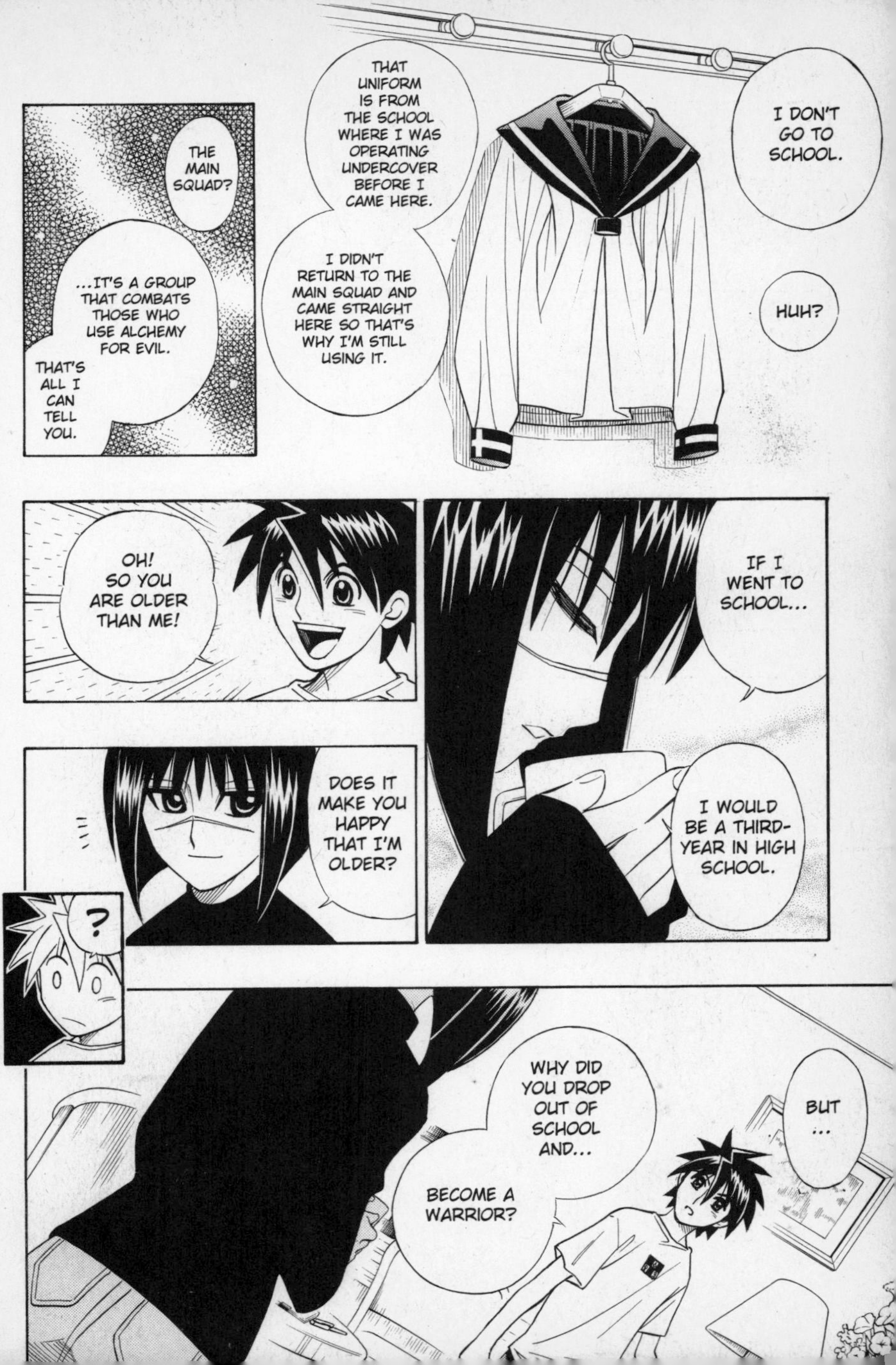
I DON'T GO TO SCHOOL.
HUH?
THAT UNIFORM IS FROM THE SCHOOL WHERE I WAS OPERATING UNDERCOVER BEFORE I CAME HERE.
I DIDN'T RETURN TO THE MAIN SQUAD AND CAME STRAIGHT HERE SO THAT'S WHY I'M STILL USING IT.
THE MAIN SQUAD?
...IT'S A GROUP THAT COMBATS THOSE WHO USE ALCHEMY FOR EVIL.
THAT'S ALL I CAN TELL YOU.
IF I WENT TO SCHOOL...
I WOULD BE A THIRD-YEAR IN HIGH SCHOOL.
OH! SO YOU ARE OLDER THAN ME!
DOES IT MAKE YOU HAPPY THAT I'M OLDER?
?
BUT...
WHY DID YOU DROP OUT OF SCHOOL AND...
BECOME A WARRIOR?

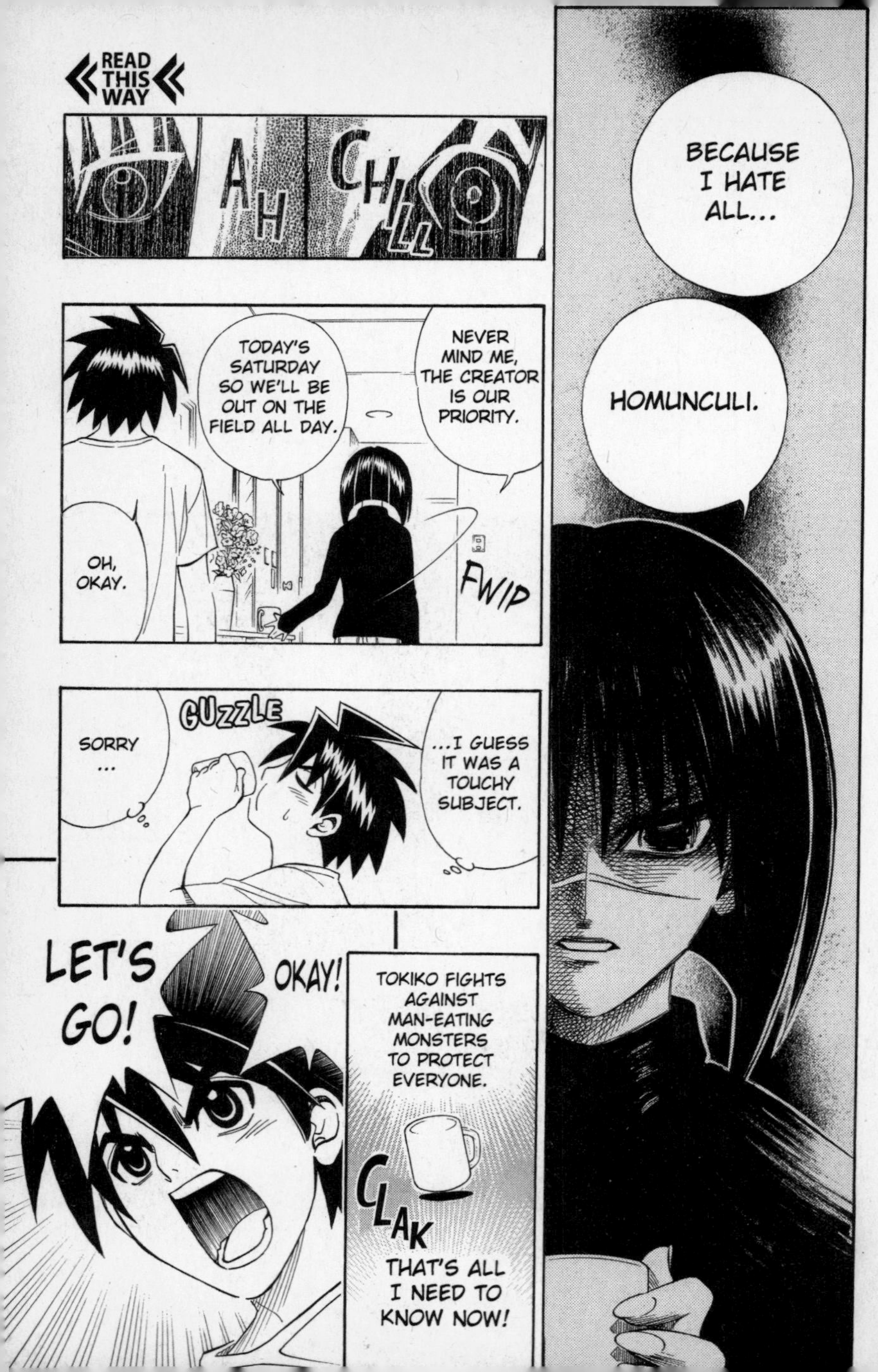
READ THIS WAY
BECAUSE I HATE ALL...
HOMUNCULI.
CHLL
AH
NEVER MIND ME, THE CREATOR IS OUR PRIORITY.
FWIP
TODAY'S SATURDAY SO WE'LL BE OUT ON THE FIELD ALL DAY.
OH, OKAY.
...I GUESS IT WAS A TOUCHY SUBJECT.
GUZZLE
SORRY...
TOKIKO FIGHTS AGAINST MAN-EATING MONSTERS TO PROTECT EVERYONE.
CLAK
THAT'S ALL I NEED TO KNOW NOW!
LET'S GO!
OKAY!

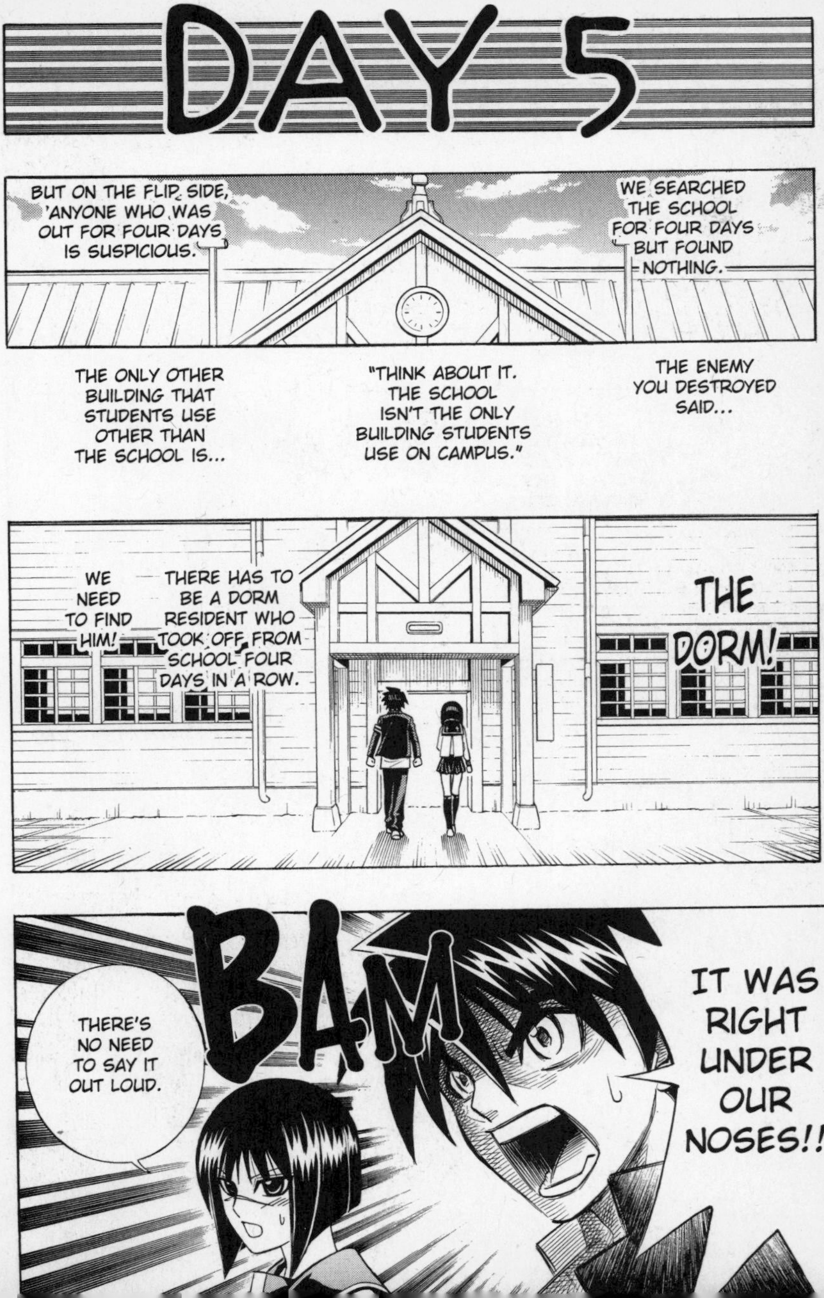
DAY 5
WE SEARCHED THE SCHOOL FOR FOUR DAYS BUT FOUND NOTHING.
BUT ON THE FLIP SIDE, ANYONE WHO WAS OUT FOR FOUR DAYS IS SUSPICIOUS.
THE ENEMY YOU DESTROYED SAID...
"THINK ABOUT IT. THE SCHOOL ISN'T THE ONLY BUILDING STUDENTS USE ON CAMPUS."
THE ONLY OTHER BUILDING THAT STUDENTS USE OTHER THAN THE SCHOOL IS...
THE DORM!
THERE HAS TO BE A DORM RESIDENT WHO TOOK OFF FROM SCHOOL FOUR DAYS IN A ROW.
WE NEED TO FIND HIM!
IT WAS RIGHT UNDER OUR NOSES!!
BAM
THERE'S NO NEED TO SAY IT OUT LOUD.

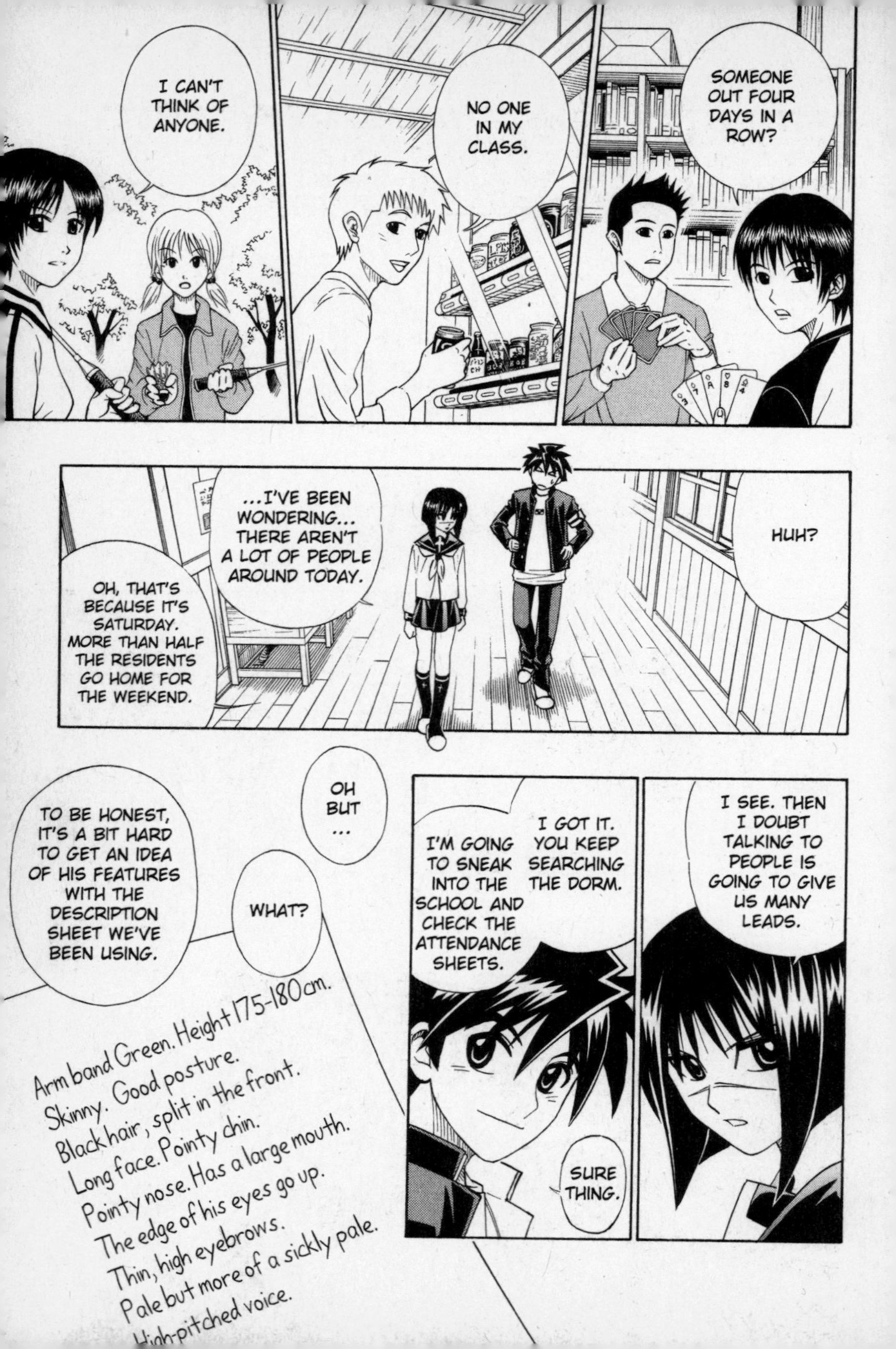
SOMEONE OUT FOUR DAYS IN A ROW?
NO ONE IN MY CLASS.
I CAN'T THINK OF ANYONE.
HUH?
...I'VE BEEN WONDERING... THERE AREN'T A LOT OF PEOPLE AROUND TODAY.
OH, THAT'S BECAUSE IT'S SATURDAY. MORE THAN HALF THE RESIDENTS GO HOME FOR THE WEEKEND.
I SEE. THEN I DOUBT TALKING TO PEOPLE IS GOING TO GIVE US MANY LEADS.
I GOT IT. YOU KEEP SEARCHING THE DORM.
I'M GOING TO SNEAK INTO THE SCHOOL AND CHECK THE ATTENDANCE SHEETS.
SURE THING.
OH BUT ...
WHAT?
TO BE HONEST, IT'S A BIT HARD TO GET AN IDEA OF HIS FEATURES WITH THE DESCRIPTION SHEET WE'VE BEEN USING.
Arm band Green. Height 175-180cm.
Skinny. Good posture.
Black hair, split in the front.
Long face. Pointy chin.
Pointy nose. Has a large mouth.
The edge of his eyes go up.
Thin, high eyebrows.
Pale but more of a sickly pale.
High-pitched voice.

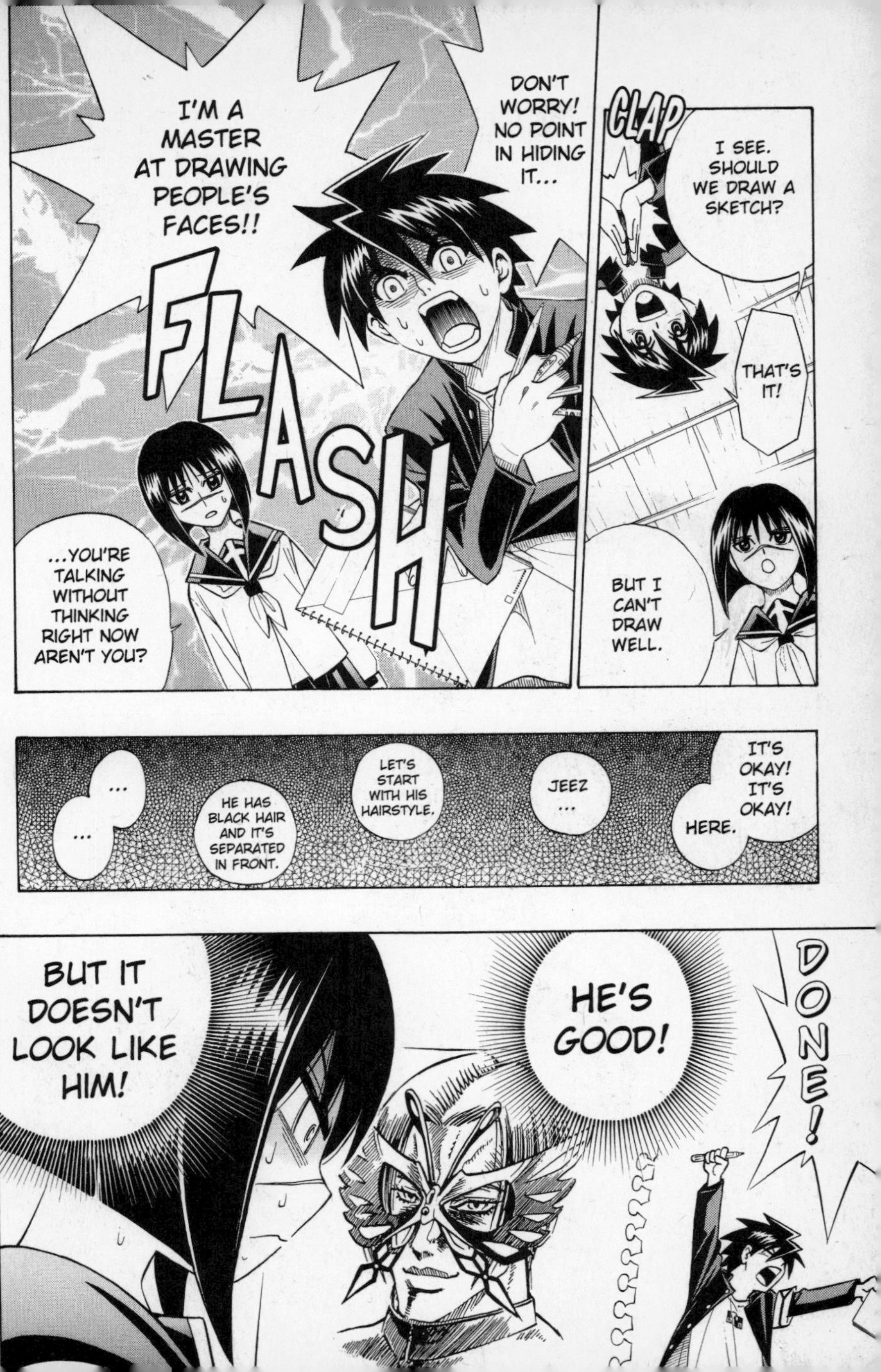
CLAP
I SEE. SHOULD WE DRAW A SKETCH?
THAT'S IT!
BUT I CAN'T DRAW WELL.
DON'T WORRY! NO POINT IN HIDING IT...
I'M A MASTER AT DRAWING PEOPLE'S FACES!!
FLASH
...YOU'RE TALKING WITHOUT THINKING RIGHT NOW AREN'T YOU?
IT'S OKAY! IT'S OKAY!
HERE.
JEEZ ...
LET'S START WITH HIS HAIRSTYLE.
HE HAS BLACK HAIR AND IT'S SEPARATED IN FRONT.
...
...
DONE!
HE'S GOOD!
BUT IT DOESN'T LOOK LIKE HIM!

READ THIS WAY

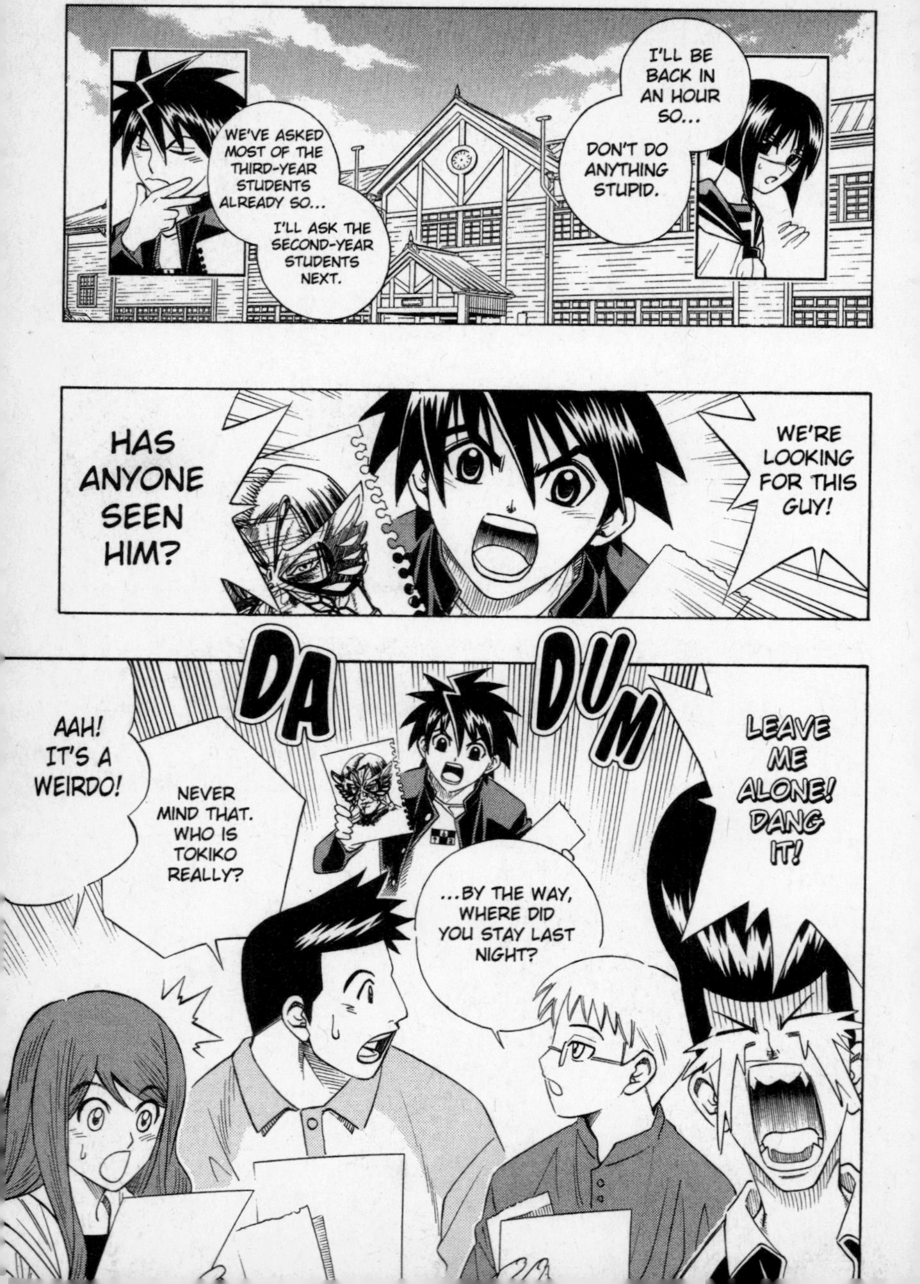
I'LL BE BACK IN AN HOUR SO...
DON'T DO ANYTHING STUPID.
WE'VE ASKED MOST OF THE THIRD-YEAR STUDENTS ALREADY SO...
I'LL ASK THE SECOND-YEAR STUDENTS NEXT.
WE'RE LOOKING FOR THIS GUY!
HAS ANYONE SEEN HIM?
DA DUM
LEAVE ME ALONE! DANG IT!
...BY THE WAY, WHERE DID YOU STAY LAST NIGHT?
NEVER MIND THAT. WHO IS TOKIKO REALLY?
AAH! IT'S A WEIRDO!

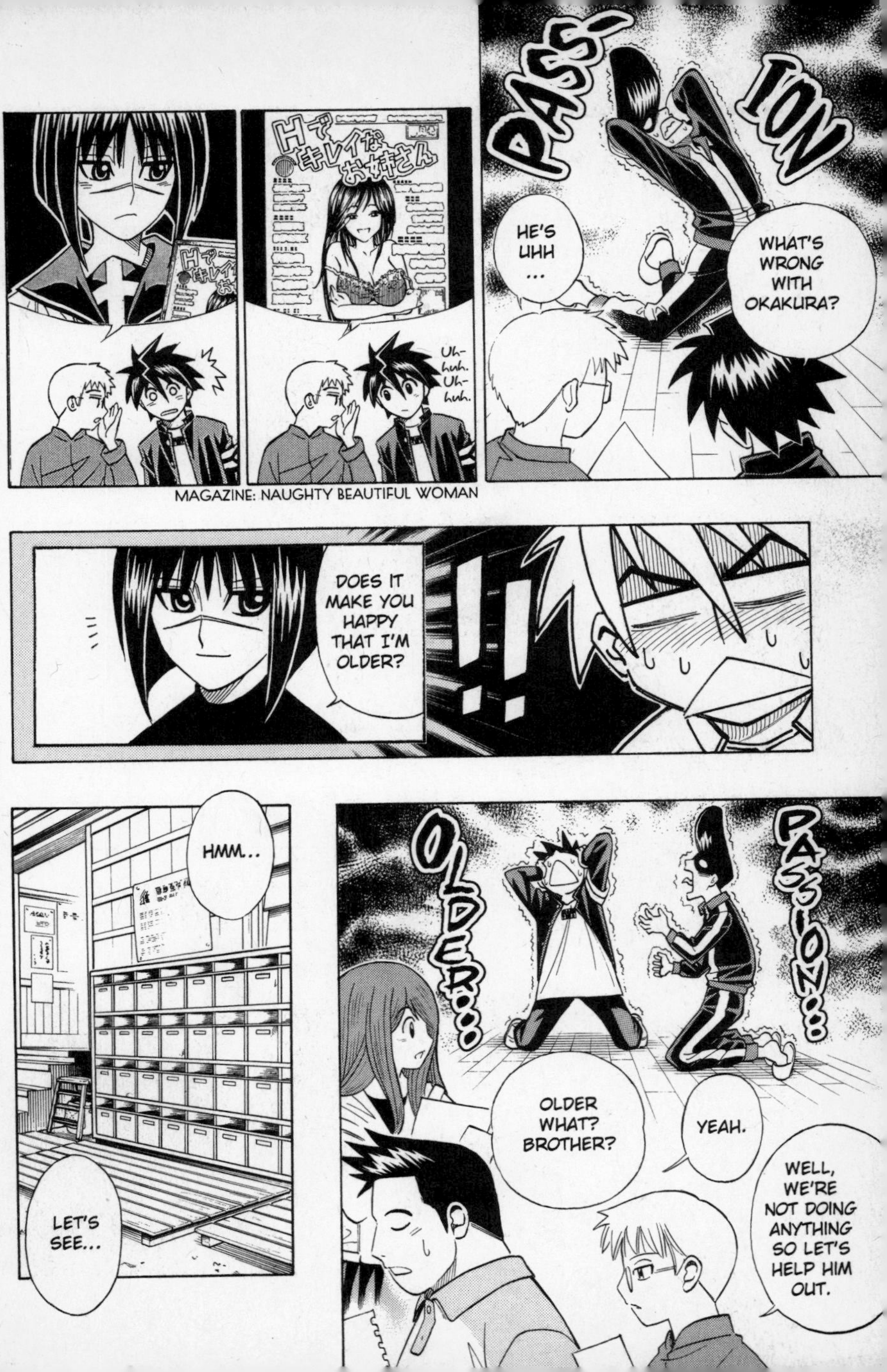
PASS-
ION
WHAT'S WRONG WITH OKAKURA?
HE'S UHH ...
Hでキレイなお姉さん
Uh-huh. Uh-huh.
Hで キレイ
MAGAZINE: NAUGHTY BEAUTIFUL WOMAN
DOES IT MAKE YOU HAPPY THAT I'M OLDER?
!!
PASSION...
OLDER...
OLDER WHAT? BROTHER?
YEAH.
WELL, WE'RE NOT DOING ANYTHING SO LET'S HELP HIM OUT.
HMM...
LET'S SEE...

READ THIS WAY

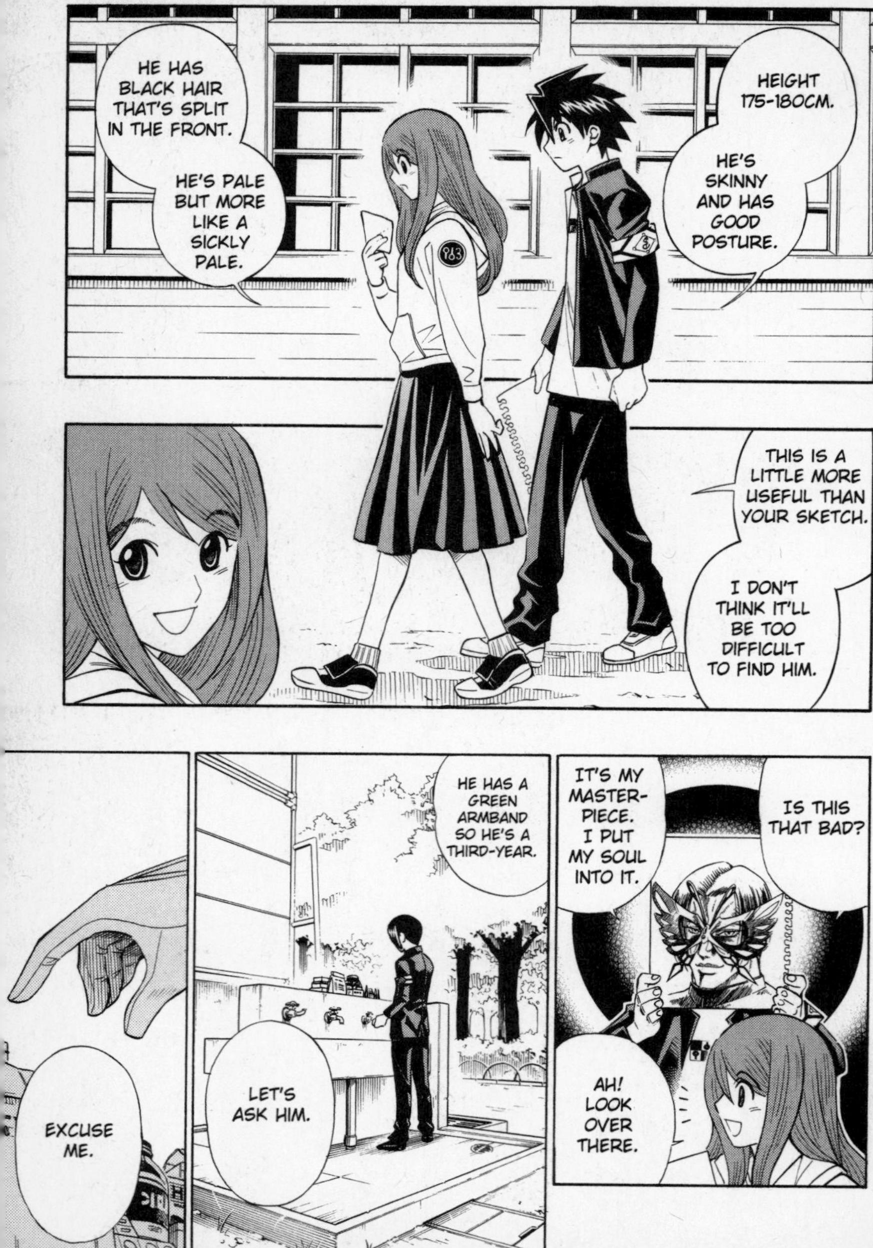
HEIGHT 175-180CM.
HE'S SKINNY AND HAS GOOD POSTURE.
HE HAS BLACK HAIR THAT'S SPLIT IN THE FRONT.
HE'S PALE BUT MORE LIKE A SICKLY PALE.
THIS IS A LITTLE MORE USEFUL THAN YOUR SKETCH.
I DON'T THINK IT'LL BE TOO DIFFICULT TO FIND HIM.
IS THIS THAT BAD?
IT'S MY MASTER-PIECE. I PUT MY SOUL INTO IT.
AH! LOOK OVER THERE.
HE HAS A GREEN ARMBAND SO HE'S A THIRD-YEAR.
LET'S ASK HIM.
EXCUSE ME.

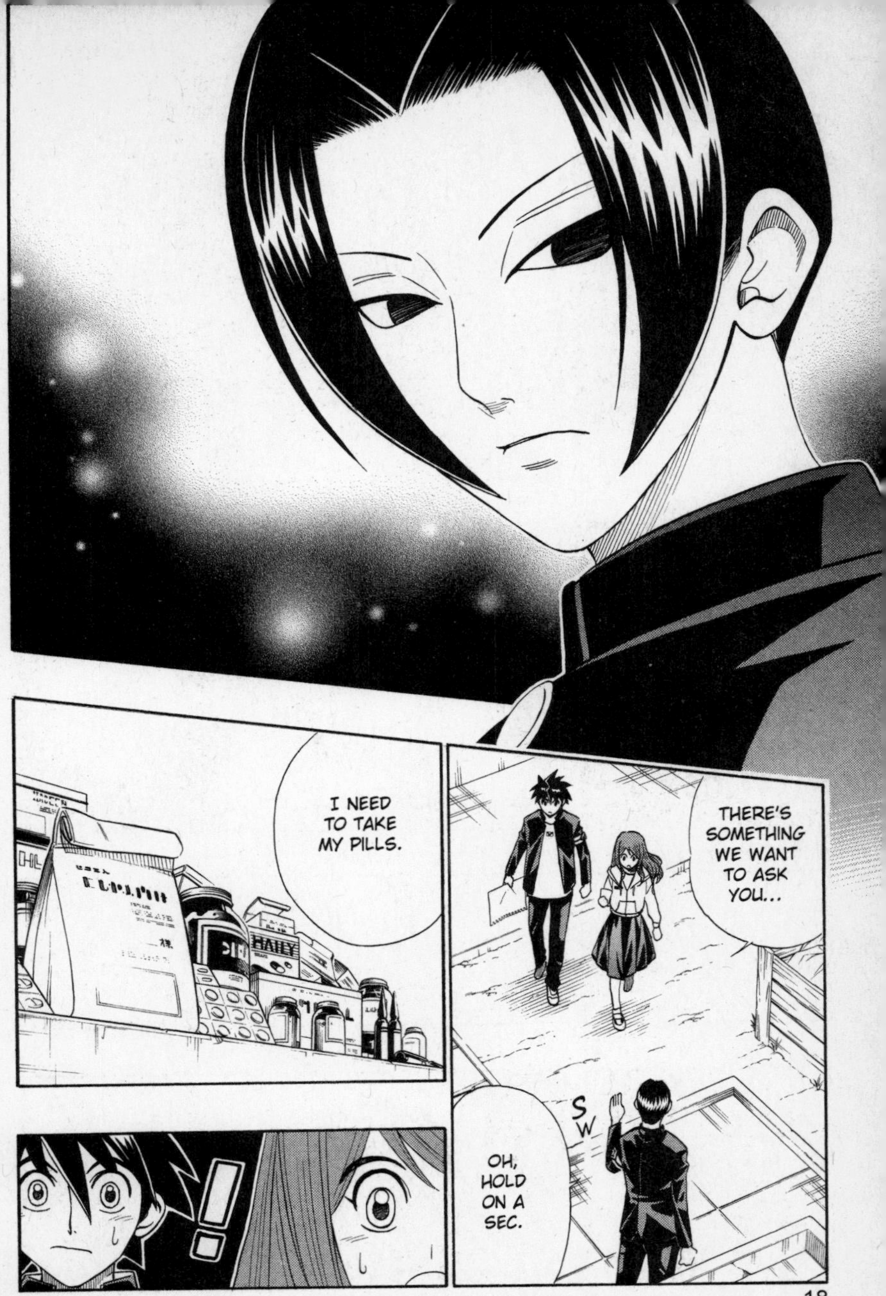
THERE'S SOMETHING WE WANT TO ASK YOU...
SW
OH, HOLD ON A SEC.
I NEED TO TAKE MY PILLS.
HAILY
!

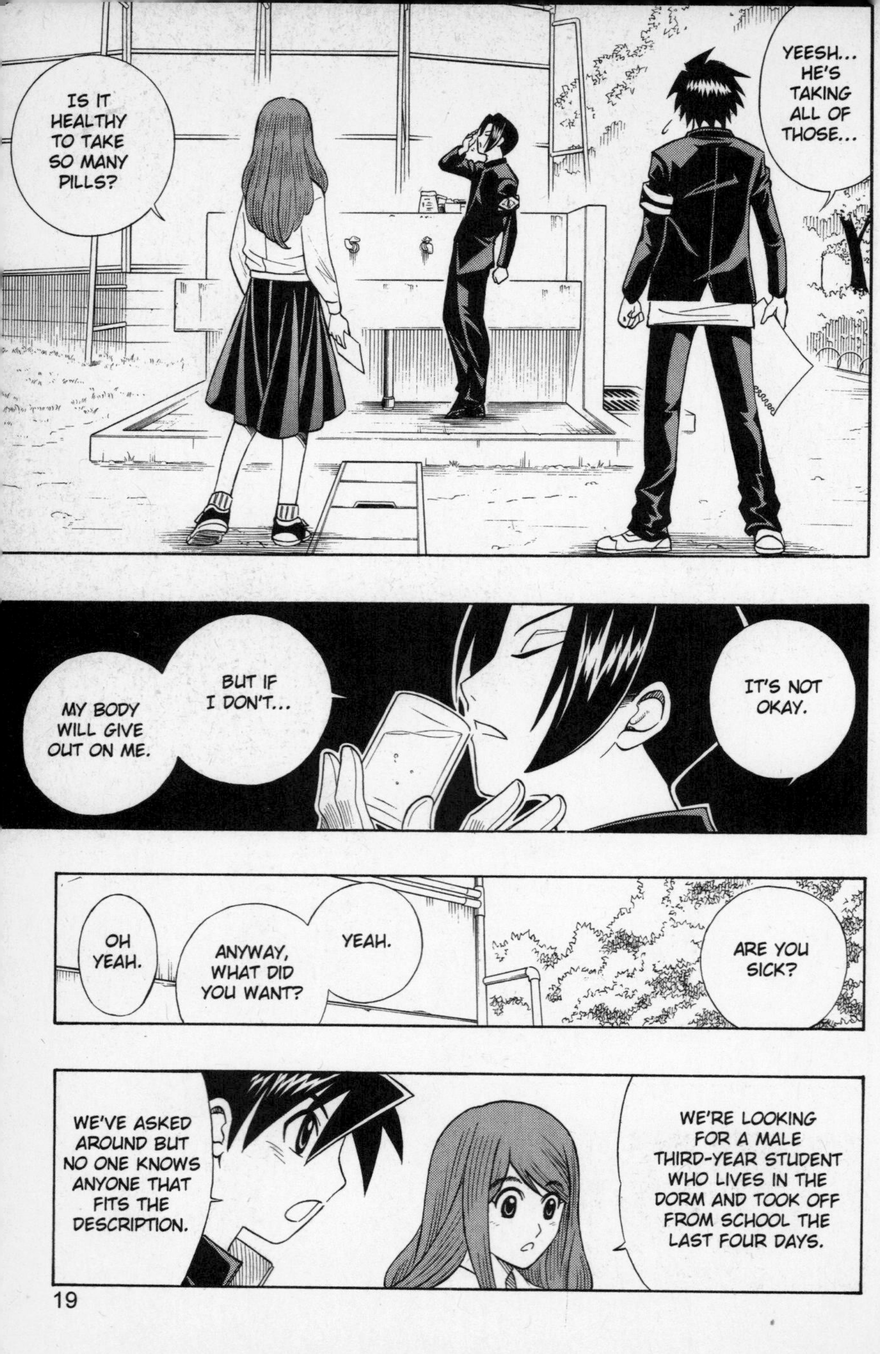
YEESH... HE'S TAKING ALL OF THOSE...
IS IT HEALTHY TO TAKE SO MANY PILLS?
IT'S NOT OKAY.
BUT IF I DON'T...
MY BODY WILL GIVE OUT ON ME.
ARE YOU SICK?
YEAH.
ANYWAY, WHAT DID YOU WANT?
OH YEAH.
WE'RE LOOKING FOR A MALE THIRD-YEAR STUDENT WHO LIVES IN THE DORM AND TOOK OFF FROM SCHOOL THE LAST FOUR DAYS.
WE'VE ASKED AROUND BUT NO ONE KNOWS ANYONE THAT FITS THE DESCRIPTION.

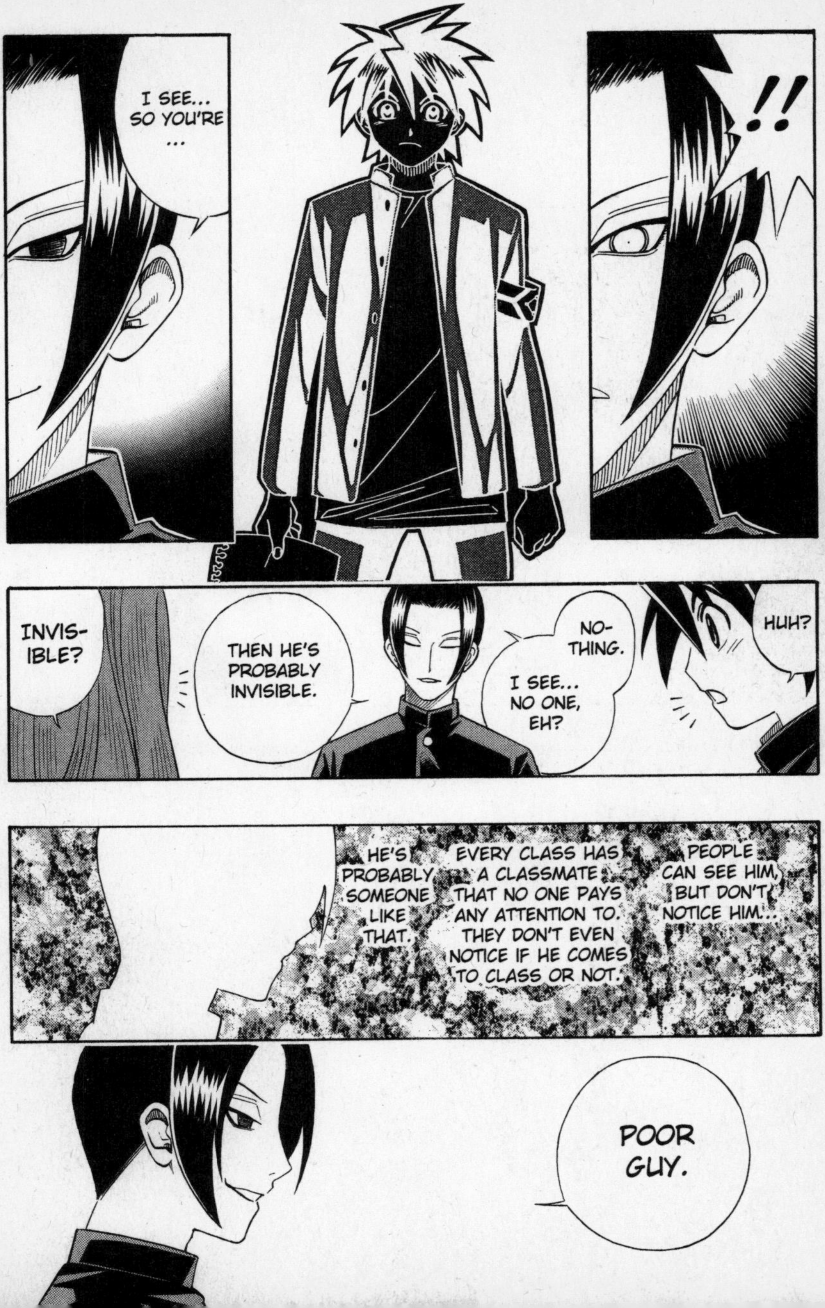
!!
I SEE... SO YOU'RE ...
HUH?
NO-THING.
I SEE... NO ONE, EH?
THEN HE'S PROBABLY INVISIBLE.
INVIS-IBLE?
PEOPLE CAN SEE HIM, BUT DON'T NOTICE HIM...
EVERY CLASS HAS A CLASSMATE THAT NO ONE PAYS ANY ATTENTION TO. THEY DON'T EVEN NOTICE IF HE COMES TO CLASS OR NOT.
HE'S PROBABLY SOMEONE LIKE THAT.
POOR GUY.

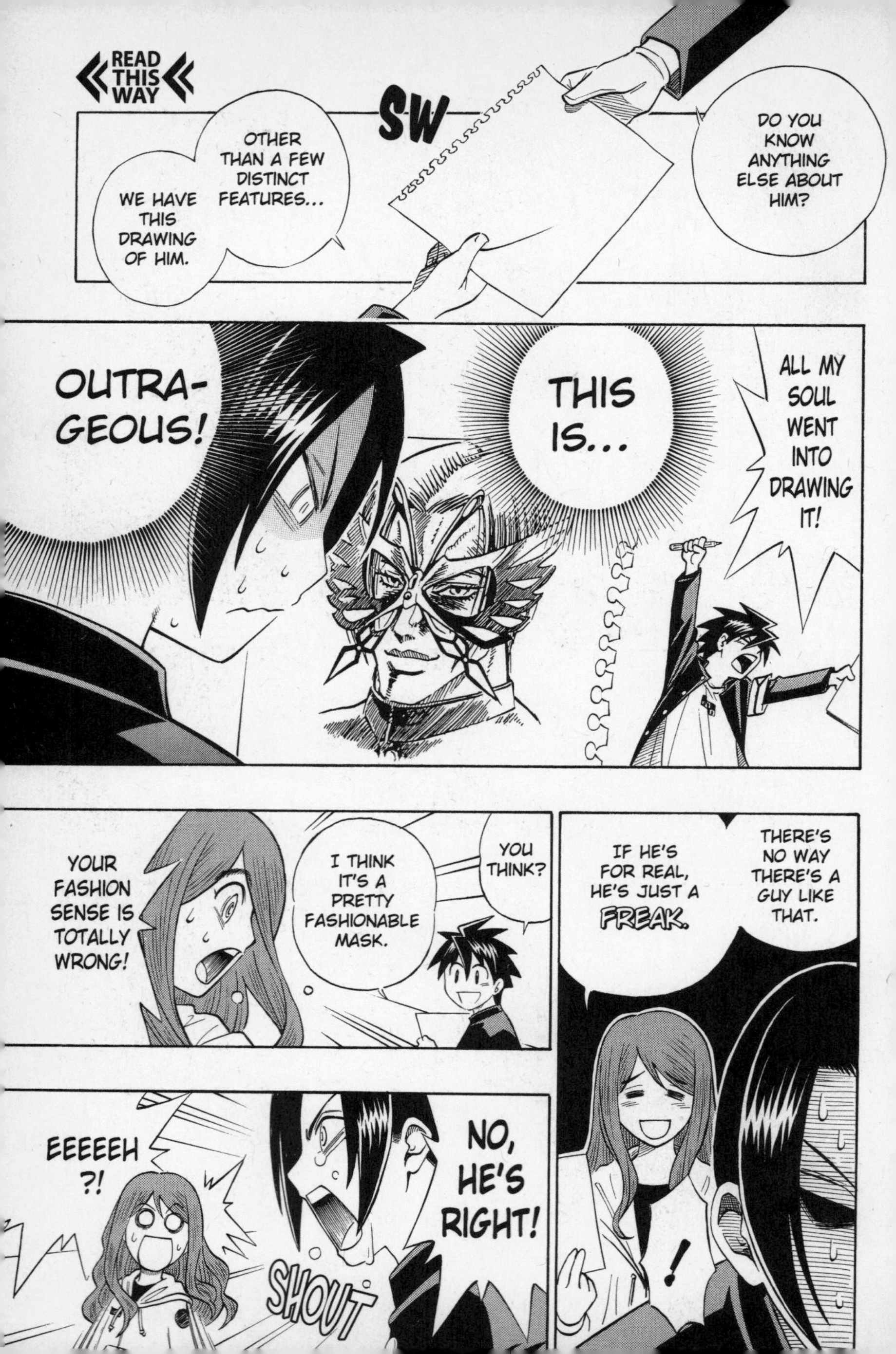
READ THIS WAY
DO YOU KNOW ANYTHING ELSE ABOUT HIM?
SW
OTHER THAN A FEW DISTINCT FEATURES...
WE HAVE THIS DRAWING OF HIM.
ALL MY SOUL WENT INTO DRAWING IT!
THIS IS...
OUTRA-GEOUS!
THERE'S NO WAY THERE'S A GUY LIKE THAT.
IF HE'S FOR REAL, HE'S JUST A FREAK.
!
YOU THINK?
I THINK IT'S A PRETTY FASHIONABLE MASK.
YOUR FASHION SENSE IS TOTALLY WRONG!
NO, HE'S RIGHT!
SHOUT
EEEEEH ?!

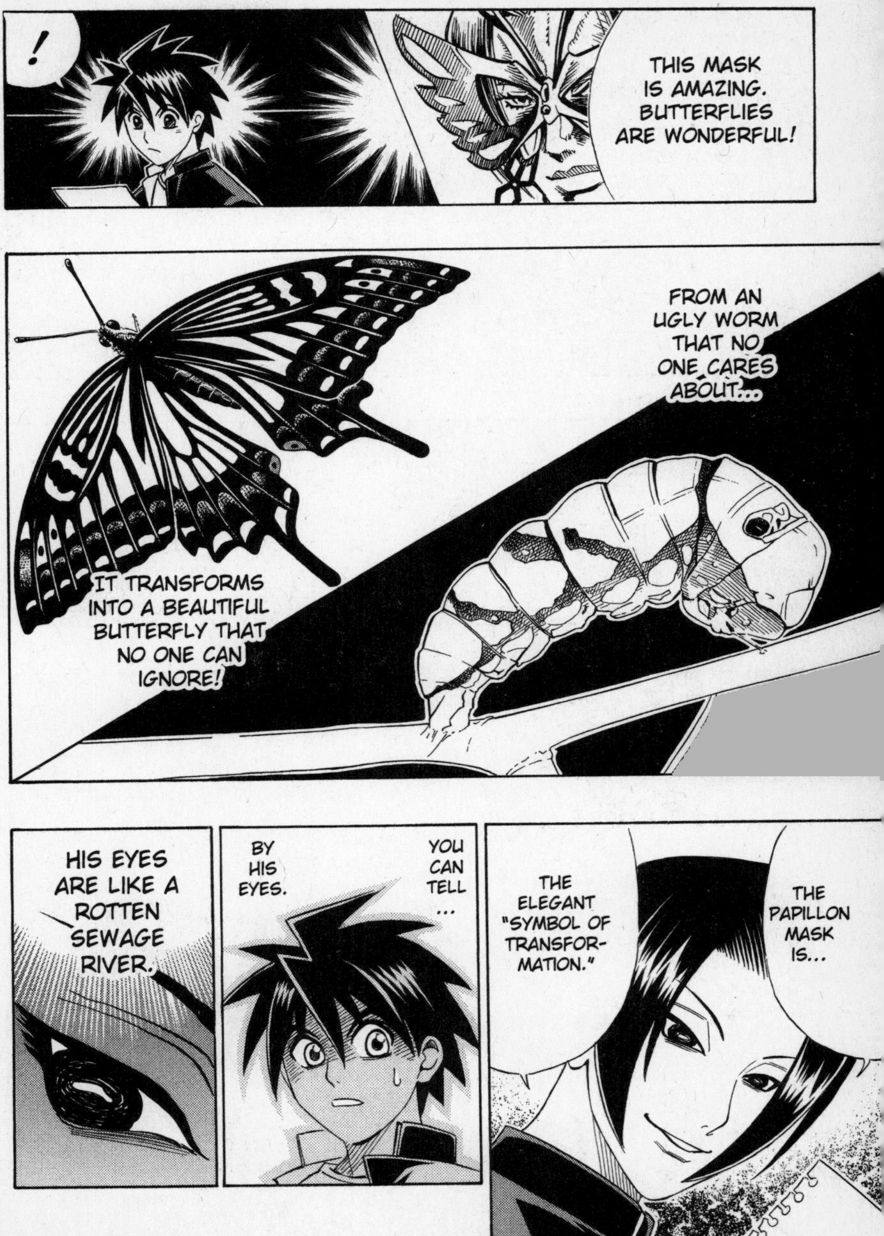
THIS MASK IS AMAZING. BUTTERFLIES ARE WONDERFUL!
!
FROM AN UGLY WORM THAT NO ONE CARES ABOUT...
IT TRANSFORMS INTO A BEAUTIFUL BUTTERFLY THAT NO ONE CAN IGNORE!
THE PAPILLON MASK IS...
THE ELEGANT "SYMBOL OF TRANSFORMATION."
YOU CAN TELL...
BY HIS EYES.
HIS EYES ARE LIKE A ROTTEN SEWAGE RIVER.

READ THIS WAY

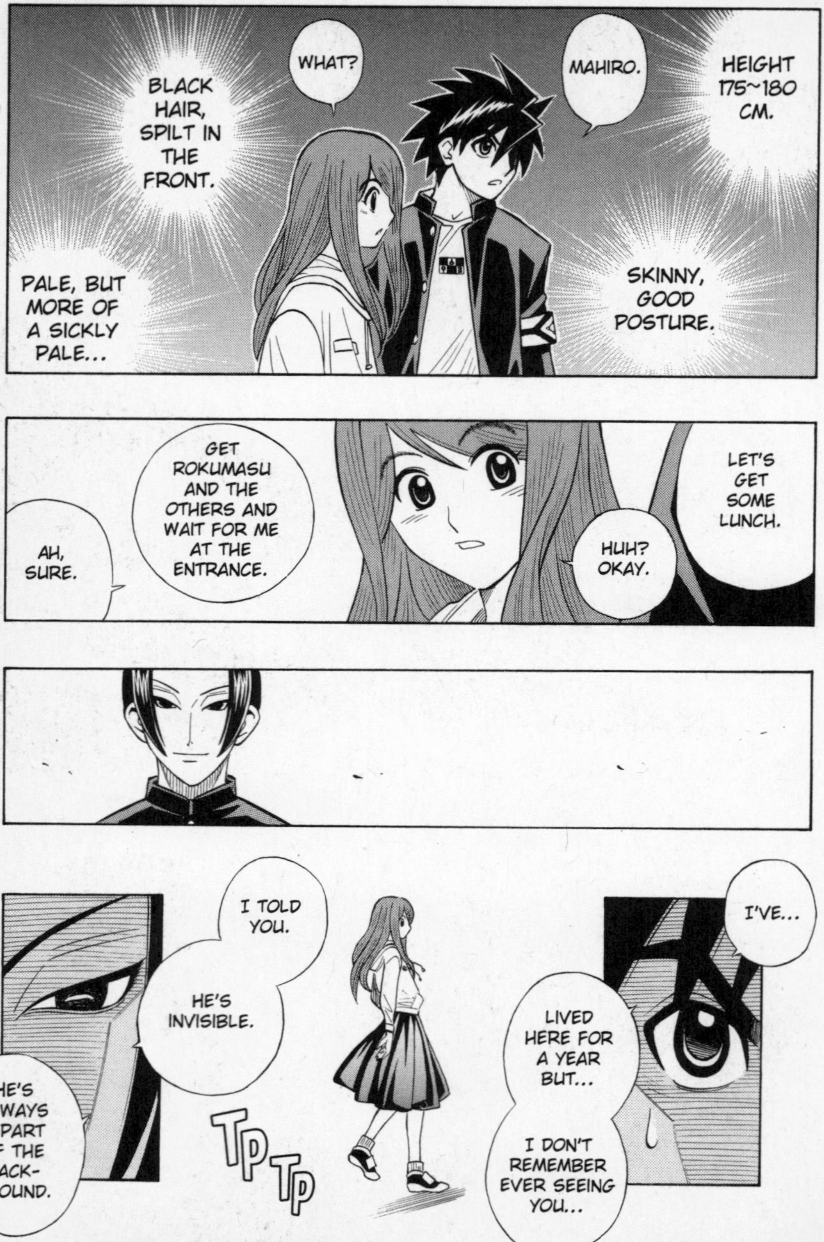

HEIGHT 175~180 CM.
MAHIRO.
WHAT?
BLACK HAIR, SPILT IN THE FRONT.
SKINNY, GOOD POSTURE.
PALE, BUT MORE OF A SICKLY PALE...
LET'S GET SOME LUNCH.
HUH? OKAY.
GET ROKUMASU AND THE OTHERS AND WAIT FOR ME AT THE ENTRANCE.
AH, SURE.
I'VE...
LIVED HERE FOR A YEAR BUT...
I DON'T REMEMBER EVER SEEING YOU...
I TOLD YOU.
HE'S INVISIBLE.
TP TP
HE'S ALWAYS A PART OF THE BACK-GROUND.

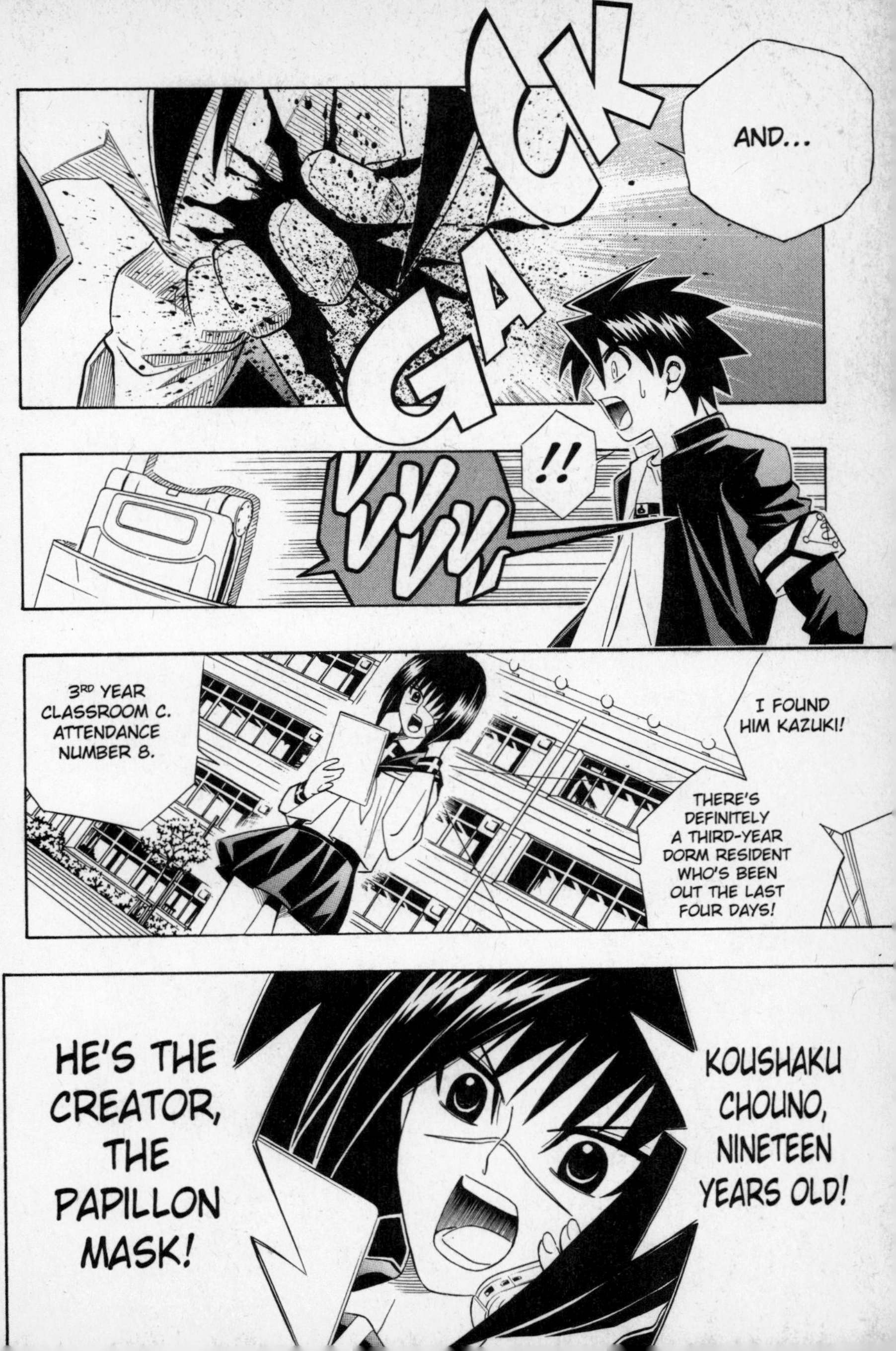
AND...
GACK
!!
VVVV
I FOUND HIM KAZUKI!
THERE'S DEFINITELY A THIRD-YEAR DORM RESIDENT WHO'S BEEN OUT THE LAST FOUR DAYS!
3RD YEAR CLASSROOM C. ATTENDANCE NUMBER 8.
KOUSHAKU CHOUNO, NINETEEN YEARS OLD!
HE'S THE CREATOR, THE PAPILLON MASK!

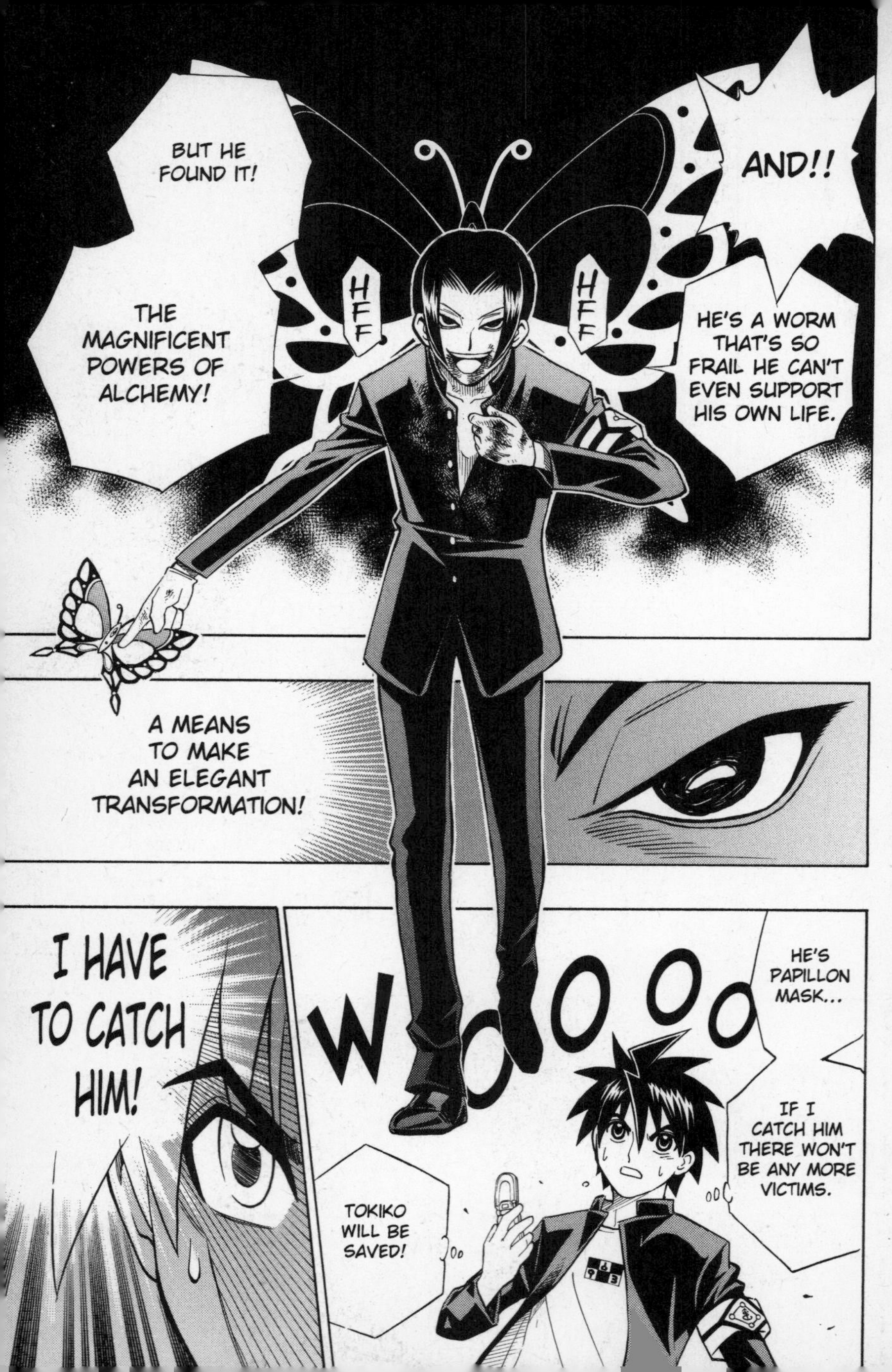

AND!!
HE'S A WORM THAT'S SO FRAIL HE CAN'T EVEN SUPPORT HIS OWN LIFE.
HFF
HFF
BUT HE FOUND IT!
THE MAGNIFICENT POWERS OF ALCHEMY!
A MEANS TO MAKE AN ELEGANT TRANSFORMATION!
HE'S PAPILLON MASK...
IF I CATCH HIM THERE WON'T BE ANY MORE VICTIMS.
TOKIKO WILL BE SAVED!
WOOOOO
I HAVE TO CATCH HIM!

- Height: 162 cm; Weight: 51kg
- Born: January 25th; Aquarius; Blood Type AB; 16 years old
- Favorites: Glay, math, and Weider (jelly-like drink)
- Dislikes: Nothing in particular
            (Wouldn't tell you even if I knew)
- Hobby: Computer stuff
- Things he's good at: Mimicking voices and much more
- Affiliation: Private Ginsei Academy 2nd Year High School
            Student Class Room B, Dorm resident

Character Profile No.8

Koji Rokumasu

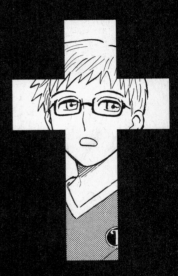

Author's Notes

- A character created to liven up Kazuki's everyday life. He has the leveled eyebrow look (the Cool Guy) and he's in charge of the joke puns.
- The unofficial leader of the group. He usually stays in the background but he gives precise directions to resolve any issues when necessary… was my initial concept but he somehow turned out to be the man with many mysteries.
- I based Rokumasu off an anime director I went to Anime Expo with (from my comments on the cover flap of Volume 1). He held the colorful group together while he enjoyed the convention himself. I wanted to incorporate that aspect of him into a character in my story so I borrowed his likeness.

CHAPTER 9: THE OTHER NEW LIFE

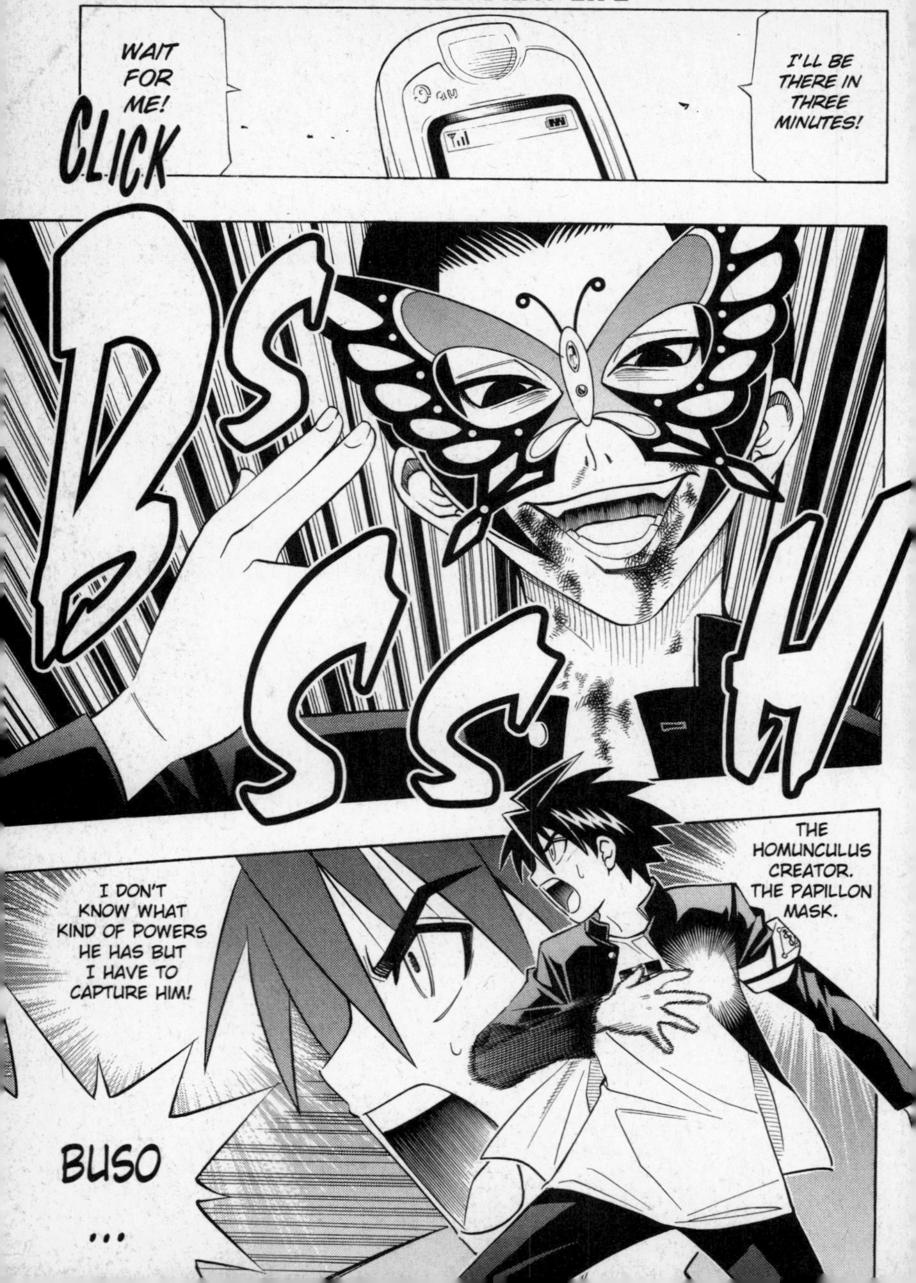
I'LL BE THERE IN THREE MINUTES!
WAIT FOR ME!
CLICK
BSSSH
THE HOMUNCULUS CREATOR. THE PAPILLON MASK.
I DON'T KNOW WHAT KIND OF POWERS HE HAS BUT I HAVE TO CAPTURE HIM!
BUSO
...

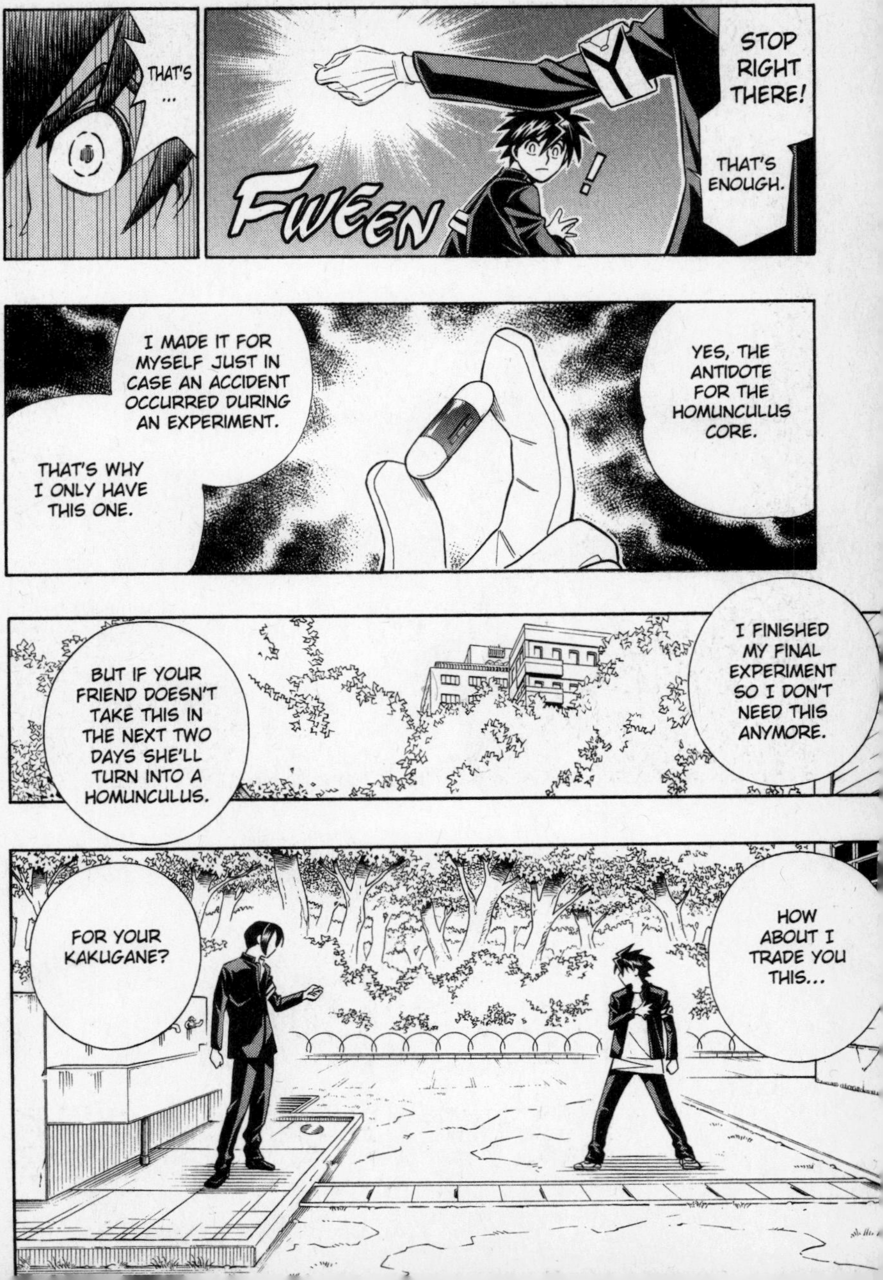
STOP RIGHT THERE!
THAT'S ENOUGH.
FWEEN
!
THAT'S ...
YES, THE ANTIDOTE FOR THE HOMUNCULUS CORE.
I MADE IT FOR MYSELF JUST IN CASE AN ACCIDENT OCCURRED DURING AN EXPERIMENT.
THAT'S WHY I ONLY HAVE THIS ONE.
I FINISHED MY FINAL EXPERIMENT SO I DON'T NEED THIS ANYMORE.
BUT IF YOUR FRIEND DOESN'T TAKE THIS IN THE NEXT TWO DAYS SHE'LL TURN INTO A HOMUNCULUS.
HOW ABOUT I TRADE YOU THIS...
FOR YOUR KAKUGANE?

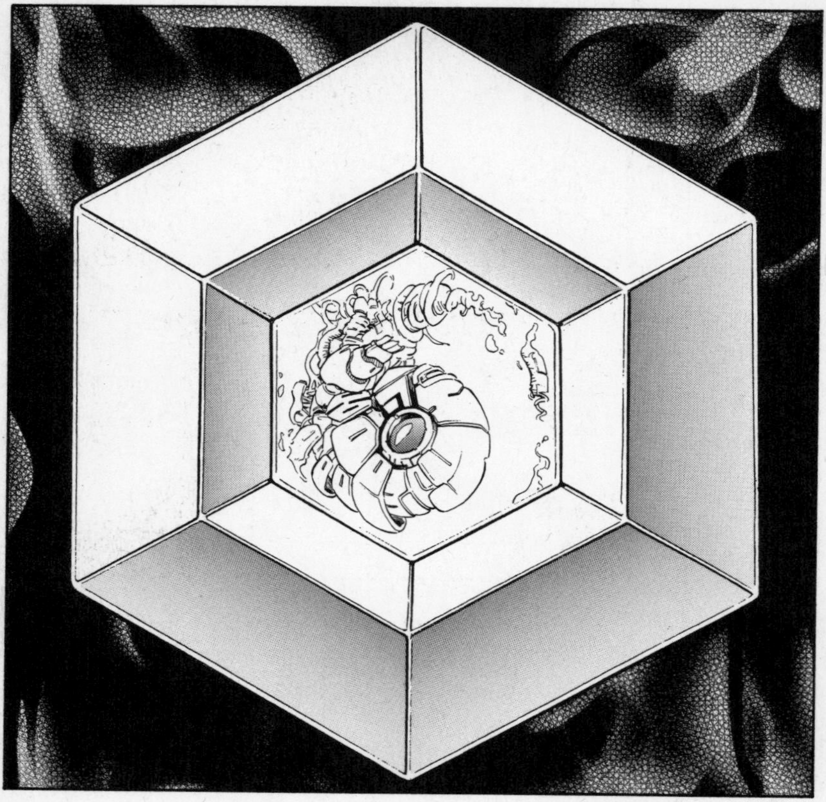

CHAPTER 9:
THE OTHER NEW LIFE

伸宏
和月

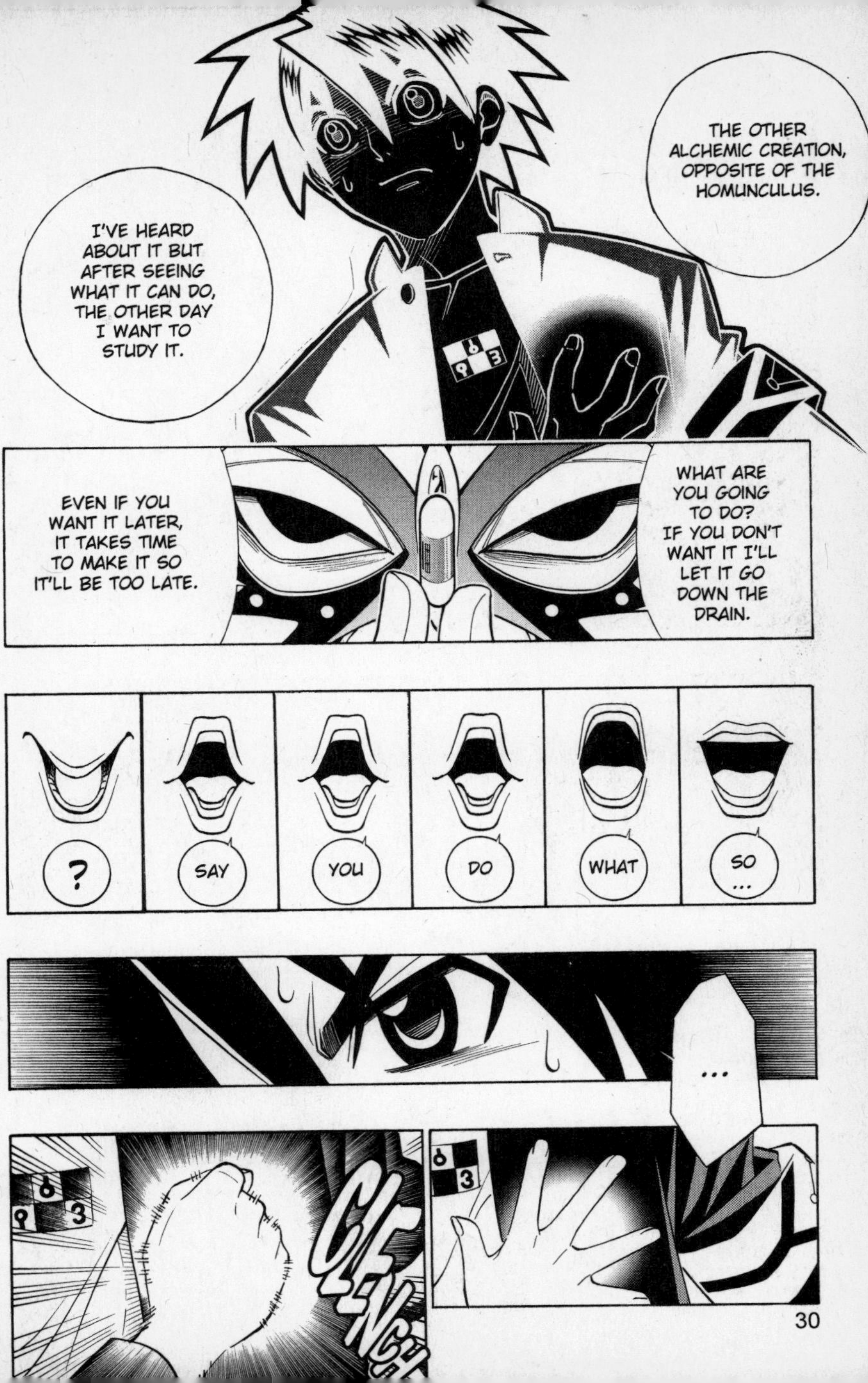
THE OTHER ALCHEMIC CREATION, OPPOSITE OF THE HOMUNCULUS.
I'VE HEARD ABOUT IT BUT AFTER SEEING WHAT IT CAN DO, THE OTHER DAY I WANT TO STUDY IT.
WHAT ARE YOU GOING TO DO? IF YOU DON'T WANT IT I'LL LET IT GO DOWN THE DRAIN.
EVEN IF YOU WANT IT LATER, IT TAKES TIME TO MAKE IT SO IT'LL BE TOO LATE.
SO ...
WHAT
DO
YOU
SAY
?
...
CLENCH

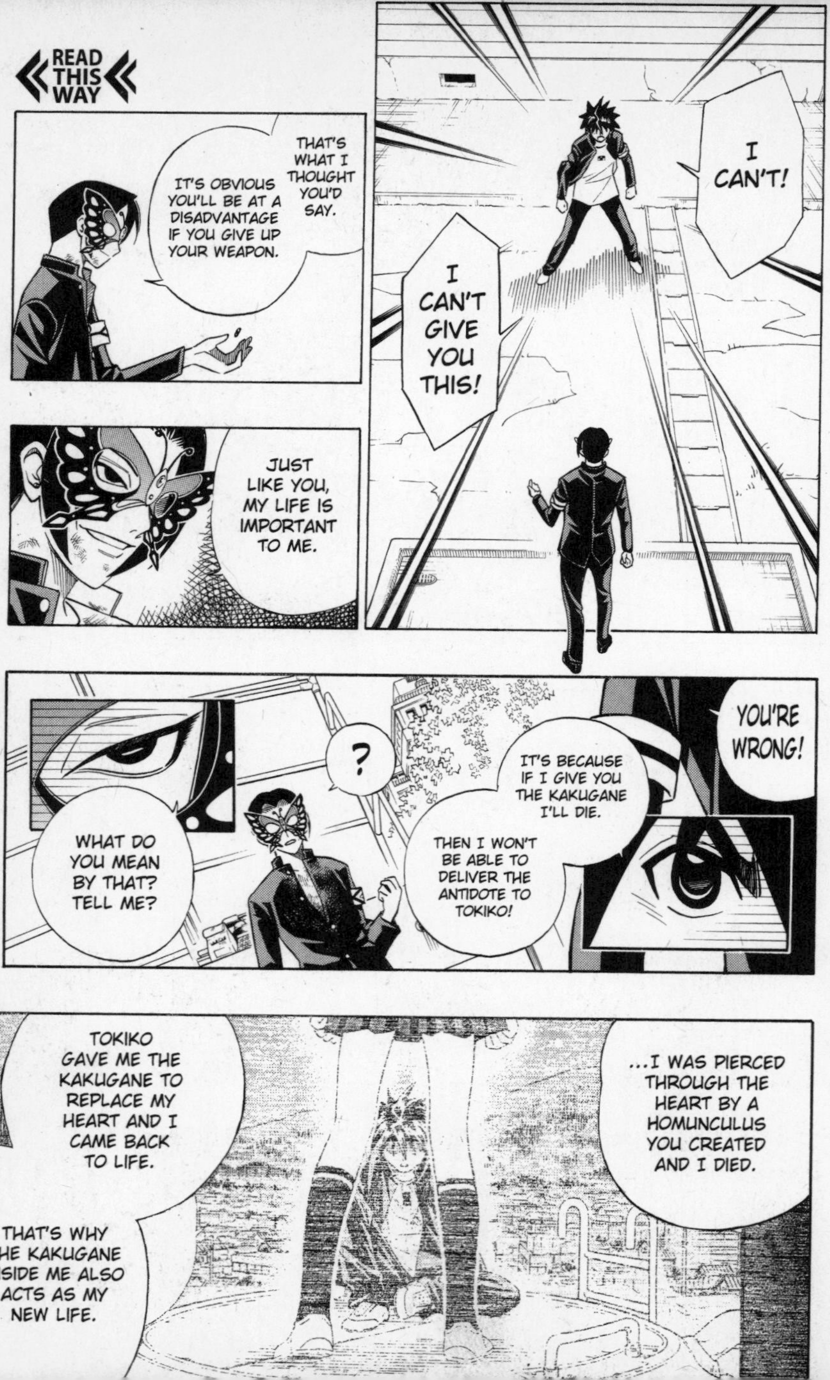
READ THIS WAY
I CAN'T!
I CAN'T GIVE YOU THIS!
THAT'S WHAT I THOUGHT YOU'D SAY.
IT'S OBVIOUS YOU'LL BE AT A DISADVANTAGE IF YOU GIVE UP YOUR WEAPON.
JUST LIKE YOU, MY LIFE IS IMPORTANT TO ME.
YOU'RE WRONG!
?
WHAT DO YOU MEAN BY THAT? TELL ME?
IT'S BECAUSE IF I GIVE YOU THE KAKUGANE I'LL DIE.
THEN I WON'T BE ABLE TO DELIVER THE ANTIDOTE TO TOKIKO!
...I WAS PIERCED THROUGH THE HEART BY A HOMUNCULUS YOU CREATED AND I DIED.
TOKIKO GAVE ME THE KAKUGANE TO REPLACE MY HEART AND I CAME BACK TO LIFE.
THAT'S WHY THE KAKUGANE INSIDE ME ALSO ACTS AS MY NEW LIFE.

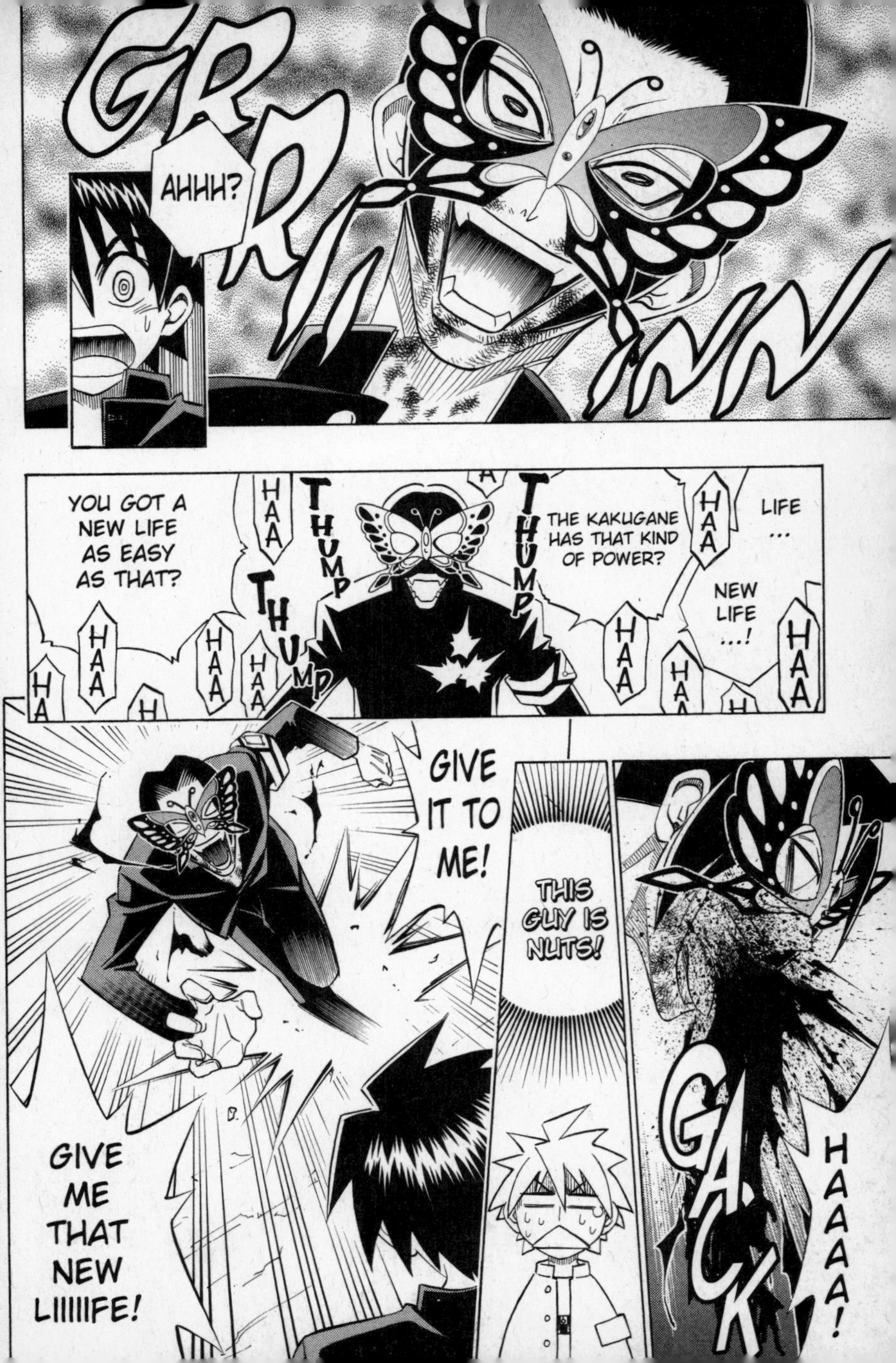

GRRINN
AHHH?
LIFE ...
NEW LIFE ...!
HAA
HAA
HAA
HAA
THE KAKUGANE HAS THAT KIND OF POWER?
THUMP
THUMP
THUMP
HAA
HAA
HAA
HAA
YOU GOT A NEW LIFE AS EASY AS THAT?
HAAAA!
GACK
THIS GUY IS NUTS!
GIVE IT TO ME!
GIVE ME THAT NEW LIIIIIFE!

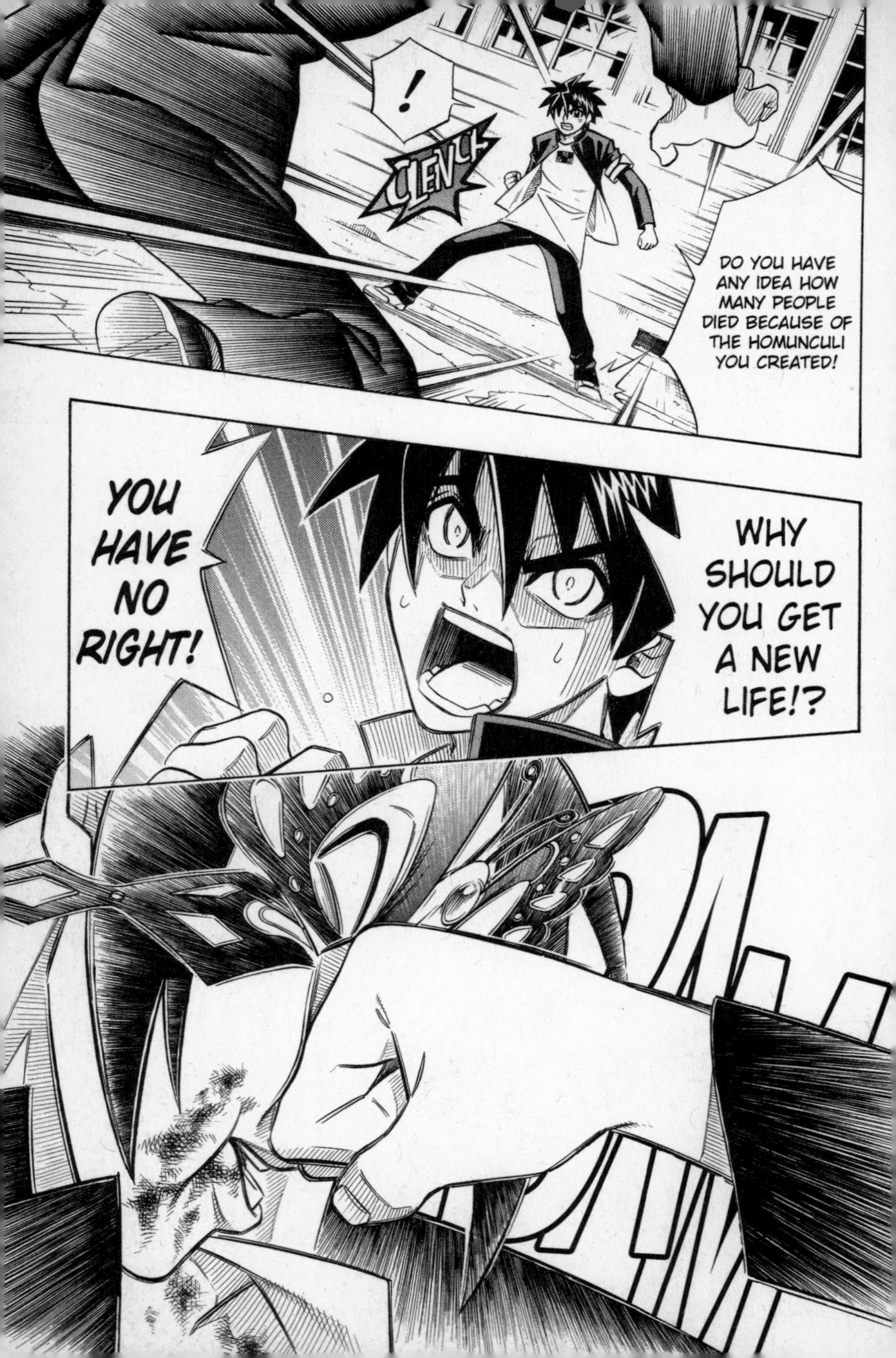
DO YOU HAVE ANY IDEA HOW MANY PEOPLE DIED BECAUSE OF THE HOMUNCULI YOU CREATED!
!
CLENCH
WHY SHOULD YOU GET A NEW LIFE!?
YOU HAVE NO RIGHT!

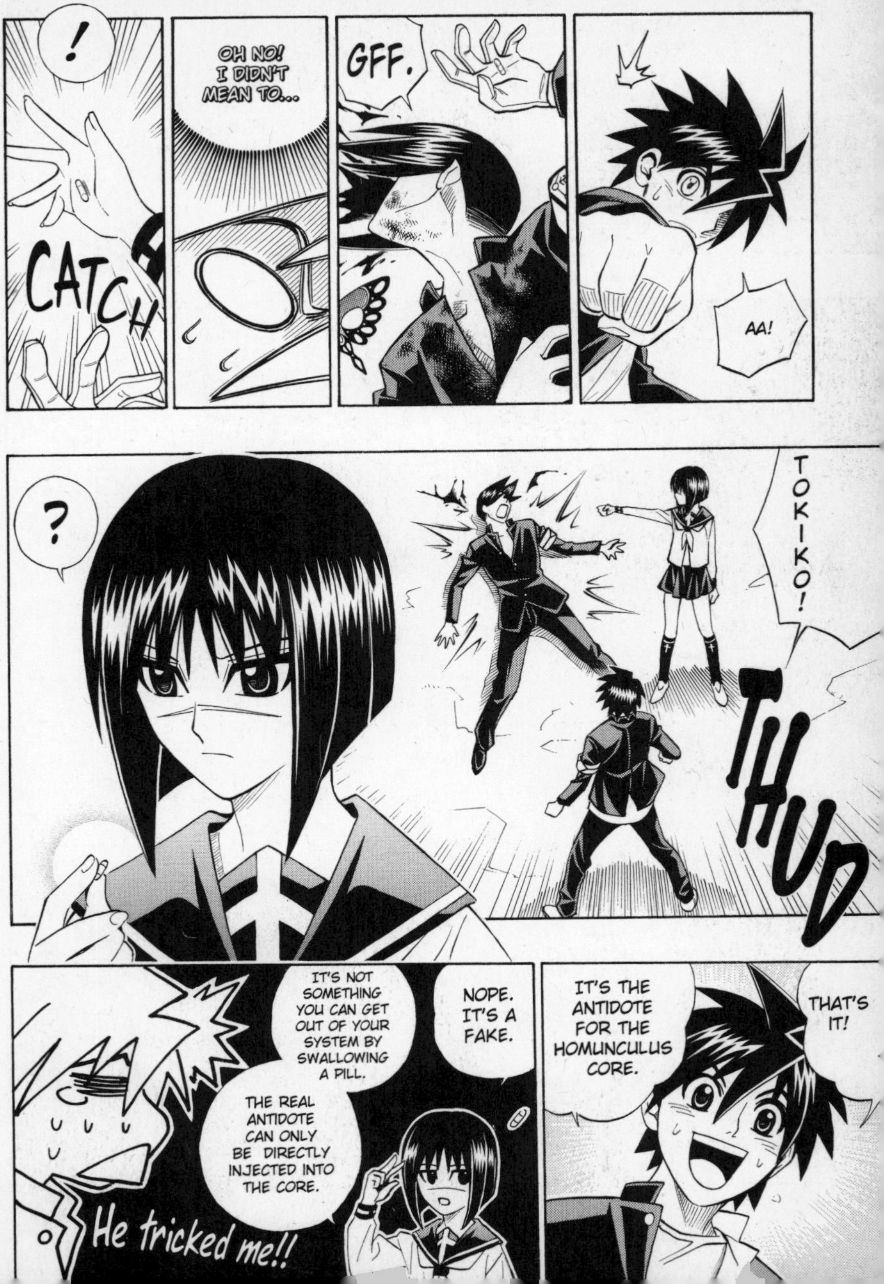
AA!
GFF.
OH NO! I DIDN'T MEAN TO...
!
CATCH
TOKIKO!
THUD
?
THAT'S IT!
IT'S THE ANTIDOTE FOR THE HOMUNCULUS CORE.
NOPE. IT'S A FAKE.
IT'S NOT SOMETHING YOU CAN GET OUT OF YOUR SYSTEM BY SWALLOWING A PILL.
THE REAL ANTIDOTE CAN ONLY BE DIRECTLY INJECTED INTO THE CORE.
He tricked me!!

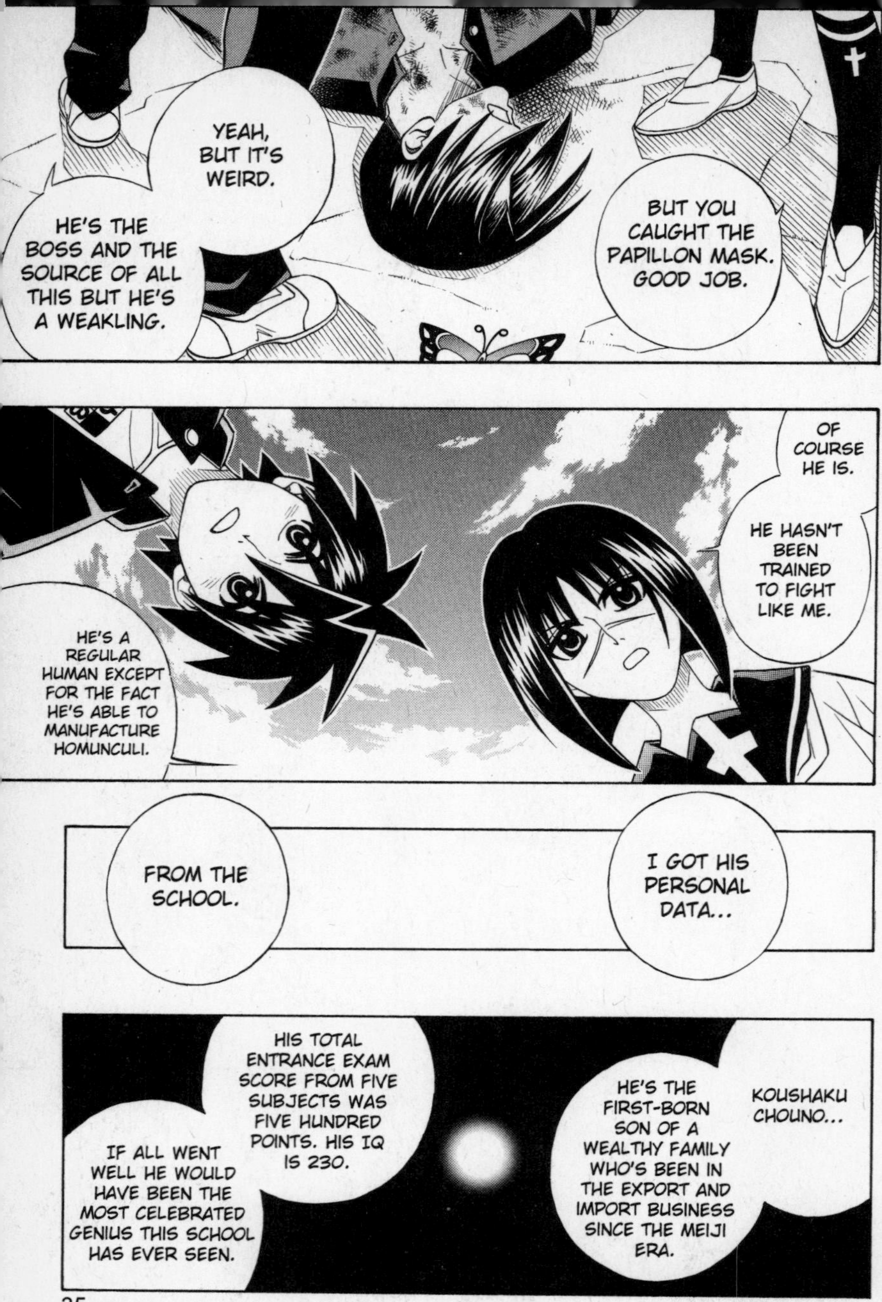

BUT YOU CAUGHT THE PAPILLON MASK. GOOD JOB.
YEAH, BUT IT'S WEIRD.
HE'S THE BOSS AND THE SOURCE OF ALL THIS BUT HE'S A WEAKLING.
OF COURSE HE IS.
HE HASN'T BEEN TRAINED TO FIGHT LIKE ME.
HE'S A REGULAR HUMAN EXCEPT FOR THE FACT HE'S ABLE TO MANUFACTURE HOMUNCULI.
I GOT HIS PERSONAL DATA...
FROM THE SCHOOL.
KOUSHAKU CHOUNO...
HE'S THE FIRST-BORN SON OF A WEALTHY FAMILY WHO'S BEEN IN THE EXPORT AND IMPORT BUSINESS SINCE THE MEIJI ERA.
HIS TOTAL ENTRANCE EXAM SCORE FROM FIVE SUBJECTS WAS FIVE HUNDRED POINTS. HIS IQ IS 230.
IF ALL WENT WELL HE WOULD HAVE BEEN THE MOST CELEBRATED GENIUS THIS SCHOOL HAS EVER SEEN.

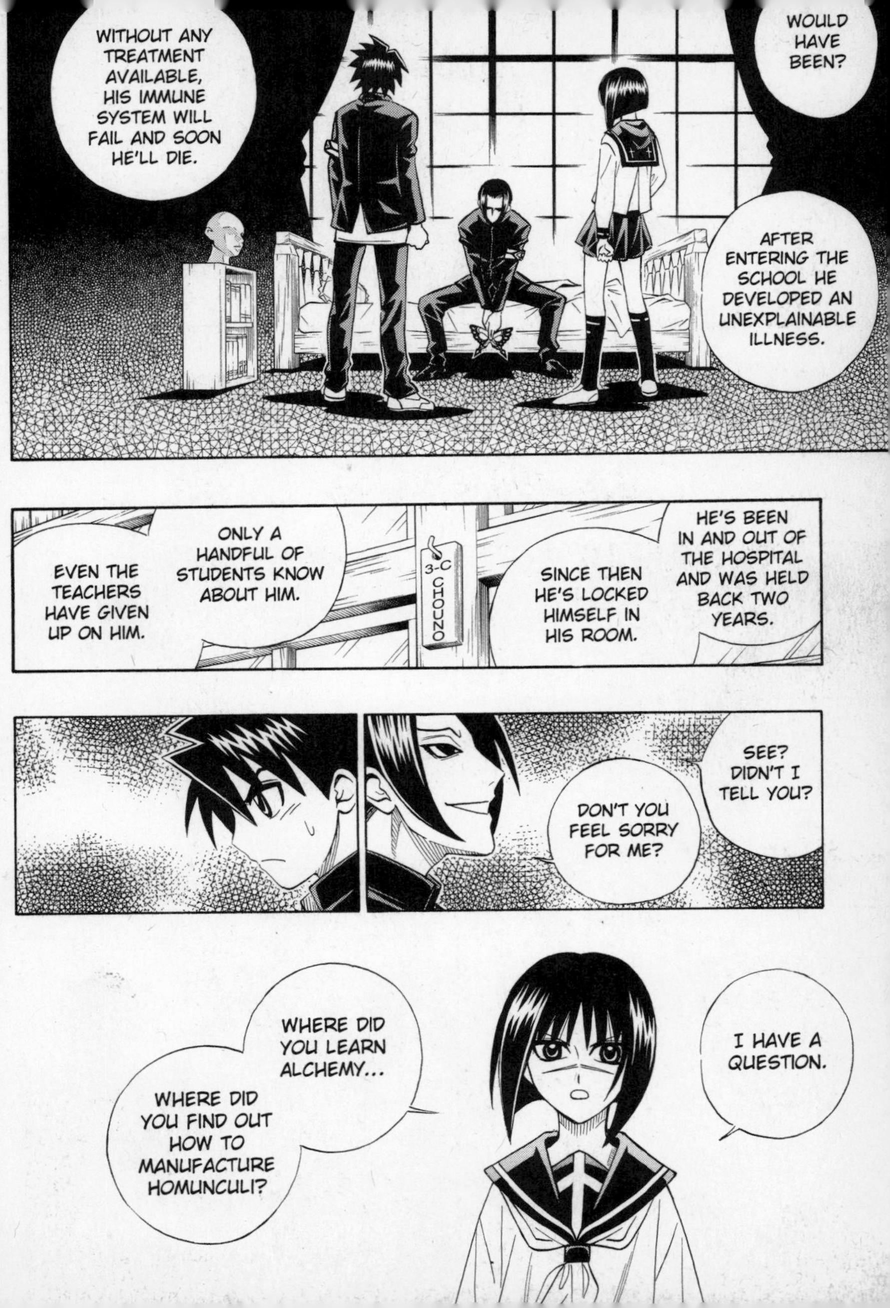
WOULD HAVE BEEN?
AFTER ENTERING THE SCHOOL HE DEVELOPED AN UNEXPLAINABLE ILLNESS.
WITHOUT ANY TREATMENT AVAILABLE, HIS IMMUNE SYSTEM WILL FAIL AND SOON HE'LL DIE.
HE'S BEEN IN AND OUT OF THE HOSPITAL AND WAS HELD BACK TWO YEARS.
SINCE THEN HE'S LOCKED HIMSELF IN HIS ROOM.
3-C CHOUNO
ONLY A HANDFUL OF STUDENTS KNOW ABOUT HIM.
EVEN THE TEACHERS HAVE GIVEN UP ON HIM.
SEE? DIDN'T I TELL YOU?
DON'T YOU FEEL SORRY FOR ME?
I HAVE A QUESTION.
WHERE DID YOU LEARN ALCHEMY...
WHERE DID YOU FIND OUT HOW TO MANUFACTURE HOMUNCULI?

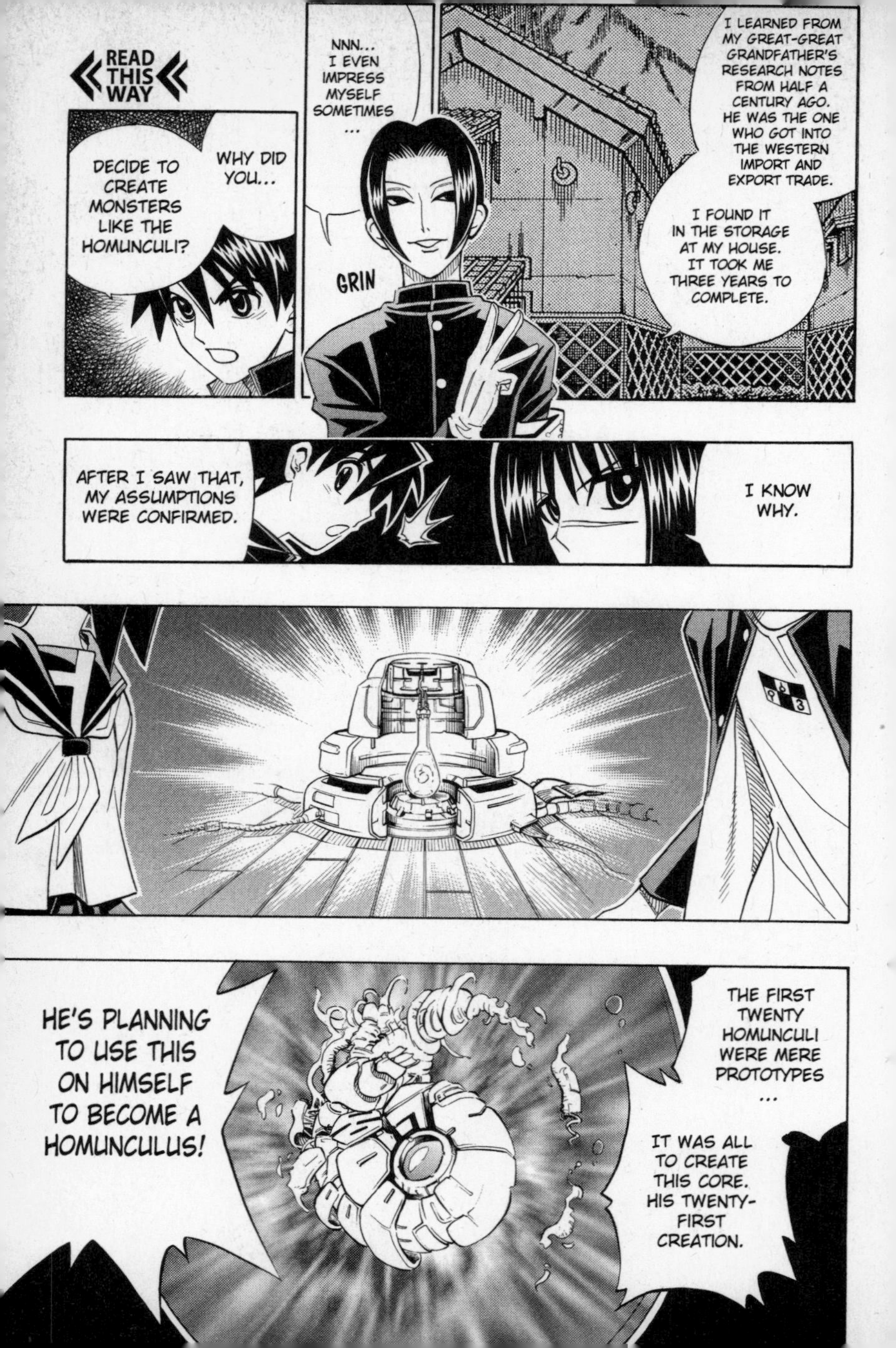
READ THIS WAY
I LEARNED FROM MY GREAT-GREAT GRANDFATHER'S RESEARCH NOTES FROM HALF A CENTURY AGO. HE WAS THE ONE WHO GOT INTO THE WESTERN IMPORT AND EXPORT TRADE.
I FOUND IT IN THE STORAGE AT MY HOUSE. IT TOOK ME THREE YEARS TO COMPLETE.
NNN... I EVEN IMPRESS MYSELF SOMETIMES...
GRIN
WHY DID YOU...
DECIDE TO CREATE MONSTERS LIKE THE HOMUNCULI?
I KNOW WHY.
AFTER I SAW THAT, MY ASSUMPTIONS WERE CONFIRMED.
THE FIRST TWENTY HOMUNCULI WERE MERE PROTOTYPES...
IT WAS ALL TO CREATE THIS CORE. HIS TWENTY-FIRST CREATION.
HE'S PLANNING TO USE THIS ON HIMSELF TO BECOME A HOMUNCULUS!

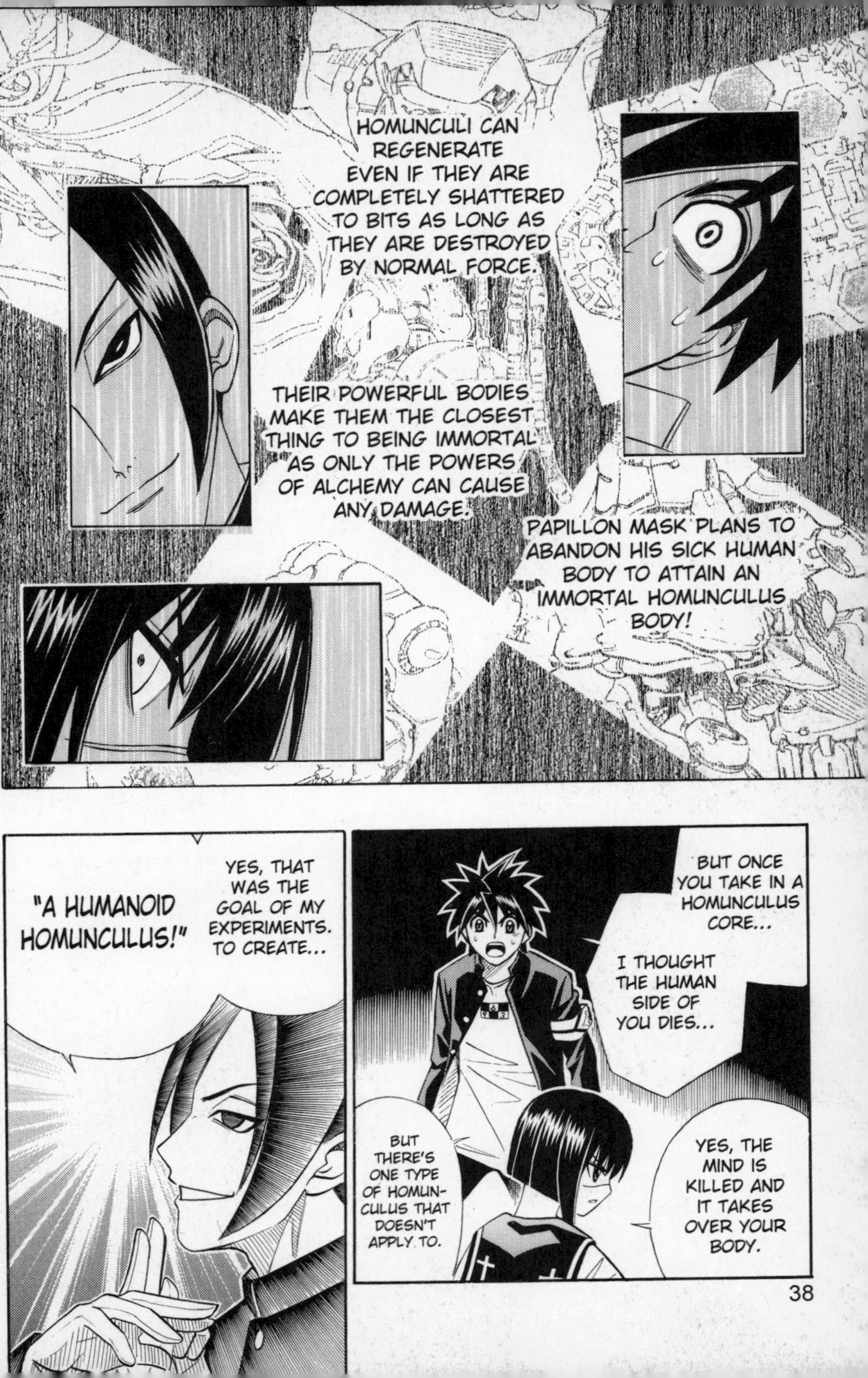
HOMUNCULI CAN REGENERATE EVEN IF THEY ARE COMPLETELY SHATTERED TO BITS AS LONG AS THEY ARE DESTROYED BY NORMAL FORCE.
THEIR POWERFUL BODIES MAKE THEM THE CLOSEST THING TO BEING IMMORTAL AS ONLY THE POWERS OF ALCHEMY CAN CAUSE ANY DAMAGE.
PAPILLON MASK PLANS TO ABANDON HIS SICK HUMAN BODY TO ATTAIN AN IMMORTAL HOMUNCULUS BODY!
BUT ONCE YOU TAKE IN A HOMUNCULUS CORE...
I THOUGHT THE HUMAN SIDE OF YOU DIES...
YES, THE MIND IS KILLED AND IT TAKES OVER YOUR BODY.
BUT THERE'S ONE TYPE OF HOMUN-CULUS THAT DOESN'T APPLY TO.
YES, THAT WAS THE GOAL OF MY EXPERIMENTS. TO CREATE...
"A HUMANOID HOMUNCULUS!"

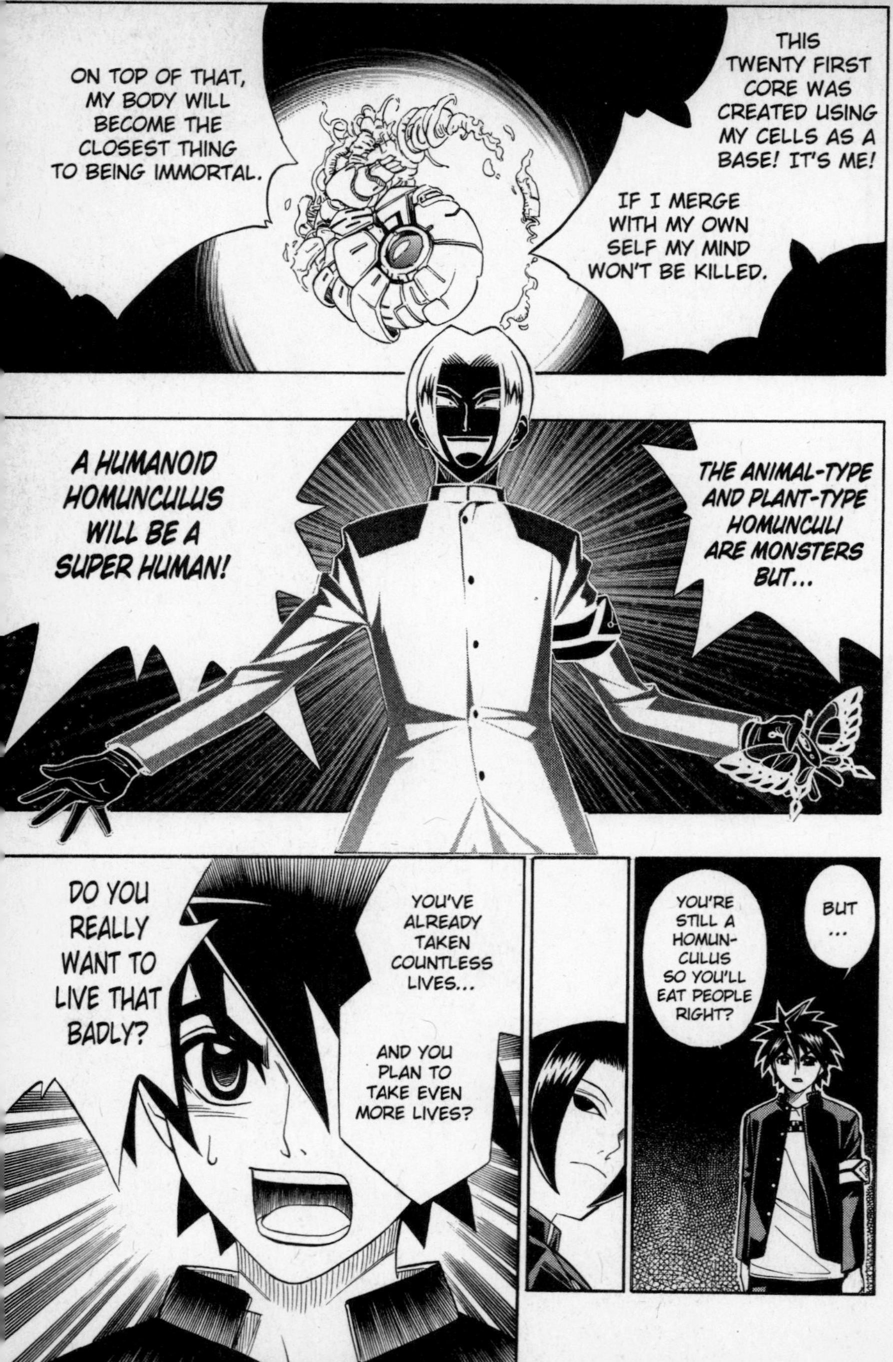
THIS TWENTY FIRST CORE WAS CREATED USING MY CELLS AS A BASE! IT'S ME!
IF I MERGE WITH MY OWN SELF MY MIND WON'T BE KILLED.
ON TOP OF THAT, MY BODY WILL BECOME THE CLOSEST THING TO BEING IMMORTAL.
THE ANIMAL-TYPE AND PLANT-TYPE HOMUNCULI ARE MONSTERS BUT...
A HUMANOID HOMUNCULUS WILL BE A SUPER HUMAN!
BUT ...
YOU'RE STILL A HOMUN-CULUS SO YOU'LL EAT PEOPLE RIGHT?
YOU'VE ALREADY TAKEN COUNTLESS LIVES...
AND YOU PLAN TO TAKE EVEN MORE LIVES?
DO YOU REALLY WANT TO LIVE THAT BADLY?

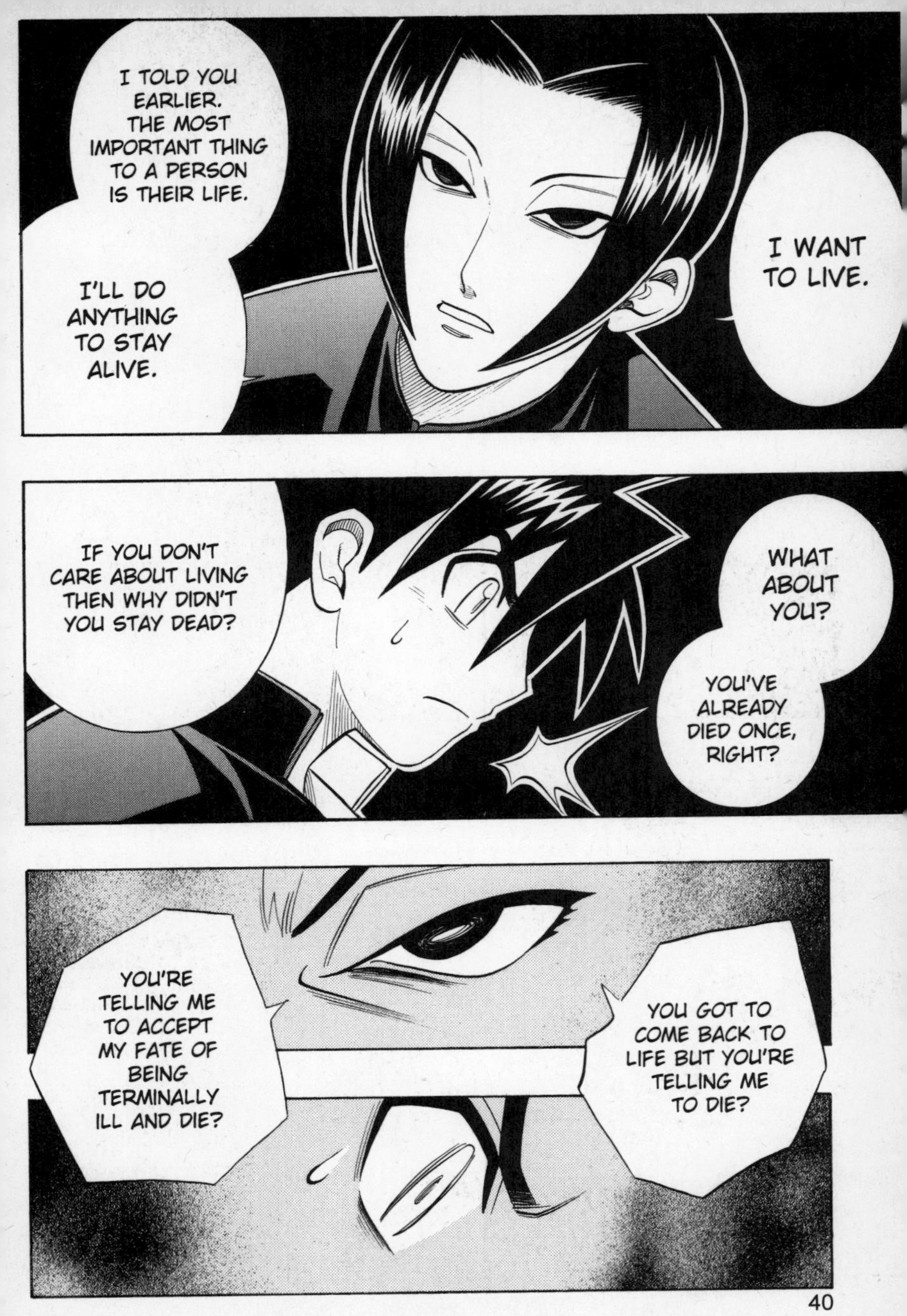
I WANT TO LIVE.
I TOLD YOU EARLIER. THE MOST IMPORTANT THING TO A PERSON IS THEIR LIFE.
I'LL DO ANYTHING TO STAY ALIVE.
WHAT ABOUT YOU?
YOU'VE ALREADY DIED ONCE, RIGHT?
IF YOU DON'T CARE ABOUT LIVING THEN WHY DIDN'T YOU STAY DEAD?
YOU GOT TO COME BACK TO LIFE BUT YOU'RE TELLING ME TO DIE?
YOU'RE TELLING ME TO ACCEPT MY FATE OF BEING TERMINALLY ILL AND DIE?

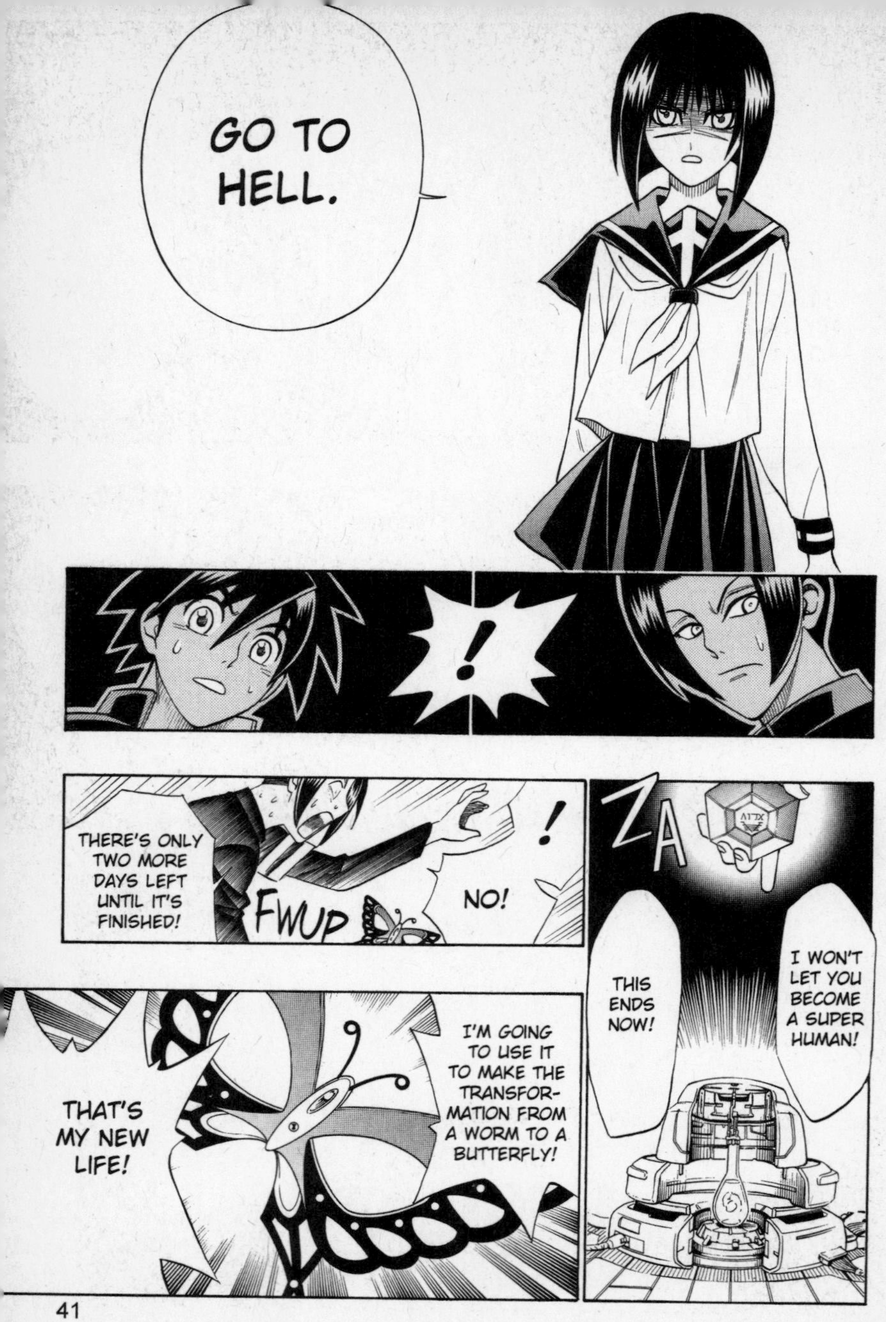
GO TO HELL.
!
ZA
I WON'T LET YOU BECOME A SUPER HUMAN!
THIS ENDS NOW!
!
NO!
FWUP
THERE'S ONLY TWO MORE DAYS LEFT UNTIL IT'S FINISHED!
I'M GOING TO USE IT TO MAKE THE TRANSFORMATION FROM A WORM TO A BUTTERFLY!
THAT'S MY NEW LIFE!

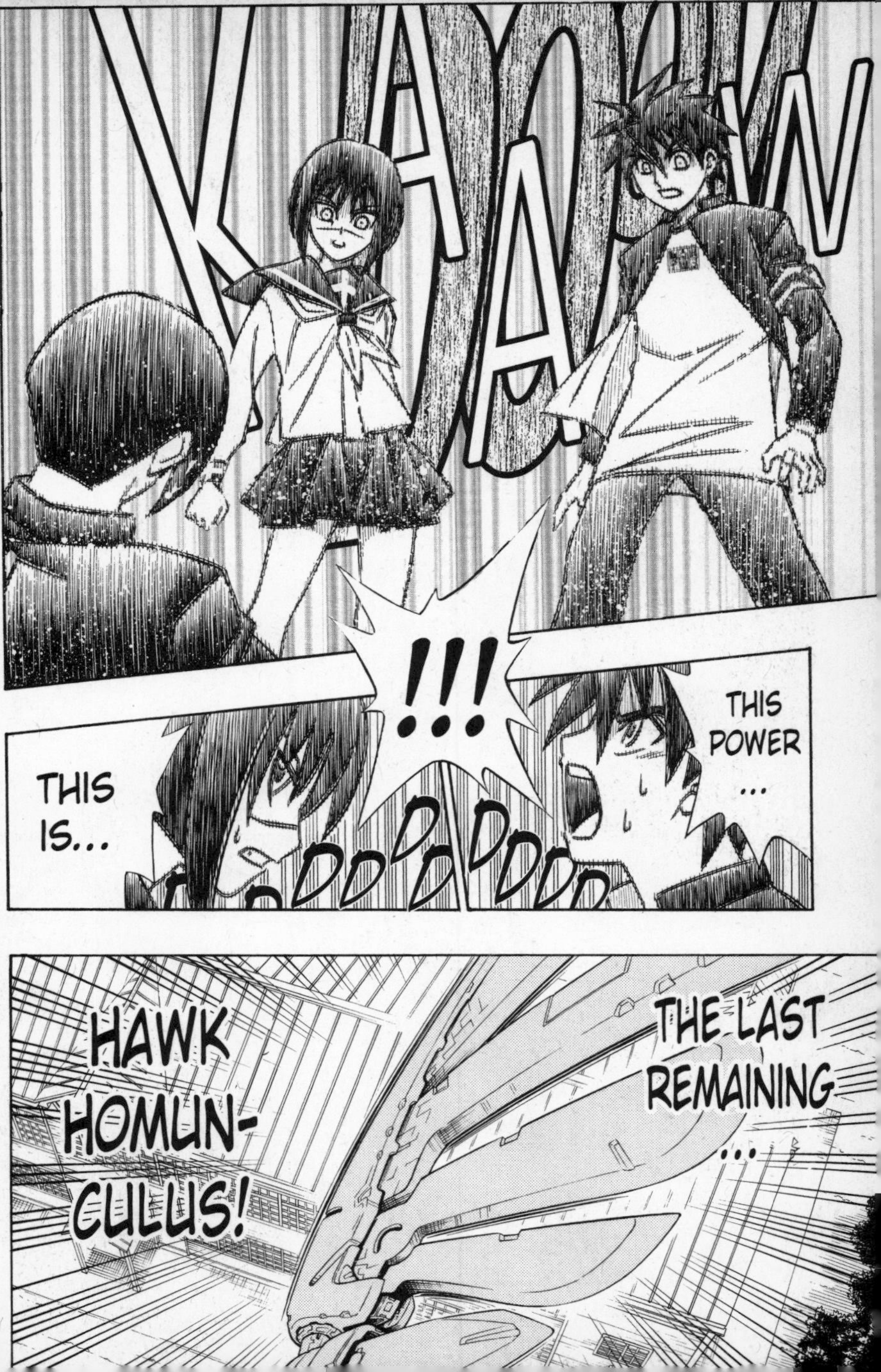
!!!
THIS POWER ...
THIS IS...
THE LAST REMAINING ...
HAWK HOMUN-CULUS!

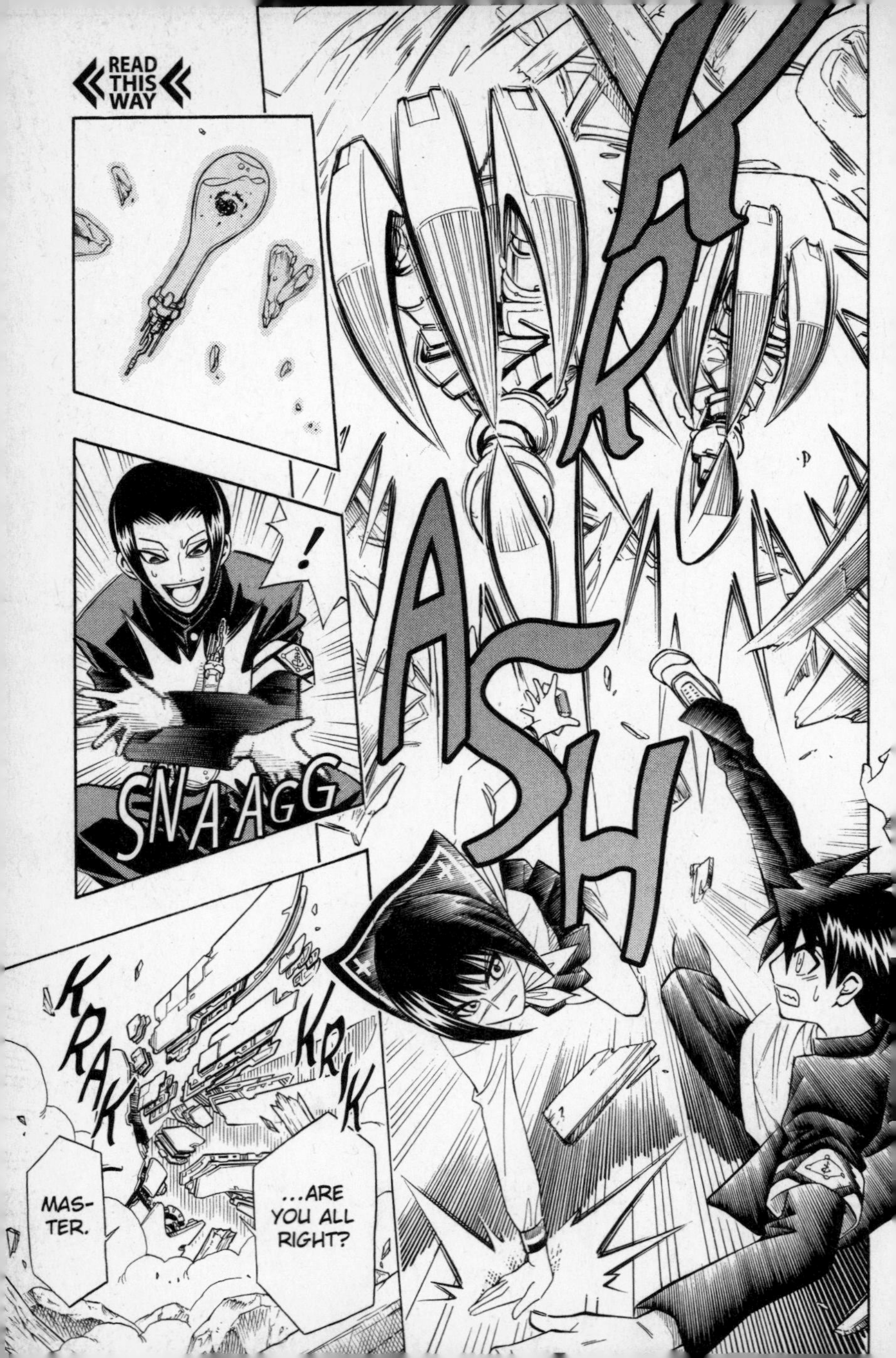
READ THIS WAY
KRASH
!
SNAAGG
KRIK
KRAK
...ARE YOU ALL RIGHT?
MASTER.

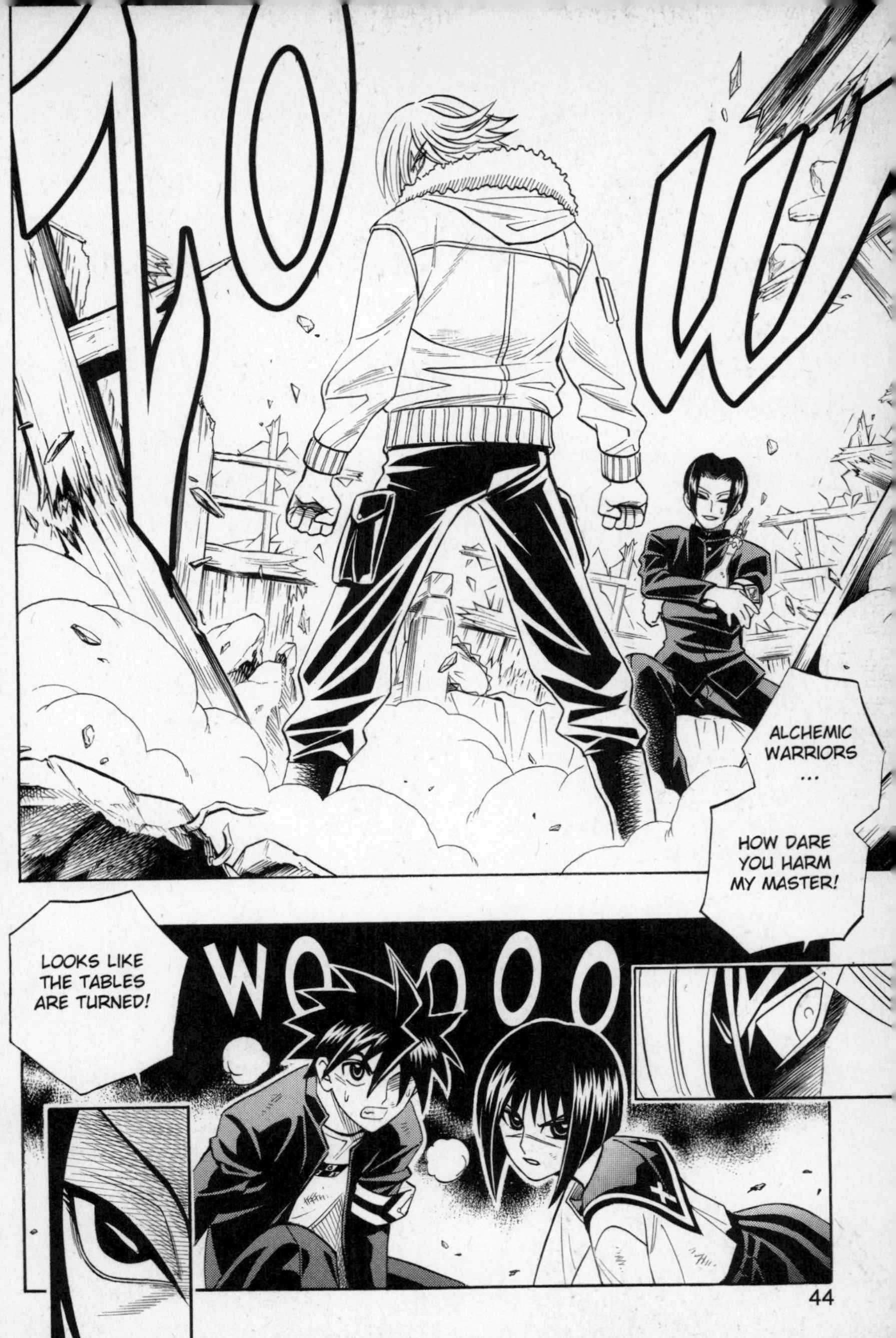
ALCHEMIC WARRIORS ...
HOW DARE YOU HARM MY MASTER!
WOOOO
LOOKS LIKE THE TABLES ARE TURNED!

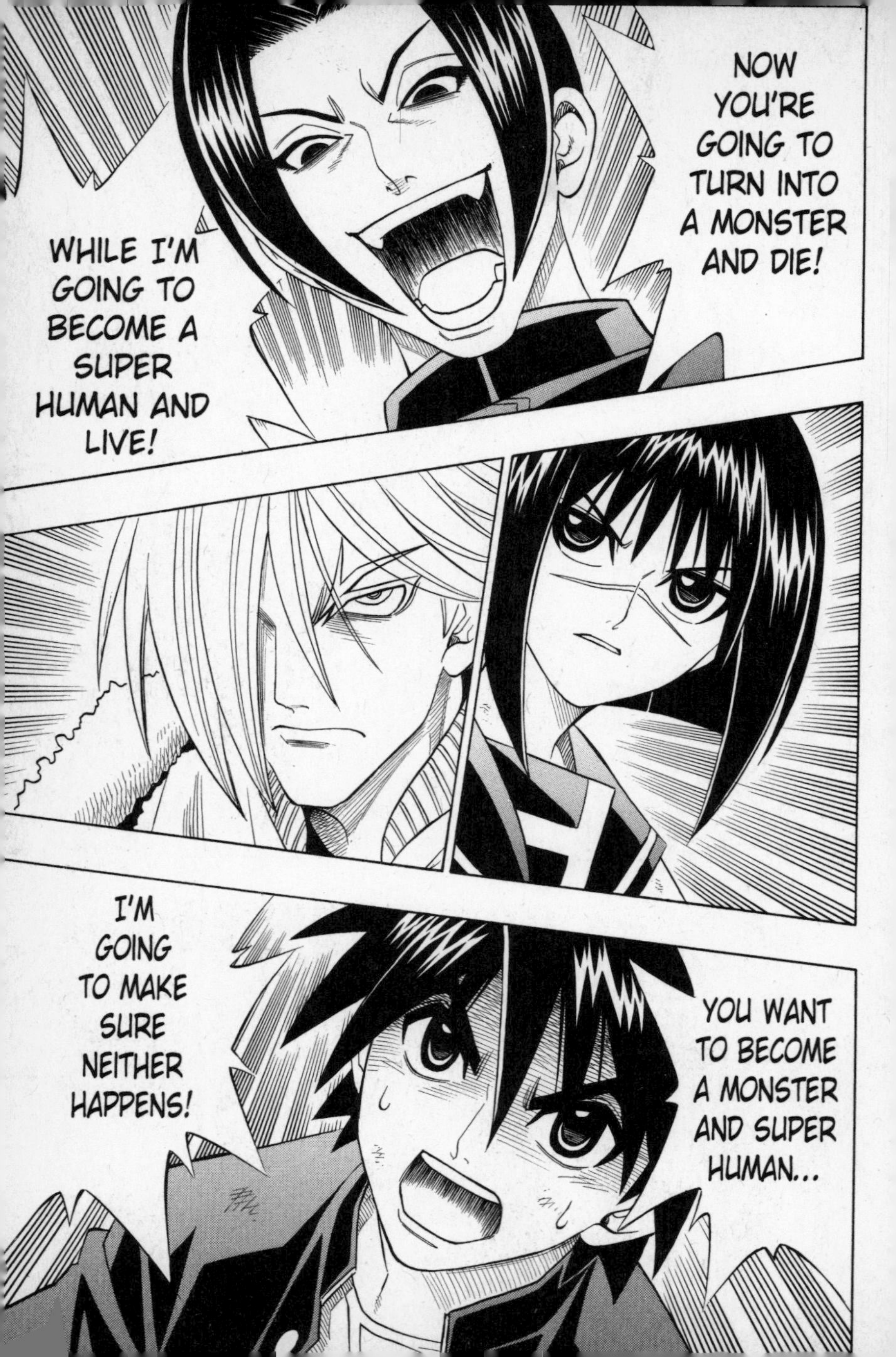
NOW YOU'RE GOING TO TURN INTO A MONSTER AND DIE!
WHILE I'M GOING TO BECOME A SUPER HUMAN AND LIVE!
YOU WANT TO BECOME A MONSTER AND SUPER HUMAN...
I'M GOING TO MAKE SURE NEITHER HAPPENS!

- Height: 172cm; Weight: 62kg
- Born: August 8th; Leo; Blood type B; 16 years old
- Favorites: Ramen, The color black, cool motorcycles
- Dislikes: Gangs, people who litter cigarette butts
- Hobby: Touring on a 50cc scooter
- Things he's good at: Breaking tiles by head-butting them (?)
- Affiliation: Private Ginsei Academy 2nd Year High School Student
  Class Room B, Dorm resident

Character File No.9
Hideyuki Okakura

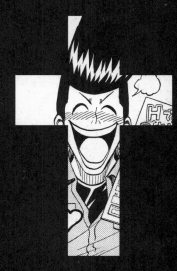

Author's Notes

- Another character created to liven up Kazuki's everyday life. He has the raised eyebrow look (the loud mouth) and he's also in charge of the joke puns.
- The more prominent one out of Kazuki's friends. Normally he's joking around with Kazuki but as an ex-delinquent he can throttle the enemy when necessary… was my initial concept but he somehow turned out to be the "So I'm controlled by passion! Damn it!" kind of guy.
- I based Hideyuki off an anime screenplay writer I went to Anime Expo with. (from my comments on the cover flap of Volume 1) He had so much character and was such a fun guy I thought if I brought his personality directly into the story he may overshadow the other characters so I ended up changing him quite a bit. But somehow, his "passionate" side stuck…

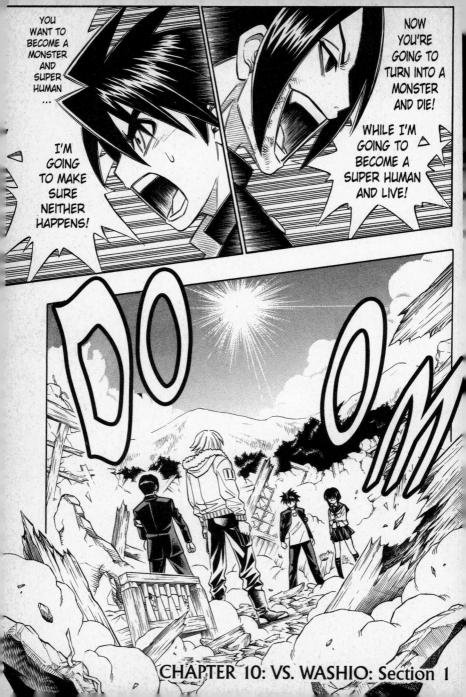

CHAPTER 10: VS. WASHIO: Section 1

CHAPTER 10

Homunculus Overview

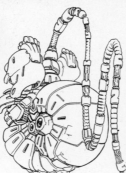

- The core is approximately 3cm and looks like a fetus. It will not survive for more than a day outside a small, enclosed space.
- Once it reaches the human brain, it overtakes the host's body and turns it into a monster that takes on traits of the base organism.

- The human's mind is killed and the mind of the base organism takes over. (i.e. – The animal/plant trait assimilates with human intelligence)
- Main diet is human but can feed off of other things. (The ultimate omnivore)
- Only the powers of Alchemy can destroy it. It's possible to inflict damage but will always regenerate. Close to being immortal.
- Homunculi are created using other organisms' cells as base.

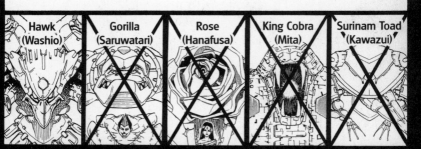

| Hawk (Washio) | Gorilla (Saruwatari) | Rose (Hanafusa) | King Cobra (Mita) | Surinam Toad (Kawazui) |

VS. WASHIO: Section 1

Humanoid Homunculus

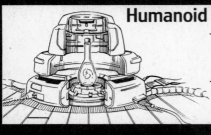

- A Homunculus that uses a human as its base enables the host to keep their mind but alters their body into being near immortal. Feeding on humans is unavoidable.
- By becoming a humanoid Homunculus Koushaku is planning to attain a new life. In two more days Koushaku's core will be complete.

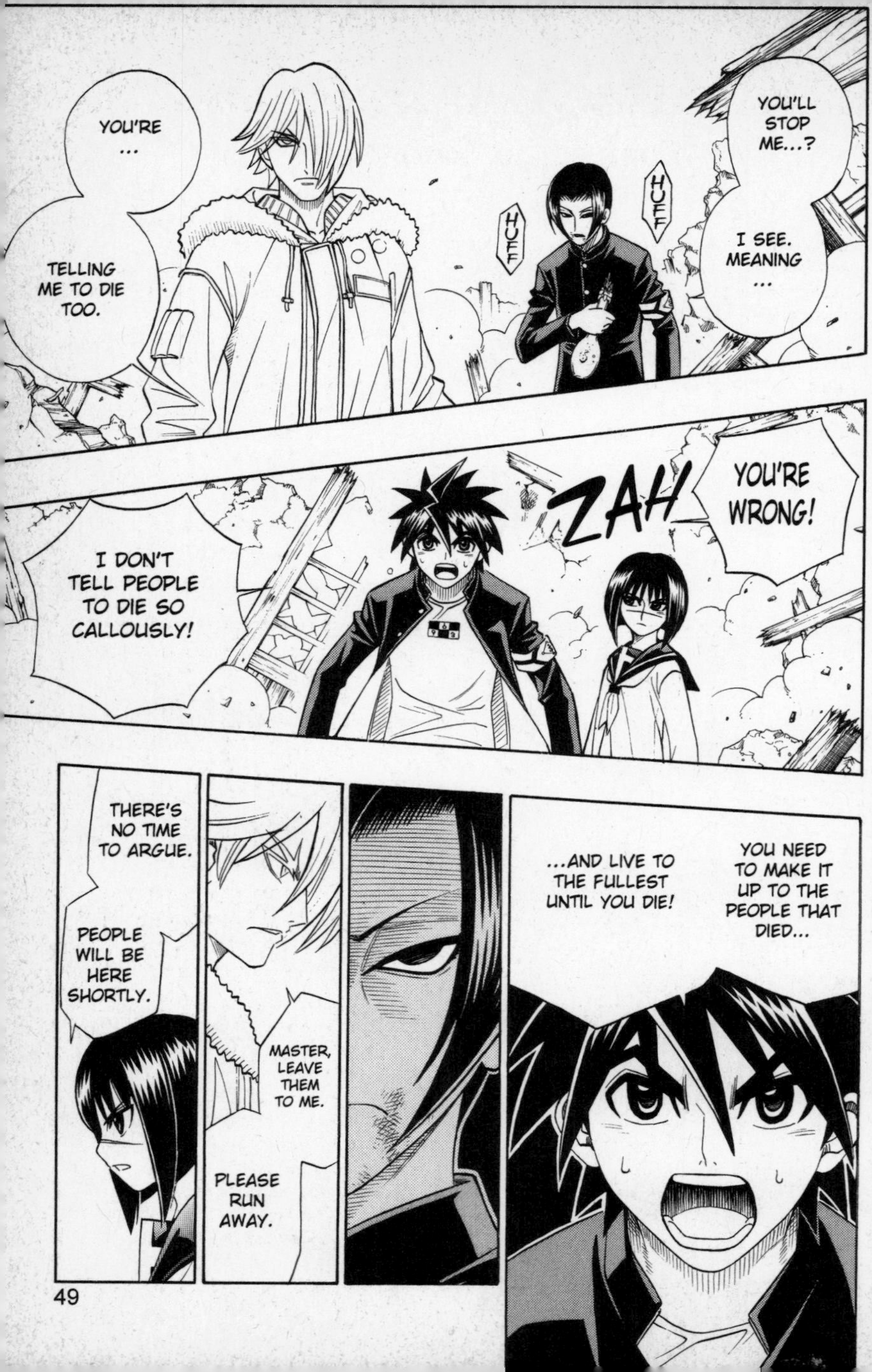
YOU'LL STOP ME...?
I SEE. MEANING ...
HUFF
HUFF
YOU'RE ...
TELLING ME TO DIE TOO.
YOU'RE WRONG!
ZAH
I DON'T TELL PEOPLE TO DIE SO CALLOUSLY!
YOU NEED TO MAKE IT UP TO THE PEOPLE THAT DIED...
...AND LIVE TO THE FULLEST UNTIL YOU DIE!
MASTER, LEAVE THEM TO ME.
PLEASE RUN AWAY.
THERE'S NO TIME TO ARGUE.
PEOPLE WILL BE HERE SHORTLY.

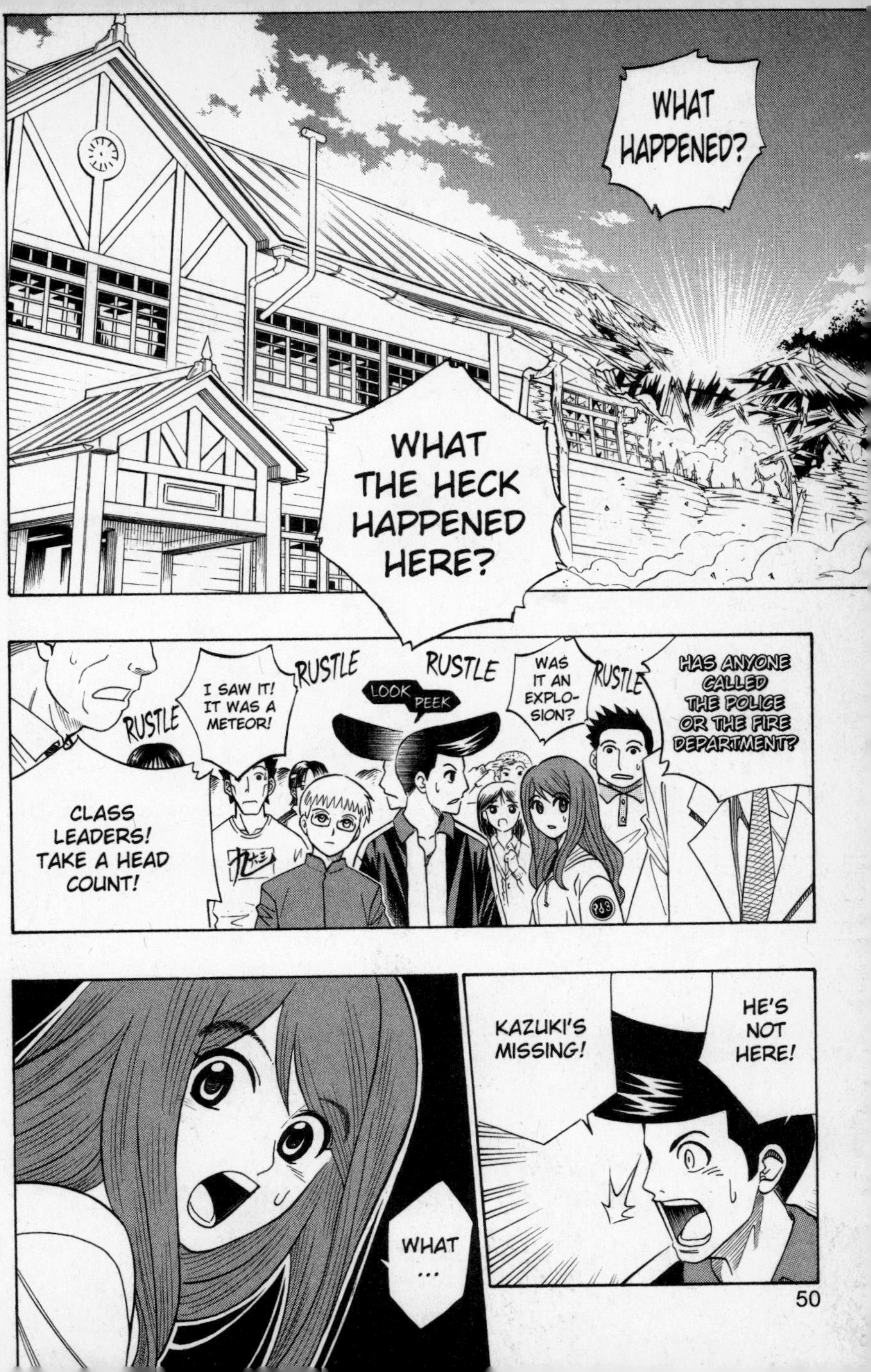
WHAT HAPPENED?
WHAT THE HECK HAPPENED HERE?
HAS ANYONE CALLED THE POLICE OR THE FIRE DEPARTMENT?
RUSTLE
WAS IT AN EXPLOSION?
RUSTLE
LOOK
PEEK
RUSTLE
I SAW IT! IT WAS A METEOR!
RUSTLE
CLASS LEADERS! TAKE A HEAD COUNT!
HE'S NOT HERE!
KAZUKI'S MISSING!
WHAT ...

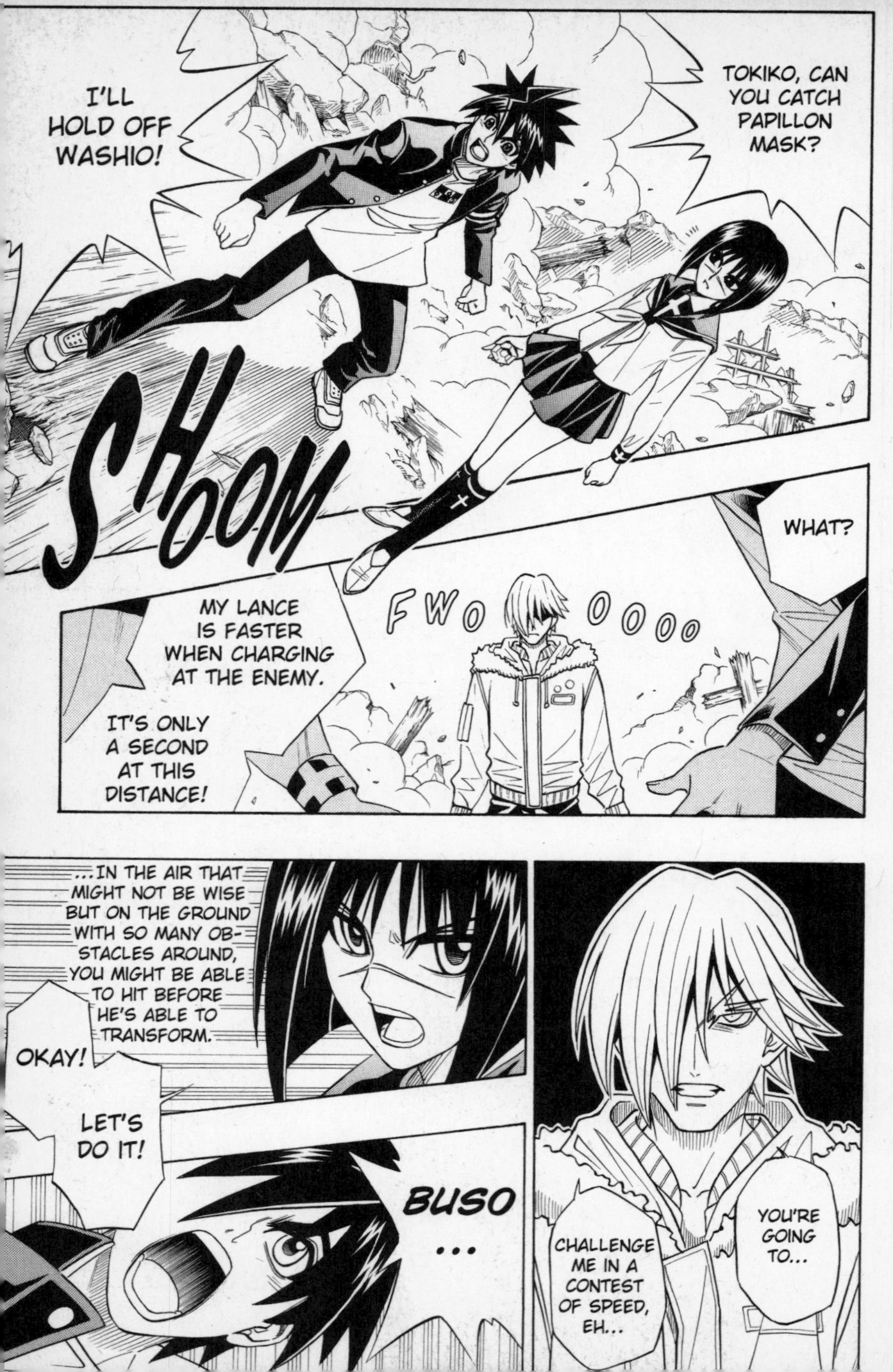
TOKIKO, CAN YOU CATCH PAPILLON MASK?
I'LL HOLD OFF WASHIO!
SHOOM
WHAT?
FWO OOOO
MY LANCE IS FASTER WHEN CHARGING AT THE ENEMY.
IT'S ONLY A SECOND AT THIS DISTANCE!
YOU'RE GOING TO...
CHALLENGE ME IN A CONTEST OF SPEED, EH...
...IN THE AIR THAT MIGHT NOT BE WISE BUT ON THE GROUND WITH SO MANY OB-STACLES AROUND, YOU MIGHT BE ABLE TO HIT BEFORE HE'S ABLE TO TRANSFORM.
OKAY!
LET'S DO IT!
BUSO ...

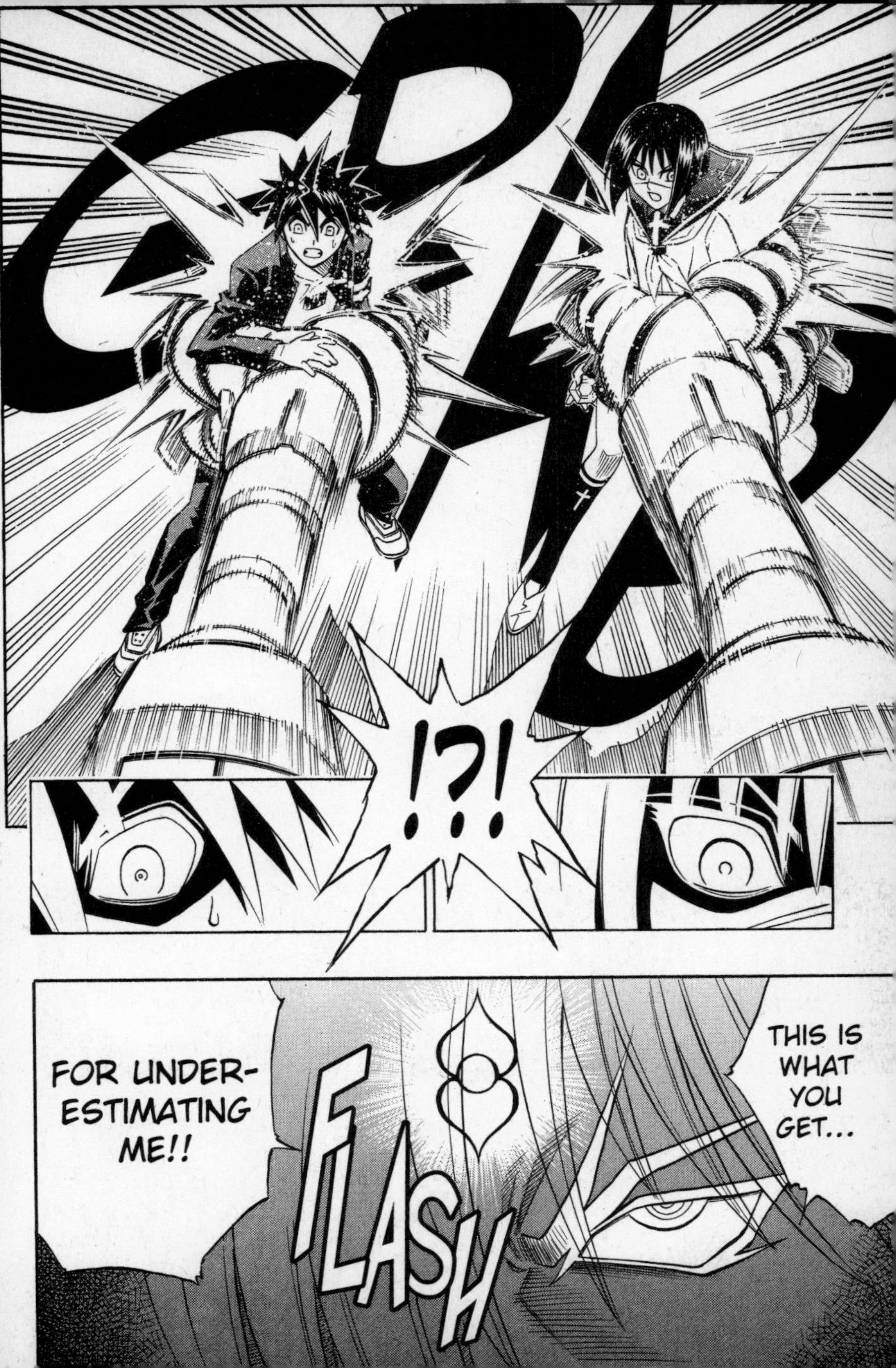
!?!
THIS IS WHAT YOU GET...
FLASH
FOR UNDER-ESTIMATING ME!!

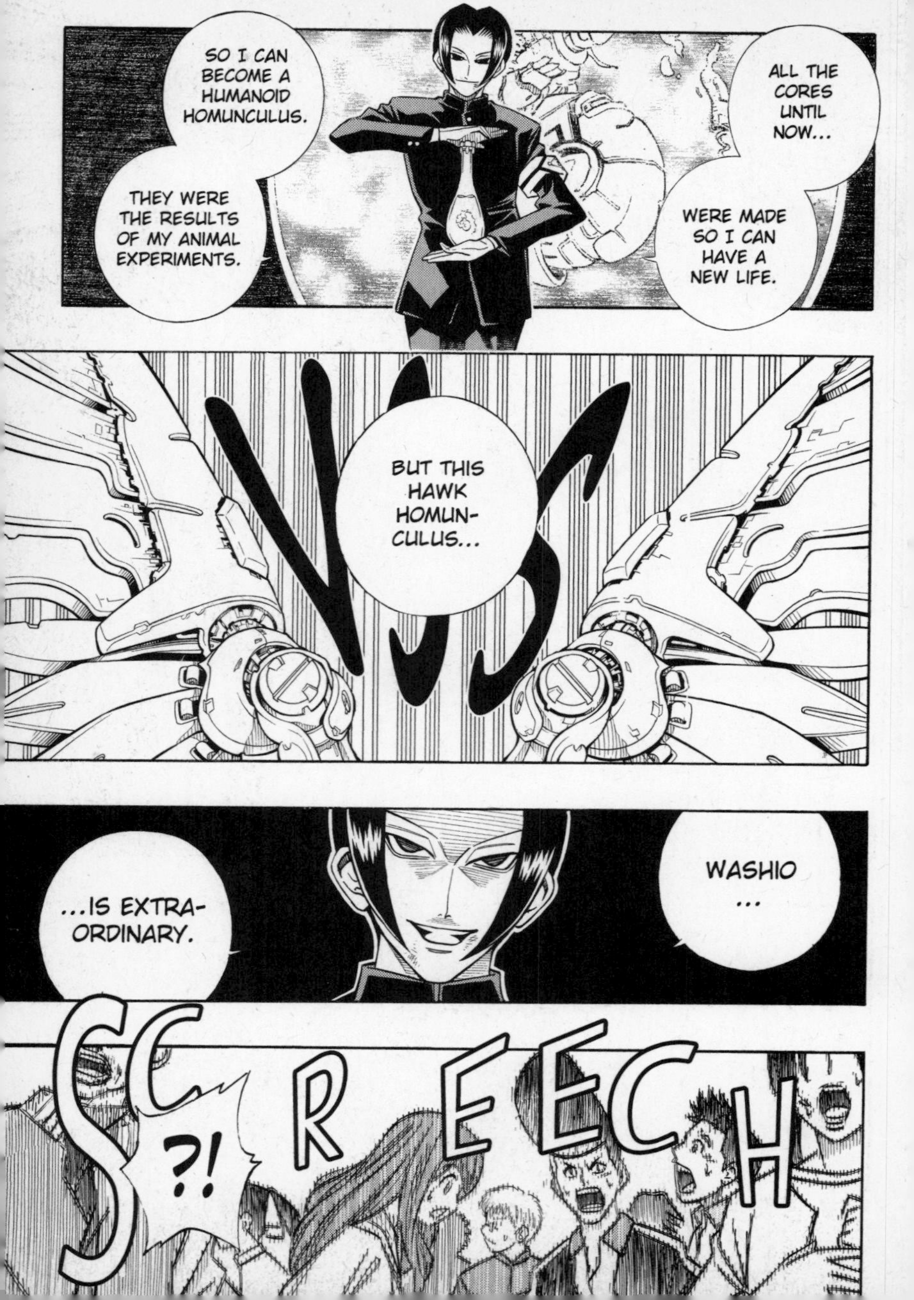
ALL THE CORES UNTIL NOW...
WERE MADE SO I CAN HAVE A NEW LIFE.
SO I CAN BECOME A HUMANOID HOMUNCULUS.
THEY WERE THE RESULTS OF MY ANIMAL EXPERIMENTS.
BUT THIS HAWK HOMUN-CULUS...
WASHIO ...
...IS EXTRA-ORDINARY.
SCREECH
?!

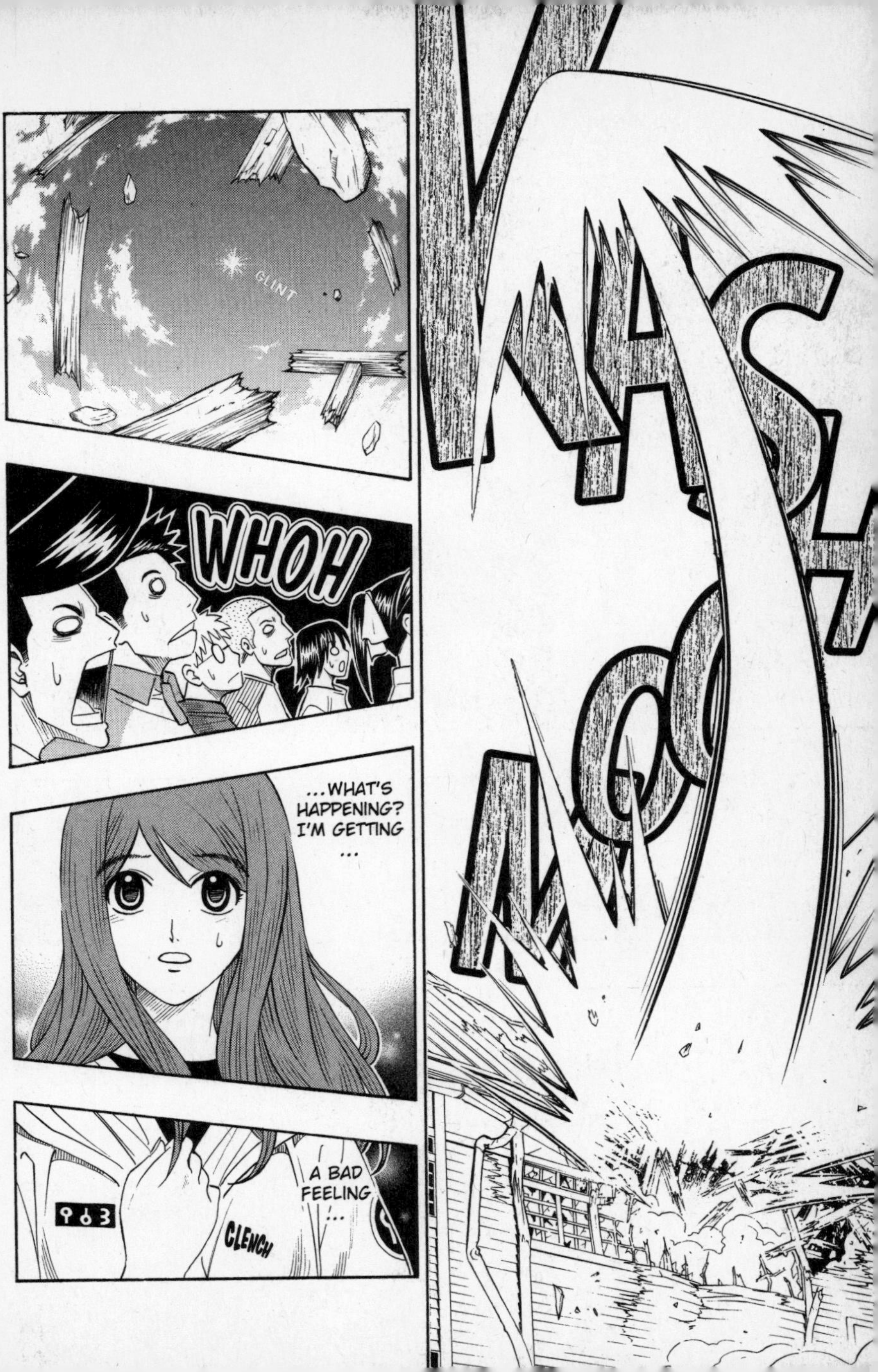
GLINT
WHOH
...WHAT'S HAPPENING? I'M GETTING ...
A BAD FEELING ...
963
CLENCH

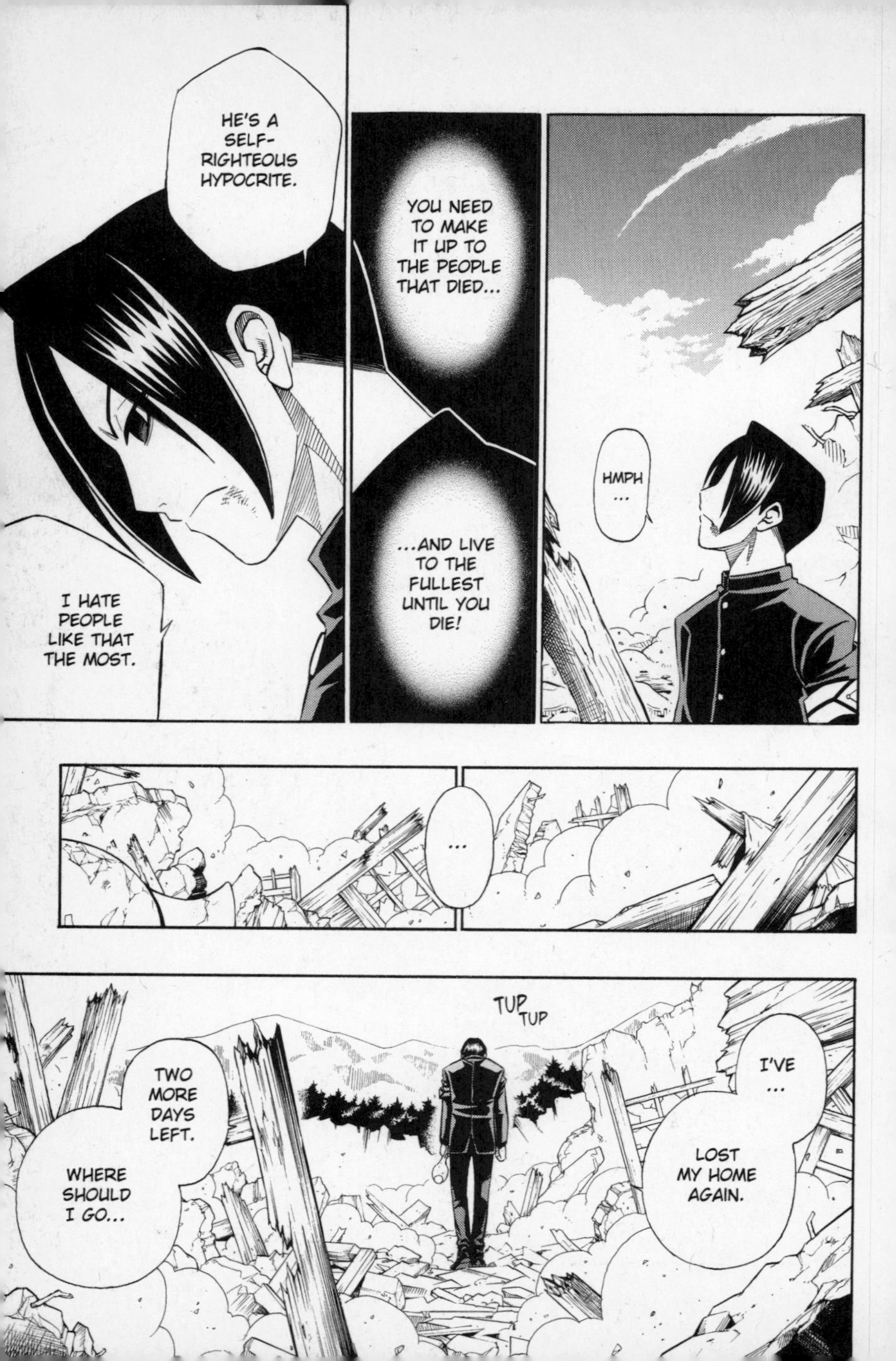
HMPH...
YOU NEED TO MAKE IT UP TO THE PEOPLE THAT DIED...
...AND LIVE TO THE FULLEST UNTIL YOU DIE!
HE'S A SELF-RIGHTEOUS HYPOCRITE.
I HATE PEOPLE LIKE THAT THE MOST.
...
TUP TUP
I'VE...
LOST MY HOME AGAIN.
TWO MORE DAYS LEFT.
WHERE SHOULD I GO...

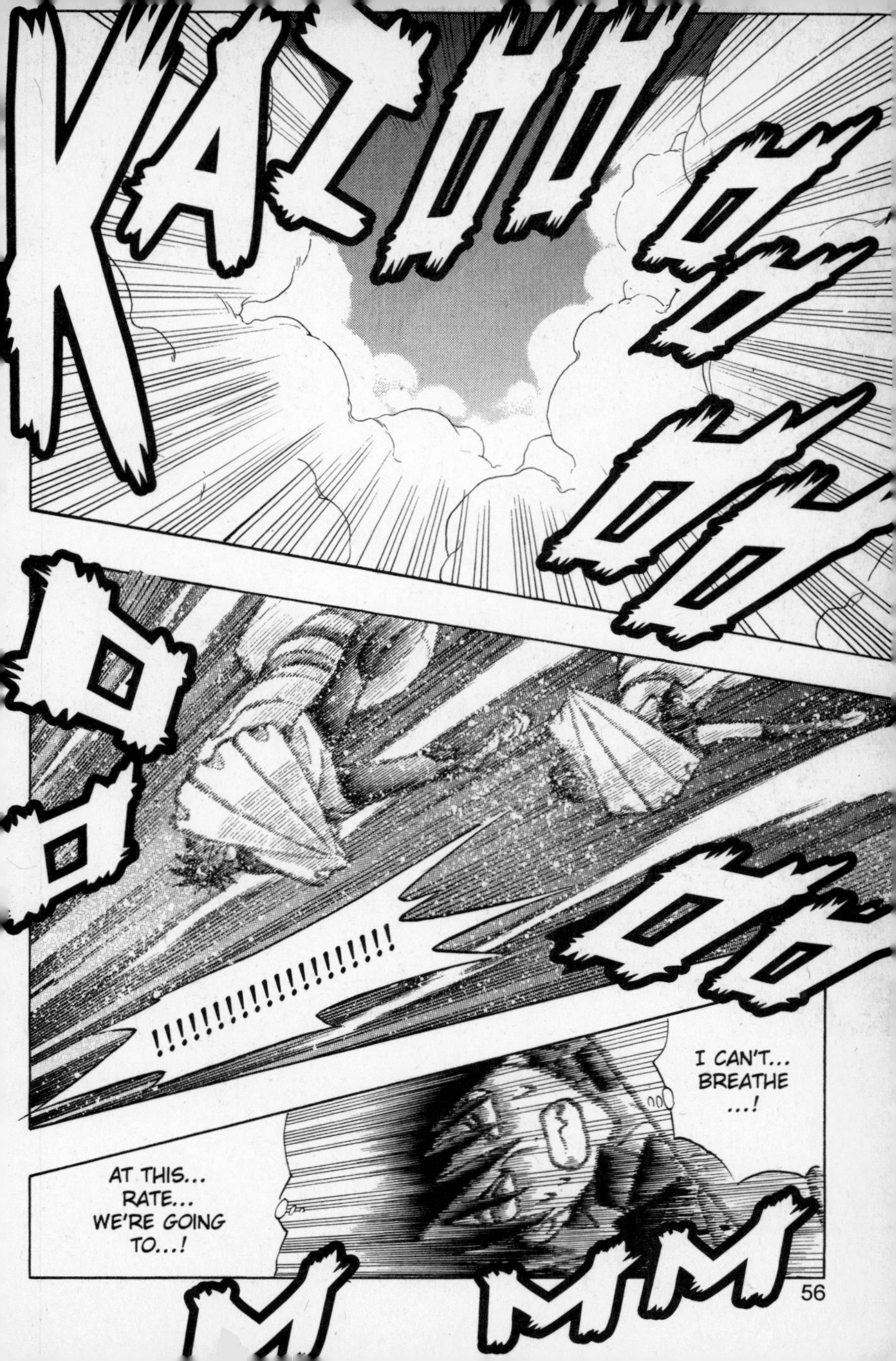
!!!!!!!!!!!!!!!!!!!!!!!!!!!
I CAN'T... BREATHE ...!
AT THIS... RATE... WE'RE GOING TO...!

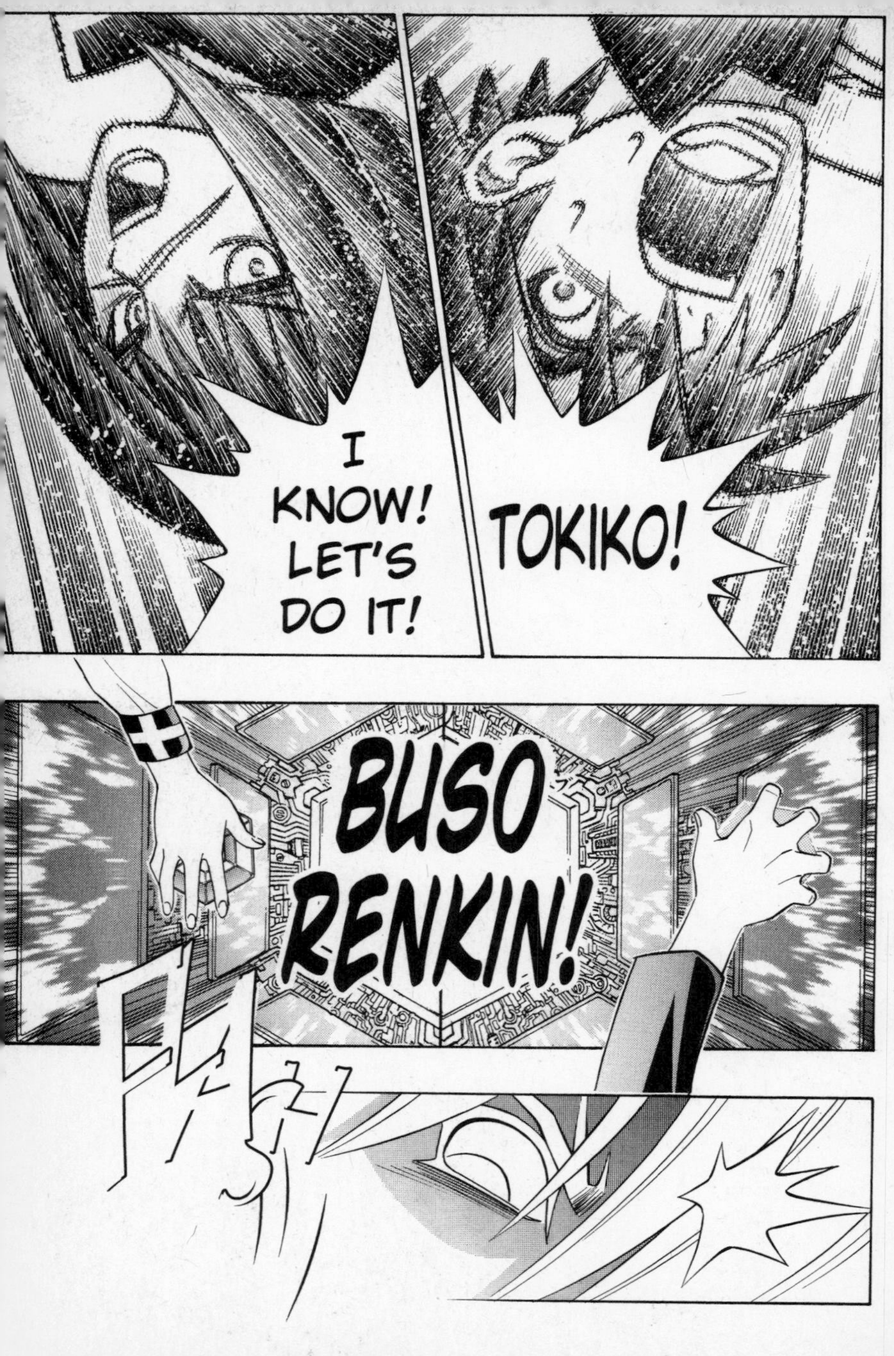
TOKIKO!
I KNOW! LET'S DO IT!
BUSO RENKIN!

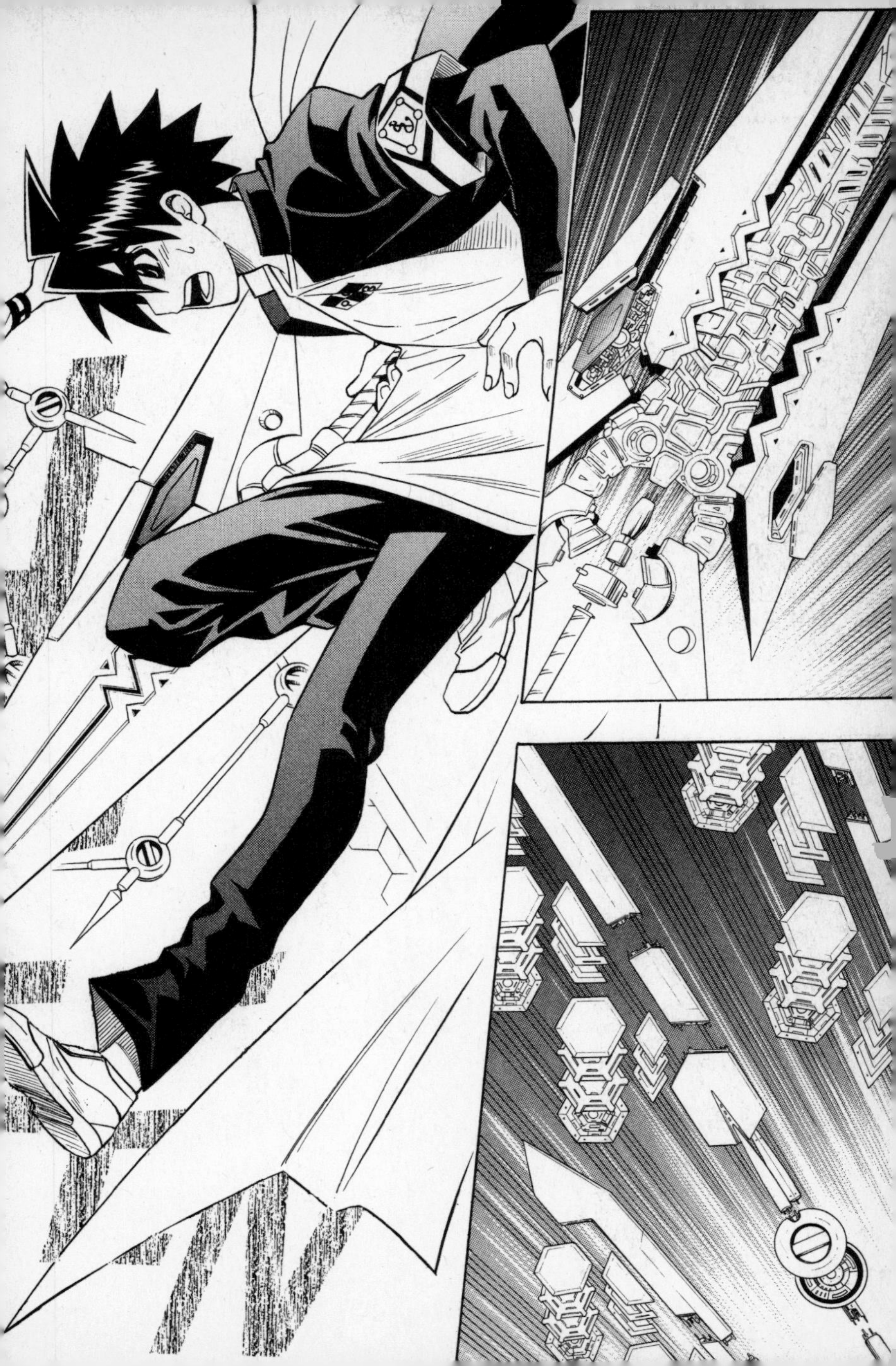

READ THIS WAY

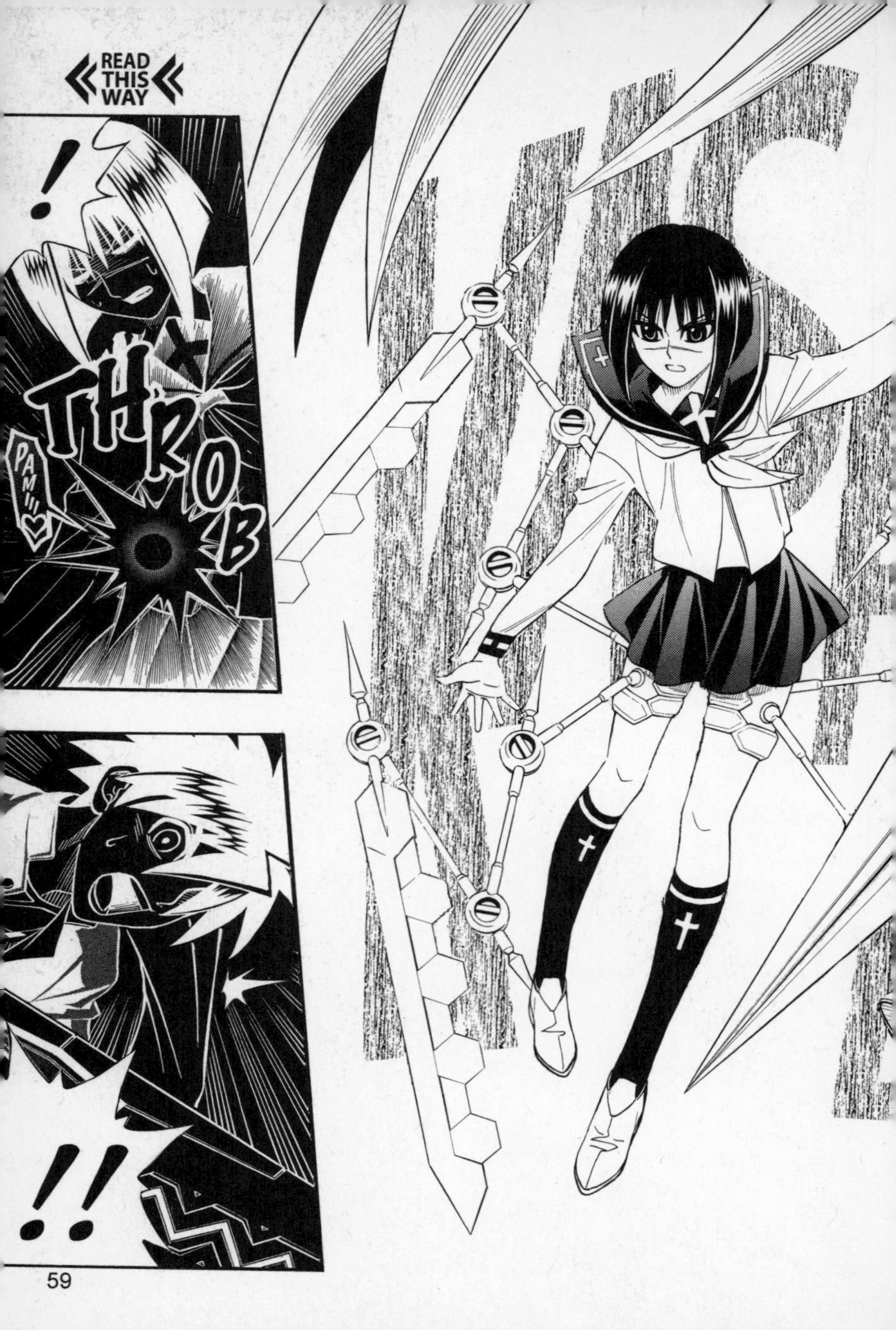
!
THROB
PAM!!!♥
!!

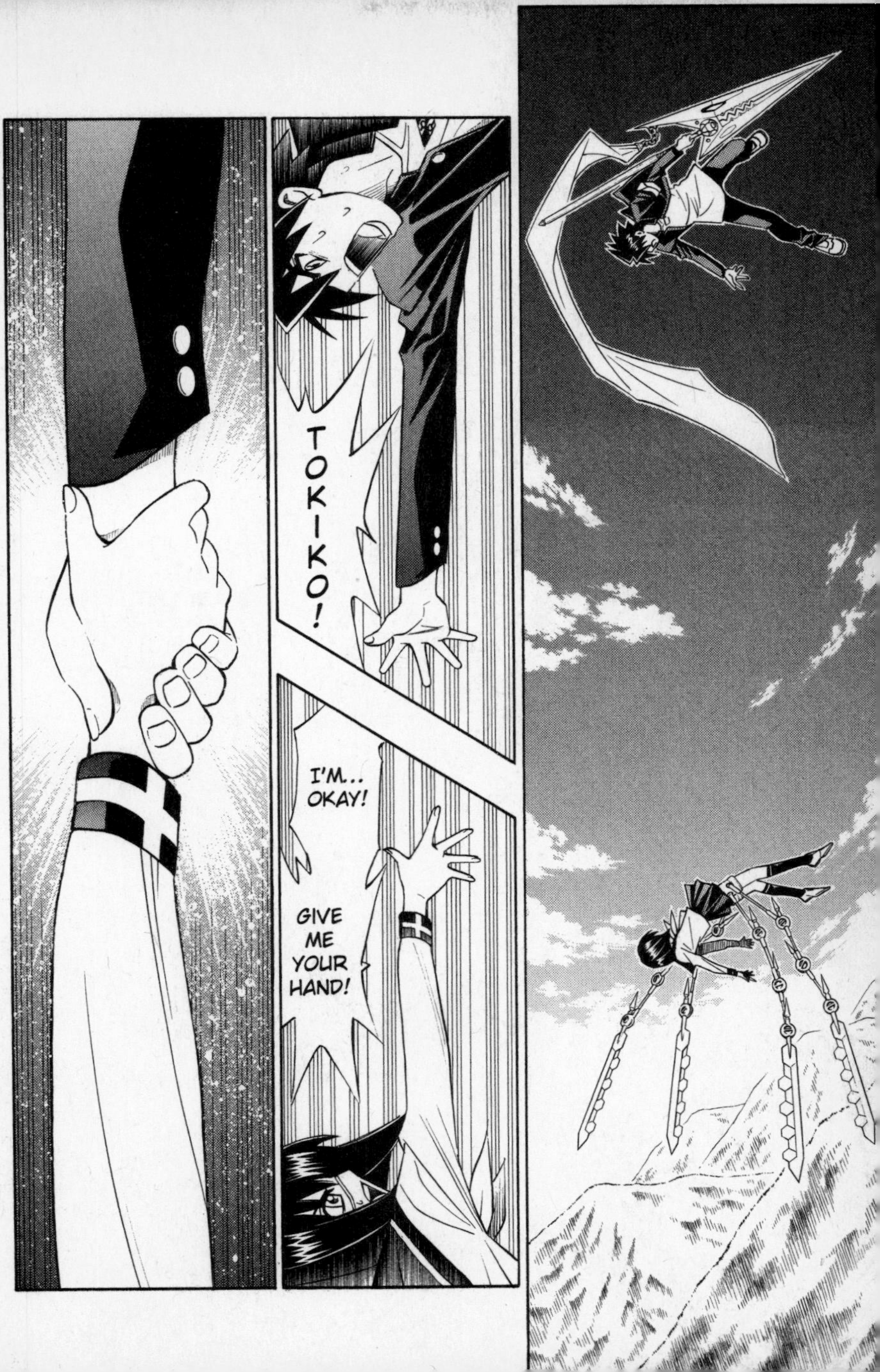
TOKIKO!
I'M... OKAY!
GIVE ME YOUR HAND!

READ THIS WAY

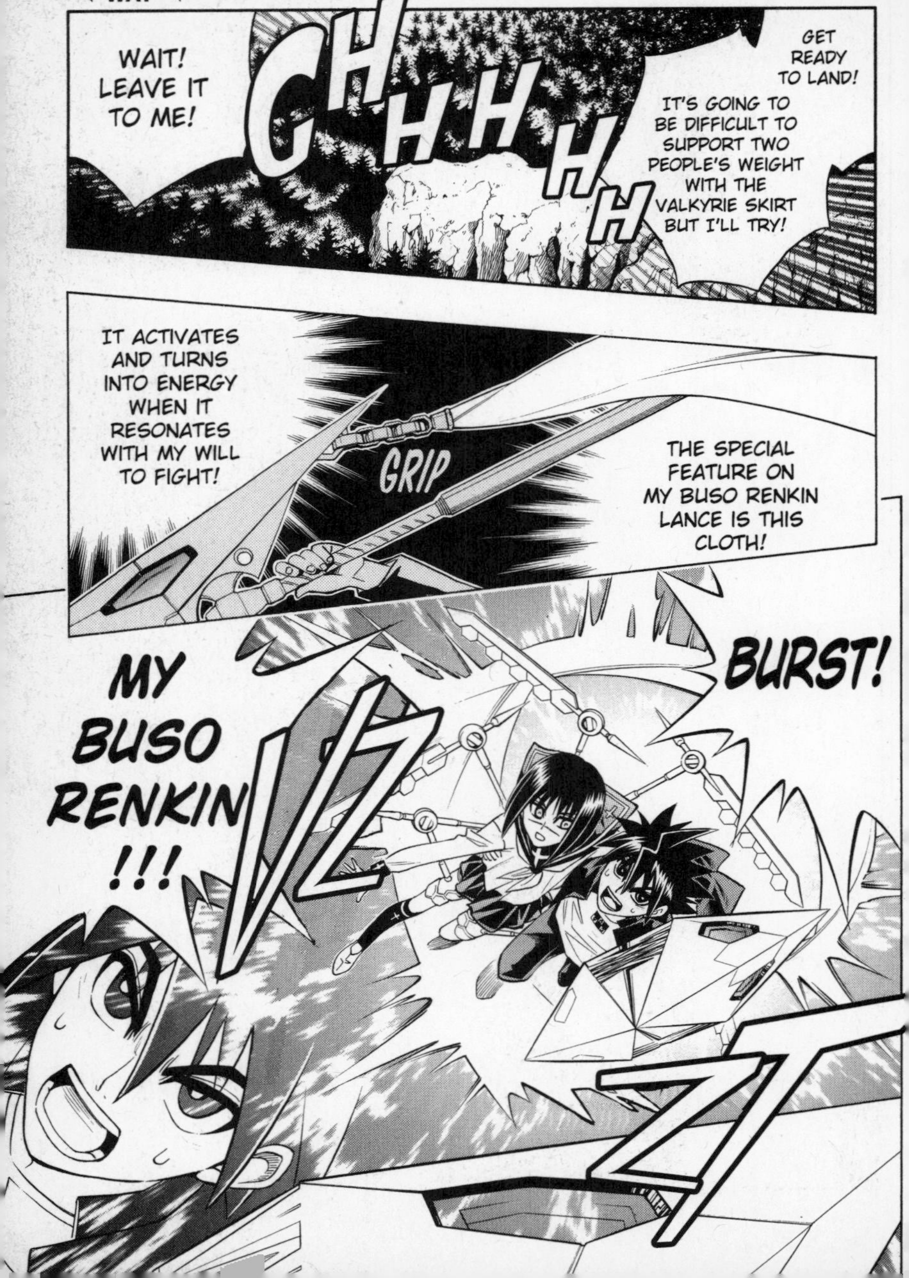
GET READY TO LAND!
IT'S GOING TO BE DIFFICULT TO SUPPORT TWO PEOPLE'S WEIGHT WITH THE VALKYRIE SKIRT BUT I'LL TRY!
CHHHHHH
WAIT! LEAVE IT TO ME!
THE SPECIAL FEATURE ON MY BUSO RENKIN LANCE IS THIS CLOTH!
GRIP
IT ACTIVATES AND TURNS INTO ENERGY WHEN IT RESONATES WITH MY WILL TO FIGHT!
BURST!
MY BUSO RENKIN !!!

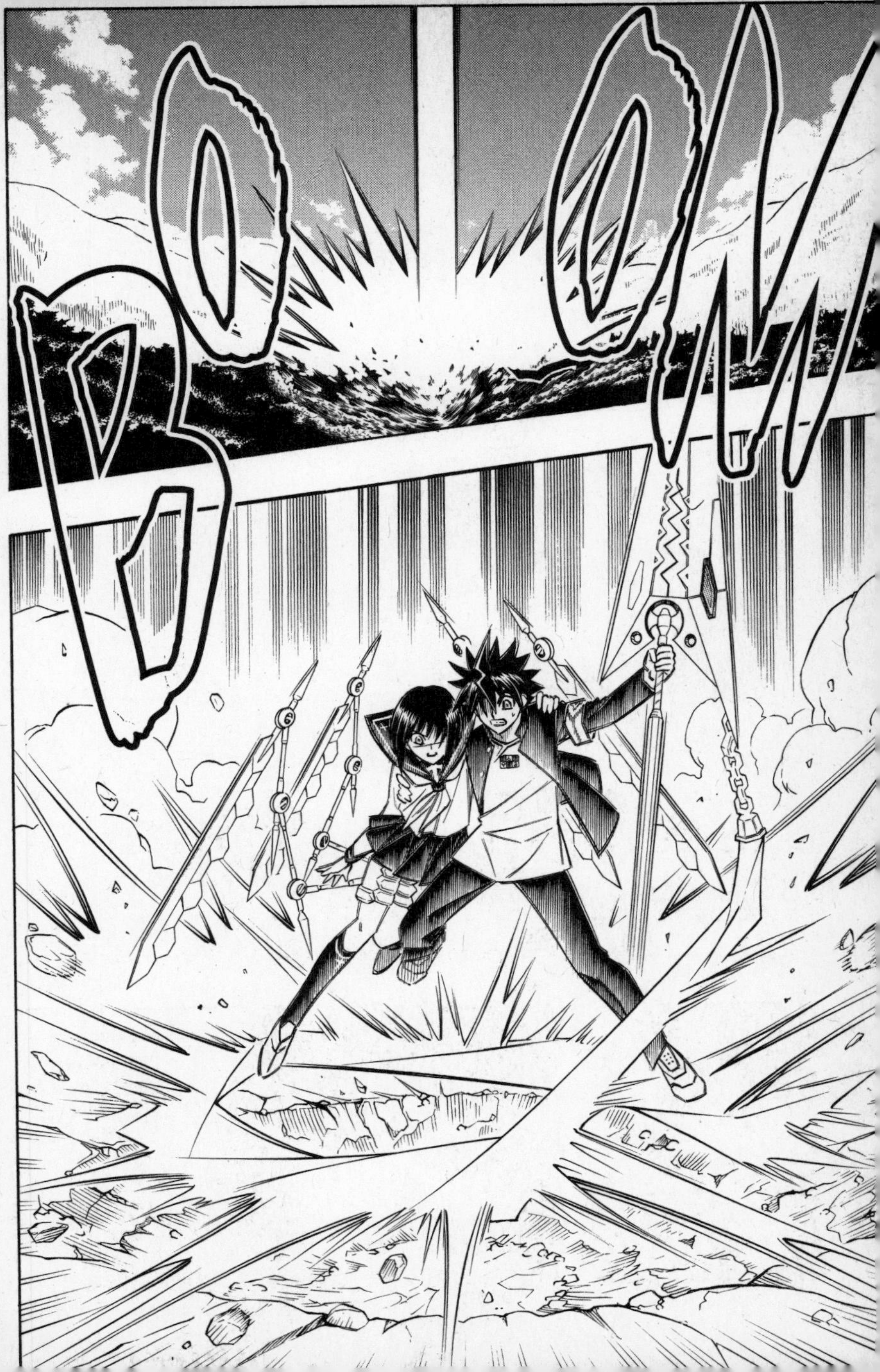
BOOM

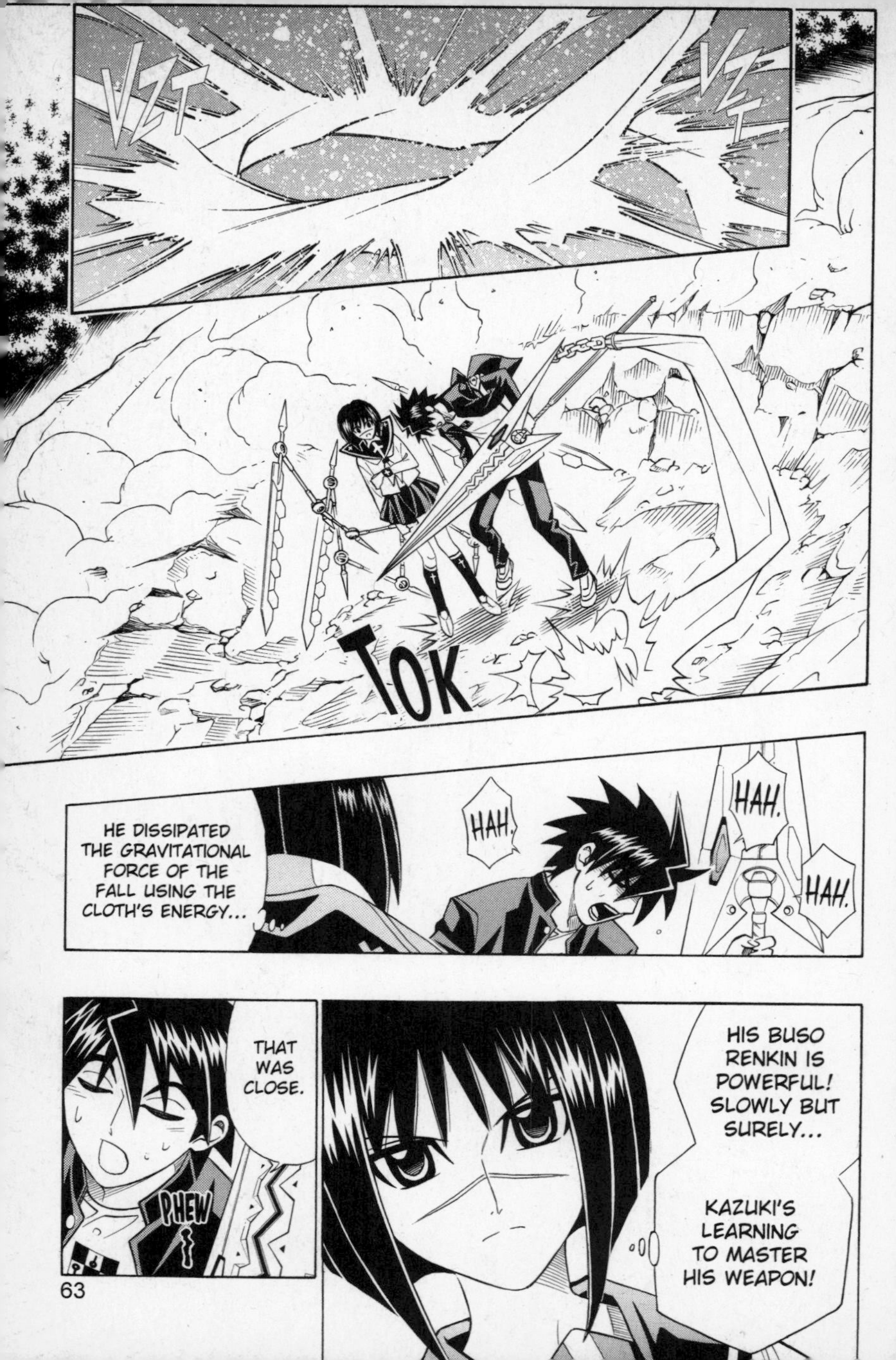
VZT
VZT
TOK
HAH.
HAH.
HAH.
HE DISSIPATED THE GRAVITATIONAL FORCE OF THE FALL USING THE CLOTH'S ENERGY...
HIS BUSO RENKIN IS POWERFUL! SLOWLY BUT SURELY...
KAZUKI'S LEARNING TO MASTER HIS WEAPON!
THAT WAS CLOSE.
PHEW

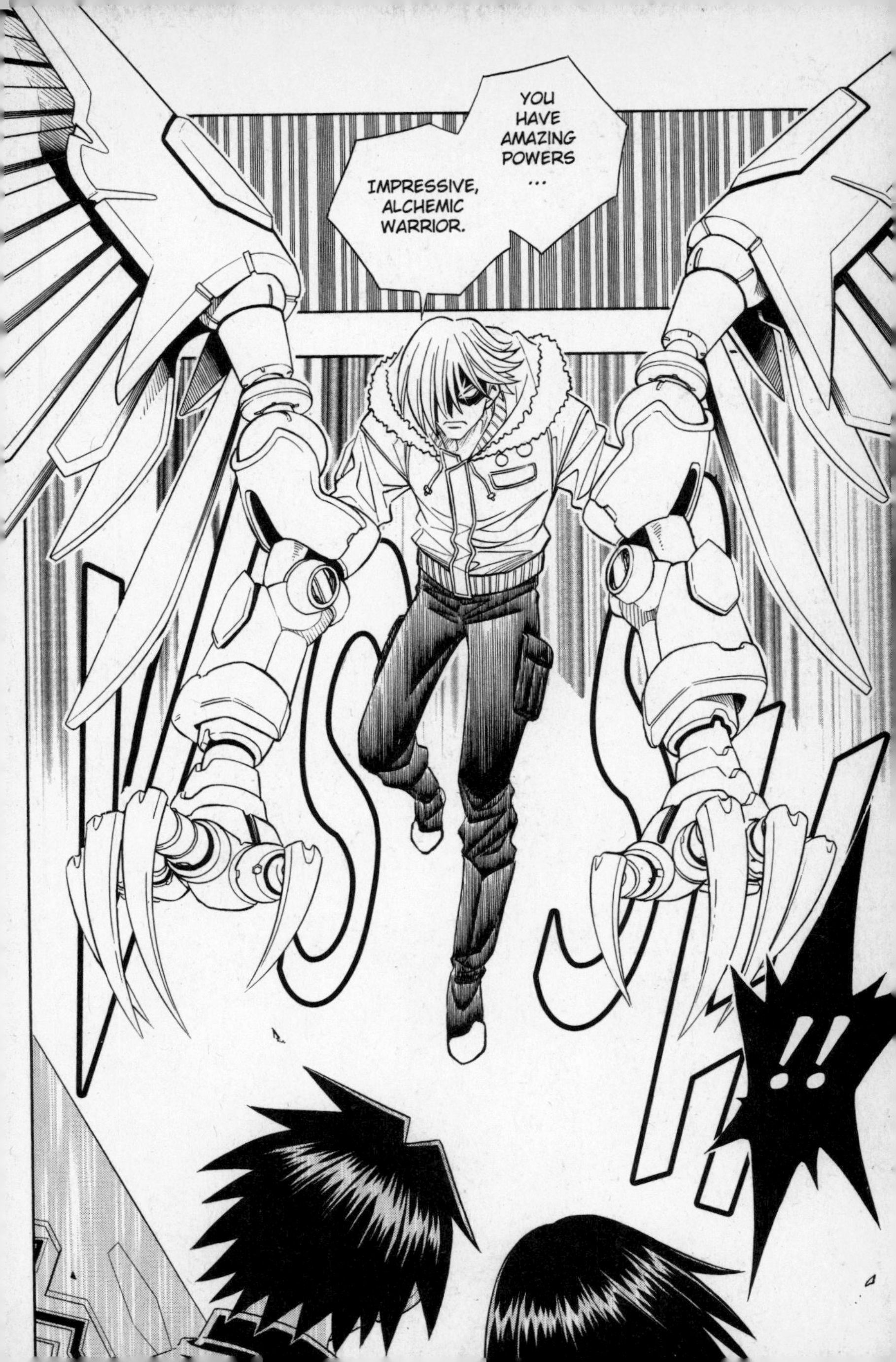
YOU HAVE AMAZING POWERS ...
IMPRESSIVE, ALCHEMIC WARRIOR.
!!

READ THIS WAY

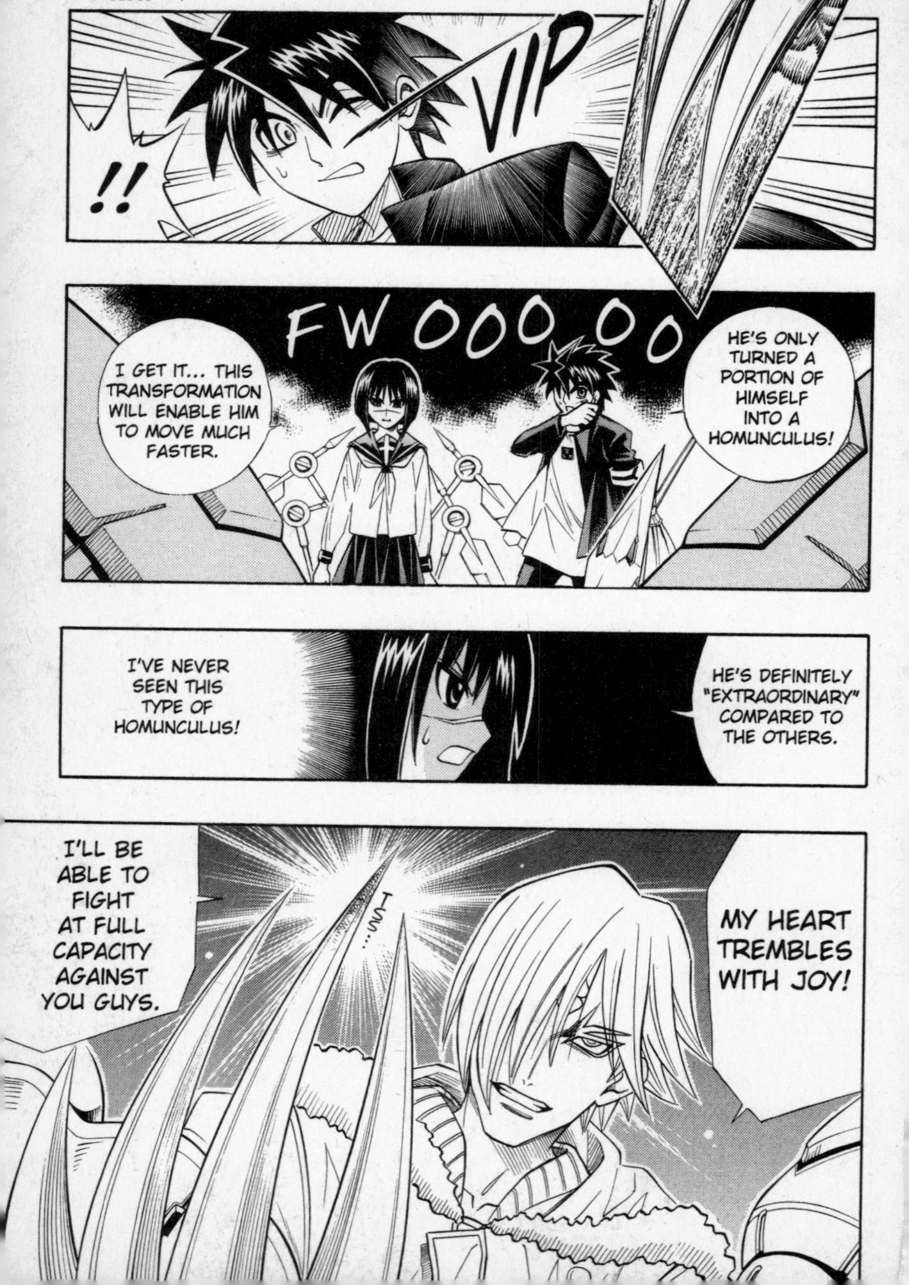
VIP
!!
HE'S ONLY TURNED A PORTION OF HIMSELF INTO A HOMUNCULUS!
FW OOO OO
I GET IT... THIS TRANSFORMATION WILL ENABLE HIM TO MOVE MUCH FASTER.
HE'S DEFINITELY "EXTRAORDINARY" COMPARED TO THE OTHERS.
I'VE NEVER SEEN THIS TYPE OF HOMUNCULUS!
MY HEART TREMBLES WITH JOY!
TSS...
I'LL BE ABLE TO FIGHT AT FULL CAPACITY AGAINST YOU GUYS.

· Height: 183cm; Weight: 85kg
· Born: September 14th; Virgo; Blood Type A; 16 years old
· Favorites: Coke, The color white, late night radio programs
· Dislikes: The eyes of broiled fish, gory horror films
· Hobby: Contributing to late night programs on the radio
· Things he's good at: Drawing, illustrating
· Affiliation: Private Ginsei Academy 2nd Year High School
             Student Class Room B, Dorm resident

Character File No.10

Masashi Daihama

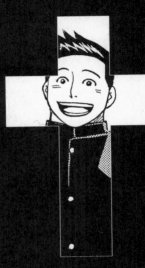

Author's Notes

· Another character created to liven up Kazuki's everyday life. He has the curved
  eyebrow look (the Worrier) and he's also in charge of the joke puns.
· The laid-back one out of Kazuki's friends. He's usually running around backing up
  Kazuki and crew but as his name suggests he'll use his large body to protect his
  friends if necessary… was my initial concept but he somehow turned out to be the
  guy who's at the mercy of Kazuki's actions and always the most surprised.
· I based Daihama off an anime character designer I went to Anime Expo with. (from
  my comments on the cover flap of Volume 1). He's reserved but yet extremely
  talented. There's a Japanese proverb that describes him well: "A great hawk hides his
  claws." I wanted to incorporate that aspect into a character in my story so I borrowed
  his likeness.

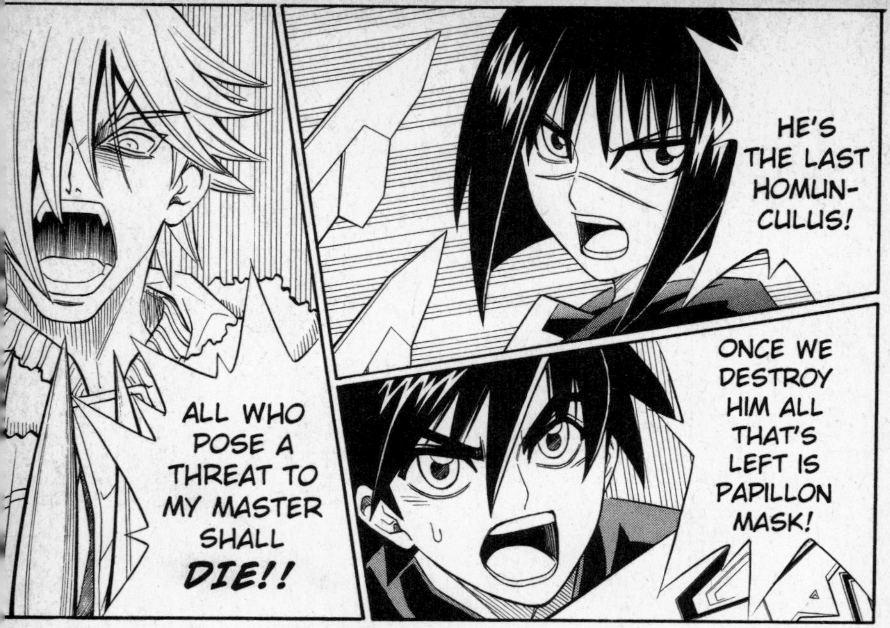
HE'S THE LAST HOMUN-CULUS!
ONCE WE DESTROY HIM ALL THAT'S LEFT IS PAPILLON MASK!
ALL WHO POSE A THREAT TO MY MASTER SHALL *DIE!!*

CHAPTER 11:
VS. WASHIO:
Part 2: Section 1

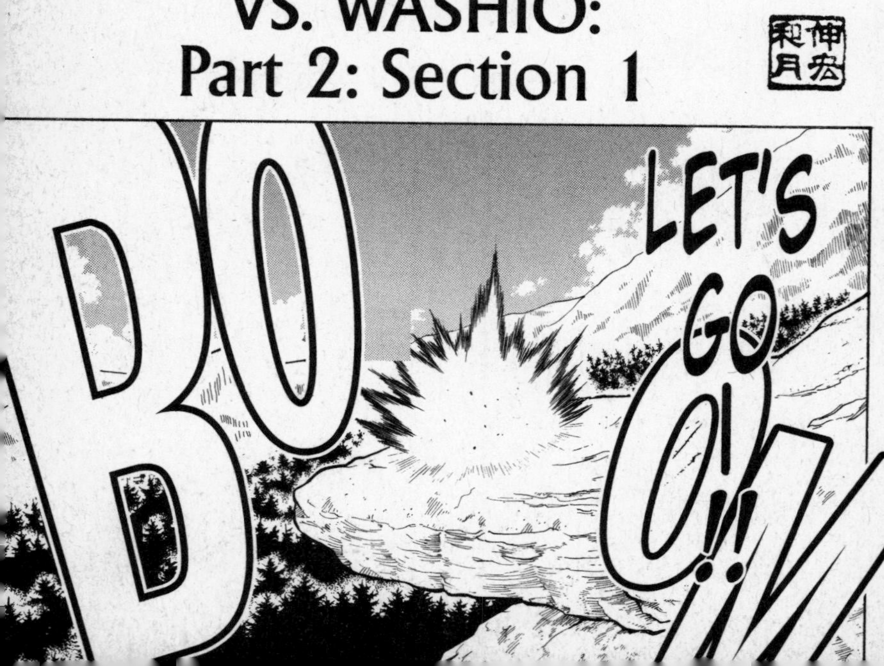
LET'S GO

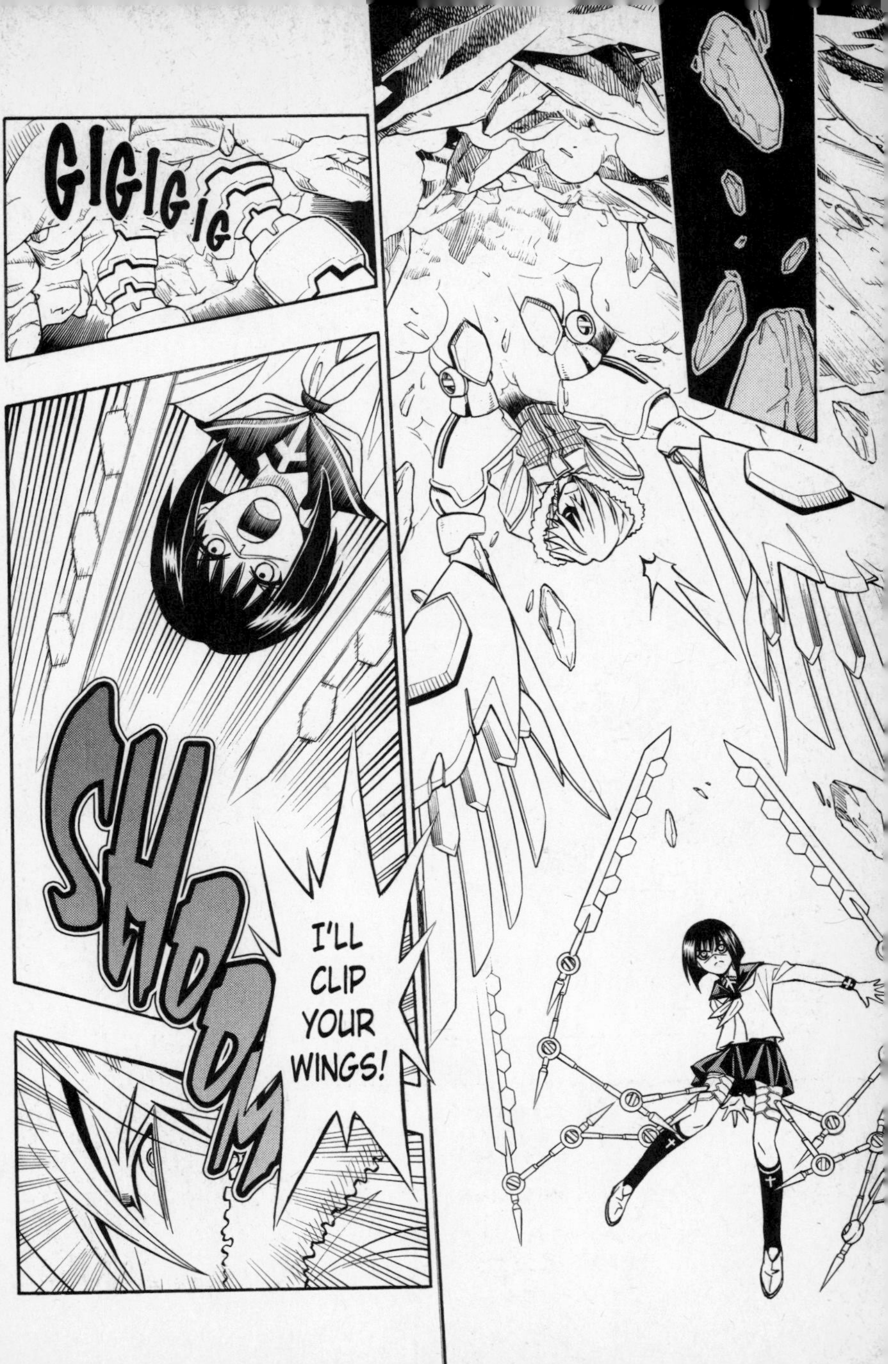
I'LL CLIP YOUR WINGS!
GIGIGIG

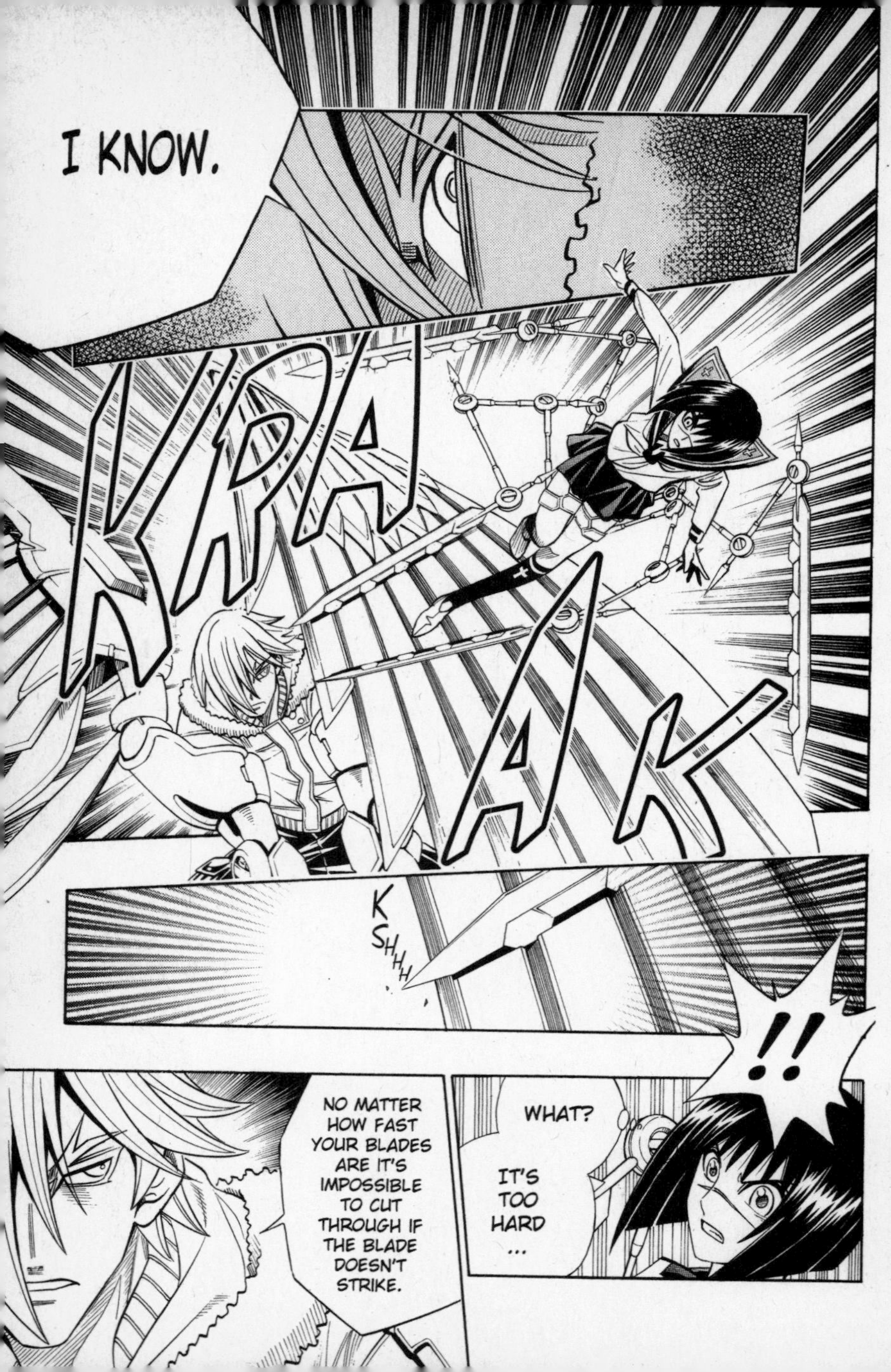
I KNOW.
KRAAAK
KSHHH
!!
WHAT?
IT'S TOO HARD ...
NO MATTER HOW FAST YOUR BLADES ARE IT'S IMPOSSIBLE TO CUT THROUGH IF THE BLADE DOESN'T STRIKE.

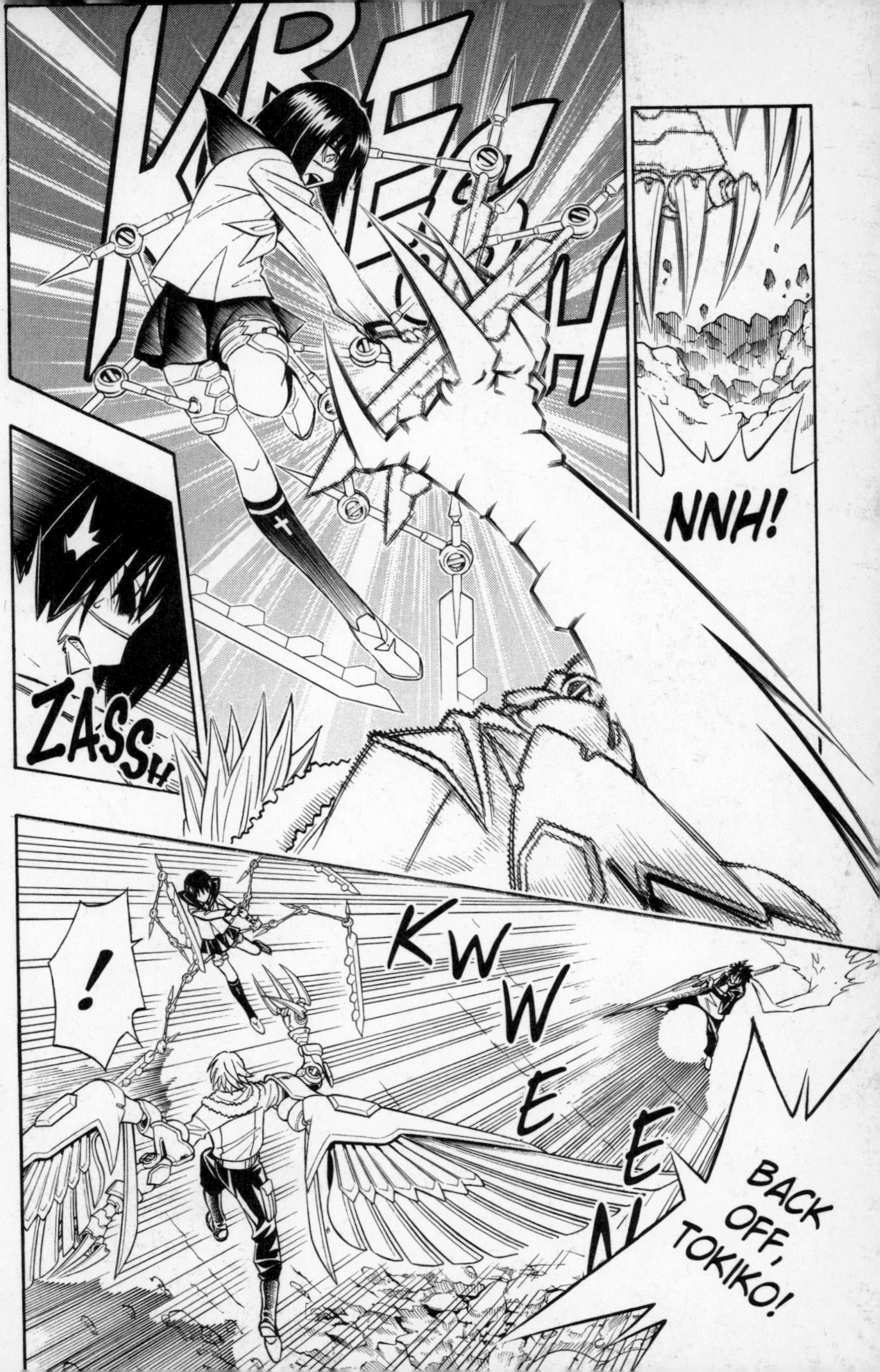
NNH!
ZASSH
BACK OFF, TOKIKO!
KWWEEN
!

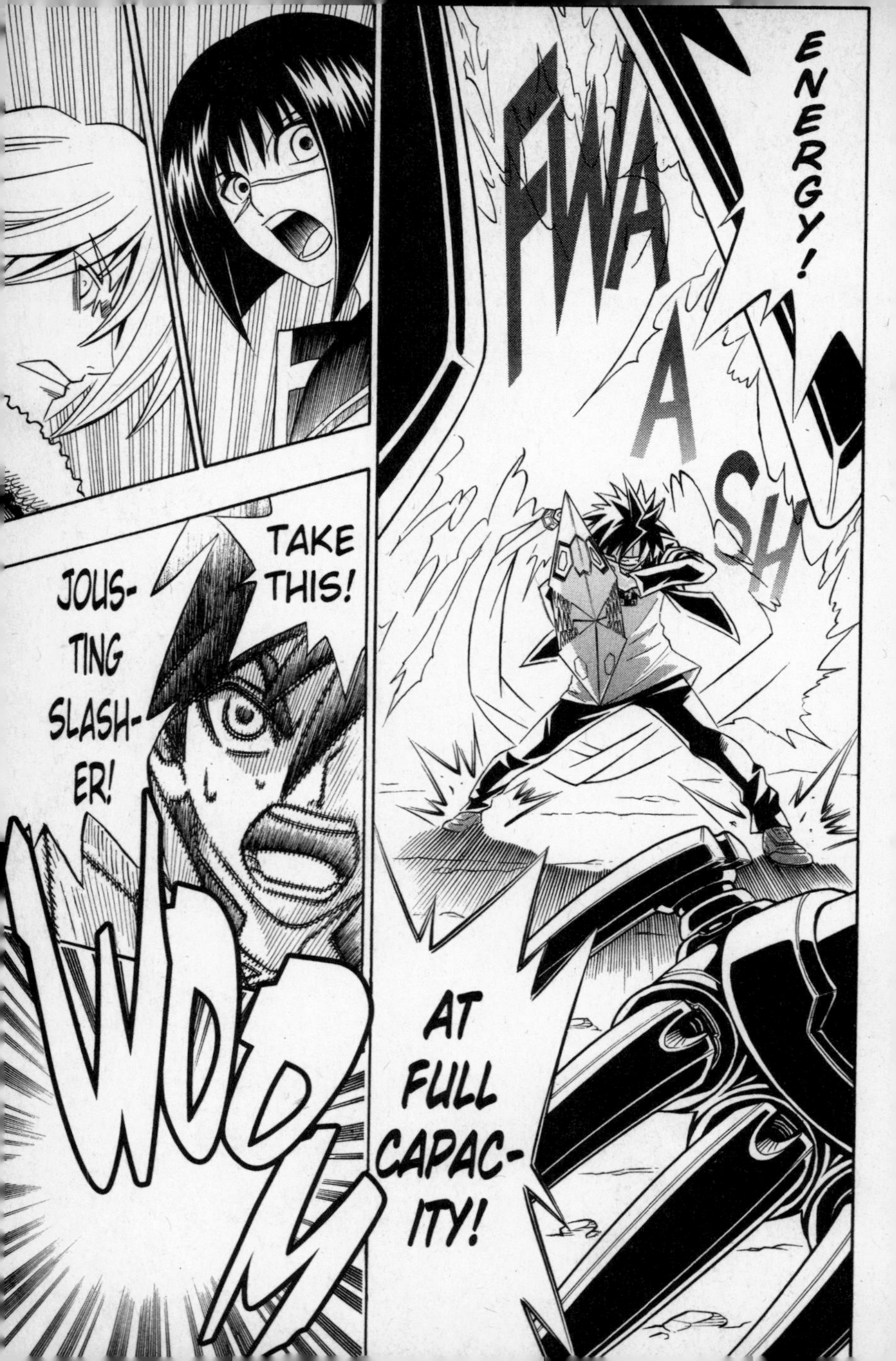
ENERGY!
FWAASH
AT FULL CAPACITY!
TAKE THIS!
JOUSTING SLASHER!

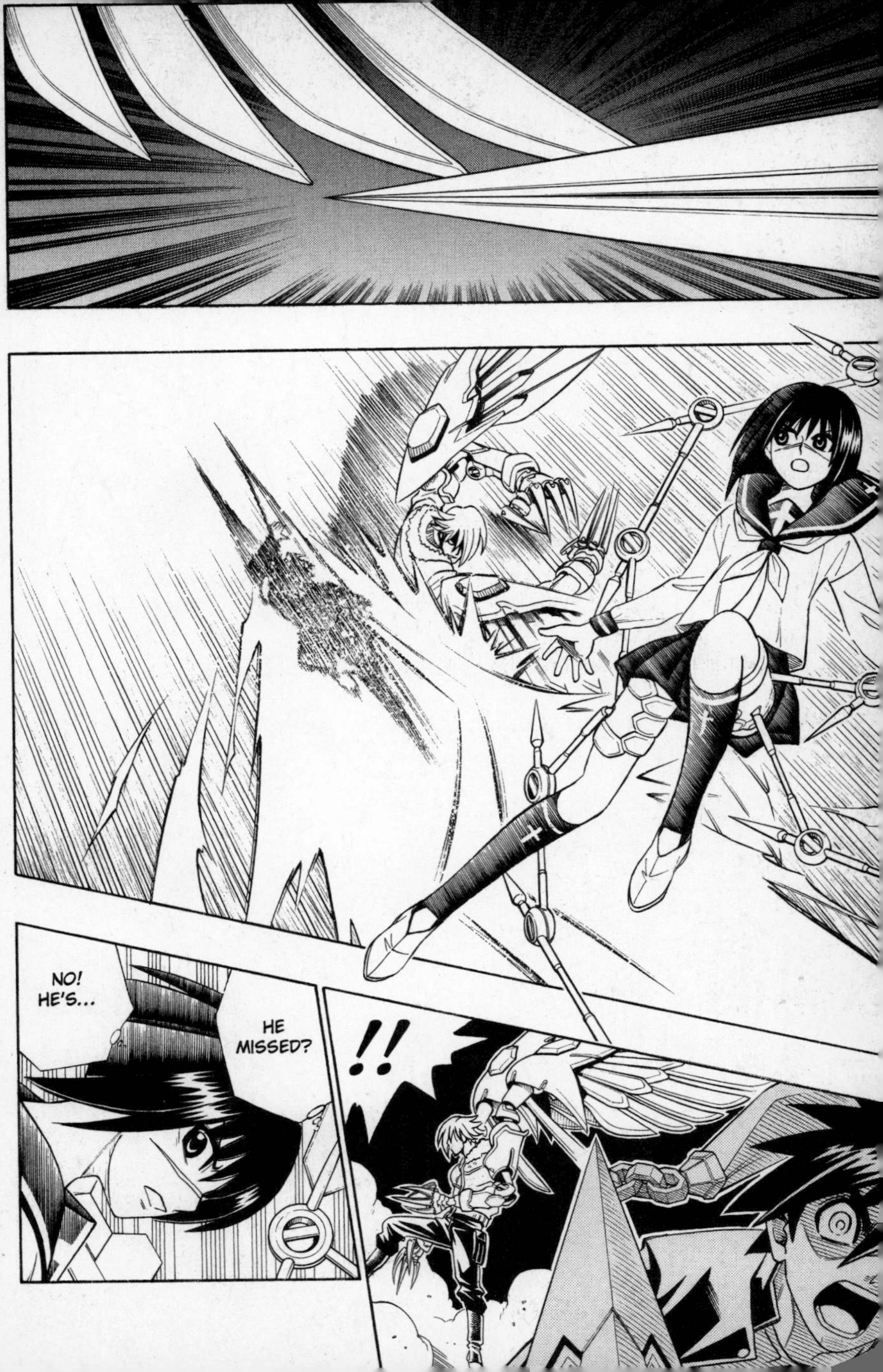
!!
HE MISSED?
NO! HE'S...

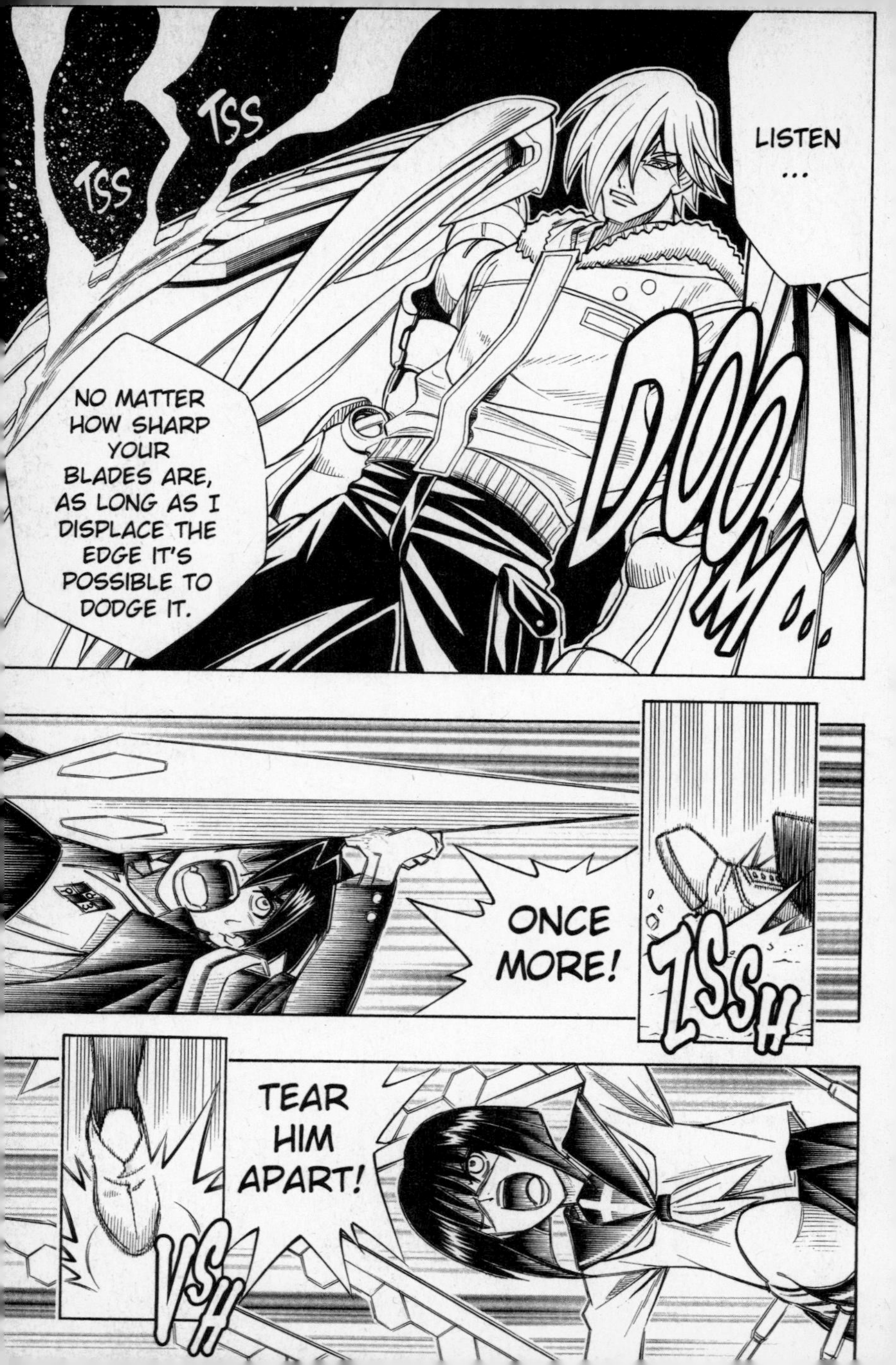

LISTEN ...
DOOM...
TSS
TSS
NO MATTER HOW SHARP YOUR BLADES ARE, AS LONG AS I DISPLACE THE EDGE IT'S POSSIBLE TO DODGE IT.
ZSSH
ONCE MORE!
TEAR HIM APART!
VSH

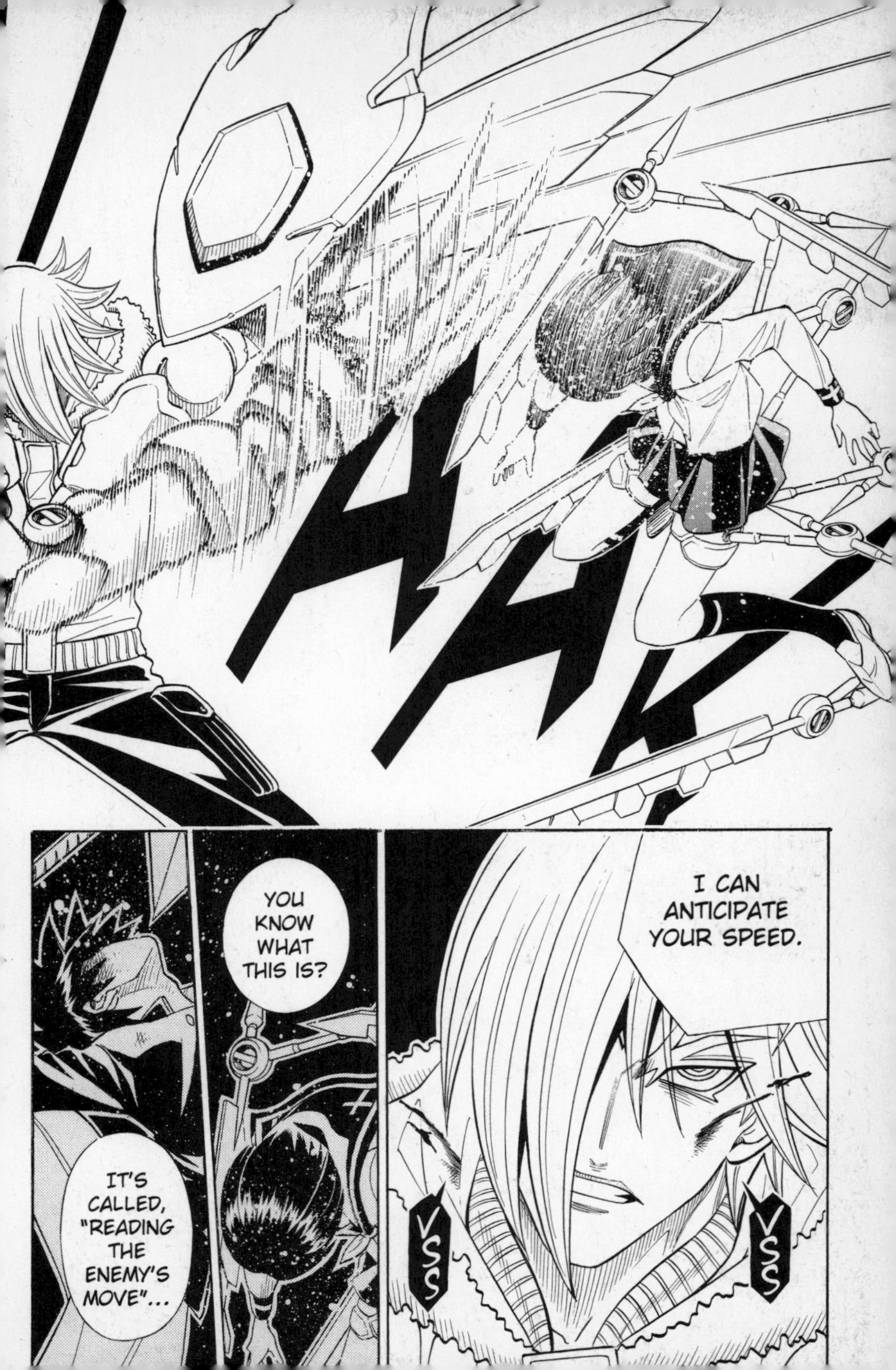
I CAN ANTICIPATE YOUR SPEED.
VSS
VSS
YOU KNOW WHAT THIS IS?
IT'S CALLED, "READING THE ENEMY'S MOVE"...

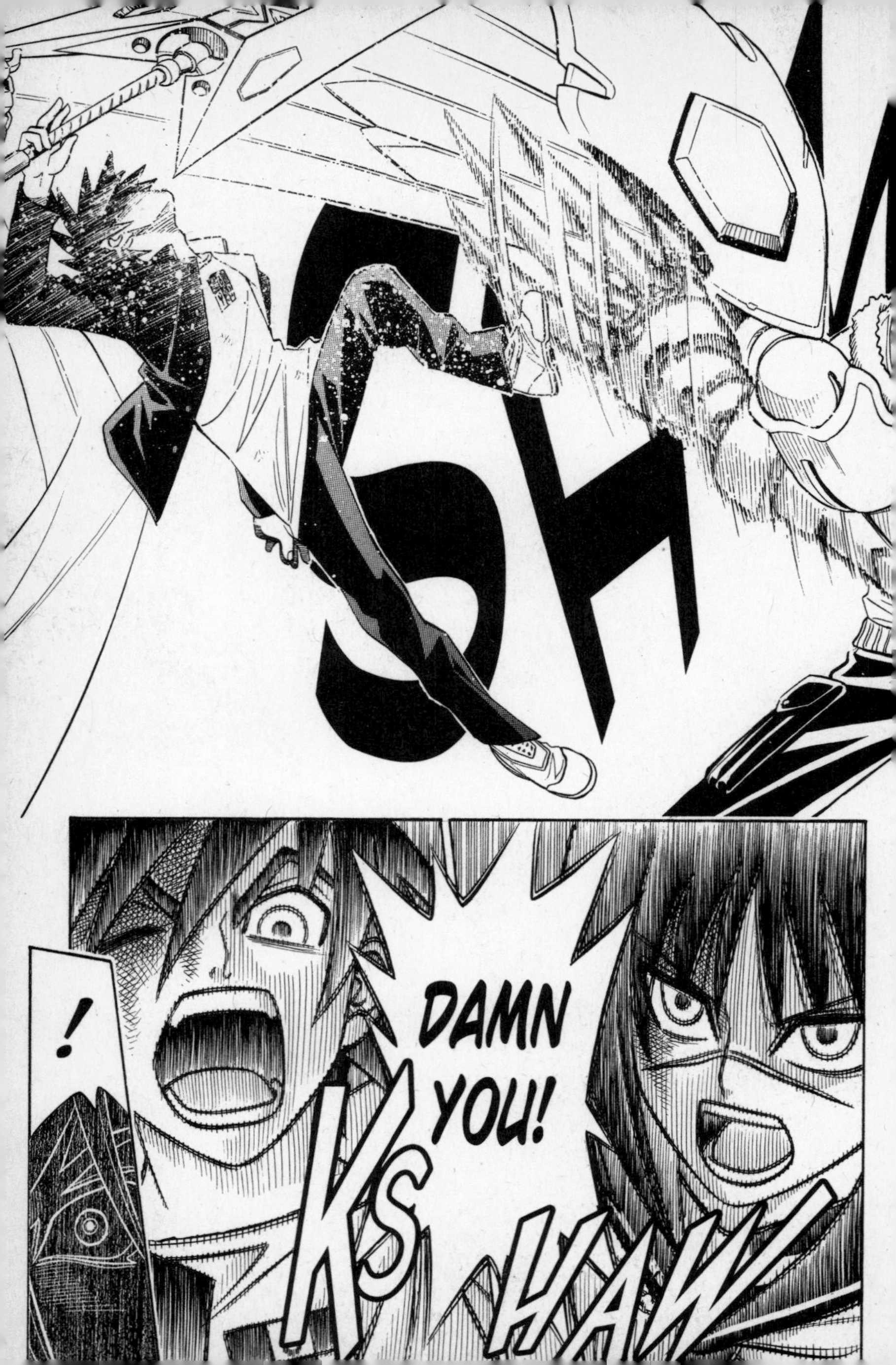
SH
DAMN YOU!
KSHAW
!

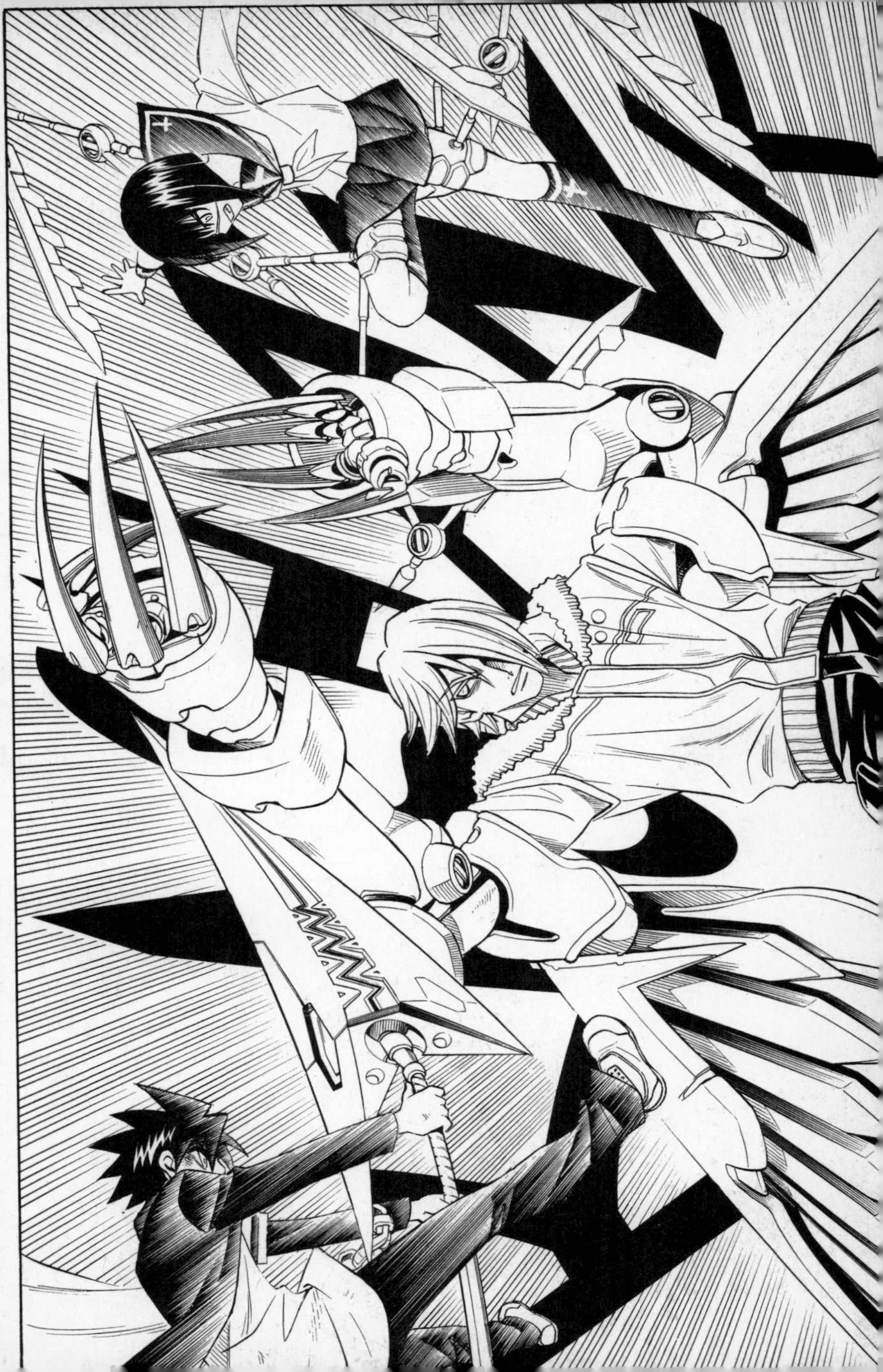

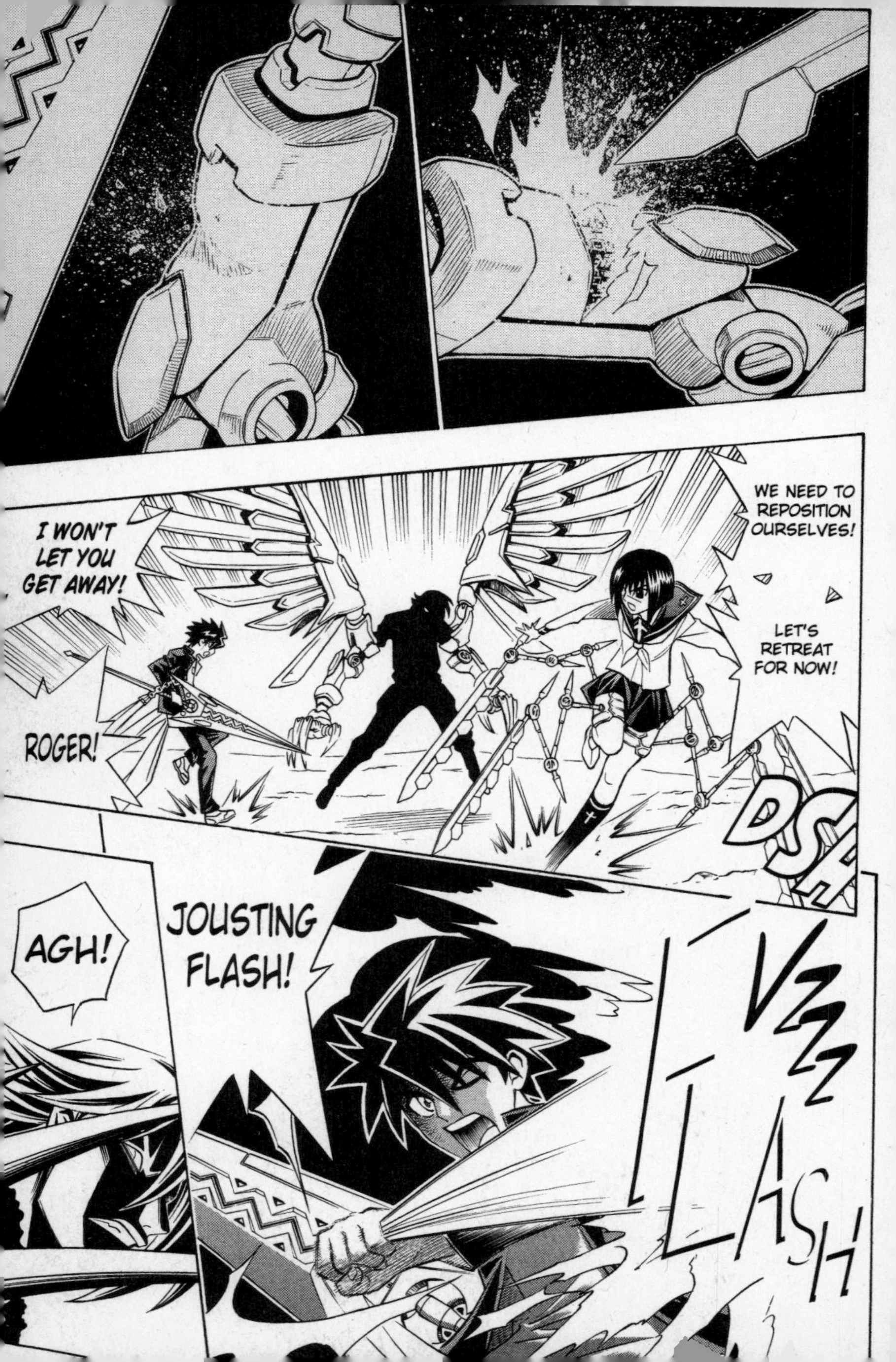
WE NEED TO REPOSITION OURSELVES!
LET'S RETREAT FOR NOW!
I WON'T LET YOU GET AWAY!
ROGER!
DSH
VZZ
FLASH
JOUSTING FLASH!
AGH!

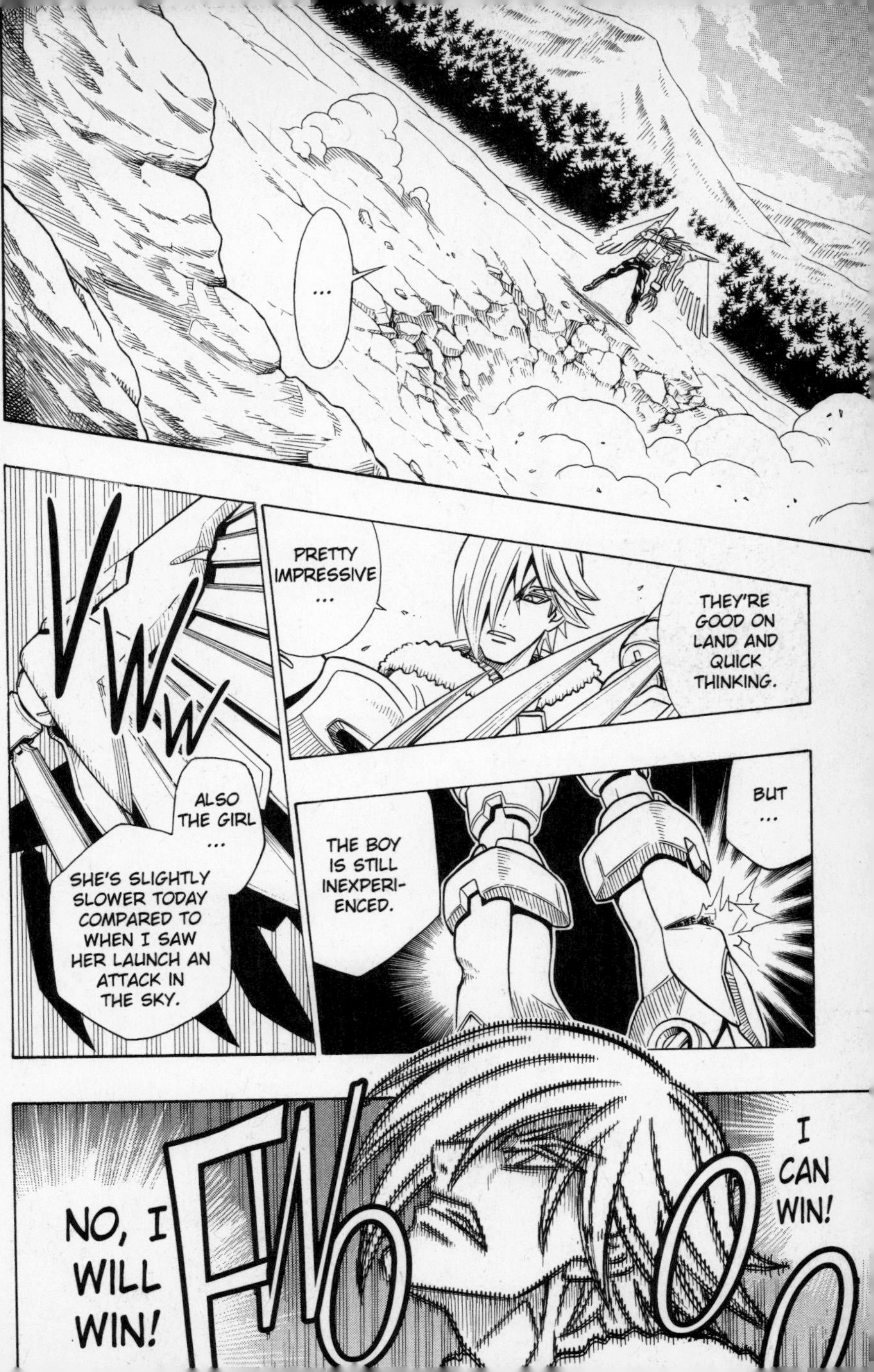
...
PRETTY IMPRESSIVE ...
THEY'RE GOOD ON LAND AND QUICK THINKING.
BUT ...
THE BOY IS STILL INEXPERIENCED.
VWWW
ALSO THE GIRL ...
SHE'S SLIGHTLY SLOWER TODAY COMPARED TO WHEN I SAW HER LAUNCH AN ATTACK IN THE SKY.
I CAN WIN!
FWOOO
NO, I WILL WIN!

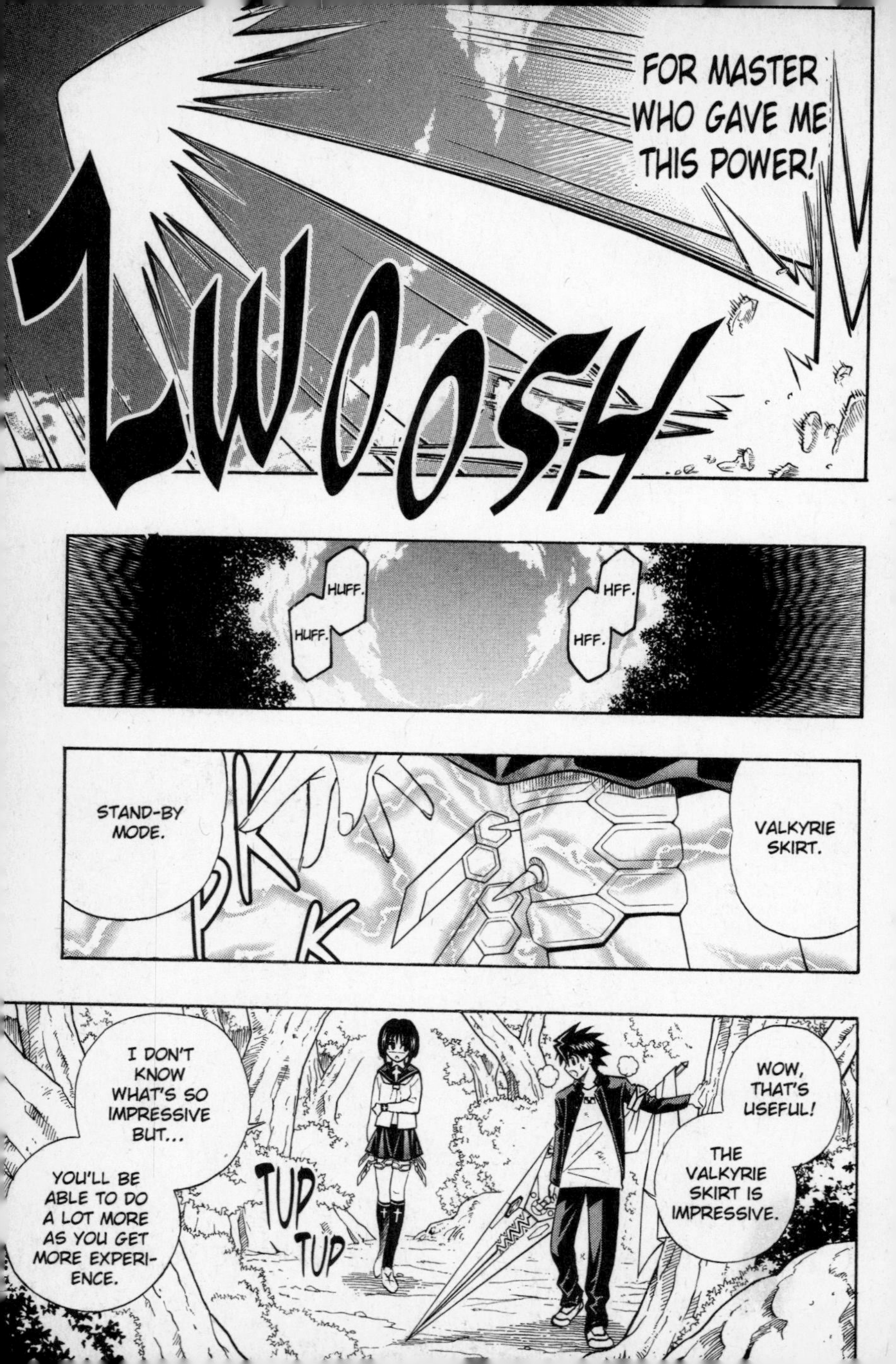
FOR MASTER WHO GAVE ME THIS POWER!
ZWOOSH
HFF. HFF.
HUFF. HUFF.
VALKYRIE SKIRT.
PK PK
STAND-BY MODE.
WOW, THAT'S USEFUL!
THE VALKYRIE SKIRT IS IMPRESSIVE.
TUP TUP
I DON'T KNOW WHAT'S SO IMPRESSIVE BUT...
YOU'LL BE ABLE TO DO A LOT MORE AS YOU GET MORE EXPERI- ENCE.

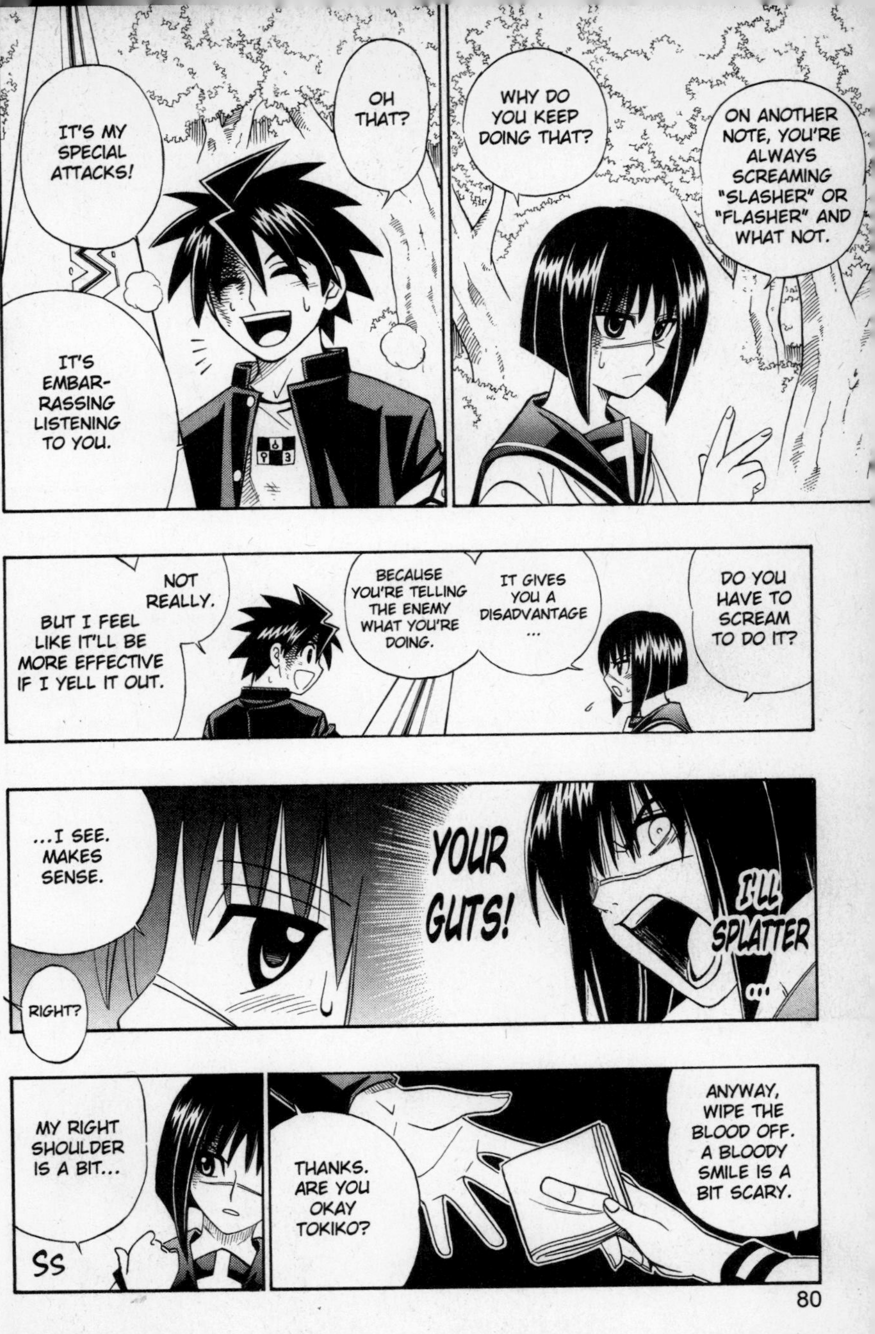
ON ANOTHER NOTE, YOU'RE ALWAYS SCREAMING "SLASHER" OR "FLASHER" AND WHAT NOT.
WHY DO YOU KEEP DOING THAT?
OH THAT?
IT'S MY SPECIAL ATTACKS!
IT'S EMBAR-RASSING LISTENING TO YOU.
DO YOU HAVE TO SCREAM TO DO IT?
IT GIVES YOU A DISADVANTAGE ...
BECAUSE YOU'RE TELLING THE ENEMY WHAT YOU'RE DOING.
NOT REALLY.
BUT I FEEL LIKE IT'LL BE MORE EFFECTIVE IF I YELL IT OUT.
I'LL SPLATTER ...
YOUR GUTS!
...I SEE. MAKES SENSE.
RIGHT?
ANYWAY, WIPE THE BLOOD OFF. A BLOODY SMILE IS A BIT SCARY.
THANKS. ARE YOU OKAY TOKIKO?
MY RIGHT SHOULDER IS A BIT...
SS

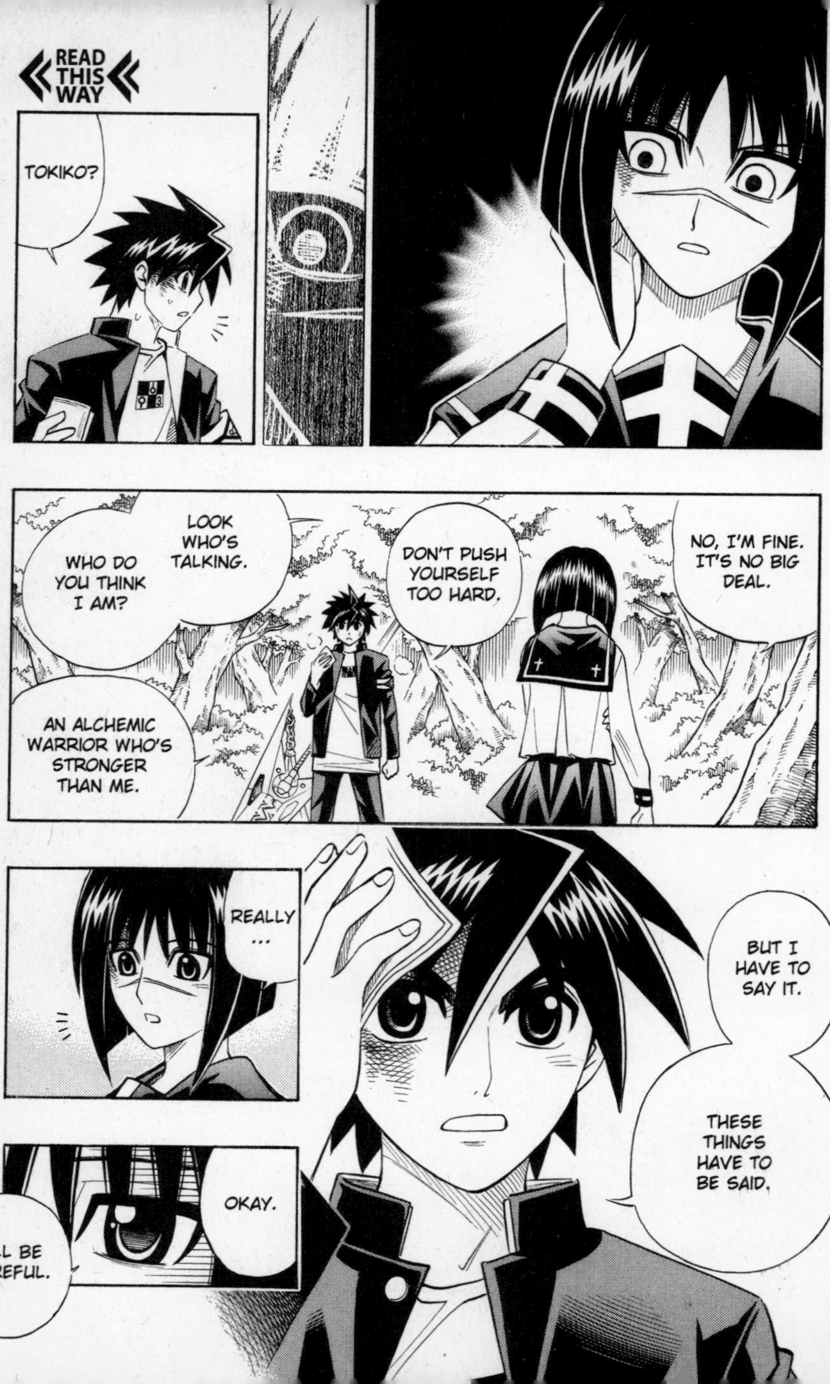
READ THIS WAY
TOKIKO?
NO, I'M FINE. IT'S NO BIG DEAL.
DON'T PUSH YOURSELF TOO HARD.
LOOK WHO'S TALKING.
WHO DO YOU THINK I AM?
AN ALCHEMIC WARRIOR WHO'S STRONGER THAN ME.
BUT I HAVE TO SAY IT.
THESE THINGS HAVE TO BE SAID.
REALLY ...
OKAY.
I'LL BE CAREFUL.

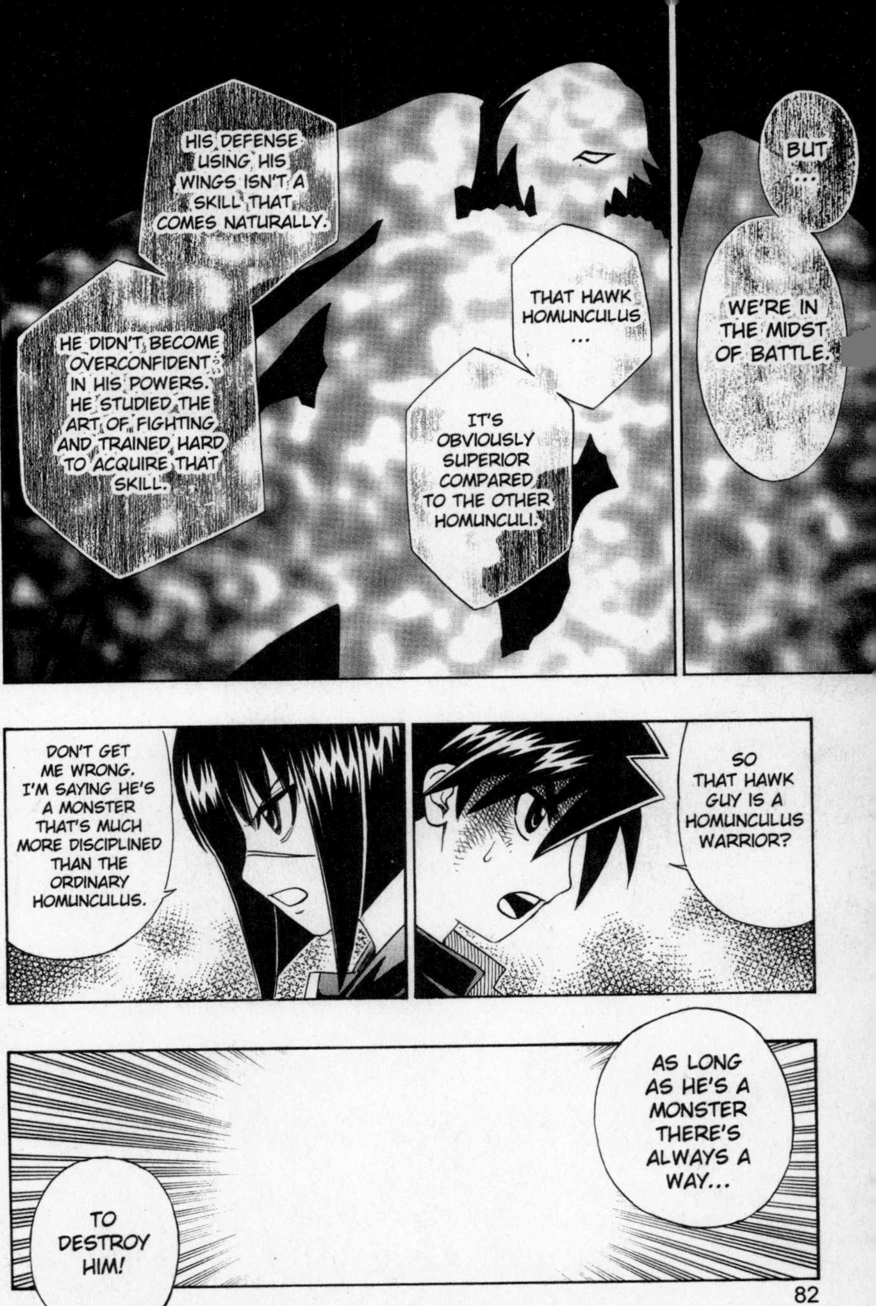
BUT ...
WE'RE IN THE MIDST OF BATTLE.
THAT HAWK HOMUNCULUS ...
IT'S OBVIOUSLY SUPERIOR COMPARED TO THE OTHER HOMUNCULI.
HIS DEFENSE USING HIS WINGS ISN'T A SKILL THAT COMES NATURALLY.
HE DIDN'T BECOME OVERCONFIDENT IN HIS POWERS. HE STUDIED THE ART OF FIGHTING AND TRAINED HARD TO ACQUIRE THAT SKILL.
SO THAT HAWK GUY IS A HOMUNCULUS WARRIOR?
DON'T GET ME WRONG. I'M SAYING HE'S A MONSTER THAT'S MUCH MORE DISCIPLINED THAN THE ORDINARY HOMUNCULUS.
AS LONG AS HE'S A MONSTER THERE'S ALWAYS A WAY...
TO DESTROY HIM!

READ THIS WAY

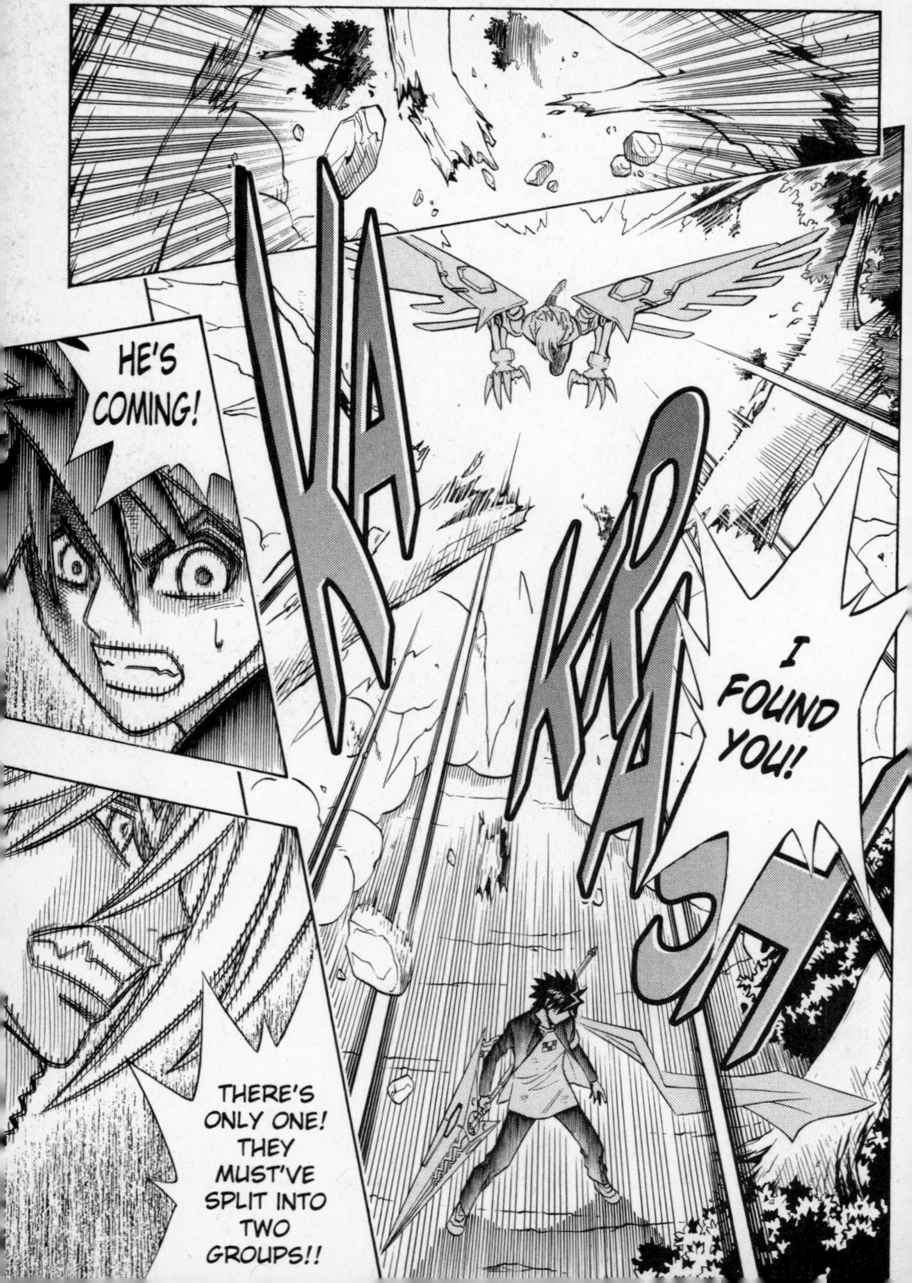
I FOUND YOU!
KA KRASH
HE'S COMING!
THERE'S ONLY ONE! THEY MUST'VE SPLIT INTO TWO GROUPS!!

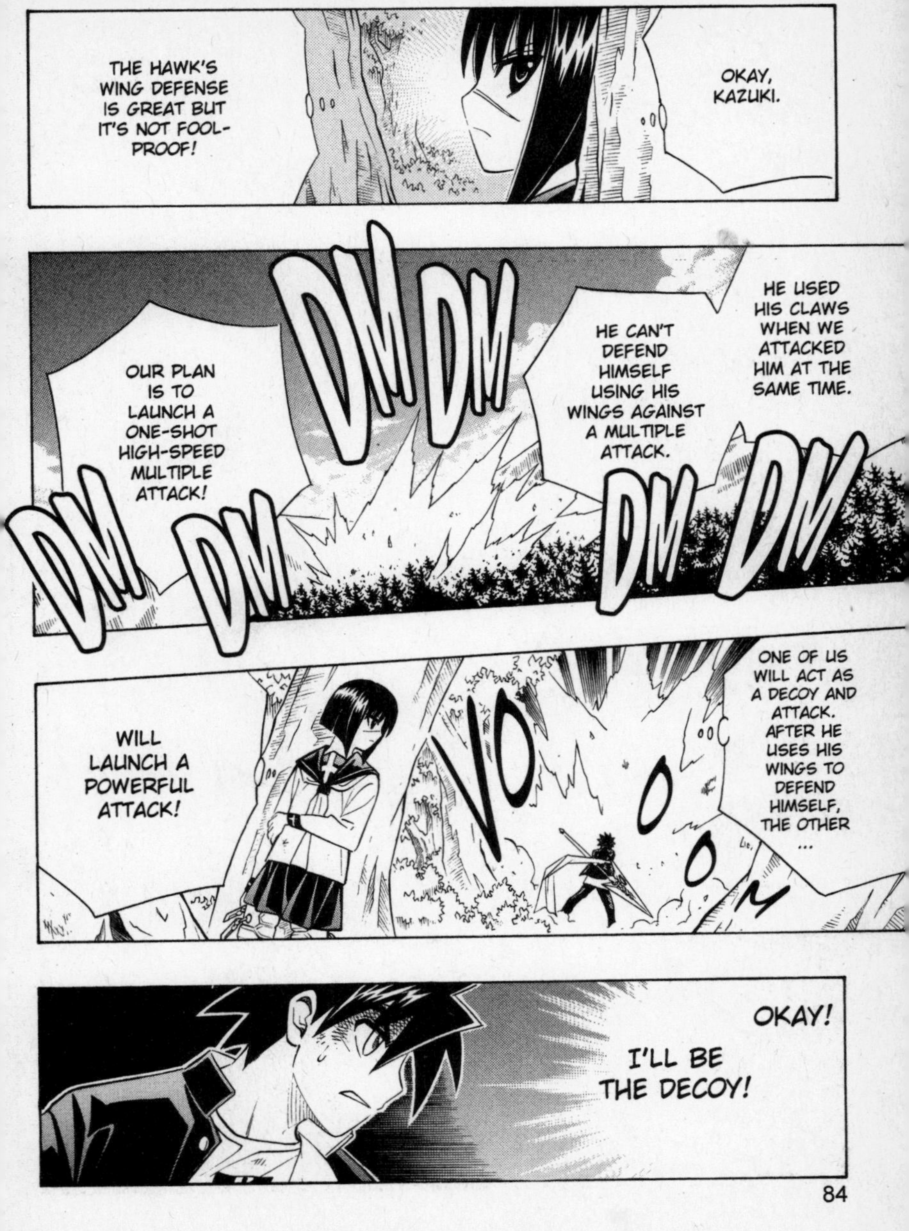
OKAY, KAZUKI.
THE HAWK'S WING DEFENSE IS GREAT BUT IT'S NOT FOOL-PROOF!
DM DM
DM DM
DM DM
HE USED HIS CLAWS WHEN WE ATTACKED HIM AT THE SAME TIME.
HE CAN'T DEFEND HIMSELF USING HIS WINGS AGAINST A MULTIPLE ATTACK.
OUR PLAN IS TO LAUNCH A ONE-SHOT HIGH-SPEED MULTIPLE ATTACK!
ONE OF US WILL ACT AS A DECOY AND ATTACK. AFTER HE USES HIS WINGS TO DEFEND HIMSELF, THE OTHER ...
VOOOM
WILL LAUNCH A POWERFUL ATTACK!
OKAY!
I'LL BE THE DECOY!

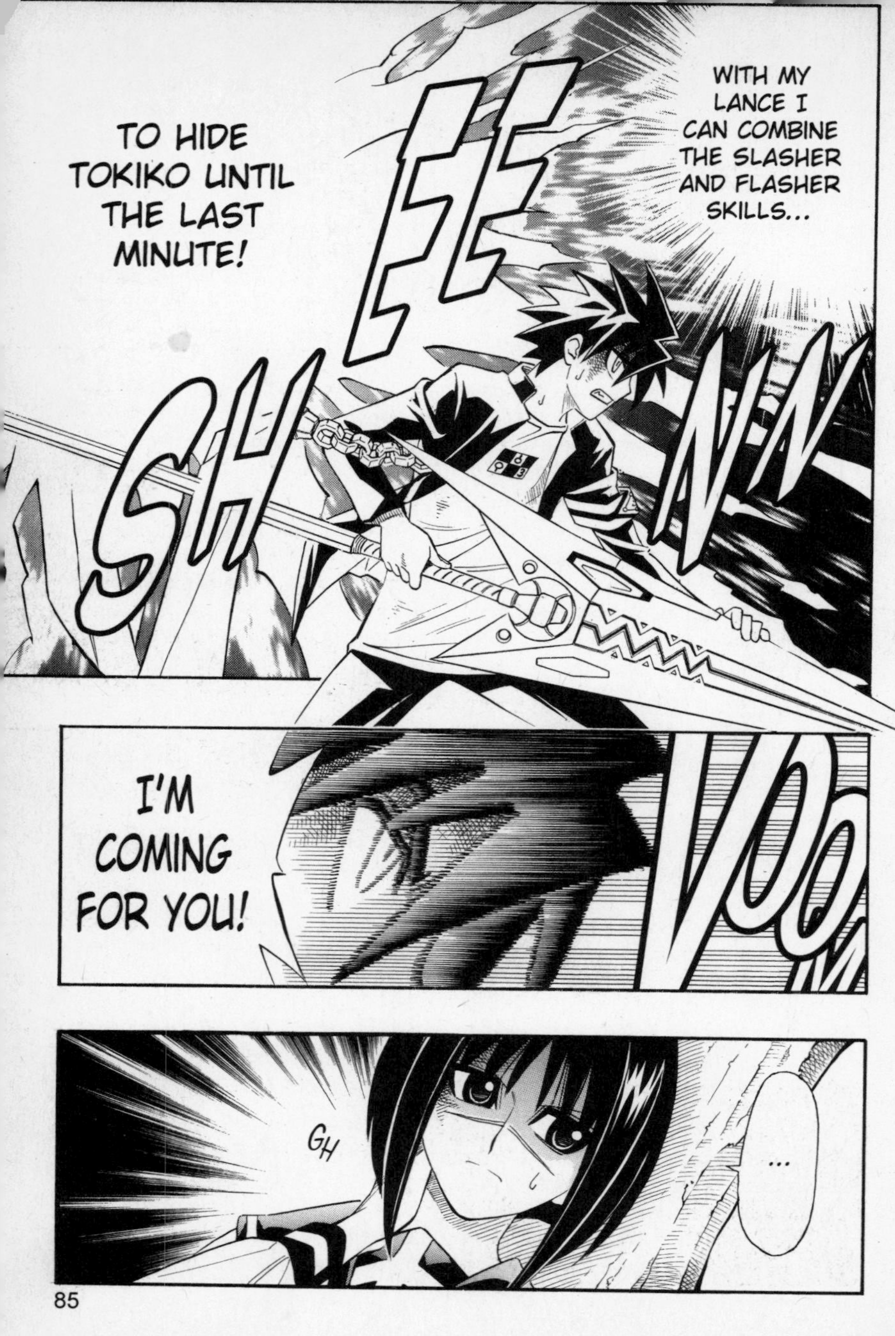
WITH MY LANCE I CAN COMBINE THE SLASHER AND FLASHER SKILLS...
TO HIDE TOKIKO UNTIL THE LAST MINUTE!
SHEENN
VOOM
I'M COMING FOR YOU!
...
GH

Chapter 8: Lock on

· This was the first chapter where there were no battles so I experimented a lot with comedic elements. The funny faces I drew were very popular. (Kazuki is a big fan of Rohan Kishibe.)

· I introduced Tokiko's background a little. I wanted to keep her the "mysterious girl" a little longer but due to the unexpected high volume of questions I inserted a little information. Tokiko is still the most popular character. You can do it Kazuki!

· Koushaku officially makes his grand entrance. I wasn't sure how I felt about him saying "Kazuki's right" for a punchline as he's supposed to be the boss character but I figured this chapter had a lot of comedy in it so I went with it. In the end, I think these words added to the type of character Papillon would be later on.

Chapter 9: The Other New Life

· Koushaku's true intentions are revealed. It's becoming more Alchemic-like with the immortality theme... I think?

· I laid out the "So, what do you say?" line like that to make it more impressionable. Normally I don't really think about matching the lips to the lines but after I got an understanding from doing this, I think I've gotten a little better at drawing the subtle facial expressions.

Chapter 10: VS. Washio: Section 1

· "Everything's in place! Time for battle!" As such, I was really pumped but the next four chapters ended up being extremely unpopular... Looking back, I could understand where people were coming from. I was honestly upset during this incident.

· I used a lot of large frames to capture the action but the content ended up being thin. It also didn't help that the previous episodes were full of content so when you read through it, it felt even thinner... (Factor 1)

· There are two reasons for Washio's partial transformation. I wanted to show he was different from the others and I also wanted to ease the amount of work put into drawing him. The reason why his wings are growing out of his arms is because I hate the "angel" design with a passion. Enough with the girls with swan wings on her back... I figured the appeal of unconventional beauty comes from "The Beauty found in the Ugly" or "The Ugly found in the Beauty?"

Chapter 11: VS. Washio: Part 2: Section 1

· "What the heck is Section 1?" I got that question A LOT. I even questioned it myself. Even my editor said "Maybe we should amend it in the tankoban?" but I decided to keep it as a reminder to myself, although embarrassing.

· I'm sure you've realized this but the VS. Washio chapters were supposed to end in three chapters. Once I started drawing, I realized how difficult the action scenes were to draw. It took a lot of work to make sure Washio's claws, wings and Kazuki's giant lance fit within the frame.

Continued on page 106

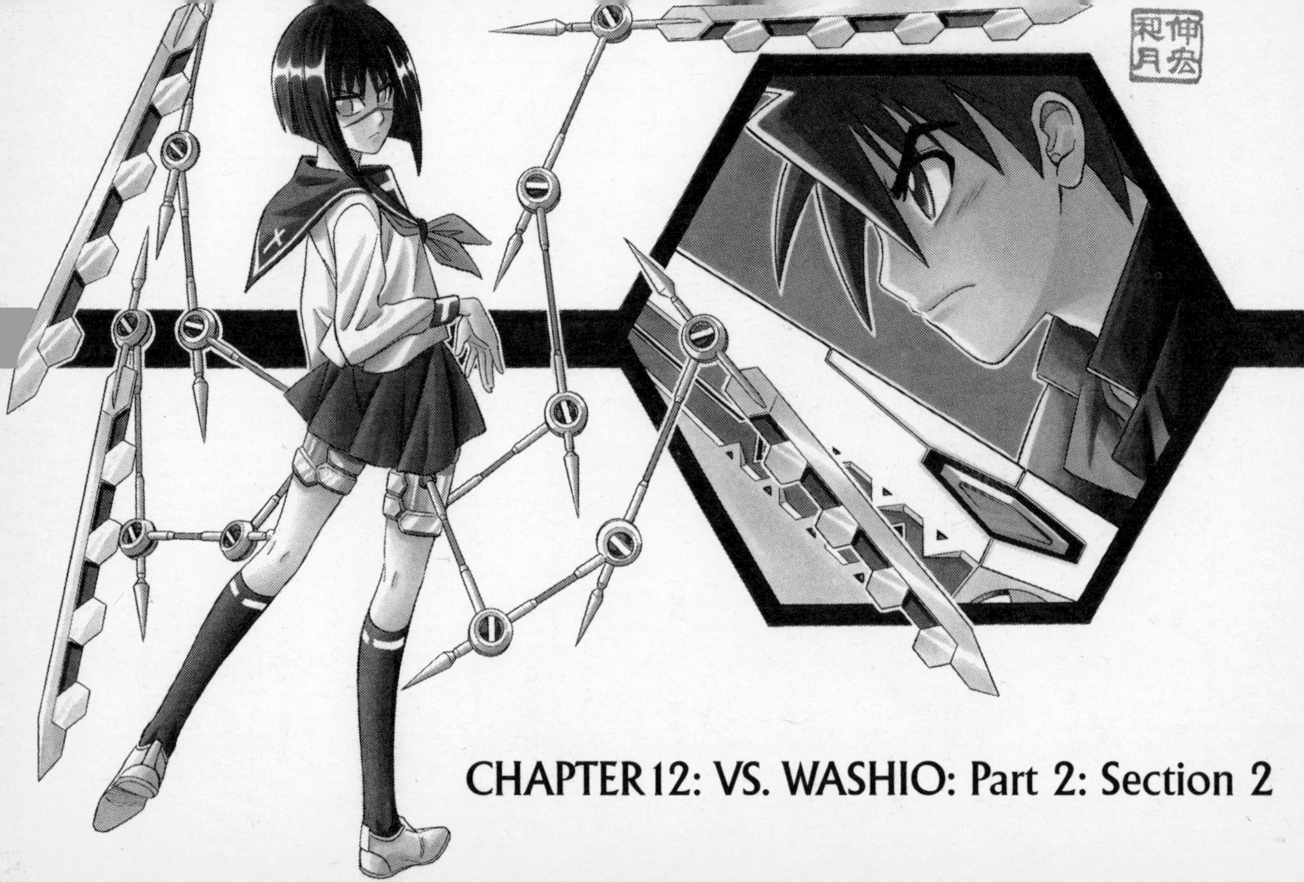
伸宏
和月

CHAPTER 12: VS. WASHIO: Part 2: Section 2

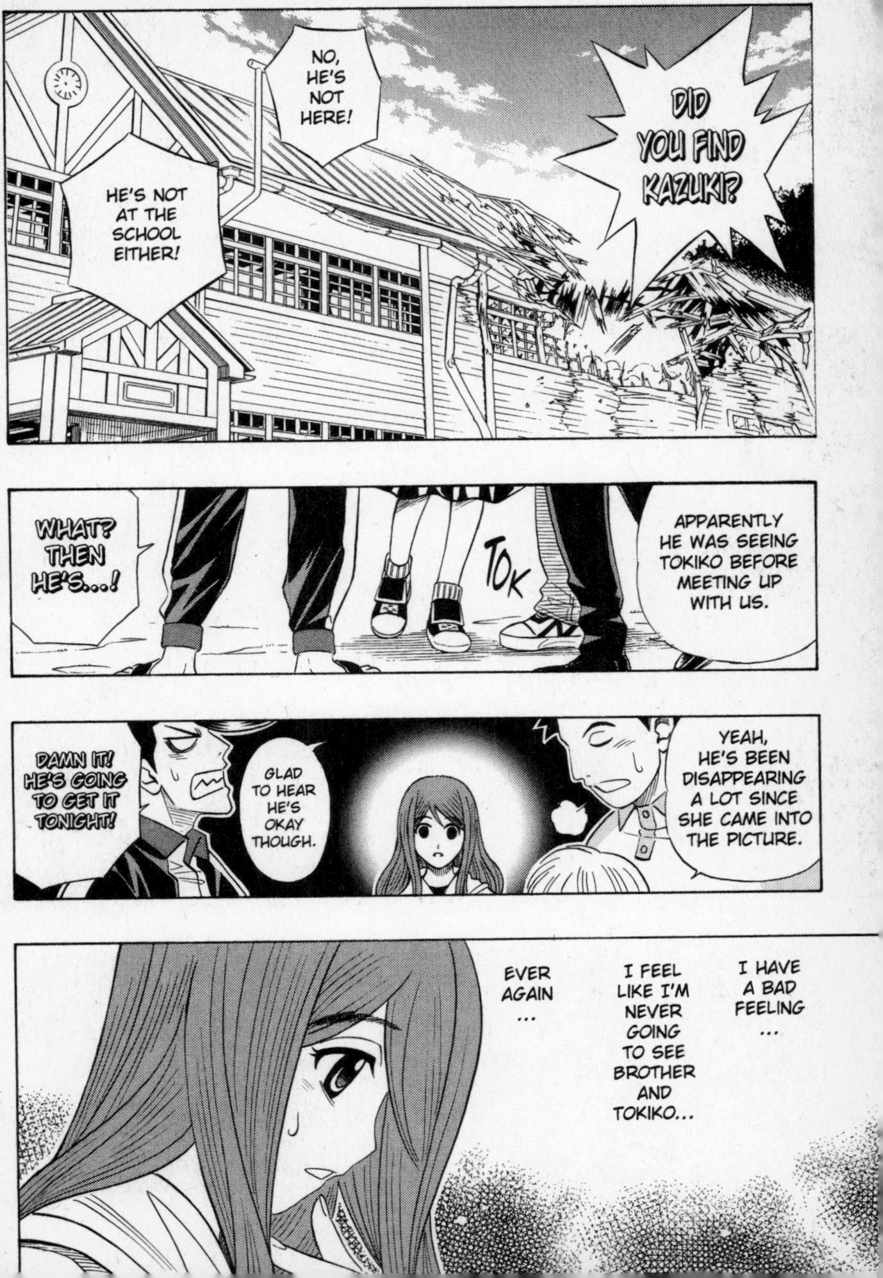
DID YOU FIND KAZUKI?
NO, HE'S NOT HERE!
HE'S NOT AT THE SCHOOL EITHER!
APPARENTLY HE WAS SEEING TOKIKO BEFORE MEETING UP WITH US.
TOK
WHAT? THEN HE'S...!
YEAH, HE'S BEEN DISAPPEARING A LOT SINCE SHE CAME INTO THE PICTURE.
GLAD TO HEAR HE'S OKAY THOUGH.
DAMN IT! HE'S GOING TO GET IT TONIGHT!
I HAVE A BAD FEELING...
I FEEL LIKE I'M NEVER GOING TO SEE BROTHER AND TOKIKO...
EVER AGAIN...

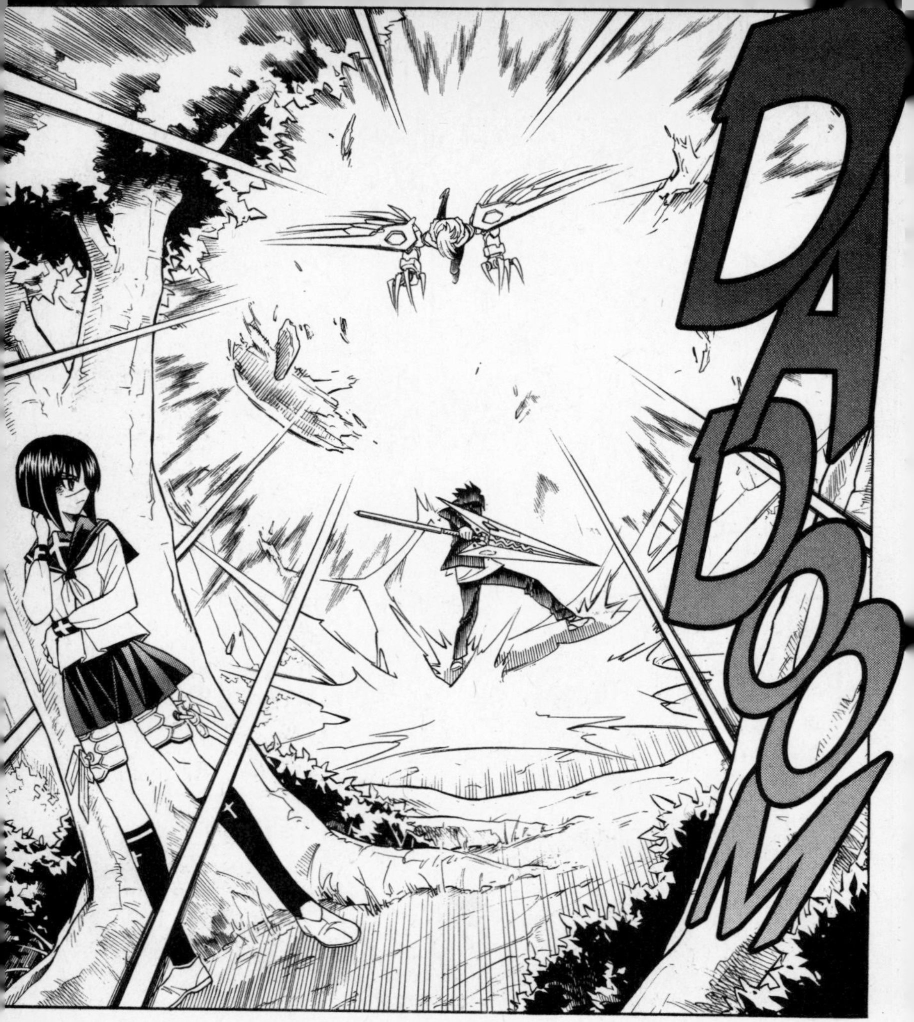
DADOOOM

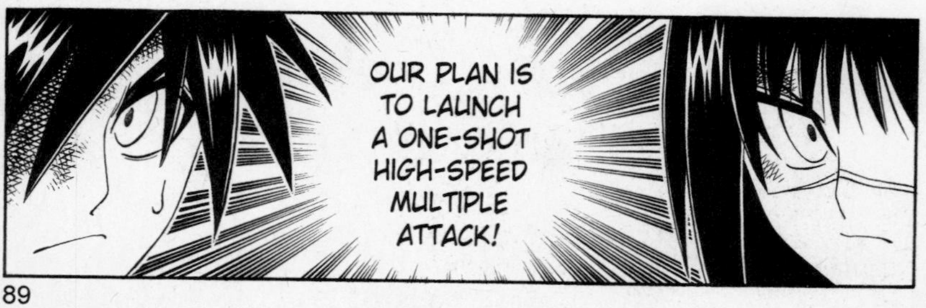
OUR PLAN IS TO LAUNCH A ONE-SHOT HIGH-SPEED MULTIPLE ATTACK!

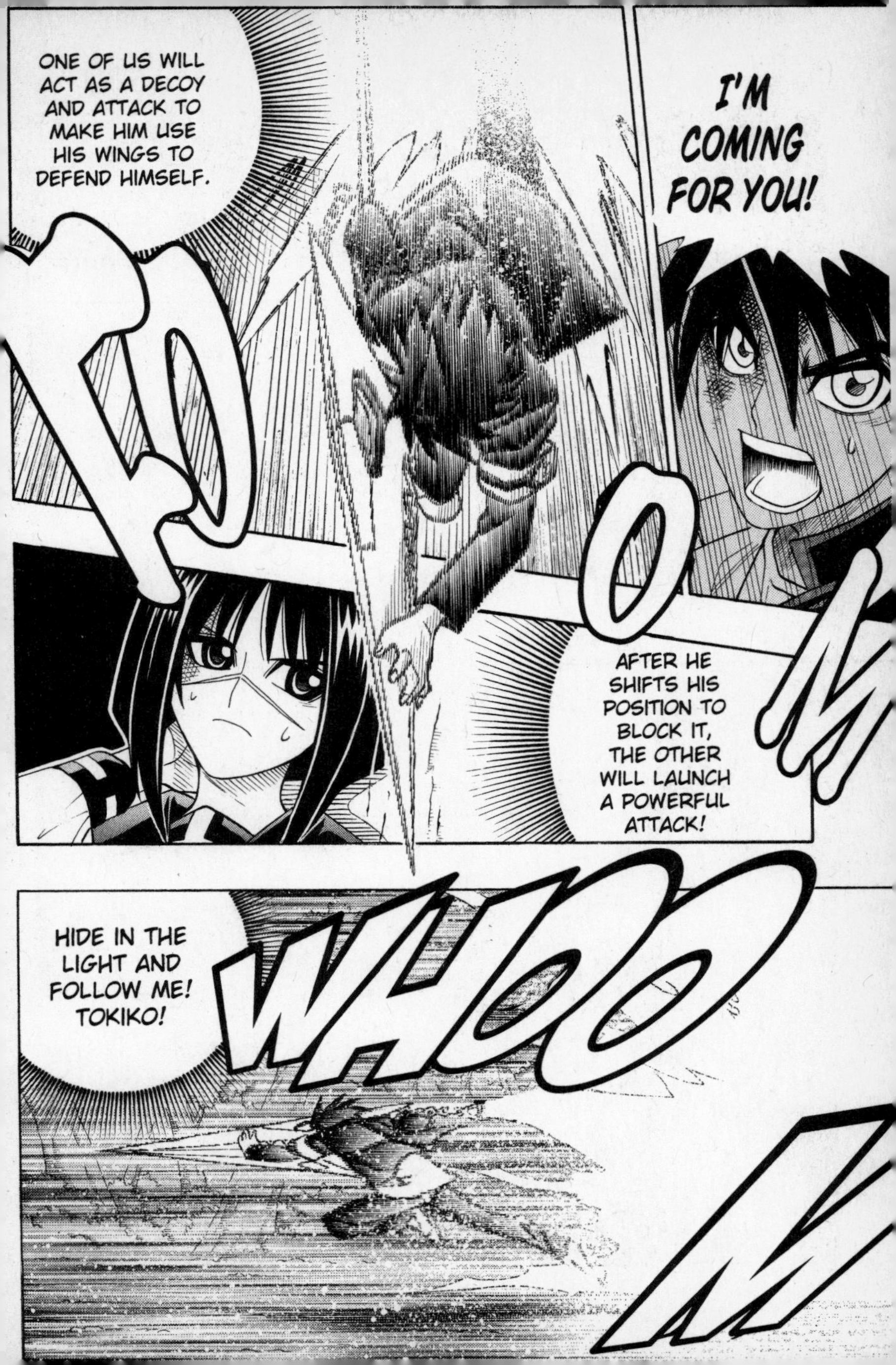
I'M COMING FOR YOU!
ONE OF US WILL ACT AS A DECOY AND ATTACK TO MAKE HIM USE HIS WINGS TO DEFEND HIMSELF.
AFTER HE SHIFTS HIS POSITION TO BLOCK IT, THE OTHER WILL LAUNCH A POWERFUL ATTACK!
HIDE IN THE LIGHT AND FOLLOW ME! TOKIKO!

ACTI-VATE!

VALKYRIE SKIRT.

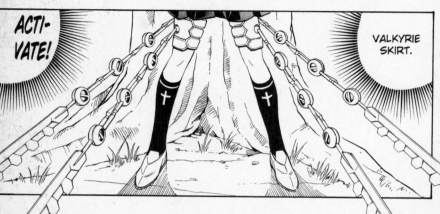

...SUCH A BEAUTIFUL GOLDEN YELLOW LIGHT.

IT'S LIKE THE RAYS OF THE SUN...

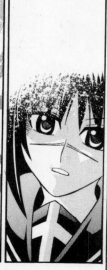

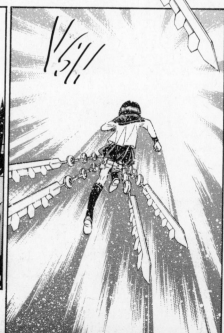

91

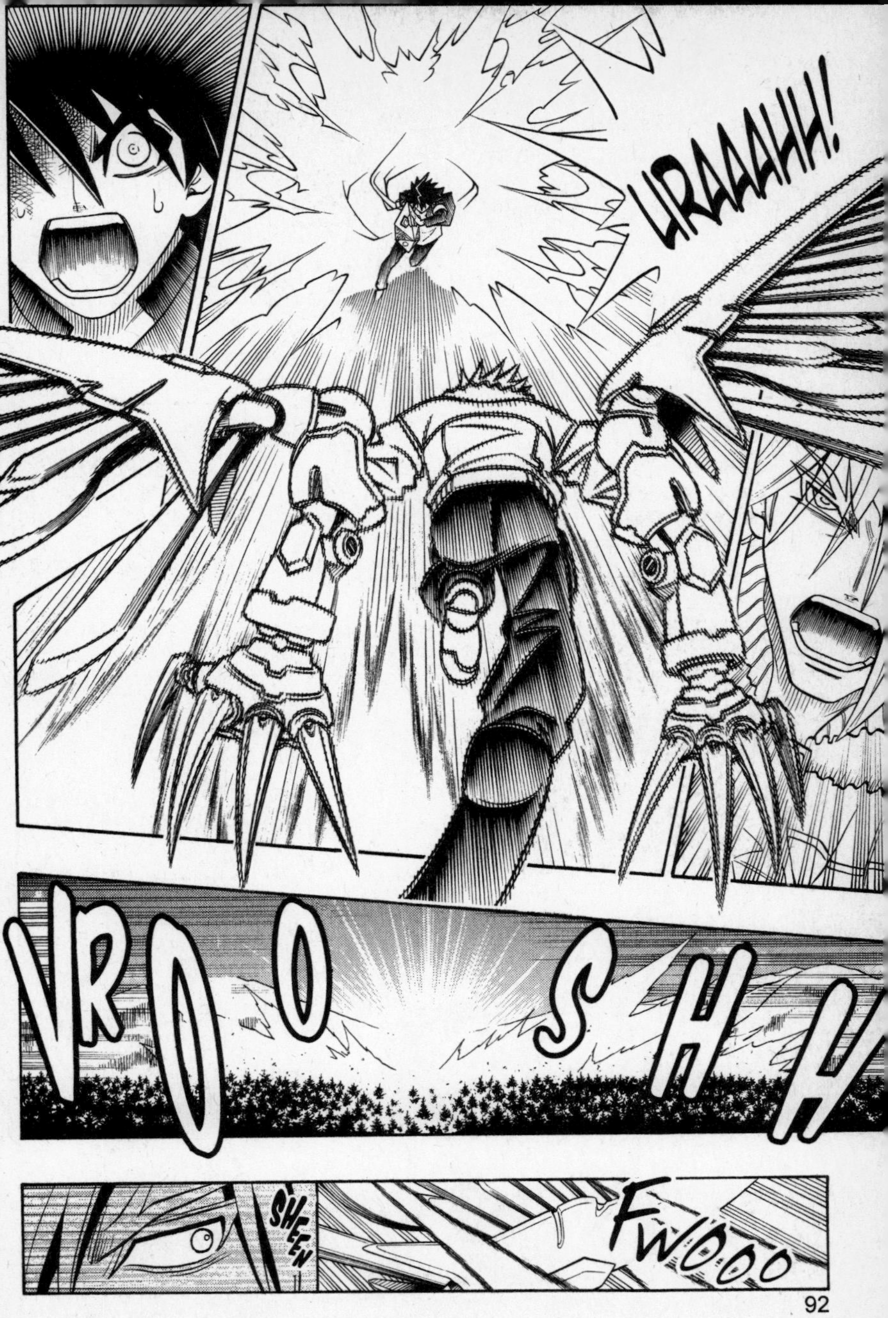
URAAAHH!
VROOSHA
FWOOO
SHEEN

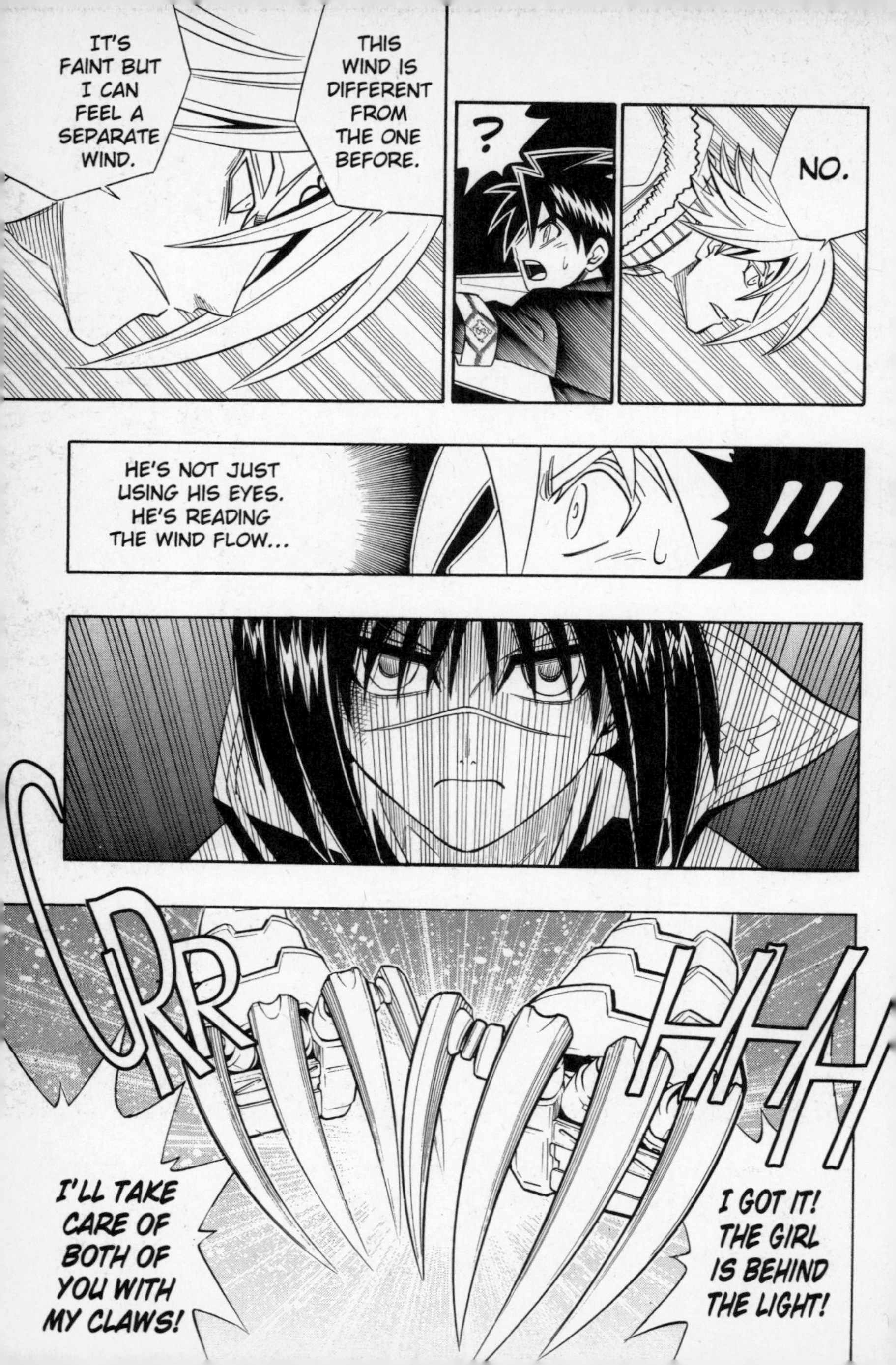
NO.
?
THIS WIND IS DIFFERENT FROM THE ONE BEFORE.
IT'S FAINT BUT I CAN FEEL A SEPARATE WIND.
!!
HE'S NOT JUST USING HIS EYES. HE'S READING THE WIND FLOW...
CRR...HH
I GOT IT! THE GIRL IS BEHIND THE LIGHT!
I'LL TAKE CARE OF BOTH OF YOU WITH MY CLAWS!

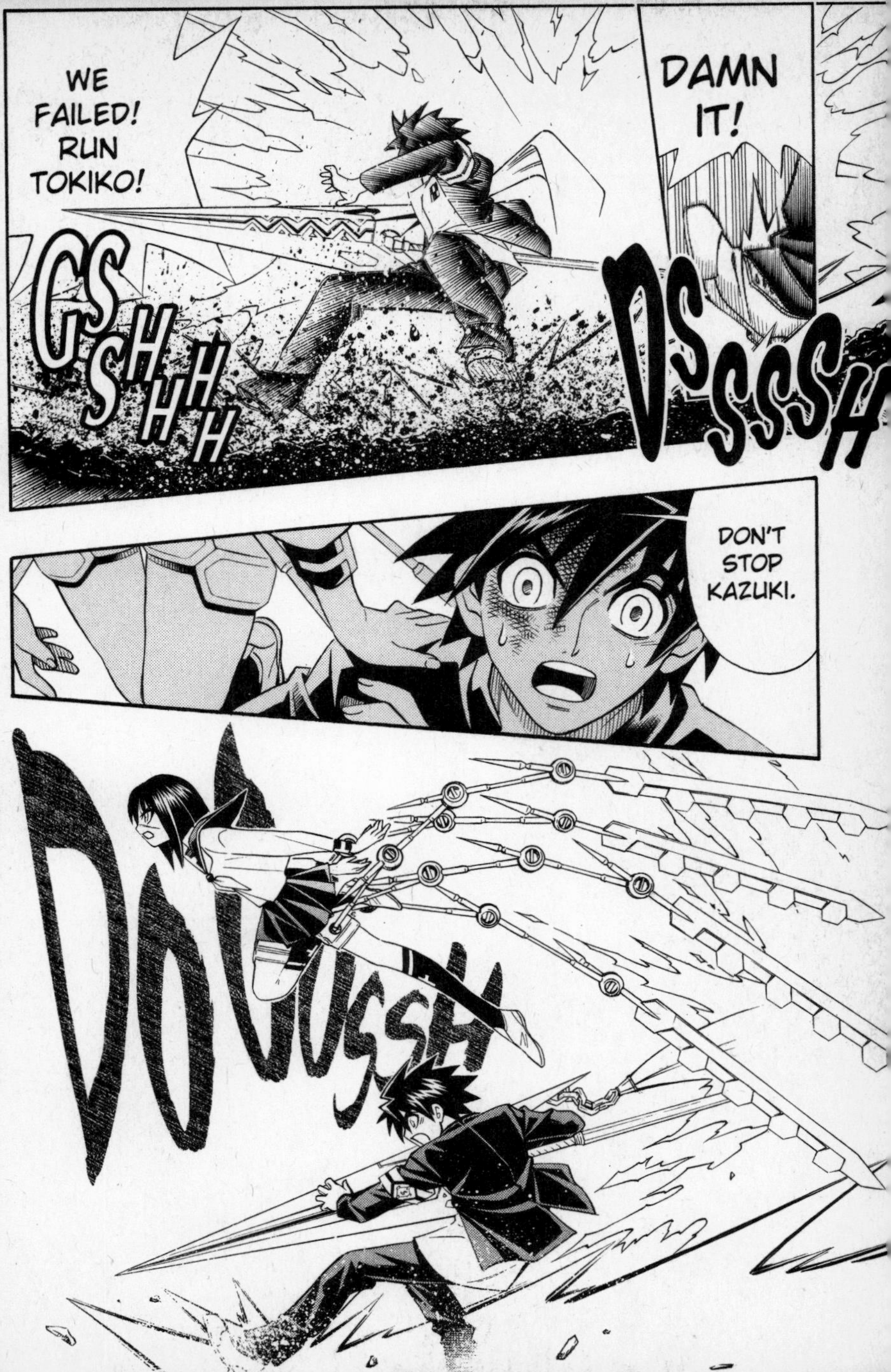
DAMN IT!
DSSSSH
WE FAILED! RUN TOKIKO!
GSSHHHHH
DON'T STOP KAZUKI.
DOUUSH

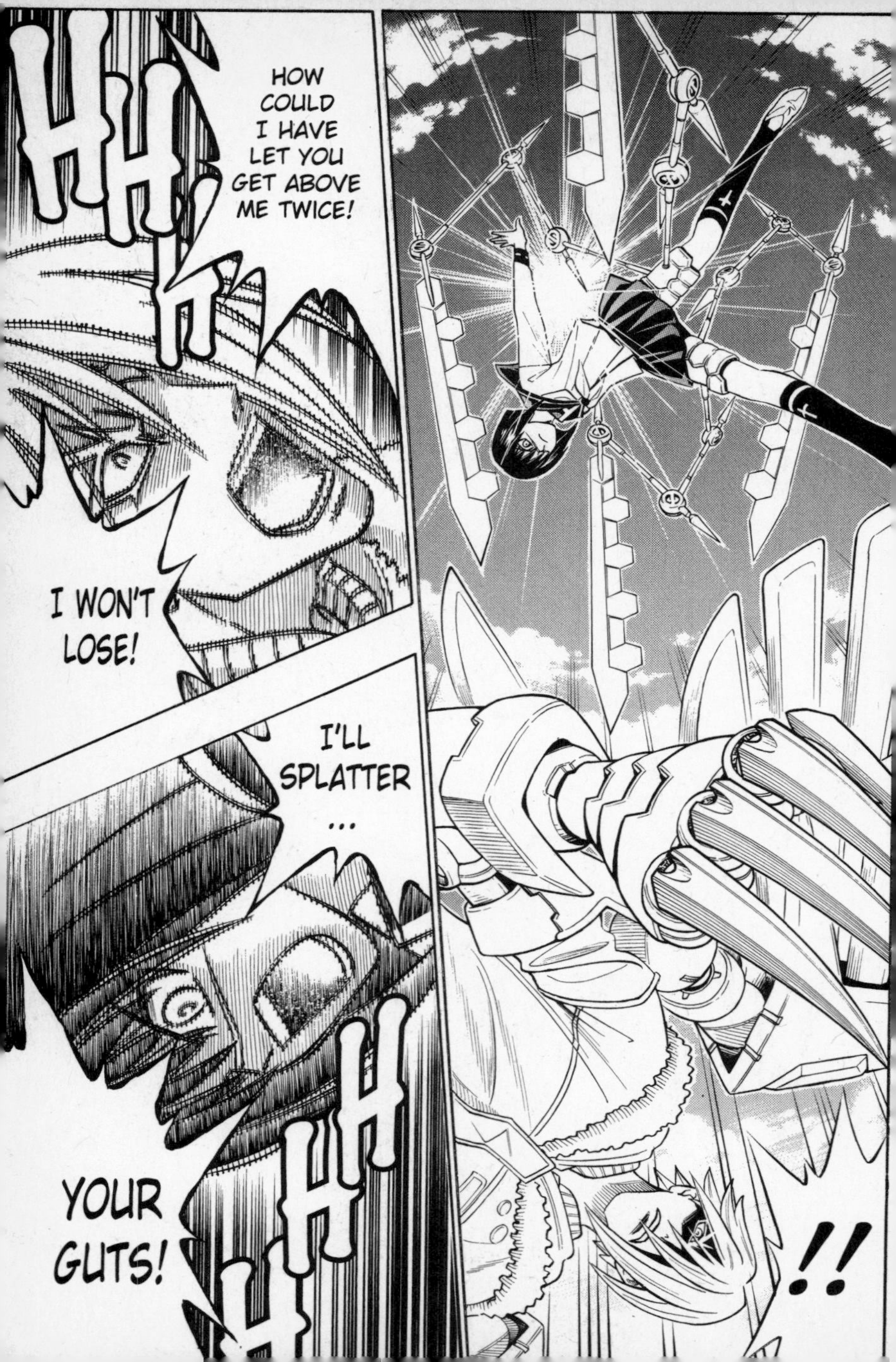
!!
HOW COULD I HAVE LET YOU GET ABOVE ME TWICE!
I WON'T LOSE!
I'LL SPLATTER ...
YOUR GUTS!

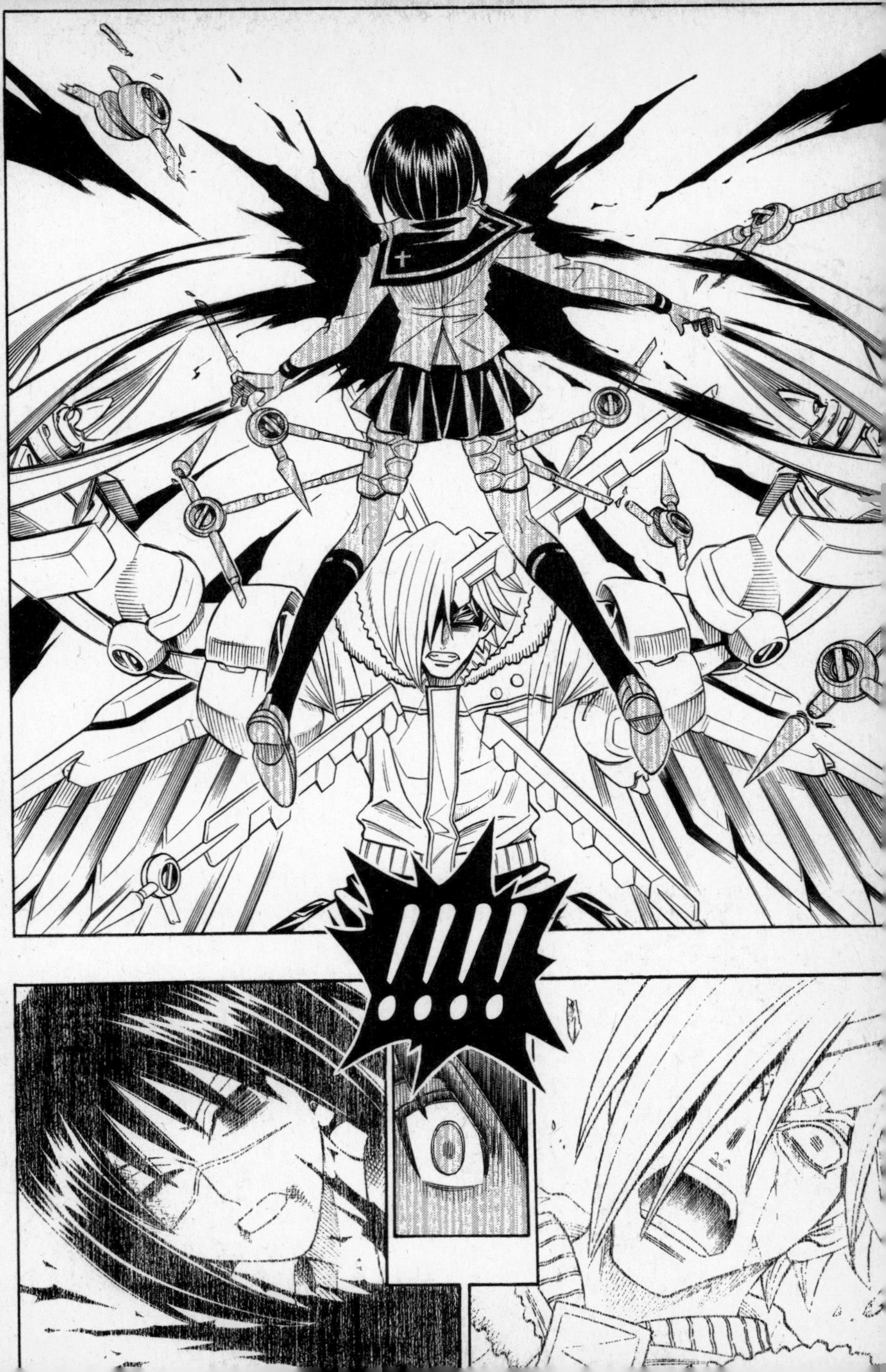
!!!!

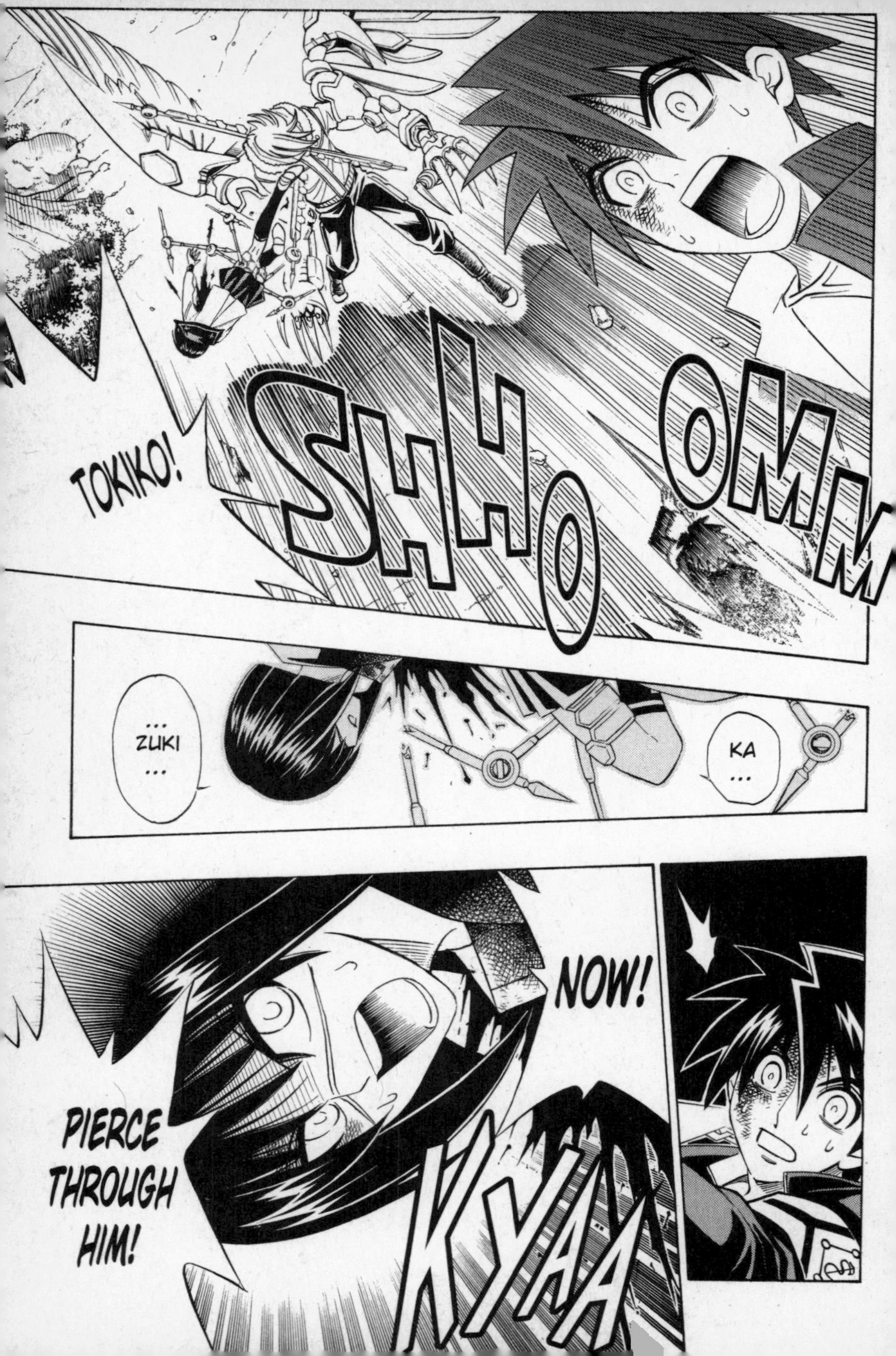
SHHOOMM
TOKIKO!
KA ...
... ZUKI ...
NOW!
PIERCE THROUGH HIM!
KYAA

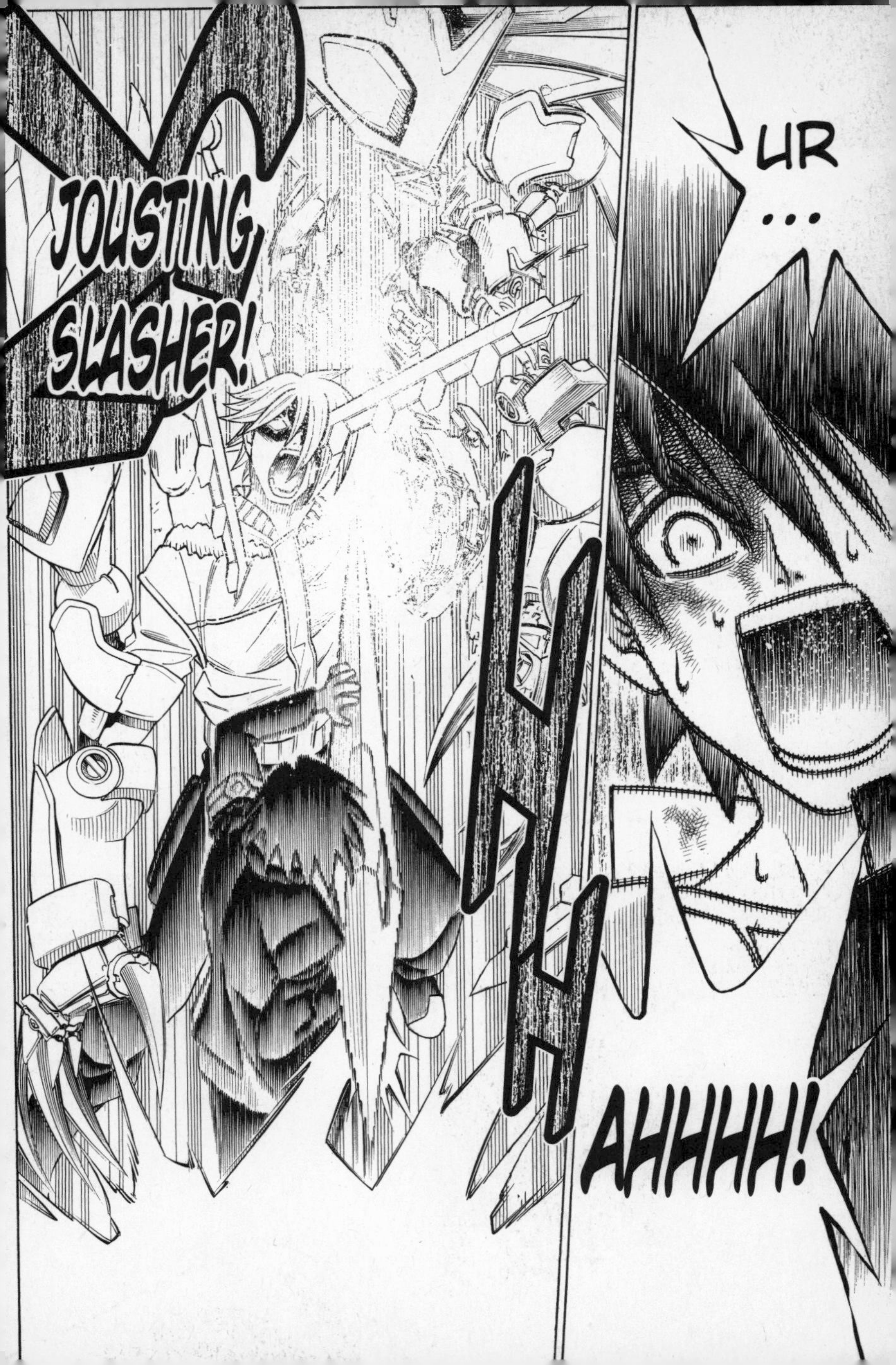
UR
...
HHH
AHHHH!
JOUSTING SLASHER!

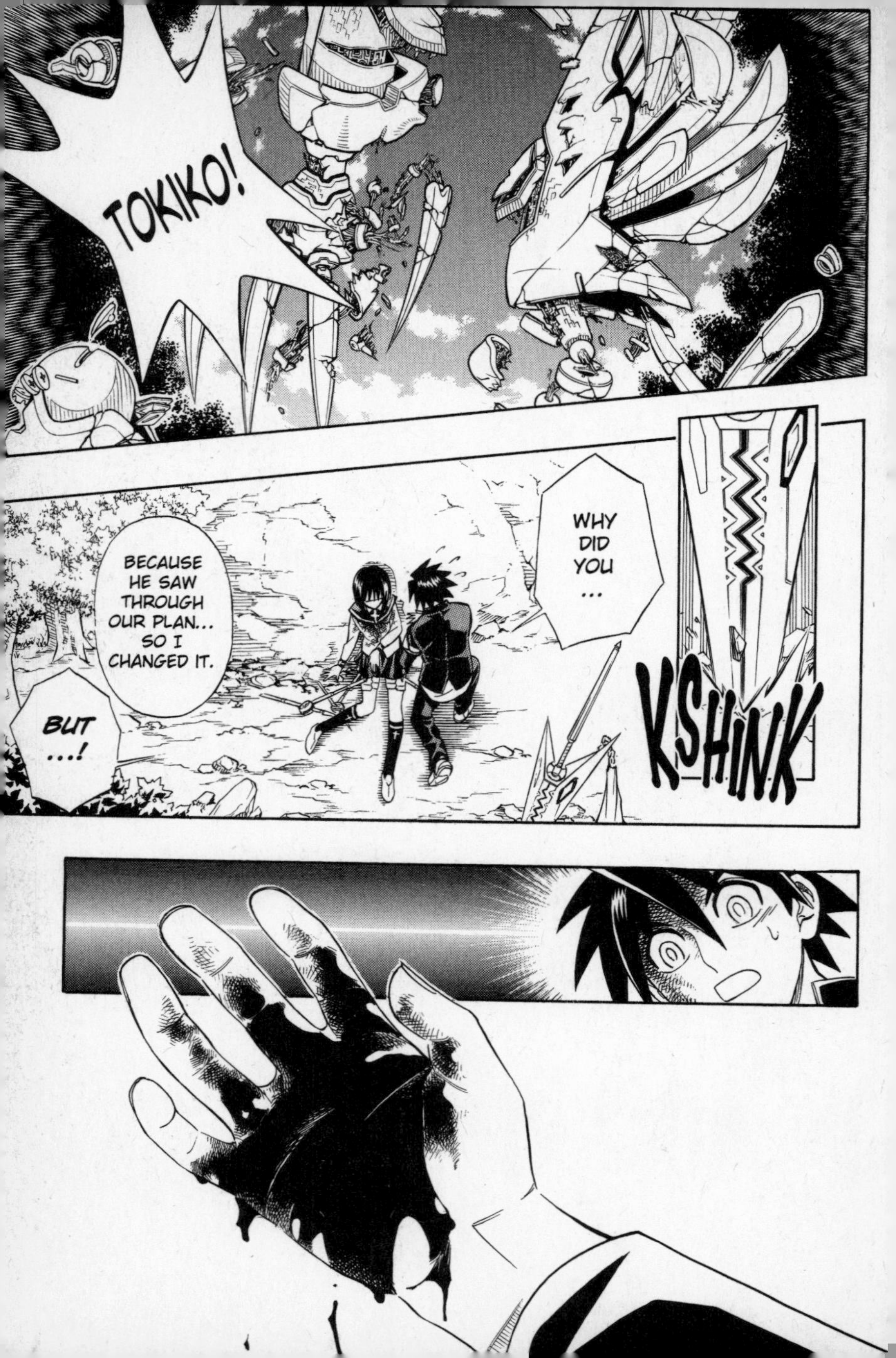
TOKIKO!
KSHINK
WHY DID YOU ...
BECAUSE HE SAW THROUGH OUR PLAN... SO I CHANGED IT.
BUT ...!

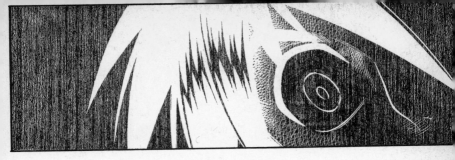

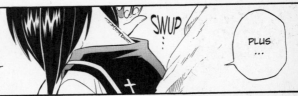

PLUS ...
SWUP
THIS IS PROBABLY THE LAST TIME I CAN REALLY FIGHT.
IT'S FINALLY REACHED MY SPINAL CORD...
HAA
I'M STARTING TO LOSE CONTROL OF MY BODY.
HAA
I COULDN'T FAIL.
THAT'S WHAT WAS GOING THROUGH MY MIND WHEN I ATTACKED BUT...

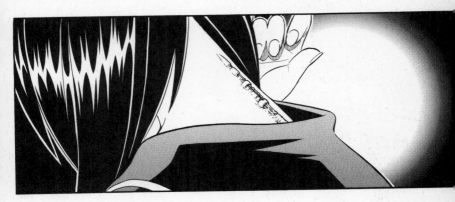

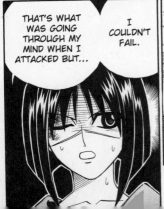

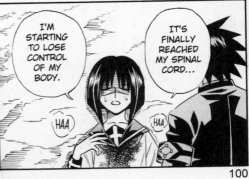

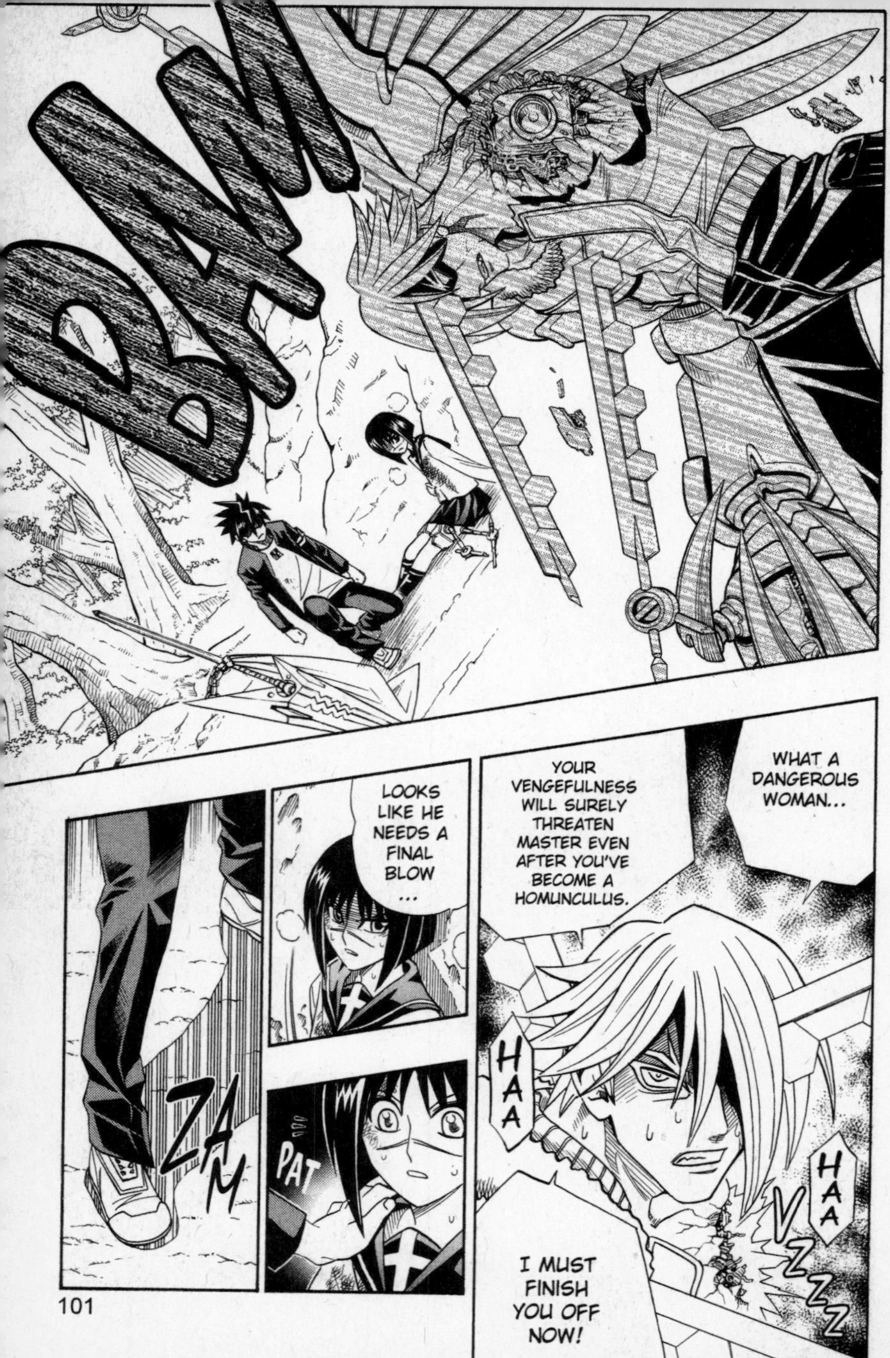
BAM
WHAT A DANGEROUS WOMAN...
YOUR VENGEFULNESS WILL SURELY THREATEN MASTER EVEN AFTER YOU'VE BECOME A HOMUNCULUS.
HAA
HAA
VZZZ
I MUST FINISH YOU OFF NOW!
LOOKS LIKE HE NEEDS A FINAL BLOW ...
PAT
ZAM

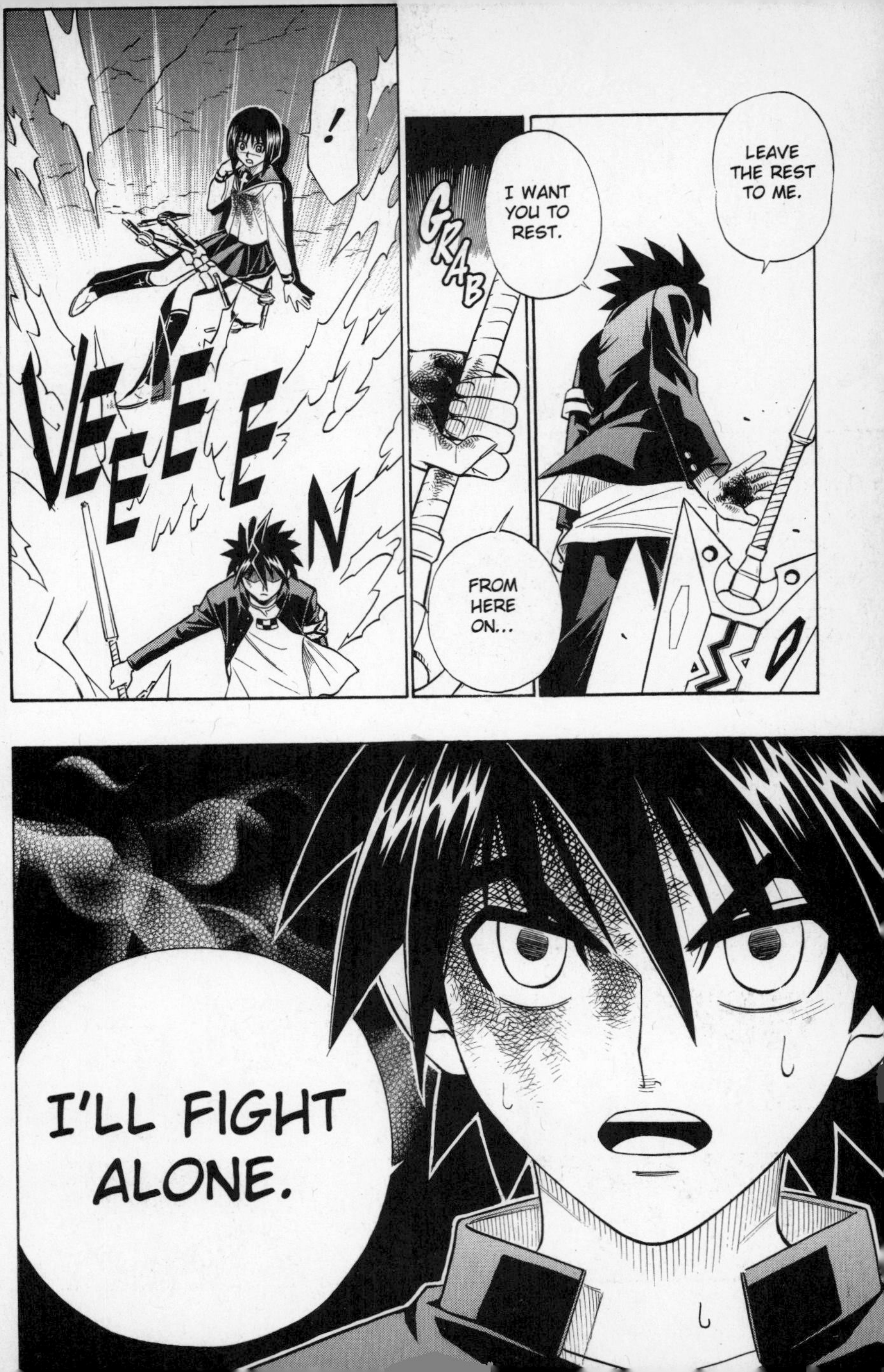
LEAVE THE REST TO ME.
I WANT YOU TO REST.
GRAB
FROM HERE ON...
!
VEEEEEN
I'LL FIGHT ALONE.

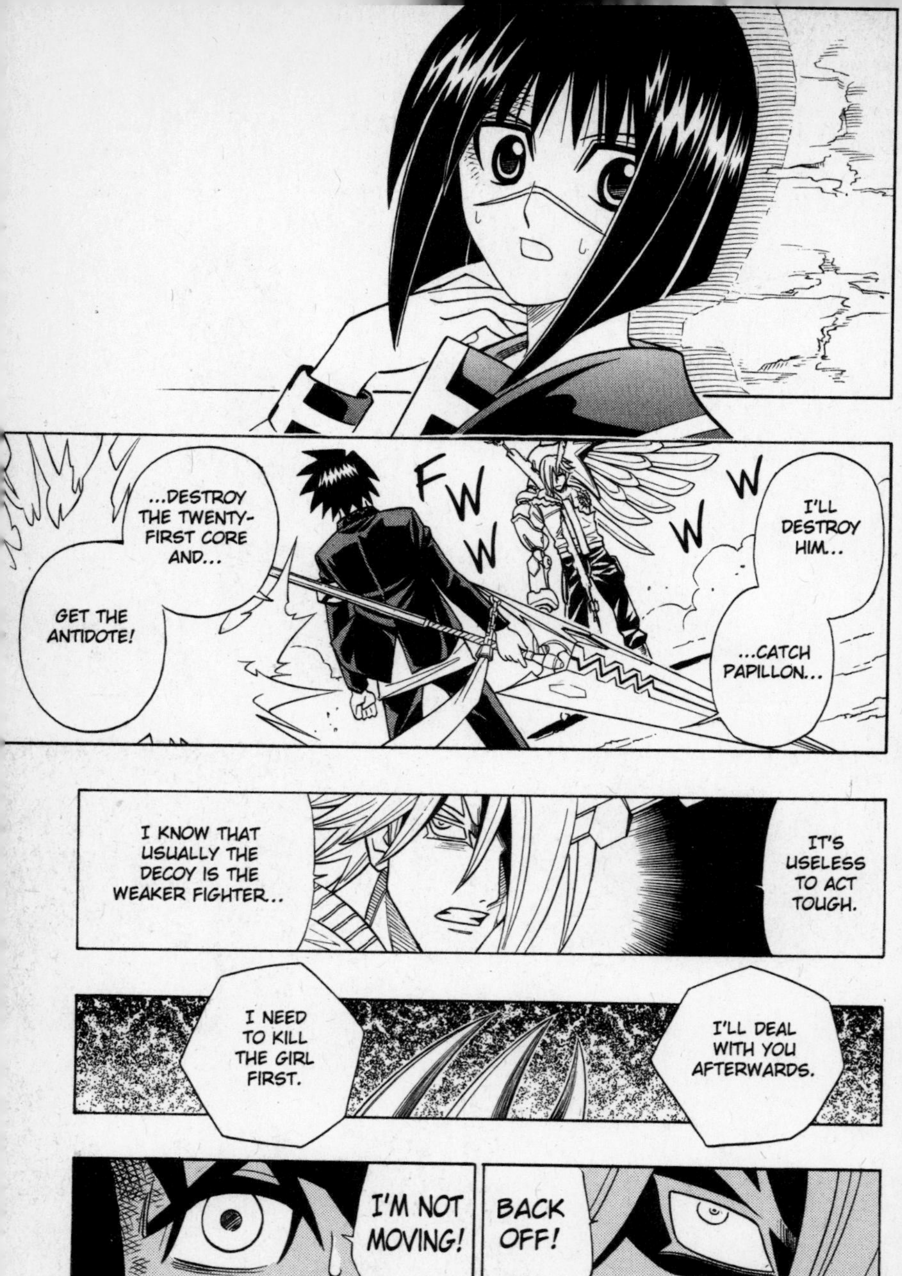
I'LL DESTROY HIM...
...CATCH PAPILLON...
...DESTROY THE TWENTY-FIRST CORE AND...
GET THE ANTIDOTE!
IT'S USELESS TO ACT TOUGH.
I KNOW THAT USUALLY THE DECOY IS THE WEAKER FIGHTER...
I'LL DEAL WITH YOU AFTERWARDS.
I NEED TO KILL THE GIRL FIRST.
BACK OFF!
I'M NOT MOVING!

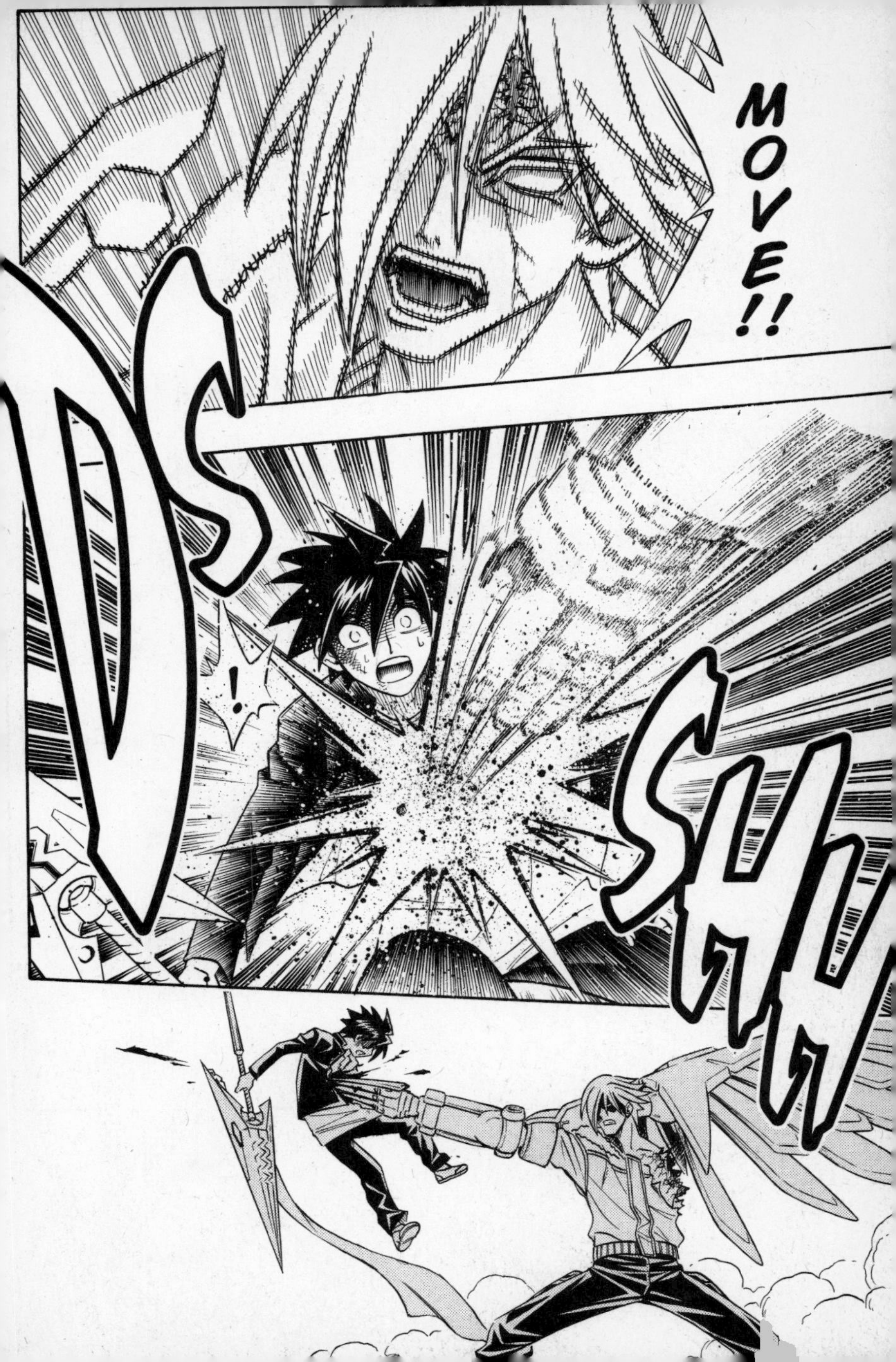
MOVE!!
DS
!
SHH

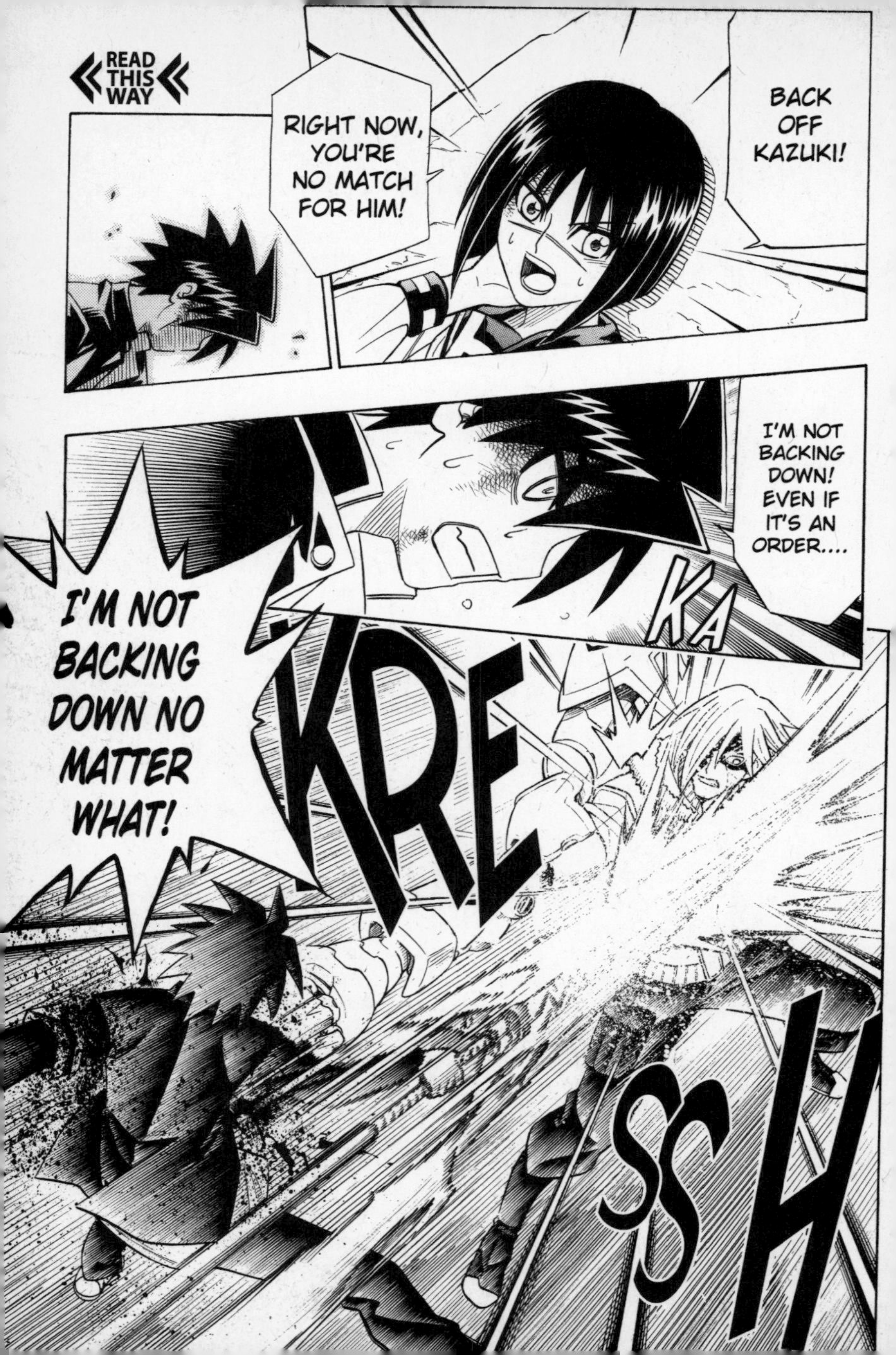

READ THIS WAY
BACK OFF KAZUKI!
RIGHT NOW, YOU'RE NO MATCH FOR HIM!
I'M NOT BACKING DOWN! EVEN IF IT'S AN ORDER....
KA
I'M NOT BACKING DOWN NO MATTER WHAT!
KRE
SSH

· (Continued from page 86) Even if I managed to fit it, the frames ended up being bigger than I thought. That's why the page count got bigger and the content got even thinner. (Factor 2)

· Kazuki's line where he says, "I feel like it'll be more effective if I yell it out" is my own comical question to my manga and to all other Battle Manga where they always announce their attack. Although in its defense, it's been proven that being vocal has a positive effect in The Hammer Throw and Weight Lifting sports.

Chapter 12: VS. Washio: Part 2: Section 2

· "What the heck is Section 2?" I got that question A LOT.

· In this chapter I continued to agonize over how to draw the battle scenes and became hesitant at times.

· Kazuki hasn't learned how to properly fight so he only has forward attacks. Washio's claws and wings are too big so it's hard to grasp what it is as a whole. Tokiko's Valkyrie Skirt is too robotic and difficult to draw in hand-to-hand combat scenes. I completely missed the above points. A lot of other things that I didn't even consider came up too. They look great by themselves but I can't manipulate them well when I combine them. (Factor 3)

· Tokiko's spine drawings were both popular and unpopular as people thought it looked painful. It's difficult to draw something that conveys pain so I'm pretty happy about this one.

Chapter 13: VS. Washio: Part 3

· Finally, the last segment.

· This chapter touches upon Washio's background. In the end where Tokiko says, "…it's instinctual for an animal to fear death but yet he put his life…" I wanted to draw the irony in what Washio was saying more dramatically but at this point I couldn't make a Section 3 so I opted not to reluctantly.

· The battle scenes were lacking contextual depth until the very end. Hmm… It's an important factor to consider moving forward.

Chapter 14: Midnight Run 2

· In the beginning I planned Kazuki to take Tokiko to the Koushaku family estate with him and settle the score. After the battle he would return to the dorm as the sun rose. Mahiro would notice a change in Kazuki as Kazuki had awakened as a Warrior and was no longer an ordinary high school student. Mahiro's "bad feeling" in Chapter 12 was actually leading up to this storyline.

· Learning my lesson from the unpopular VS. Washio chapters I decided to change it. My editor at the time and I discussed and came to the conclusion that "the readers weren't ready to have Kazuki part from his ordinary life. Perhaps the readers had their expectations betrayed by having Kazuki taken away from that to fight Washio in the mountains?" (Factor 4) That's why I decided to change the story progression by incorporating "ordinary life, meaning Mahiro and the three guys at the dorm."

· I changed Mahiro's character to be the space cadet character.

· I threw out an entire side story, changed the progression and altered a character. After doing everything I can to make it more interesting, it finally got back the popularity level before the VS. Washio chapters. I learned a very valuable lesson.

CHAPTER 13: VS. WASHIO: Part 3

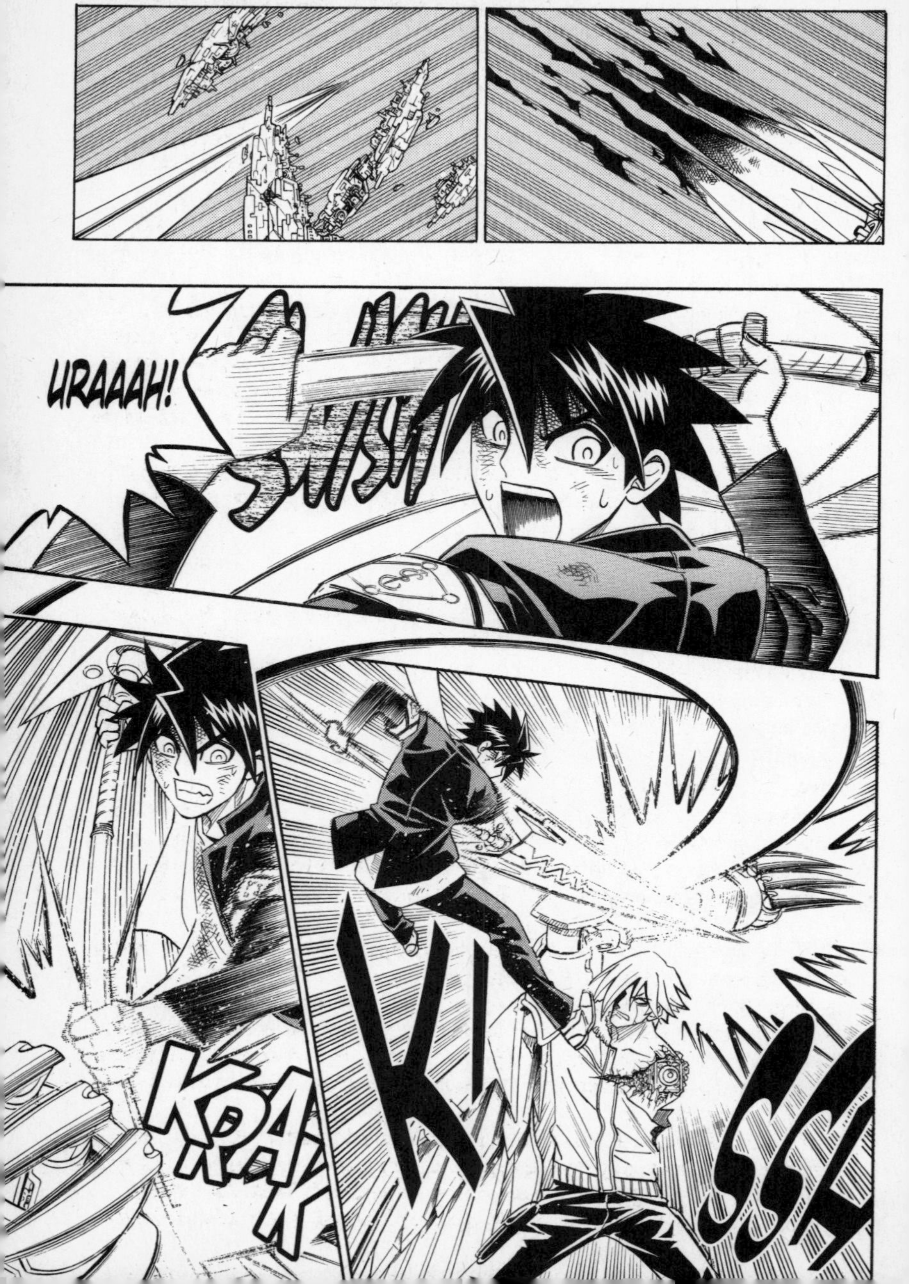
URAAAH!
SWISH
KI
SSH
KRAK

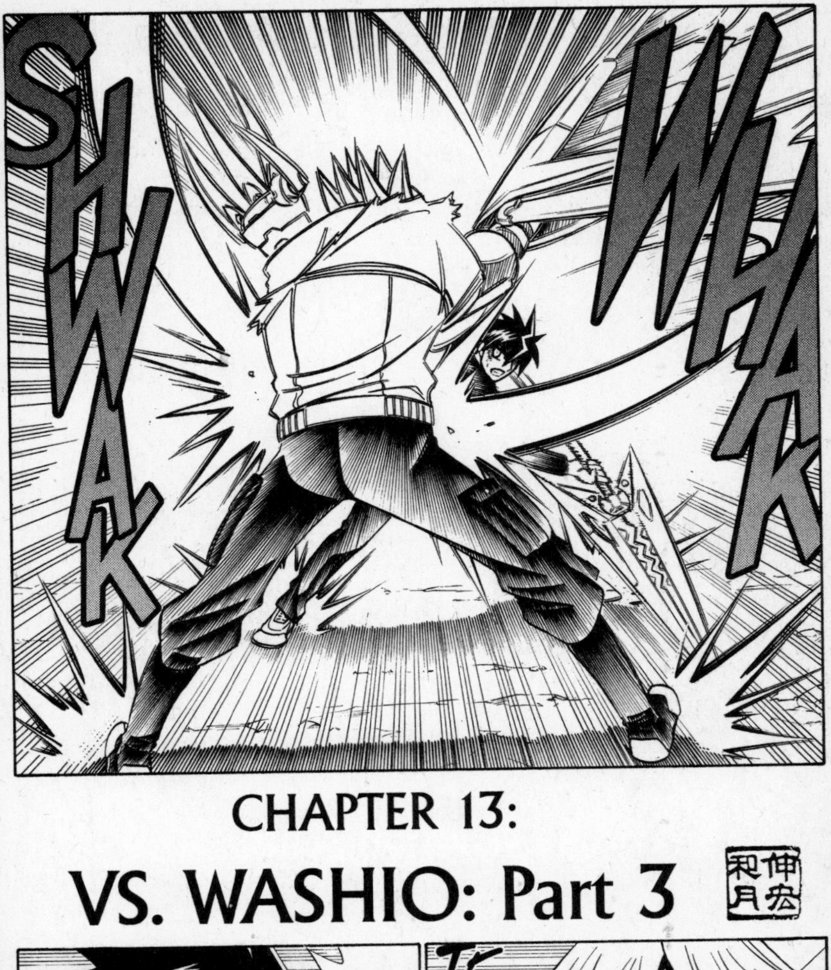
WHAK
SHWAK

CHAPTER 13:
VS. WASHIO: Part 3

伸宏和月

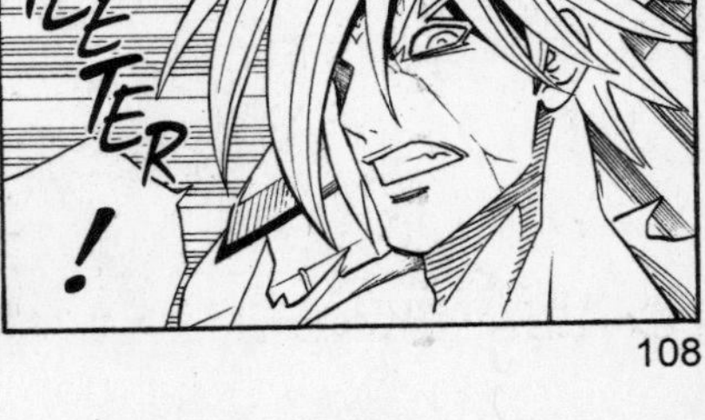
TEETER!

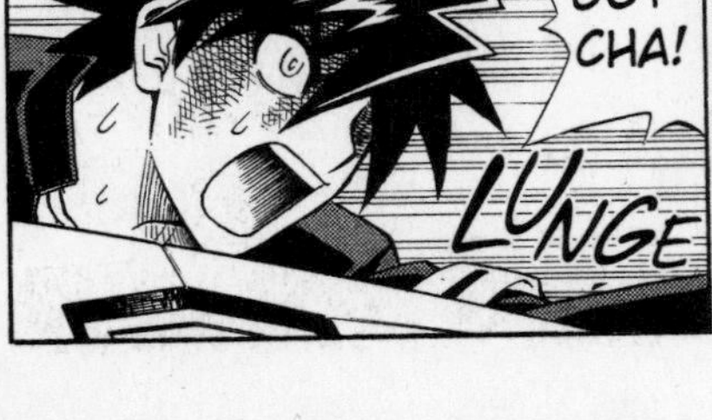
GOT-CHA!
LUNGE

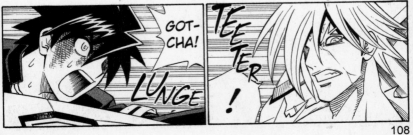

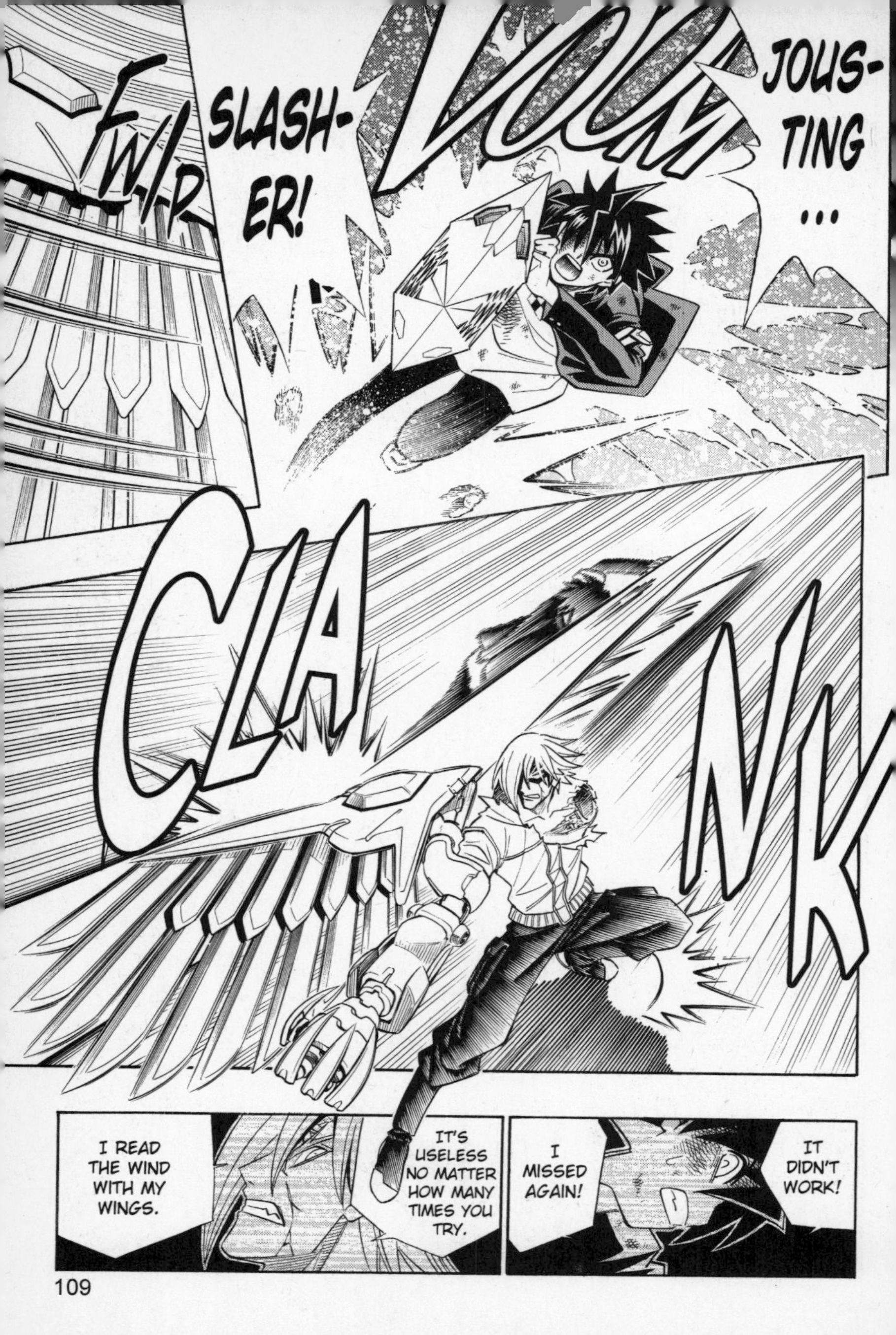

JOUS-TING ...
VOOM
SLASH-ER!
FWIP
CLANK
IT DIDN'T WORK!
I MISSED AGAIN!
IT'S USELESS NO MATTER HOW MANY TIMES YOU TRY.
I READ THE WIND WITH MY WINGS.

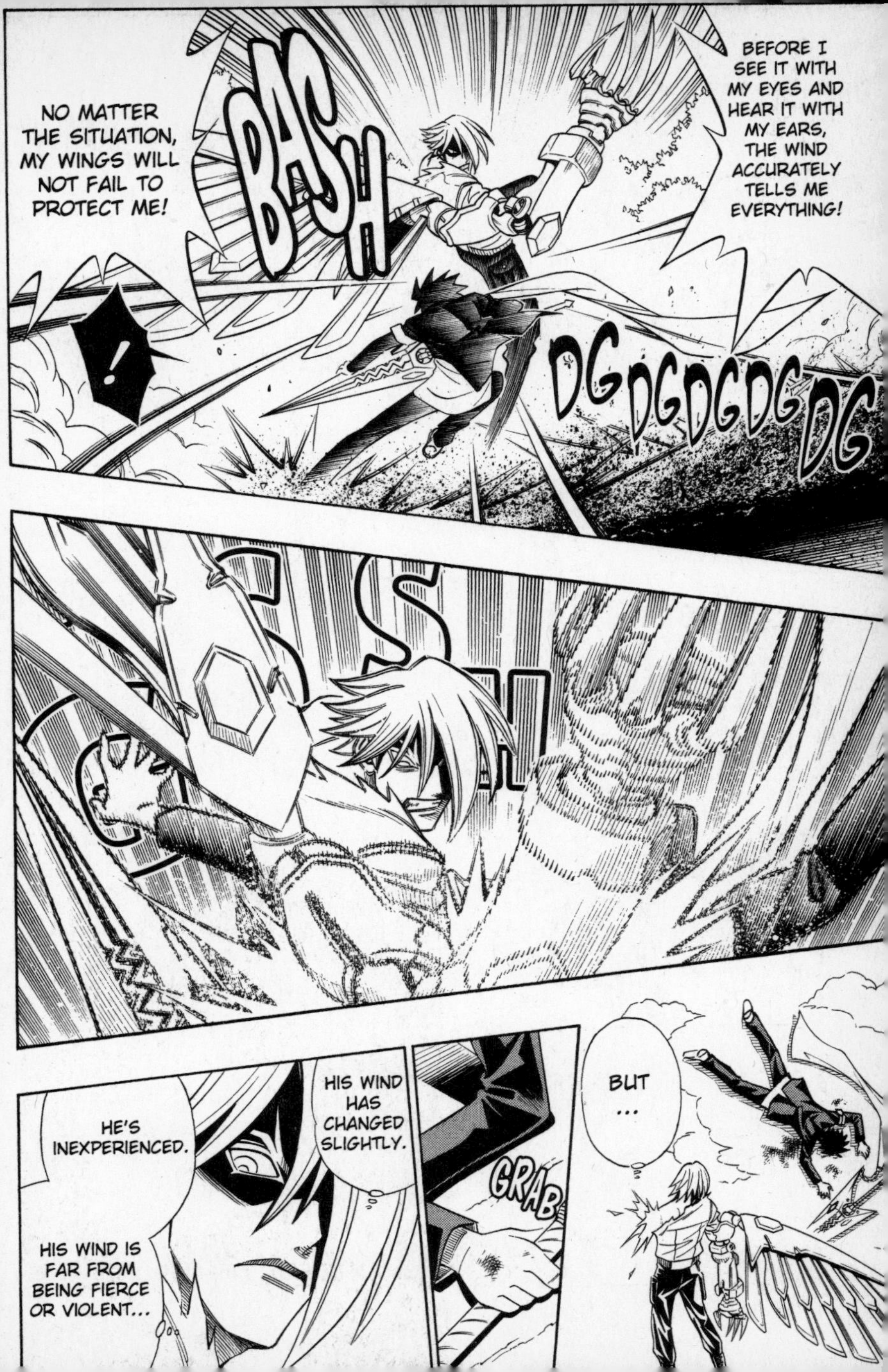
BEFORE I SEE IT WITH MY EYES AND HEAR IT WITH MY EARS, THE WIND ACCURATELY TELLS ME EVERYTHING!
BASH
NO MATTER THE SITUATION, MY WINGS WILL NOT FAIL TO PROTECT ME!
!
DG DG DG DG DG
BUT ...
HIS WIND HAS CHANGED SLIGHTLY.
GRAB
HE'S INEXPERIENCED.
HIS WIND IS FAR FROM BEING FIERCE OR VIOLENT...

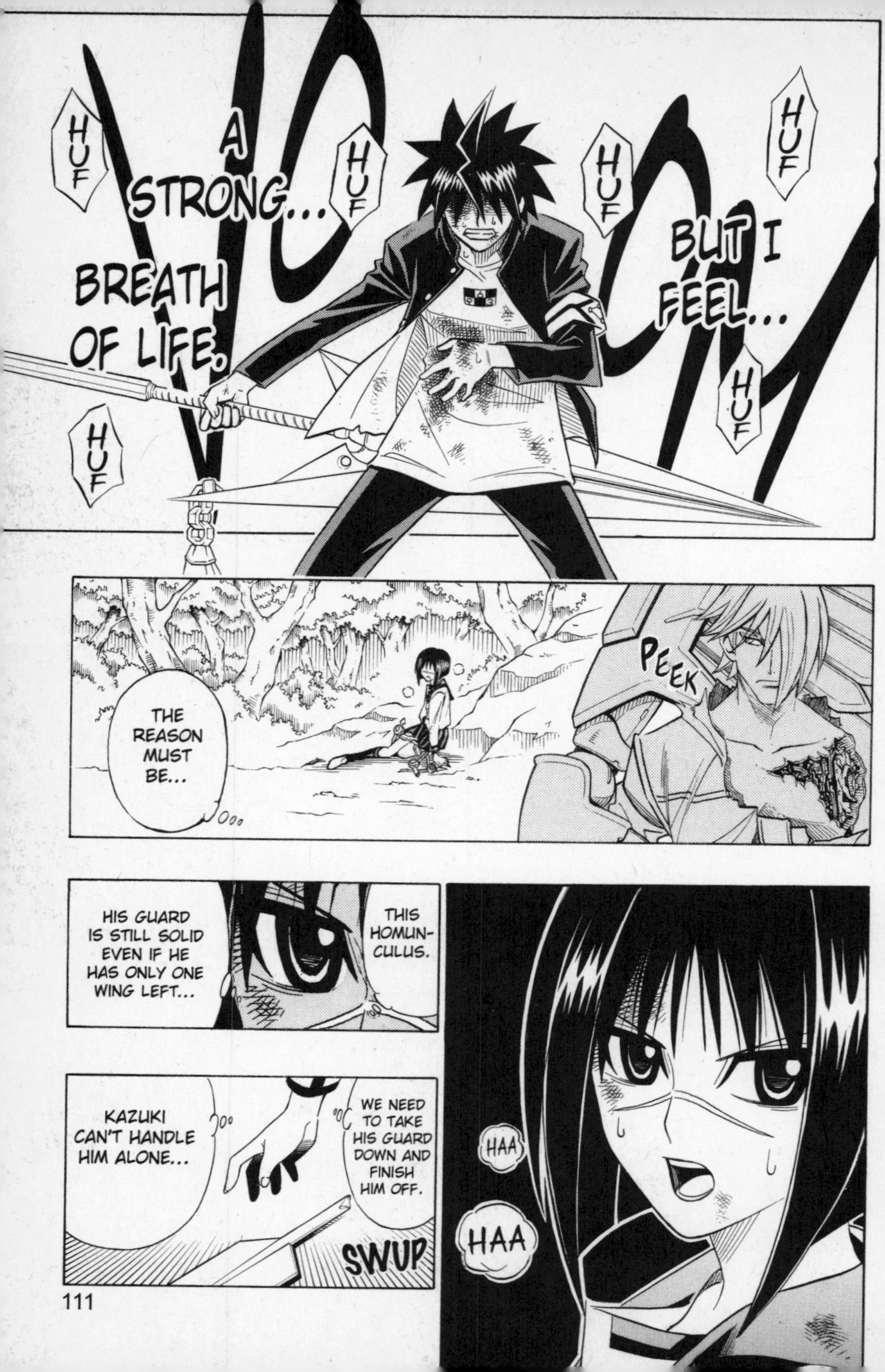
HUF
HUF
BUT I FEEL...
HUF
HUF
A STRONG... BREATH OF LIFE.
HUF
HUF
PEEK
THE REASON MUST BE...
HAA
HAA
THIS HOMUNCULUS.
HIS GUARD IS STILL SOLID EVEN IF HE HAS ONLY ONE WING LEFT...
WE NEED TO TAKE HIS GUARD DOWN AND FINISH HIM OFF.
KAZUKI CAN'T HANDLE HIM ALONE...
SWUP

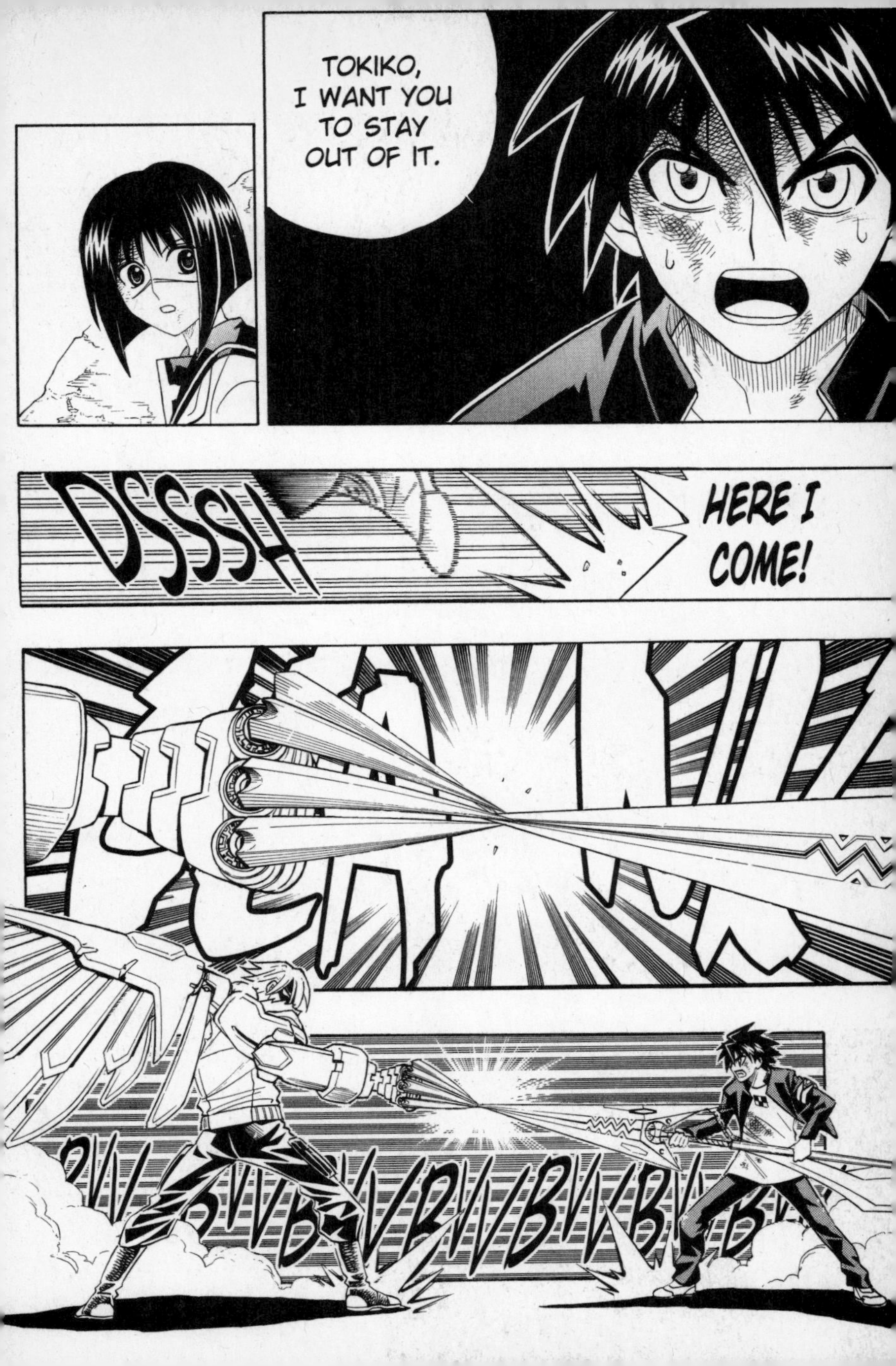
TOKIKO, I WANT YOU TO STAY OUT OF IT.
HERE I COME!
DSSSH

READ THIS WAY

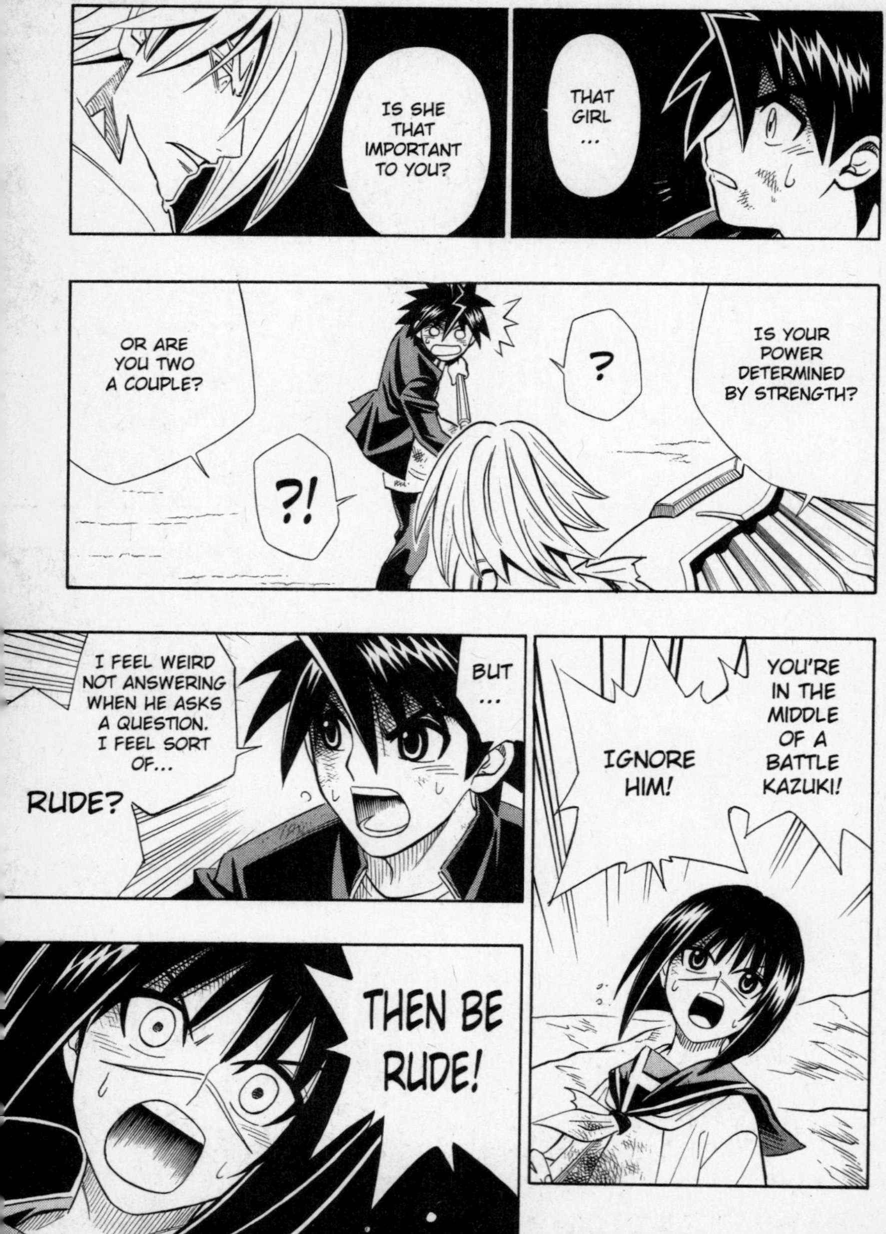
THAT GIRL ...
IS SHE THAT IMPORTANT TO YOU?
IS YOUR POWER DETERMINED BY STRENGTH?
?
OR ARE YOU TWO A COUPLE?
?!
YOU'RE IN THE MIDDLE OF A BATTLE KAZUKI!
IGNORE HIM!
BUT ...
I FEEL WEIRD NOT ANSWERING WHEN HE ASKS A QUESTION. I FEEL SORT OF...
RUDE?
THEN BE RUDE!

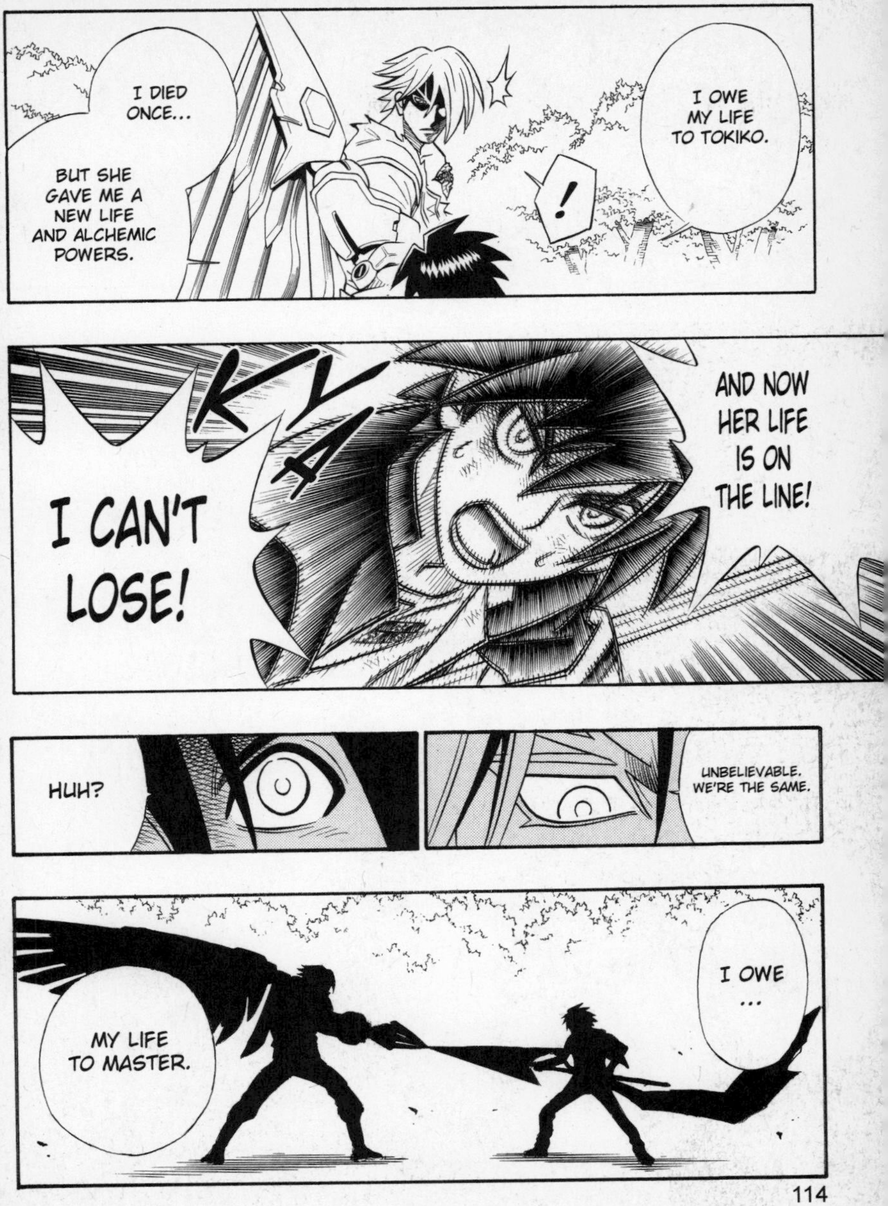
I OWE MY LIFE TO TOKIKO.
!
I DIED ONCE...
BUT SHE GAVE ME A NEW LIFE AND ALCHEMIC POWERS.
AND NOW HER LIFE IS ON THE LINE!
KYA
I CAN'T LOSE!
UNBELIEVABLE. WE'RE THE SAME.
HUH?
I OWE ...
MY LIFE TO MASTER.

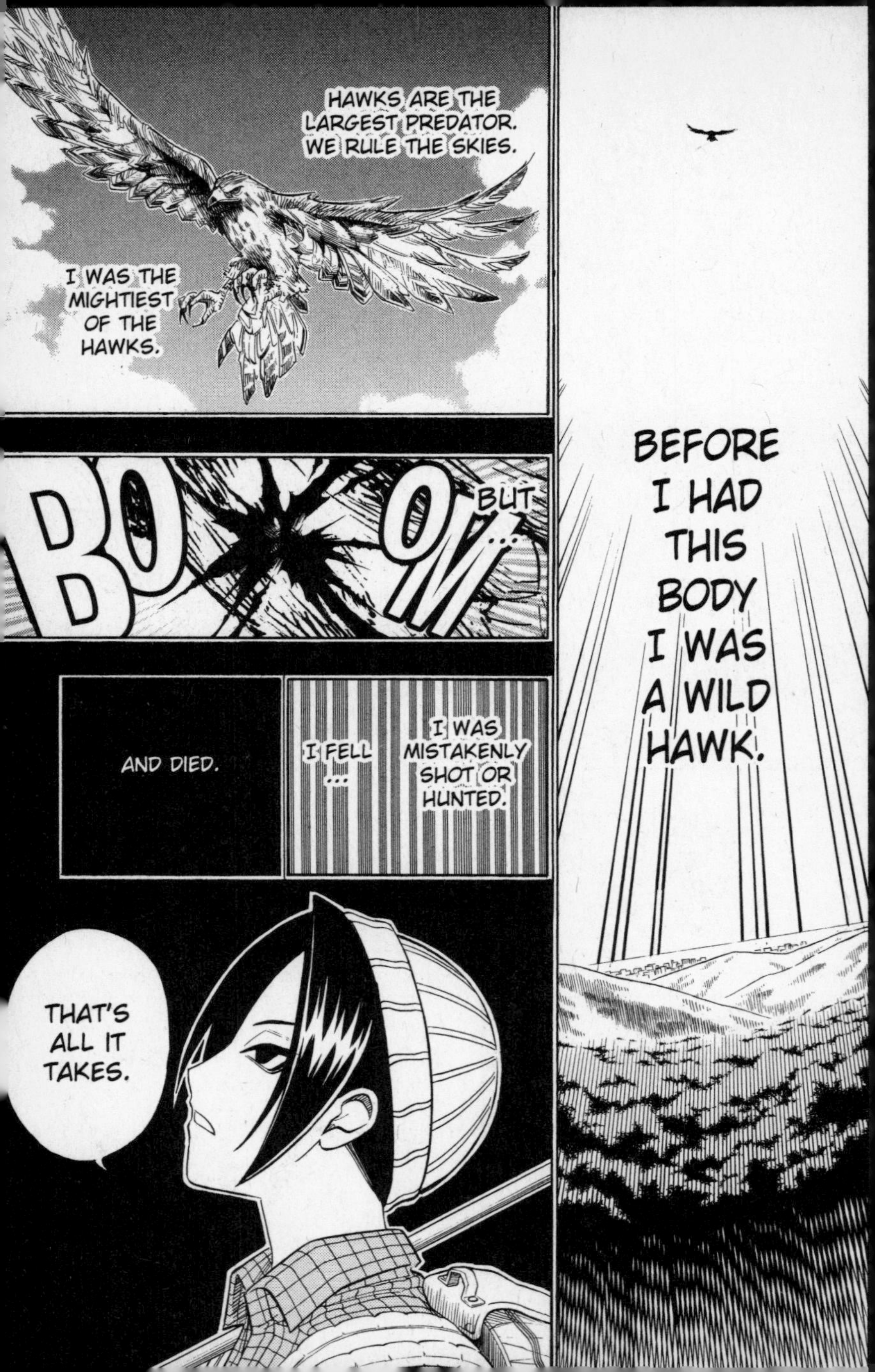
BEFORE I HAD THIS BODY I WAS A WILD HAWK.
HAWKS ARE THE LARGEST PREDATOR. WE RULE THE SKIES.
I WAS THE MIGHTIEST OF THE HAWKS.
BUT...
BOOM
I WAS MISTAKENLY SHOT OR HUNTED.
I FELL ...
AND DIED.
THAT'S ALL IT TAKES.

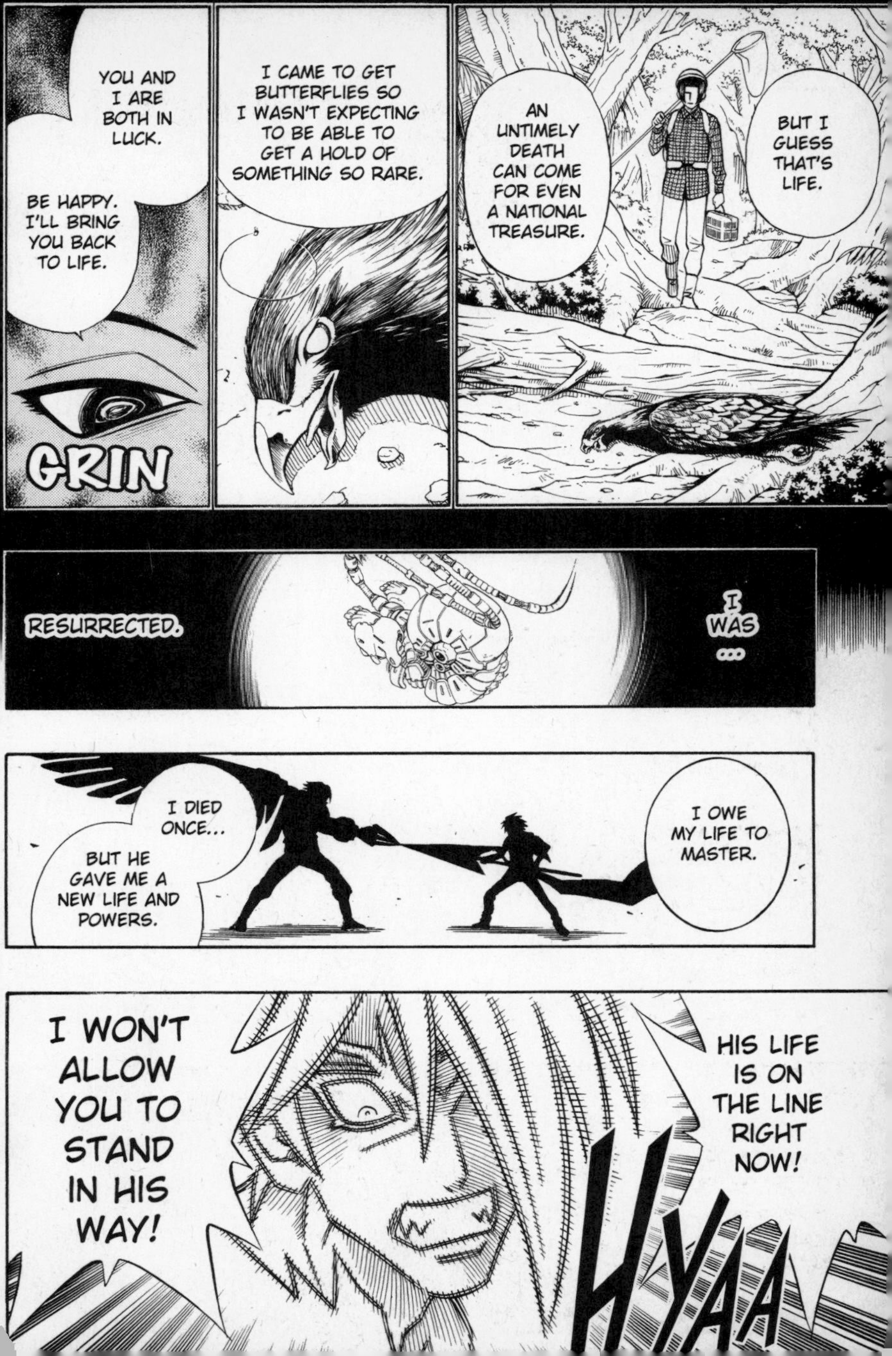

BUT I GUESS THAT'S LIFE.
AN UNTIMELY DEATH CAN COME FOR EVEN A NATIONAL TREASURE.
I CAME TO GET BUTTERFLIES SO I WASN'T EXPECTING TO BE ABLE TO GET A HOLD OF SOMETHING SO RARE.
YOU AND I ARE BOTH IN LUCK.
BE HAPPY. I'LL BRING YOU BACK TO LIFE.
GRIN
I WAS...
RESURRECTED.
I OWE MY LIFE TO MASTER.
I DIED ONCE...
BUT HE GAVE ME A NEW LIFE AND POWERS.
HIS LIFE IS ON THE LINE RIGHT NOW!
HIYAA
I WON'T ALLOW YOU TO STAND IN HIS WAY!

READ THIS WAY

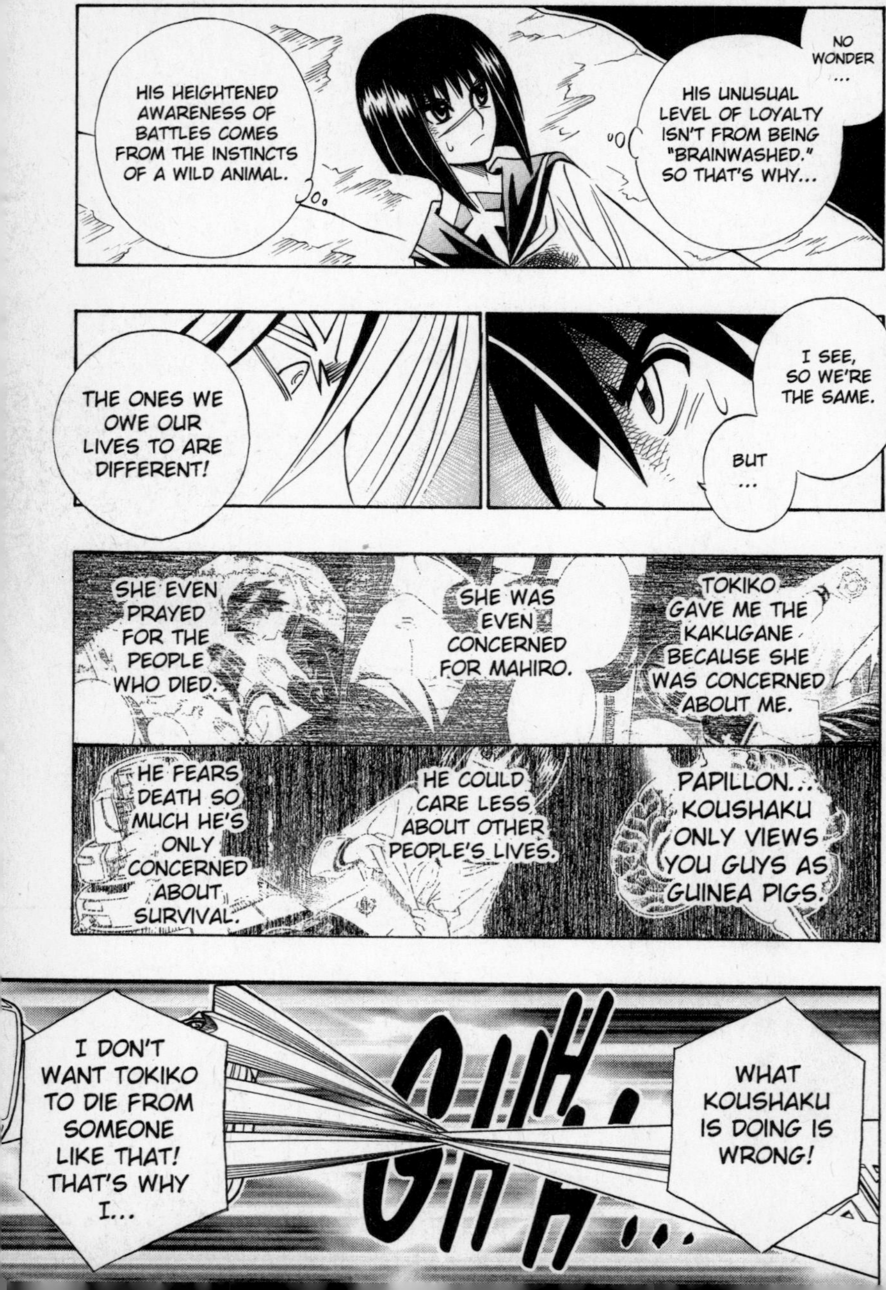
NO WONDER ...
HIS UNUSUAL LEVEL OF LOYALTY ISN'T FROM BEING "BRAINWASHED." SO THAT'S WHY...
HIS HEIGHTENED AWARENESS OF BATTLES COMES FROM THE INSTINCTS OF A WILD ANIMAL.
I SEE, SO WE'RE THE SAME.
BUT ...
THE ONES WE OWE OUR LIVES TO ARE DIFFERENT!
TOKIKO GAVE ME THE KAKUGANE BECAUSE SHE WAS CONCERNED ABOUT ME.
SHE WAS EVEN CONCERNED FOR MAHIRO.
SHE EVEN PRAYED FOR THE PEOPLE WHO DIED.
PAPILLON... KOUSHAKU ONLY VIEWS YOU GUYS AS GUINEA PIGS.
HE COULD CARE LESS ABOUT OTHER PEOPLE'S LIVES.
HE FEARS DEATH SO MUCH HE'S ONLY CONCERNED ABOUT SURVIVAL.
WHAT KOUSHAKU IS DOING IS WRONG!
I DON'T WANT TOKIKO TO DIE FROM SOMEONE LIKE THAT! THAT'S WHY I...

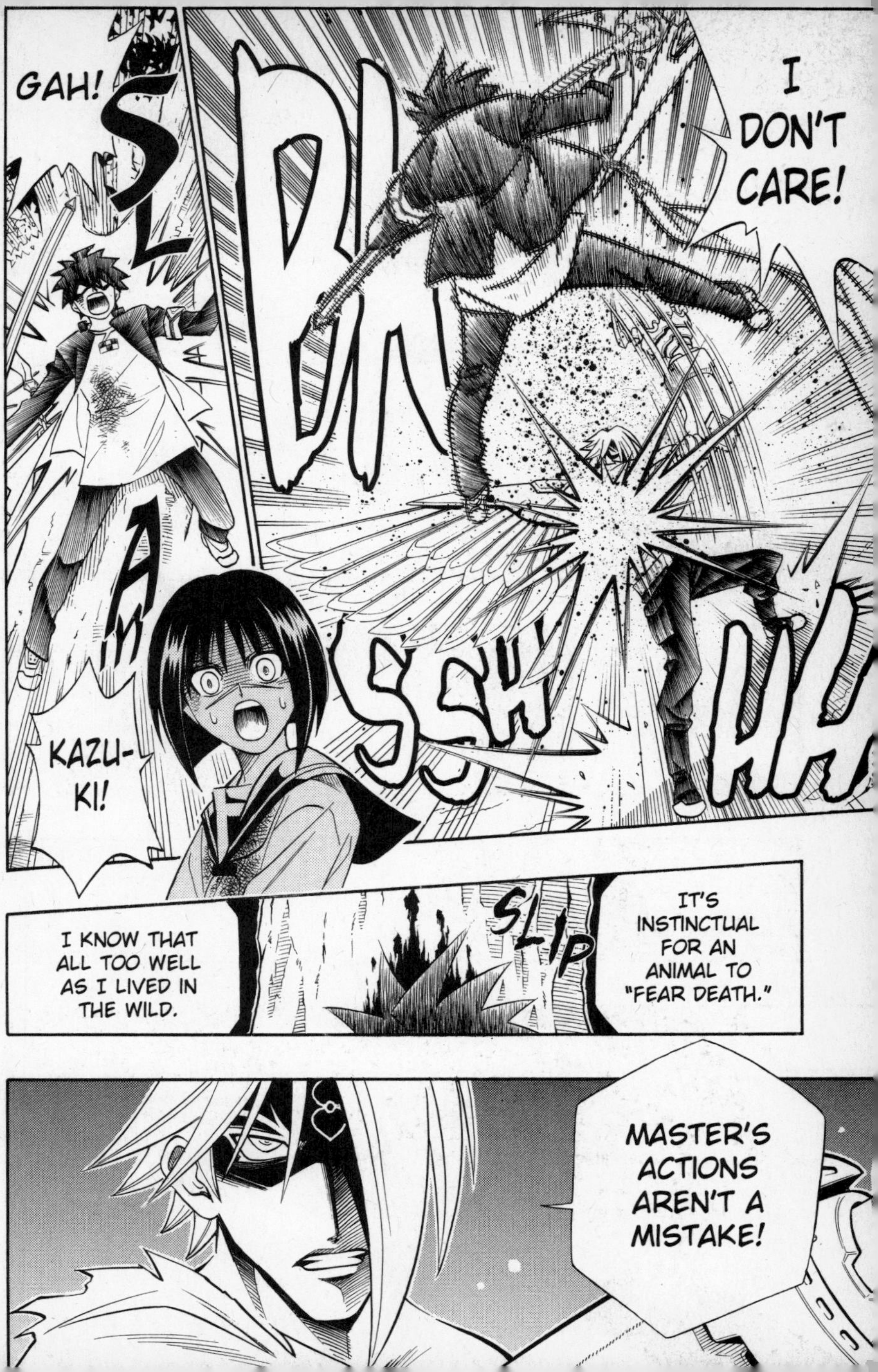
I DON'T CARE!
GAH!
SSH
KAZU-KI!
IT'S INSTINCTUAL FOR AN ANIMAL TO "FEAR DEATH."
SLIP
I KNOW THAT ALL TOO WELL AS I LIVED IN THE WILD.
MASTER'S ACTIONS AREN'T A MISTAKE!

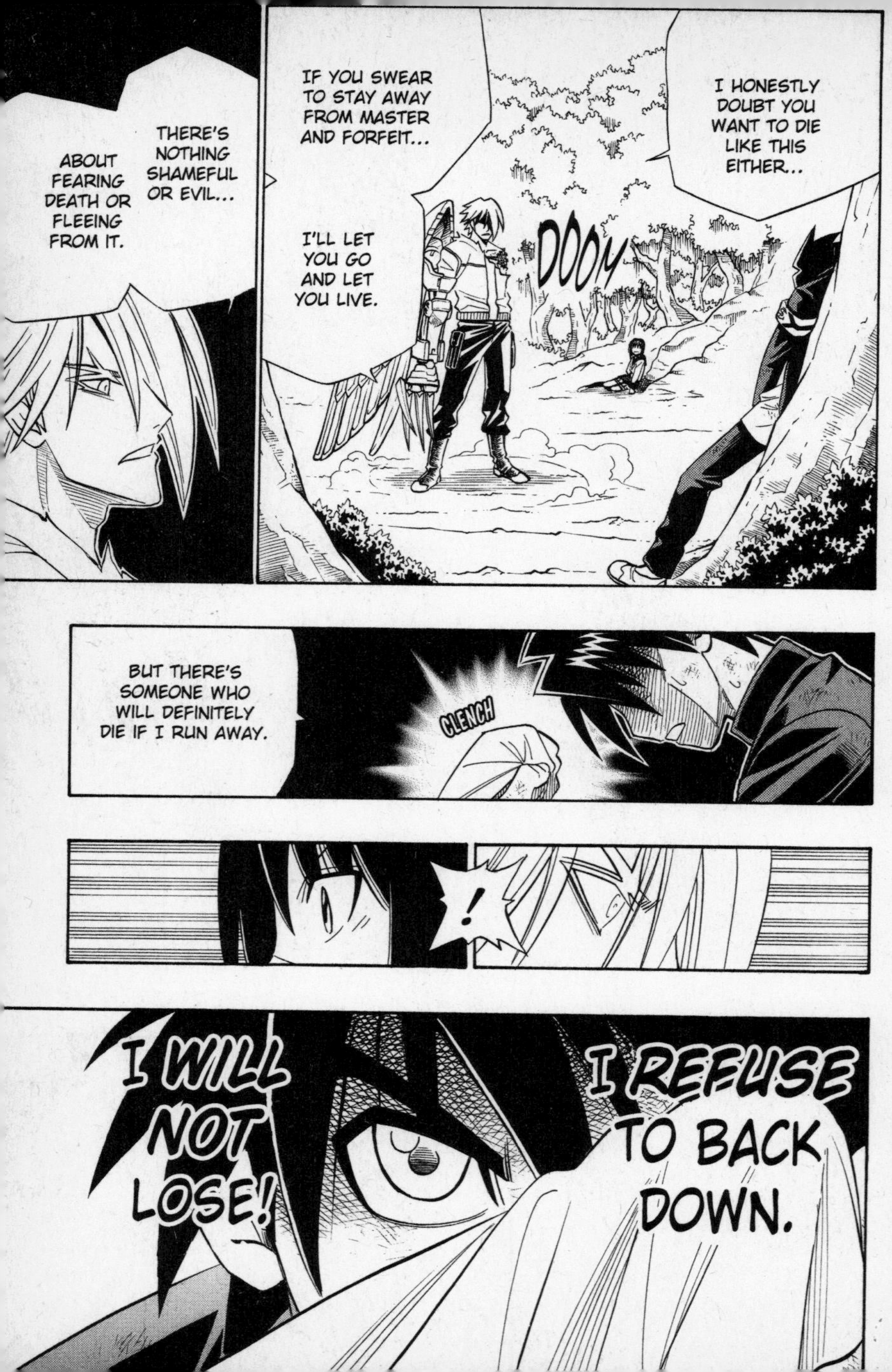
I HONESTLY DOUBT YOU WANT TO DIE LIKE THIS EITHER...
IF YOU SWEAR TO STAY AWAY FROM MASTER AND FORFEIT...
I'LL LET YOU GO AND LET YOU LIVE.
DOOM
THERE'S NOTHING SHAMEFUL OR EVIL...
ABOUT FEARING DEATH OR FLEEING FROM IT.
BUT THERE'S SOMEONE WHO WILL DEFINITELY DIE IF I RUN AWAY.
CLENCH
!
I REFUSE TO BACK DOWN.
I WILL NOT LOSE!

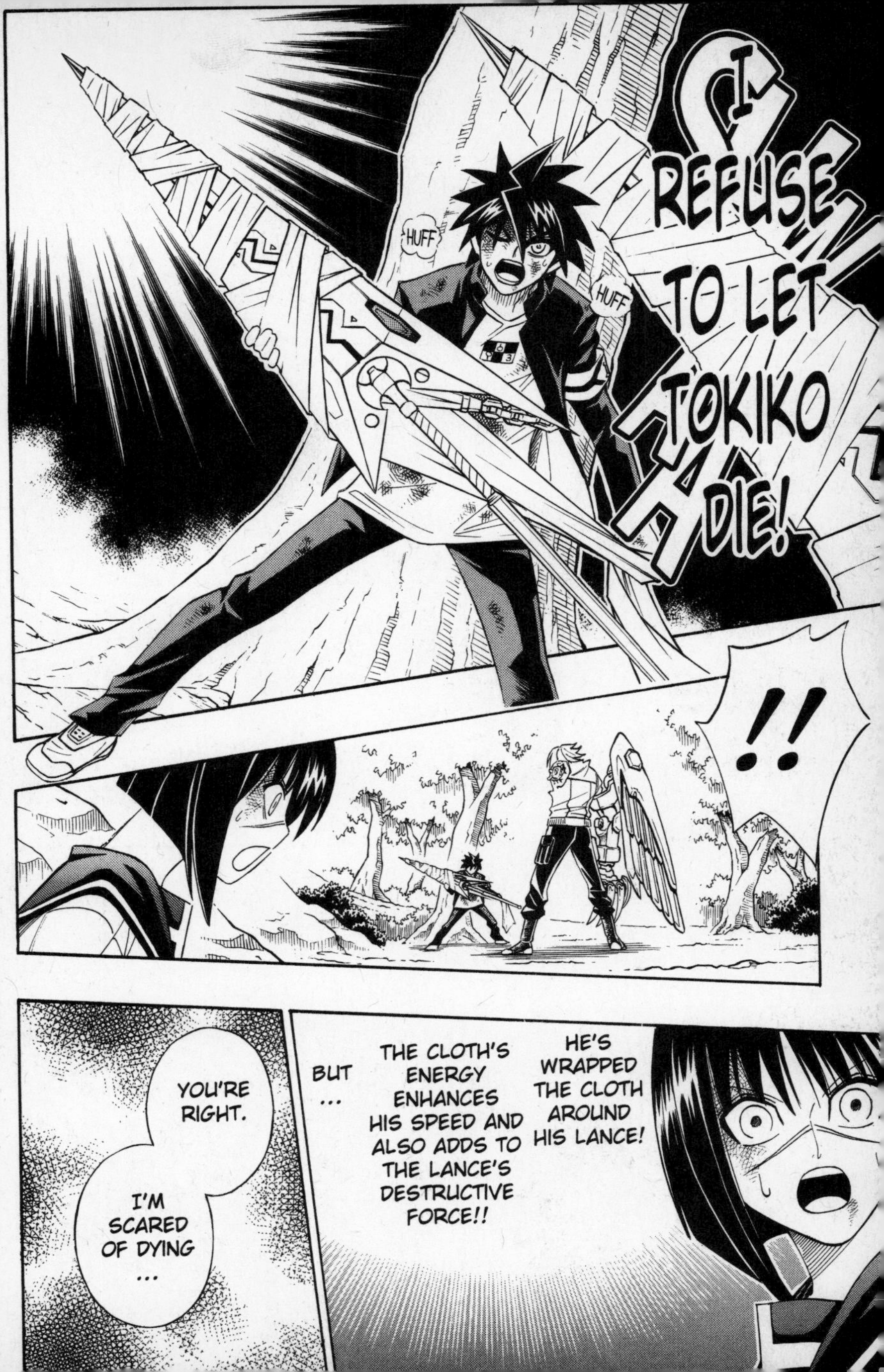
I REFUSE TO LET TOKIKO DIE!
HUFF
HUFF
!!
HE'S WRAPPED THE CLOTH AROUND HIS LANCE!
THE CLOTH'S ENERGY ENHANCES HIS SPEED AND ALSO ADDS TO THE LANCE'S DESTRUCTIVE FORCE!!
BUT ...
YOU'RE RIGHT.
I'M SCARED OF DYING ...

READ THIS WAY

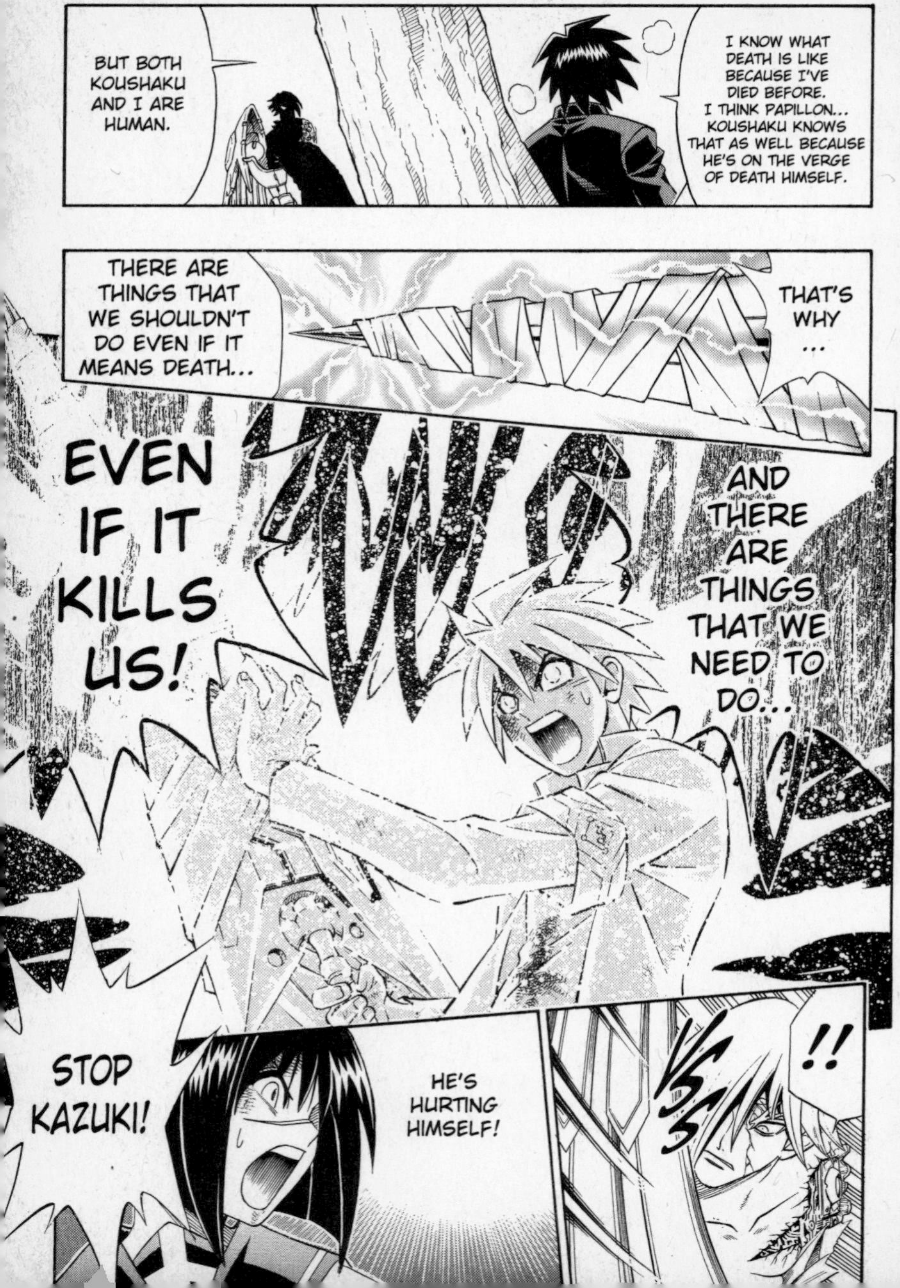

I KNOW WHAT DEATH IS LIKE BECAUSE I'VE DIED BEFORE. I THINK PAPILLON... KOUSHAKU KNOWS THAT AS WELL BECAUSE HE'S ON THE VERGE OF DEATH HIMSELF.
BUT BOTH KOUSHAKU AND I ARE HUMAN.
THAT'S WHY ...
THERE ARE THINGS THAT WE SHOULDN'T DO EVEN IF IT MEANS DEATH...
AND THERE ARE THINGS THAT WE NEED TO DO...
EVEN IF IT KILLS US!
!!
HE'S HURTING HIMSELF!
STOP KAZUKI!

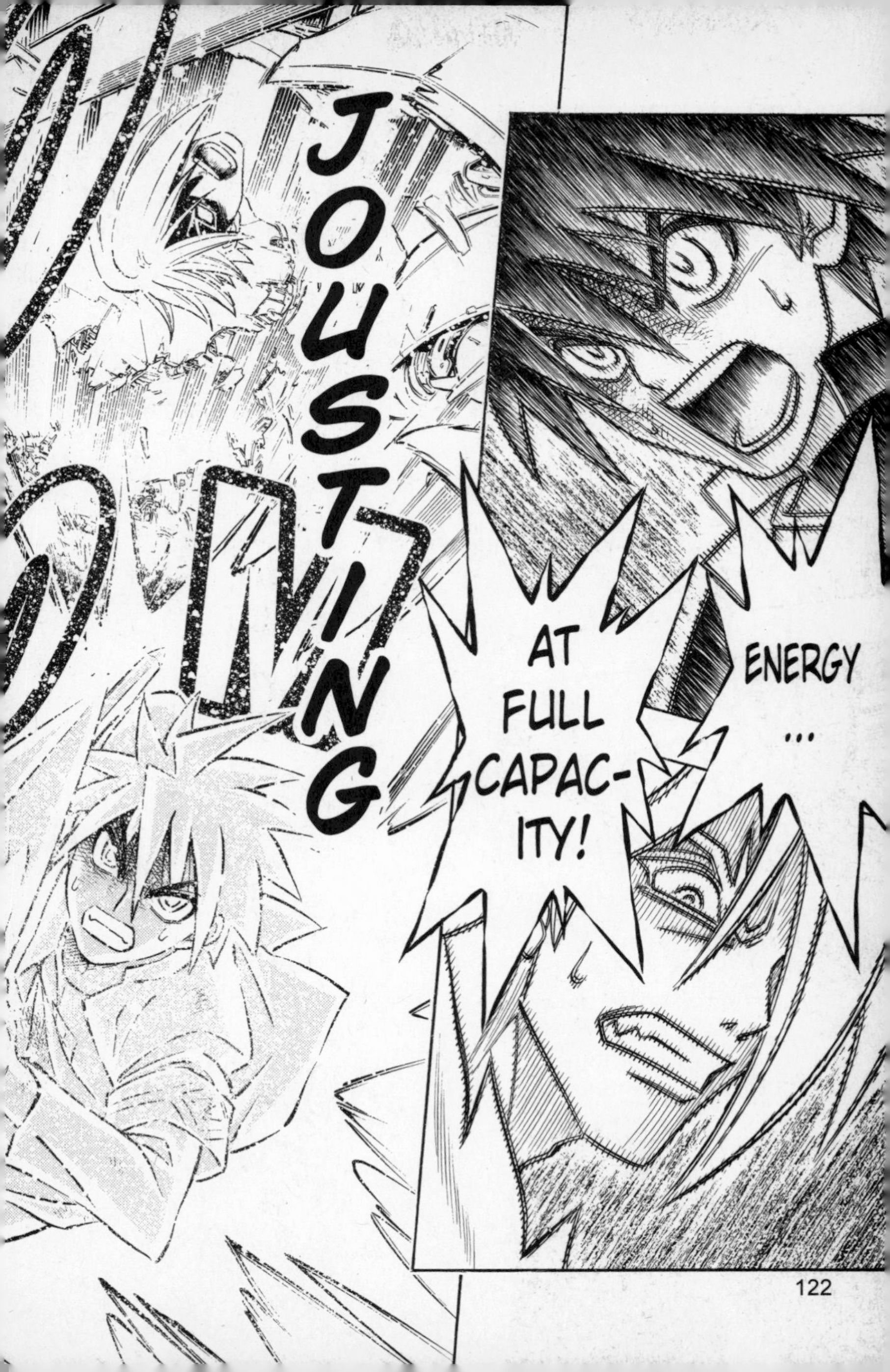
ENERGY
...
AT FULL CAPAC-ITY!
JOUSTING

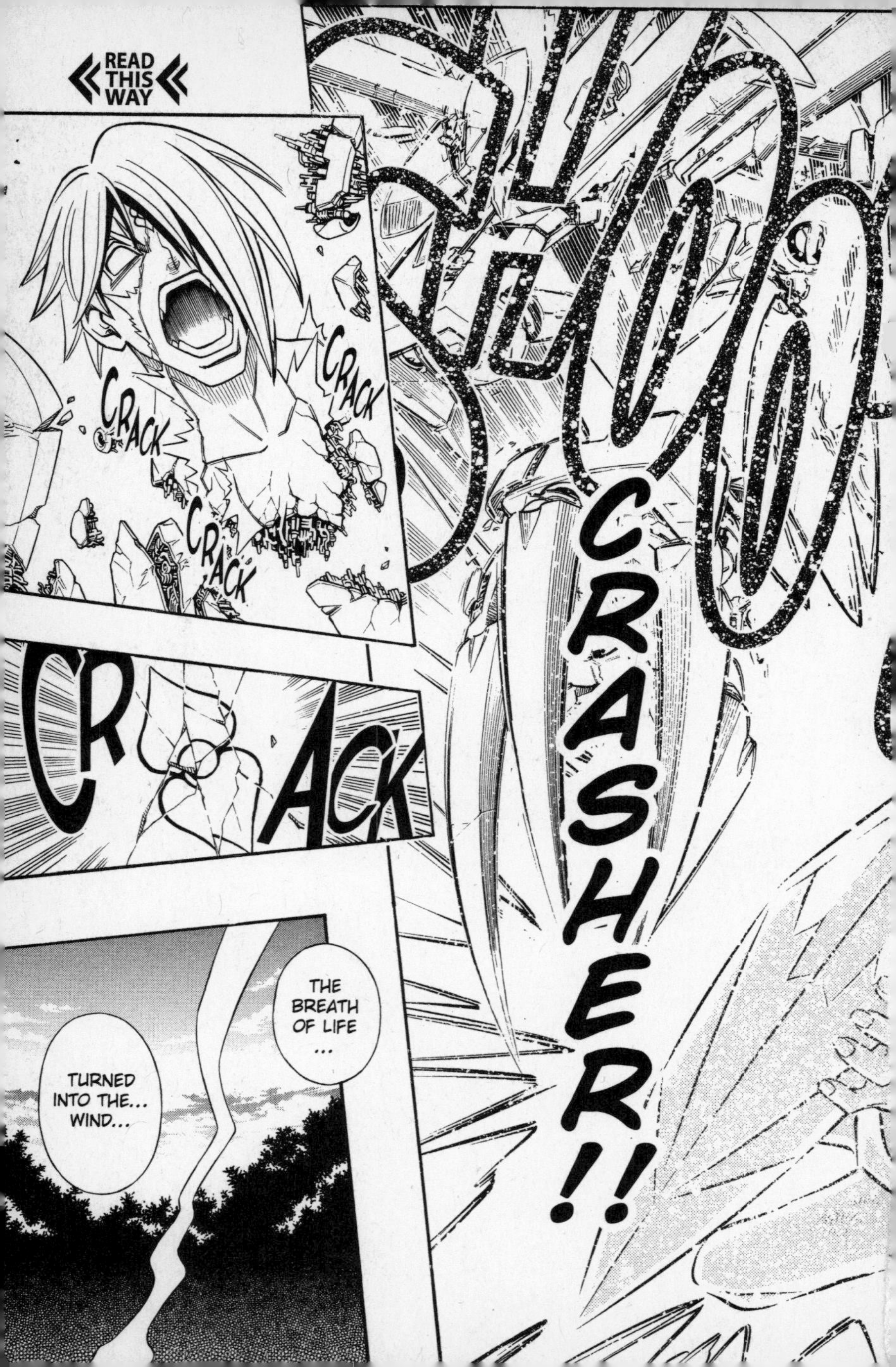
READ THIS WAY
CRASHER!!
CRACK
CRACK
CRACK
CR ACK
THE BREATH OF LIFE ...
TURNED INTO THE... WIND...

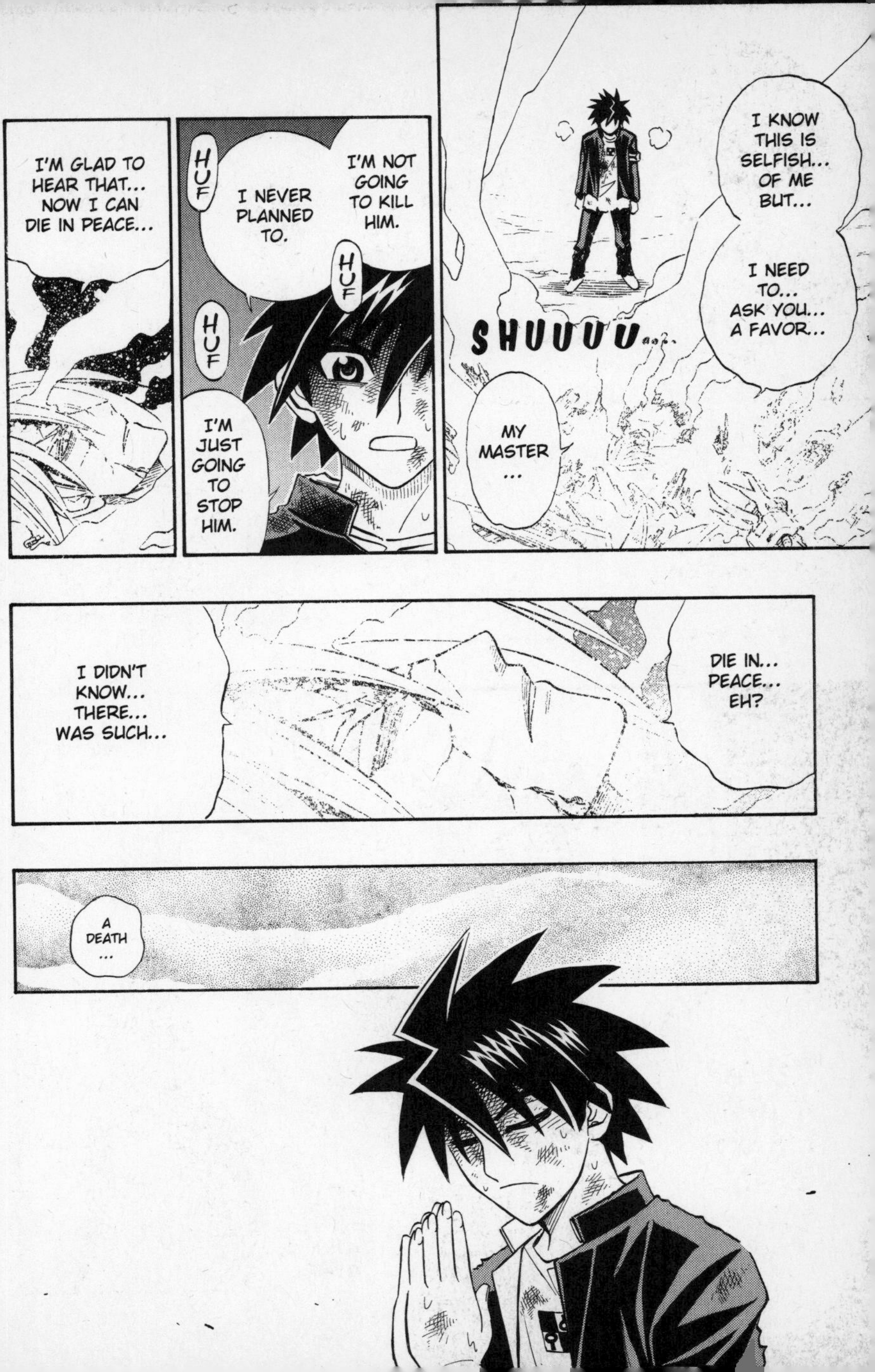
I KNOW THIS IS SELFISH... OF ME BUT...
I NEED TO... ASK YOU... A FAVOR...
SHUUUU...
MY MASTER ...
I'M NOT GOING TO KILL HIM.
I NEVER PLANNED TO.
HUF
HUF
HUF
I'M JUST GOING TO STOP HIM.
I'M GLAD TO HEAR THAT... NOW I CAN DIE IN PEACE...
DIE IN... PEACE... EH?
I DIDN'T KNOW... THERE... WAS SUCH...
A DEATH ...

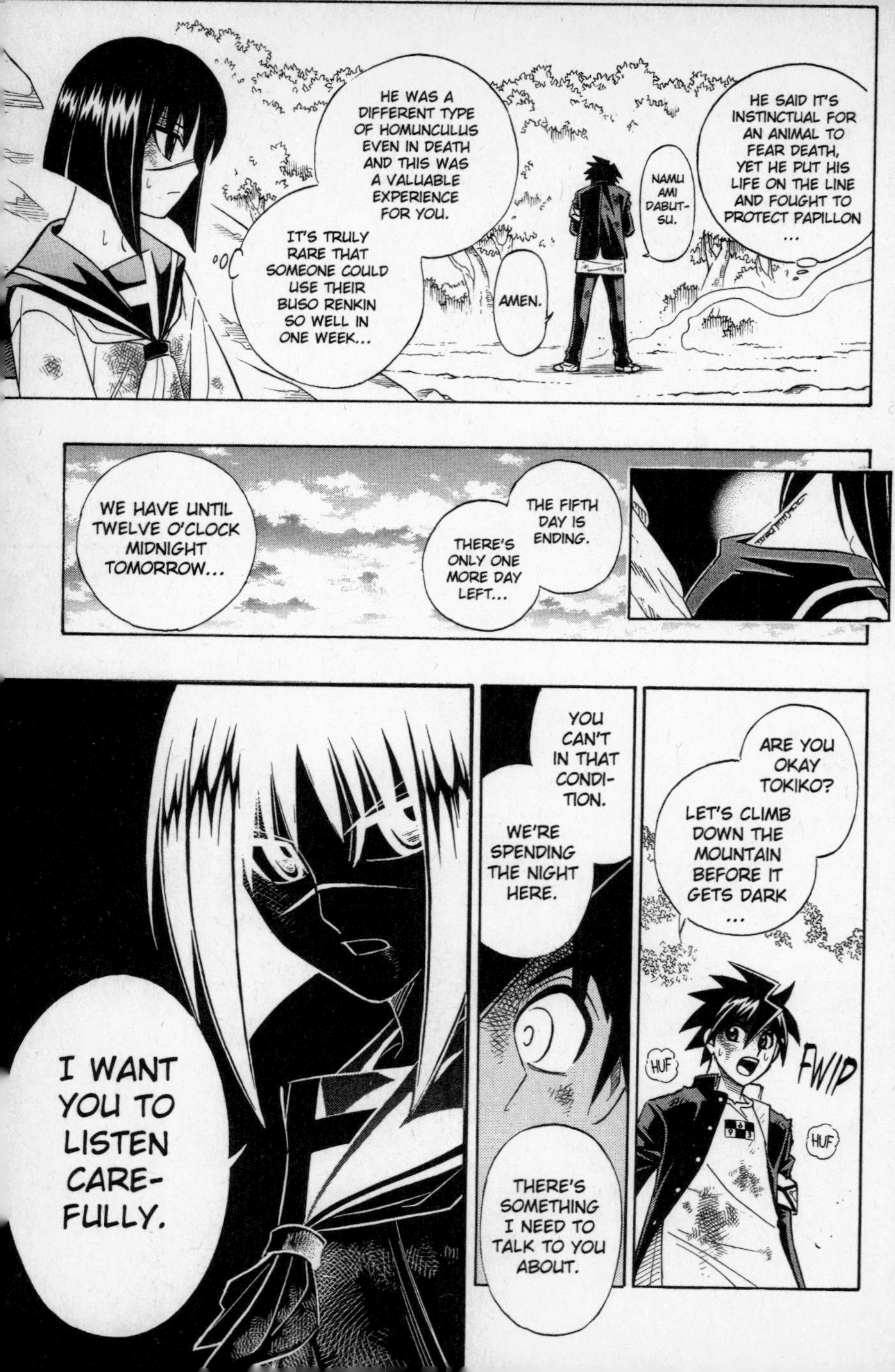
HE SAID IT'S INSTINCTUAL FOR AN ANIMAL TO FEAR DEATH, YET HE PUT HIS LIFE ON THE LINE AND FOUGHT TO PROTECT PAPILLON ...
NAMU AMI DABUT-SU.
AMEN.
HE WAS A DIFFERENT TYPE OF HOMUNCULUS EVEN IN DEATH AND THIS WAS A VALUABLE EXPERIENCE FOR YOU.
IT'S TRULY RARE THAT SOMEONE COULD USE THEIR BUSO RENKIN SO WELL IN ONE WEEK...
THE FIFTH DAY IS ENDING.
THERE'S ONLY ONE MORE DAY LEFT...
WE HAVE UNTIL TWELVE O'CLOCK MIDNIGHT TOMORROW...
ARE YOU OKAY TOKIKO?
LET'S CLIMB DOWN THE MOUNTAIN BEFORE IT GETS DARK ...
FWIP
HUF
HUF
YOU CAN'T IN THAT CONDI-TION.
WE'RE SPENDING THE NIGHT HERE.
THERE'S SOMETHING I NEED TO TALK TO YOU ABOUT.
I WANT YOU TO LISTEN CARE-FULLY.

Character File No.11

Homunculus Washio

- Height: 195cm; Weight: 90kg
- Born: January 10th; Capricorn; Blood Type A; 25 years old
  Above is an assumption of his human form
- Favorites: Rabbits (yummy), the will to fight for survival
- Dislikes: Any threat to the Creator, hunting rifles, unnecessary battles
- Hobby: Flying around
- Things he's good at: Partial transformation into a Homunculus.

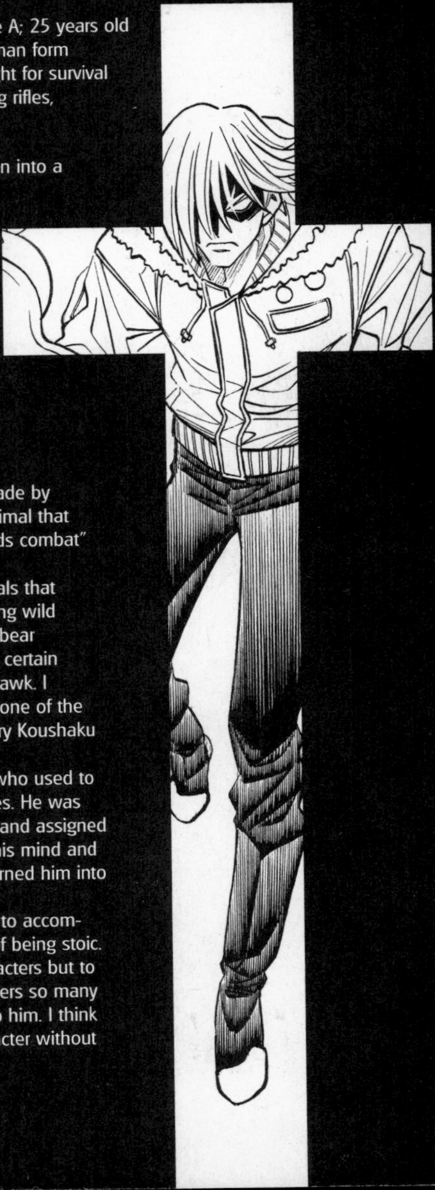

Author's Notes

- As the most powerful Homunculus made by Koushaku, it needed to be "a wild animal that has a strong affinity and talent towards combat" so I put some thoughts into it.
- Hawks and bears were the two animals that came to mind when I thought of strong wild animals that live in Japan. I figured a bear would be too similar to Saruwatari in certain respects so instead I went with the hawk. I figured it would have speed, which none of the other Homunculi have, and could carry Koushaku who's sick.
- Originally he was a Yakuza member who used to be a soldier in the Self-Defense Forces. He was sent to work at the Koushaku family and assigned as Koushaku's trainer to strengthen his mind and body. Koushaku resented him and turned him into a Homunculus.
- He is extremely loyal and committed to accomplishing a goal, almost to the point of being stoic. I've always liked these types of characters but to be honest, I've drawn similar characters so many times before, I really couldn't get into him. I think he turned out really good for a character without a design motif but...

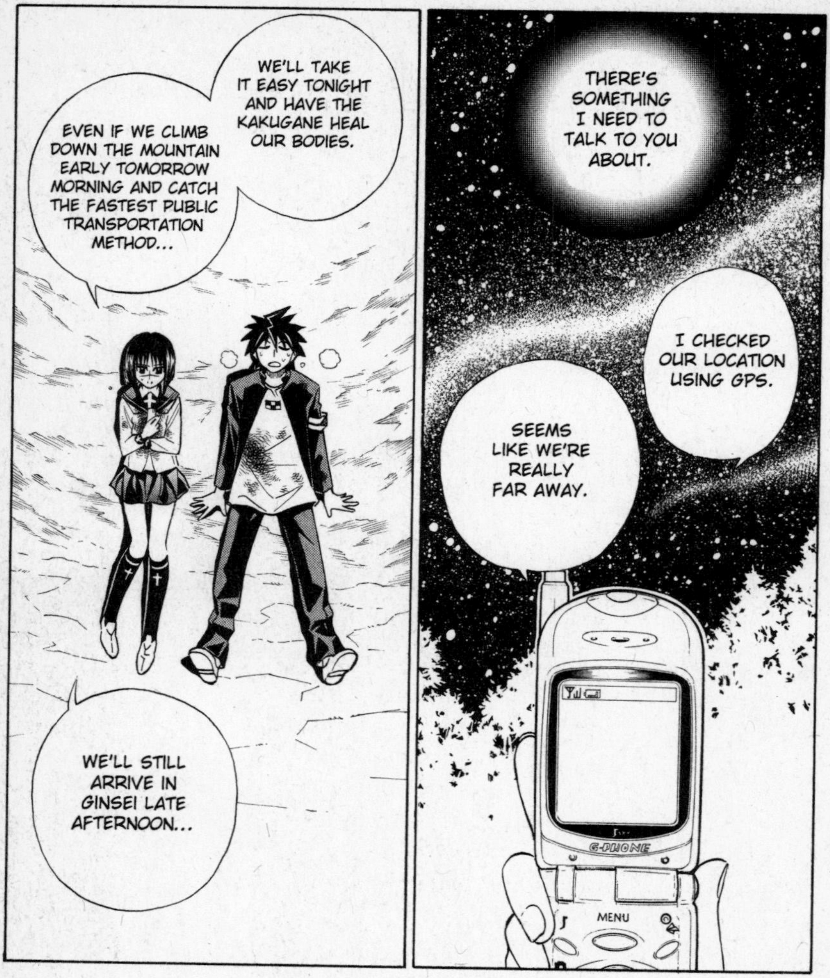
THERE'S SOMETHING I NEED TO TALK TO YOU ABOUT.
I CHECKED OUR LOCATION USING GPS.
SEEMS LIKE WE'RE REALLY FAR AWAY.
G-PHONE
MENU
WE'LL TAKE IT EASY TONIGHT AND HAVE THE KAKUGANE HEAL OUR BODIES.
EVEN IF WE CLIMB DOWN THE MOUNTAIN EARLY TOMORROW MORNING AND CATCH THE FASTEST PUBLIC TRANSPORTATION METHOD...
WE'LL STILL ARRIVE IN GINSEI LATE AFTERNOON...

CHAPTER 14:
MIDNIGHT RUN 2

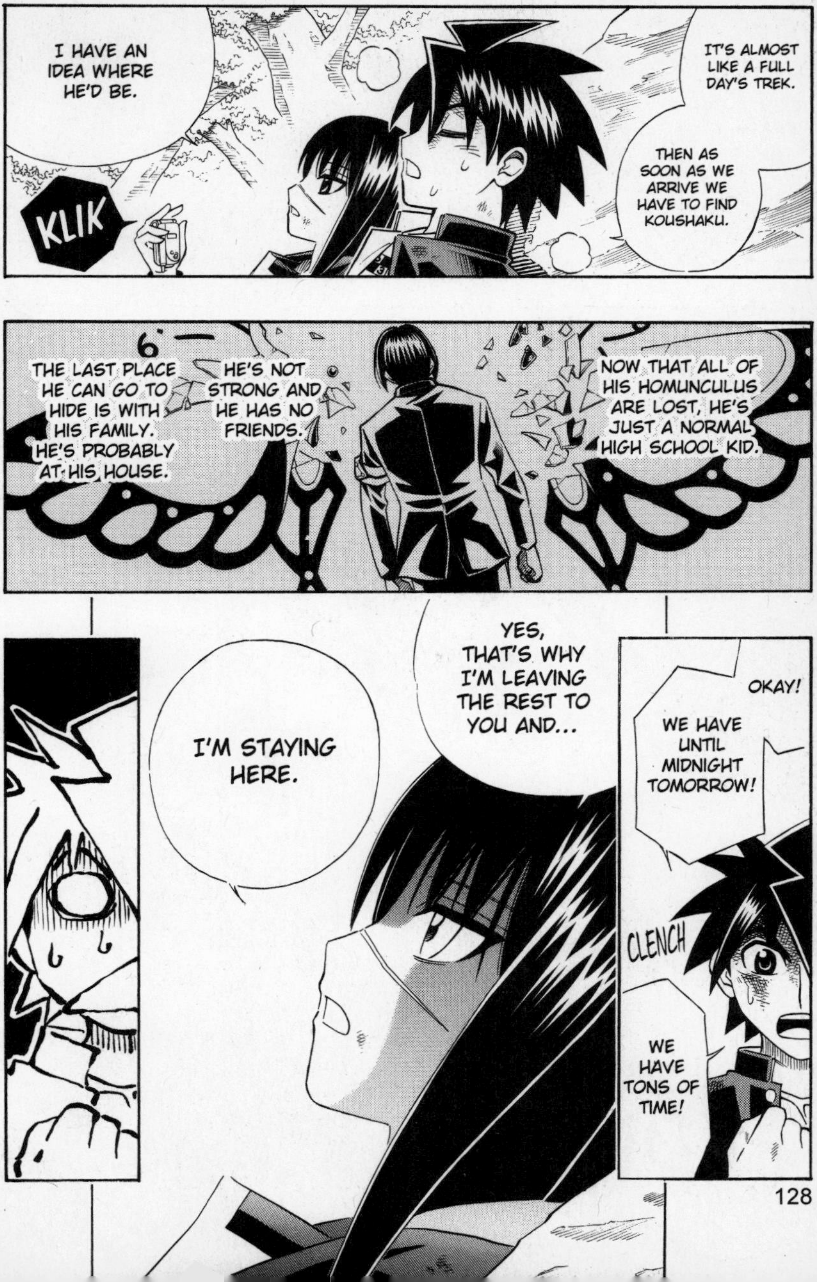
IT'S ALMOST LIKE A FULL DAY'S TREK.
THEN AS SOON AS WE ARRIVE WE HAVE TO FIND KOUSHAKU.
I HAVE AN IDEA WHERE HE'D BE.
KLIK
NOW THAT ALL OF HIS HOMUNCULUS ARE LOST, HE'S JUST A NORMAL HIGH SCHOOL KID.
HE'S NOT STRONG AND HE HAS NO FRIENDS.
THE LAST PLACE HE CAN GO TO HIDE IS WITH HIS FAMILY. HE'S PROBABLY AT HIS HOUSE.
OKAY!
WE HAVE UNTIL MIDNIGHT TOMORROW!
CLENCH
WE HAVE TONS OF TIME!
YES, THAT'S WHY I'M LEAVING THE REST TO YOU AND...
I'M STAYING HERE.

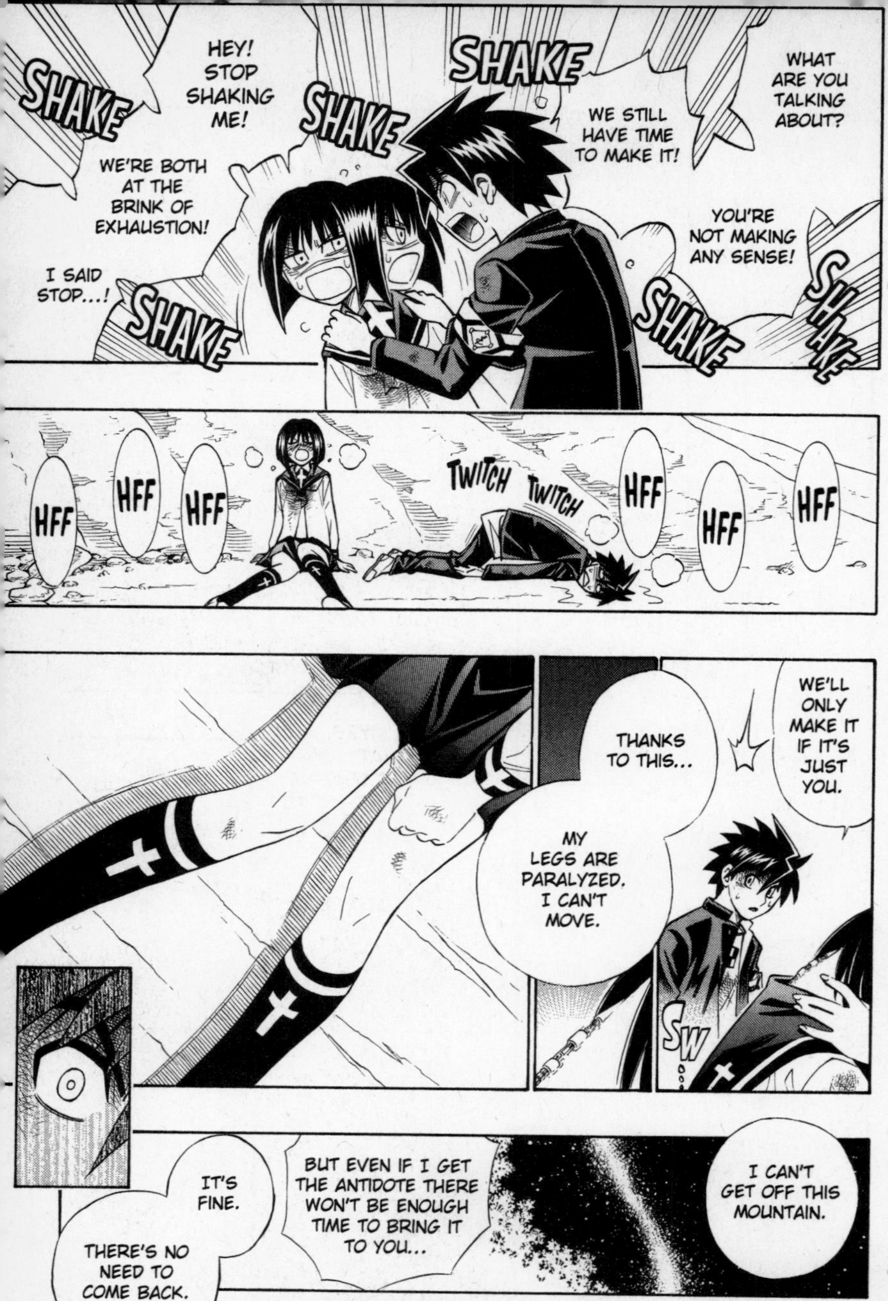
WHAT ARE YOU TALKING ABOUT?
SHAKE
WE STILL HAVE TIME TO MAKE IT!
YOU'RE NOT MAKING ANY SENSE!
SHAKE
SHAKE
SHAKE
HEY! STOP SHAKING ME!
SHAKE
WE'RE BOTH AT THE BRINK OF EXHAUSTION!
I SAID STOP...!
SHAKE
HFF
HFF
HFF
TWITCH
TWITCH
HFF
HFF
HFF
WE'LL ONLY MAKE IT IF IT'S JUST YOU.
THANKS TO THIS...
MY LEGS ARE PARALYZED. I CAN'T MOVE.
SW
I CAN'T GET OFF THIS MOUNTAIN.
BUT EVEN IF I GET THE ANTIDOTE THERE WON'T BE ENOUGH TIME TO BRING IT TO YOU...
IT'S FINE.
THERE'S NO NEED TO COME BACK.

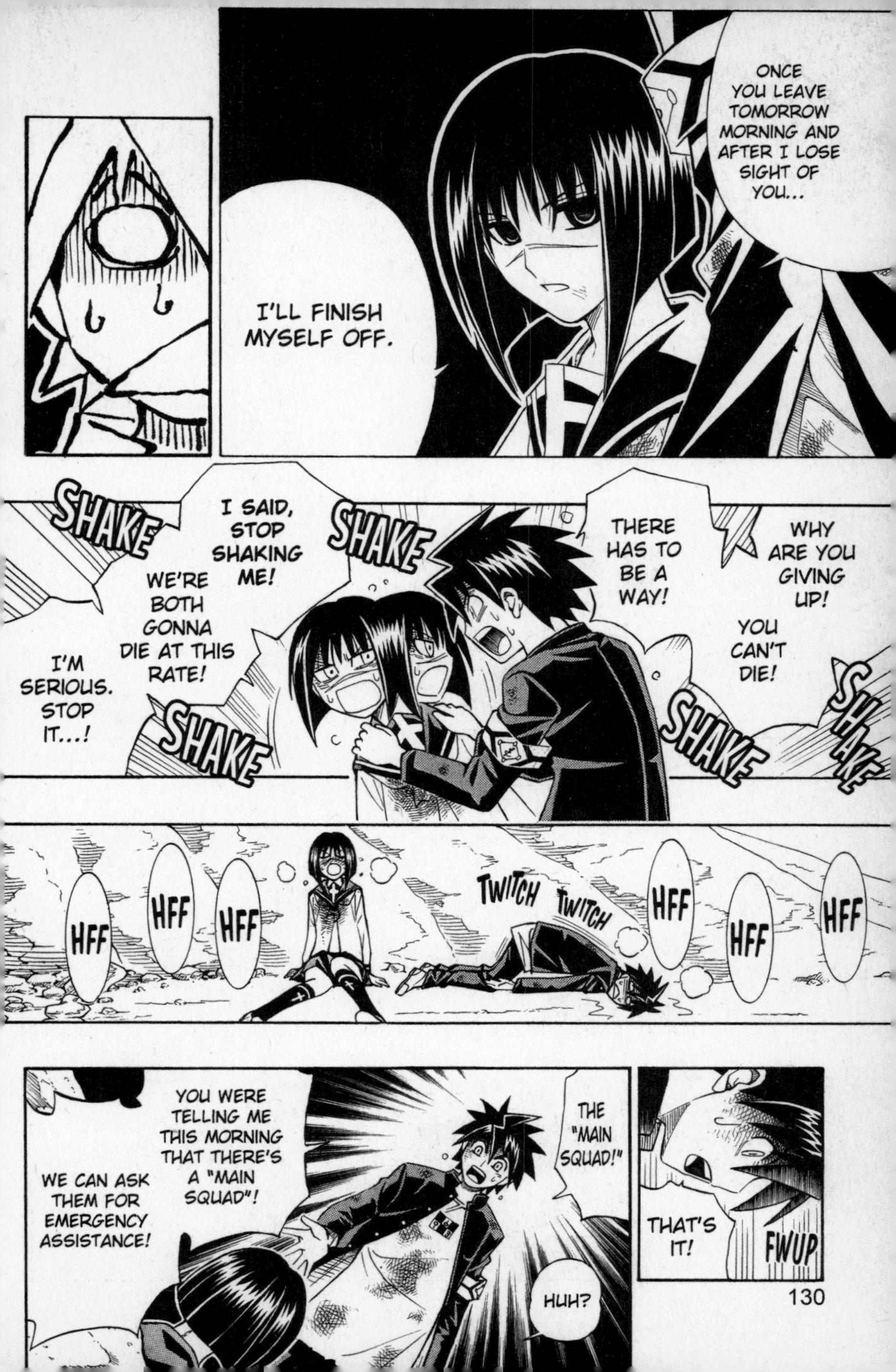
ONCE YOU LEAVE TOMORROW MORNING AND AFTER I LOSE SIGHT OF YOU...
I'LL FINISH MYSELF OFF.
WHY ARE YOU GIVING UP!
YOU CAN'T DIE!
SHAKE
SHAKE
THERE HAS TO BE A WAY!
SHAKE
I SAID, STOP SHAKING ME!
WE'RE BOTH GONNA DIE AT THIS RATE!
SHAKE
I'M SERIOUS. STOP IT...!
SHAKE
HFF
HFF
HFF
TWITCH
TWITCH
HFF
HFF
HFF
HFF
FWUP
THAT'S IT!
THE "MAIN SQUAD!"
YOU WERE TELLING ME THIS MORNING THAT THERE'S A "MAIN SQUAD"!
WE CAN ASK THEM FOR EMERGENCY ASSISTANCE!
HUH?

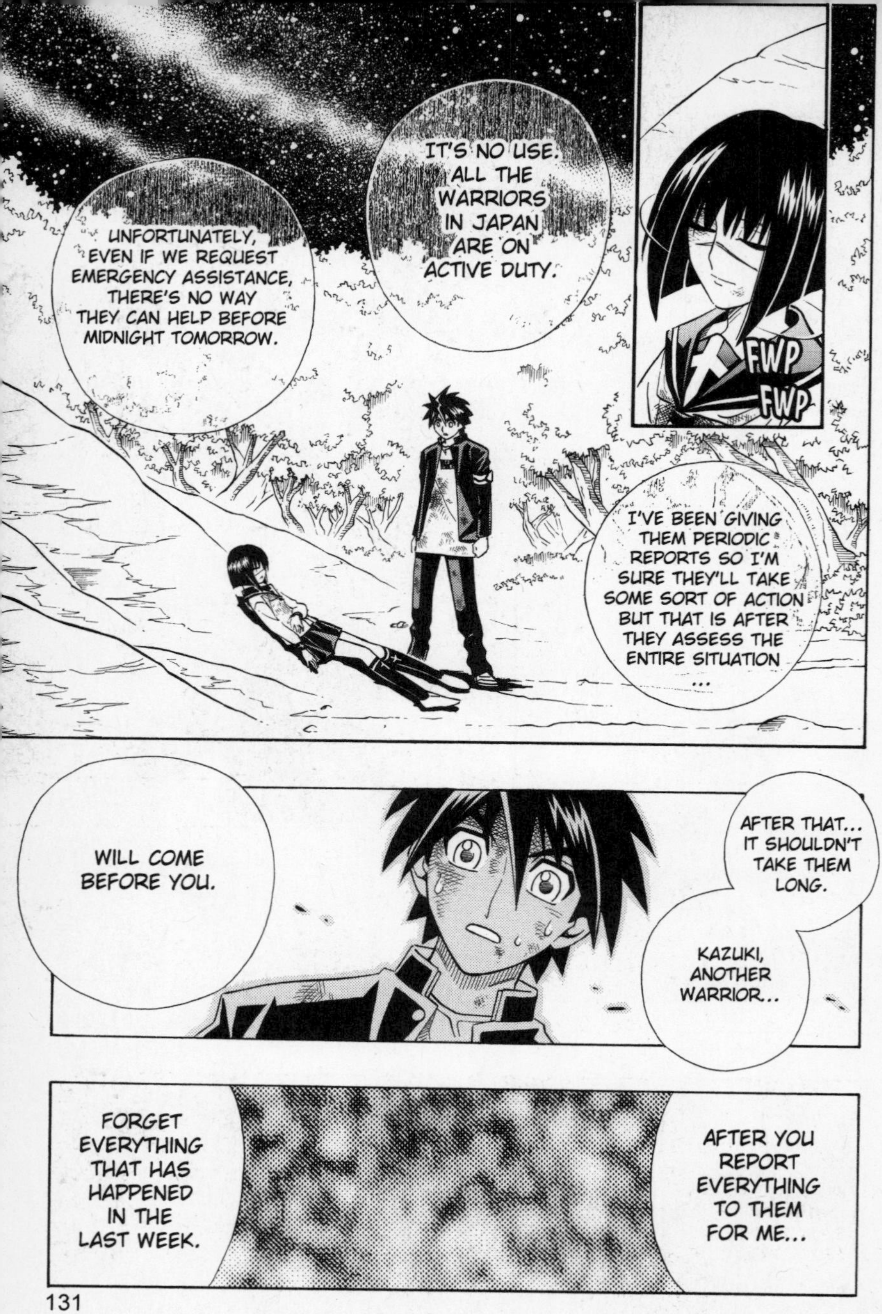
FWP
FWP
IT'S NO USE. ALL THE WARRIORS IN JAPAN ARE ON ACTIVE DUTY.
UNFORTUNATELY, EVEN IF WE REQUEST EMERGENCY ASSISTANCE, THERE'S NO WAY THEY CAN HELP BEFORE MIDNIGHT TOMORROW.
I'VE BEEN GIVING THEM PERIODIC REPORTS SO I'M SURE THEY'LL TAKE SOME SORT OF ACTION BUT THAT IS AFTER THEY ASSESS THE ENTIRE SITUATION ...
AFTER THAT... IT SHOULDN'T TAKE THEM LONG.
KAZUKI, ANOTHER WARRIOR...
WILL COME BEFORE YOU.
AFTER YOU REPORT EVERYTHING TO THEM FOR ME...
FORGET EVERYTHING THAT HAS HAPPENED IN THE LAST WEEK.

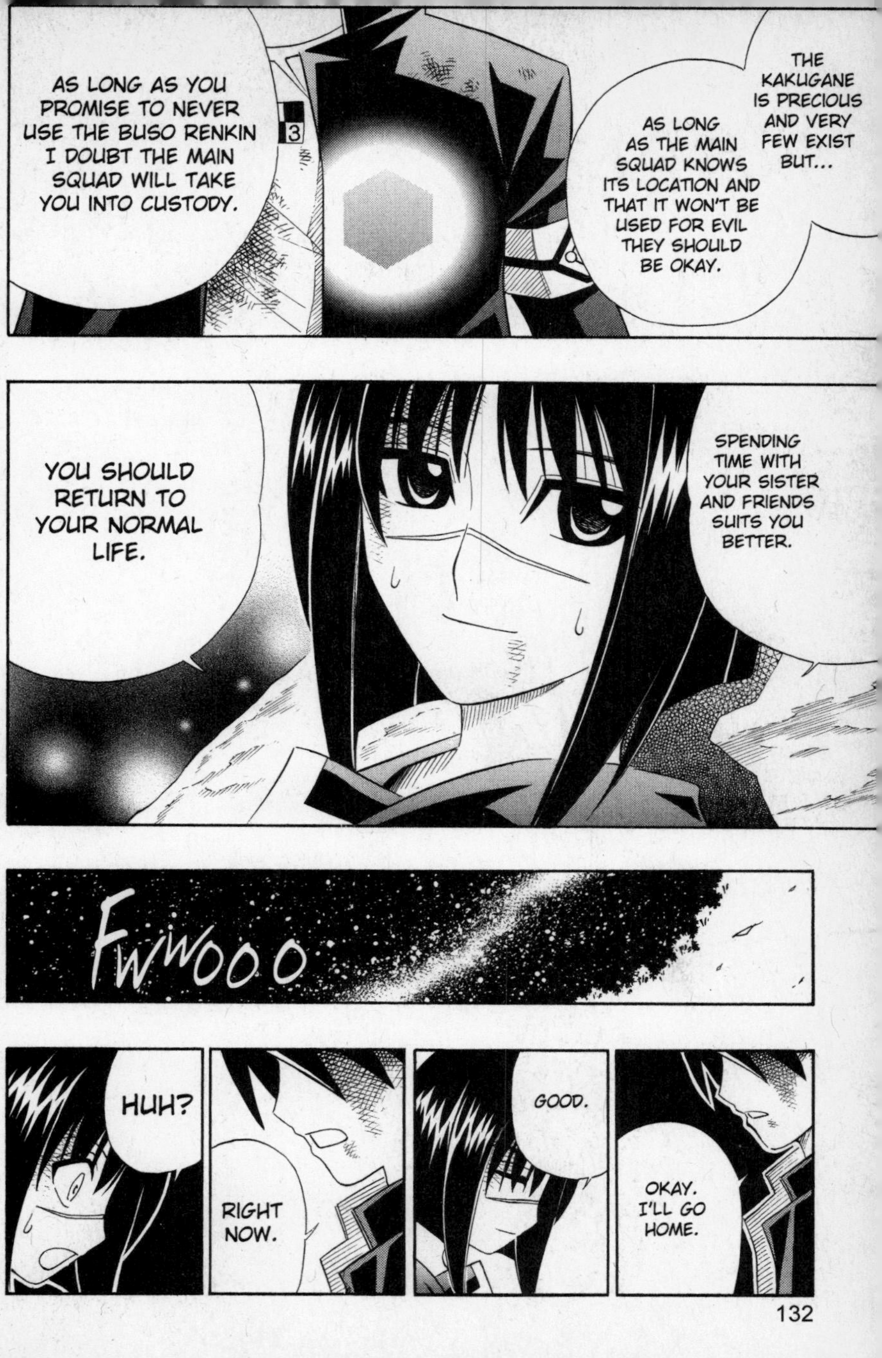
THE KAKUGANE IS PRECIOUS AND VERY FEW EXIST BUT...
AS LONG AS THE MAIN SQUAD KNOWS ITS LOCATION AND THAT IT WON'T BE USED FOR EVIL THEY SHOULD BE OKAY.
AS LONG AS YOU PROMISE TO NEVER USE THE BUSO RENKIN I DOUBT THE MAIN SQUAD WILL TAKE YOU INTO CUSTODY.
SPENDING TIME WITH YOUR SISTER AND FRIENDS SUITS YOU BETTER.
YOU SHOULD RETURN TO YOUR NORMAL LIFE.
FWWOOO
OKAY. I'LL GO HOME.
GOOD.
RIGHT NOW.
HUH?

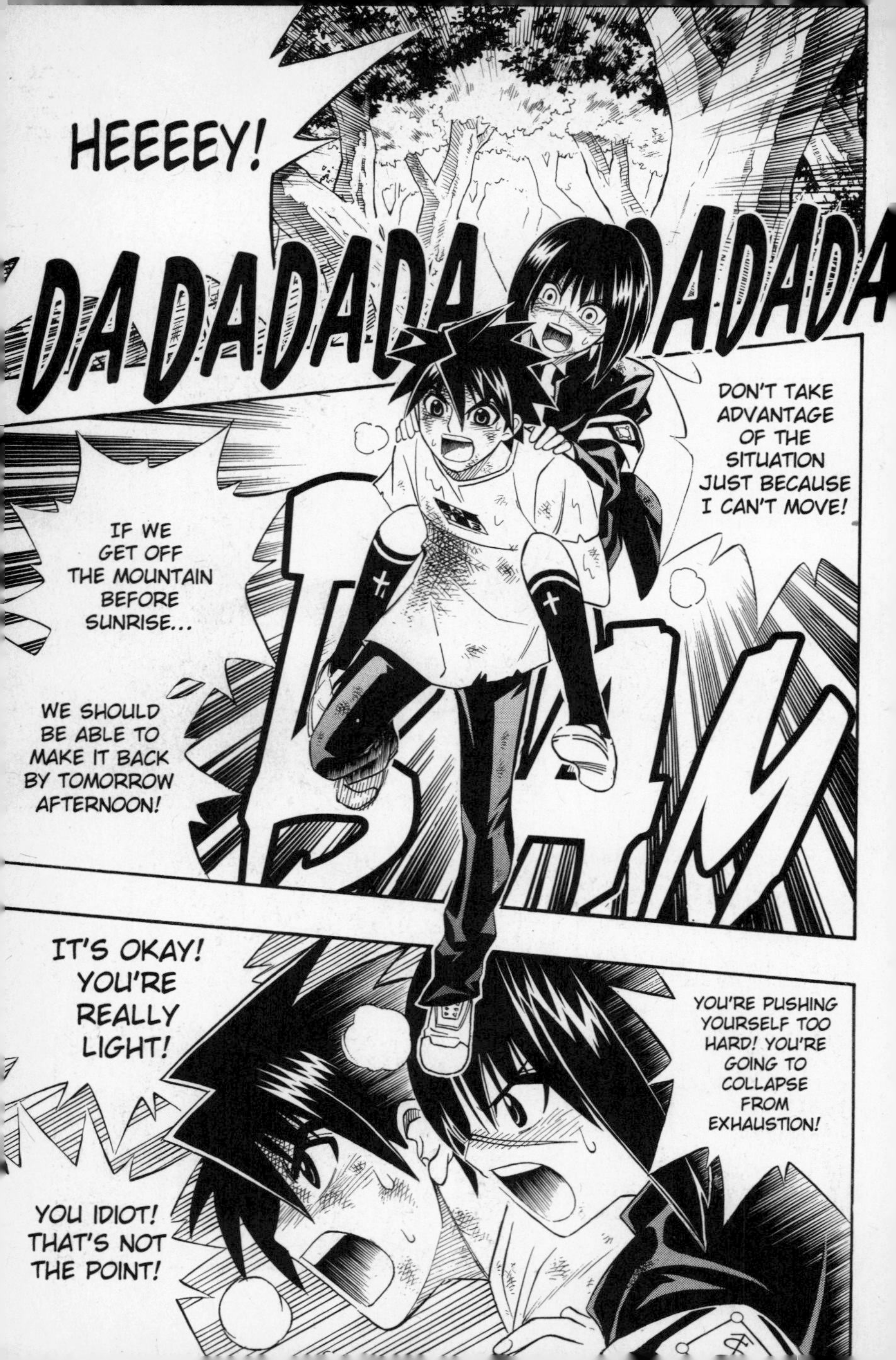
HEEEEY!
DADADA
ADADA
DON'T TAKE ADVANTAGE OF THE SITUATION JUST BECAUSE I CAN'T MOVE!
IF WE GET OFF THE MOUNTAIN BEFORE SUNRISE...
WE SHOULD BE ABLE TO MAKE IT BACK BY TOMORROW AFTERNOON!
YOU'RE PUSHING YOURSELF TOO HARD! YOU'RE GOING TO COLLAPSE FROM EXHAUSTION!
IT'S OKAY! YOU'RE REALLY LIGHT!
YOU IDIOT! THAT'S NOT THE POINT!

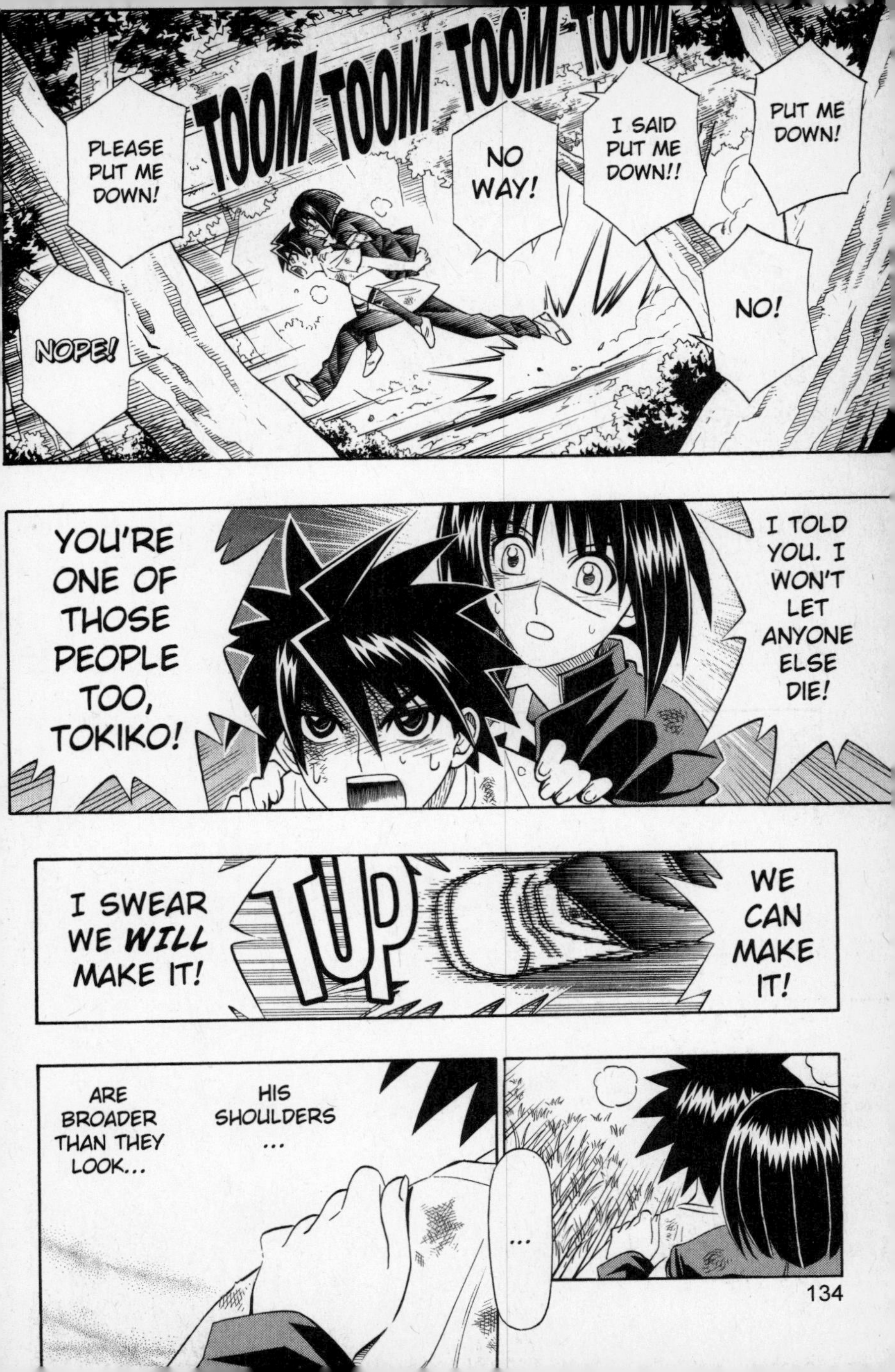
PUT ME DOWN!
NO!
I SAID PUT ME DOWN!!
NO WAY!
TOOM TOOM TOOM TOOM
PLEASE PUT ME DOWN!
NOPE!
I TOLD YOU. I WON'T LET ANYONE ELSE DIE!
YOU'RE ONE OF THOSE PEOPLE TOO, TOKIKO!
WE CAN MAKE IT!
TUP
I SWEAR WE *WILL* MAKE IT!
...
HIS SHOULDERS...
ARE BROADER THAN THEY LOOK...

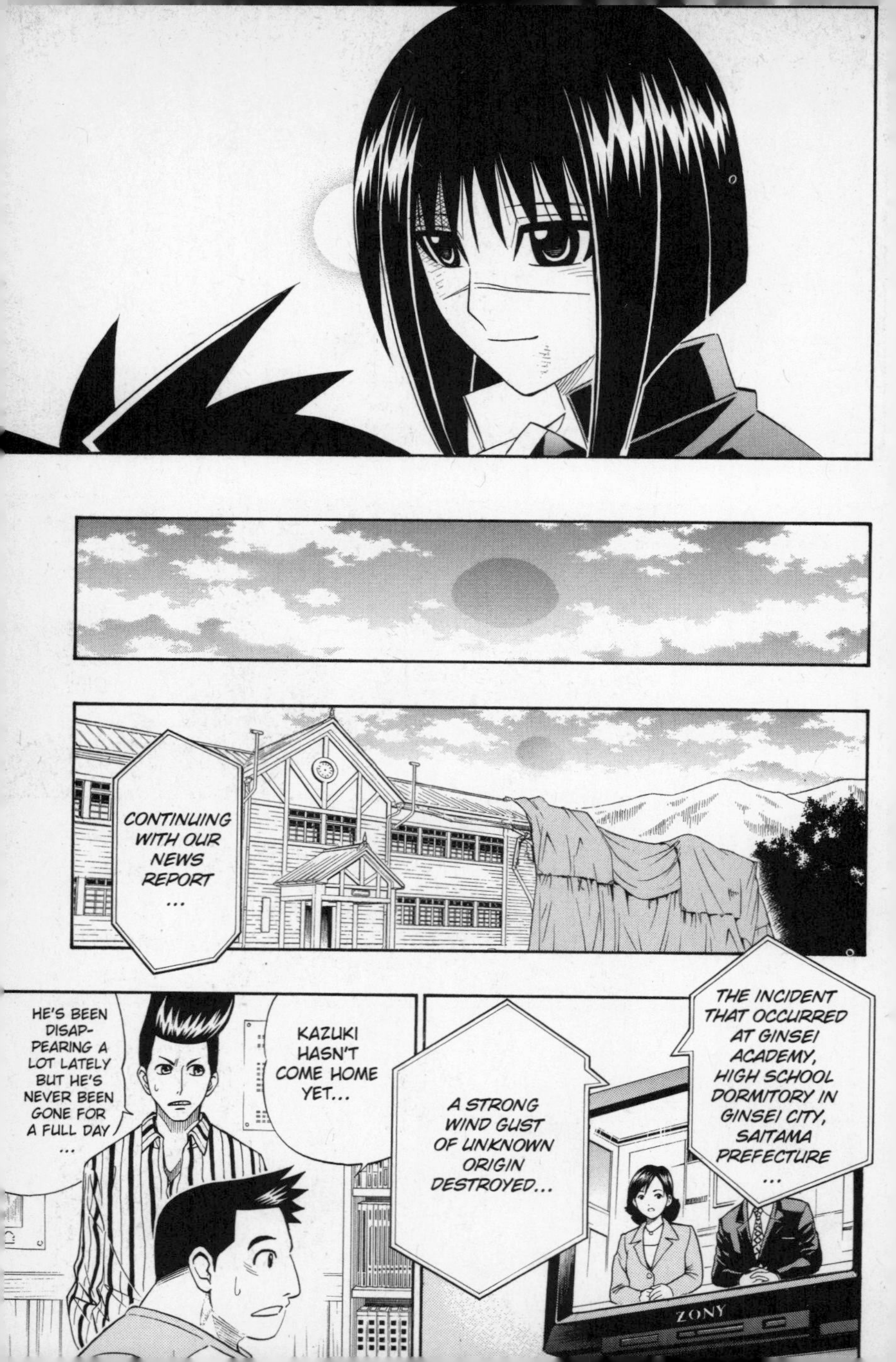
CONTINUING WITH OUR NEWS REPORT ...
THE INCIDENT THAT OCCURRED AT GINSEI ACADEMY, HIGH SCHOOL DORMITORY IN GINSEI CITY, SAITAMA PREFECTURE ...
A STRONG WIND GUST OF UNKNOWN ORIGIN DESTROYED...
ZONY
KAZUKI HASN'T COME HOME YET...
HE'S BEEN DISAP-PEARING A LOT LATELY BUT HE'S NEVER BEEN GONE FOR A FULL DAY ...

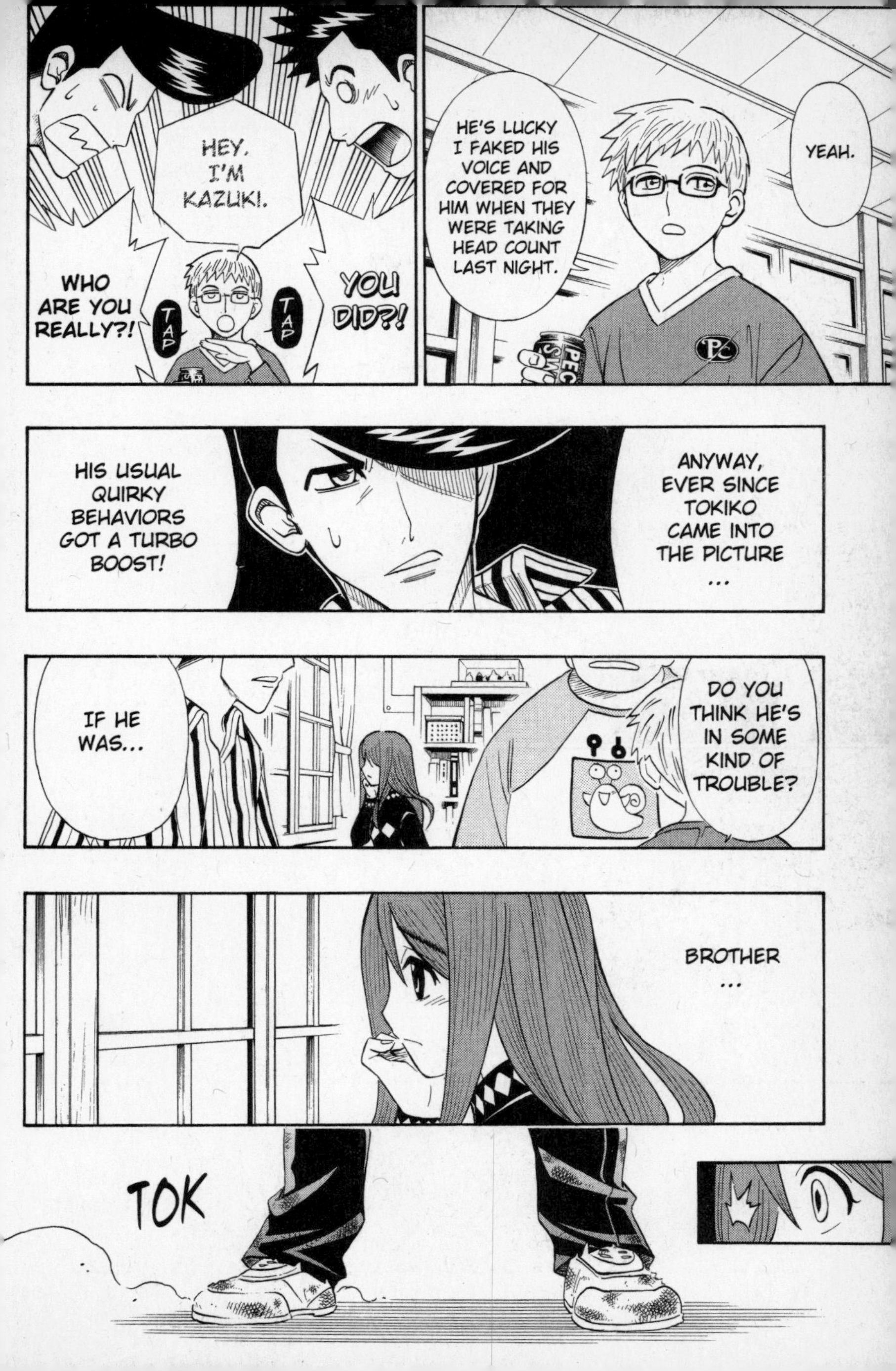
YEAH.
HE'S LUCKY I FAKED HIS VOICE AND COVERED FOR HIM WHEN THEY WERE TAKING HEAD COUNT LAST NIGHT.
HEY. I'M KAZUKI.
YOU DID?!
TAP
TAP
WHO ARE YOU REALLY?!
ANYWAY, EVER SINCE TOKIKO CAME INTO THE PICTURE ...
HIS USUAL QUIRKY BEHAVIORS GOT A TURBO BOOST!
DO YOU THINK HE'S IN SOME KIND OF TROUBLE?
IF HE WAS...
BROTHER ...
TOK

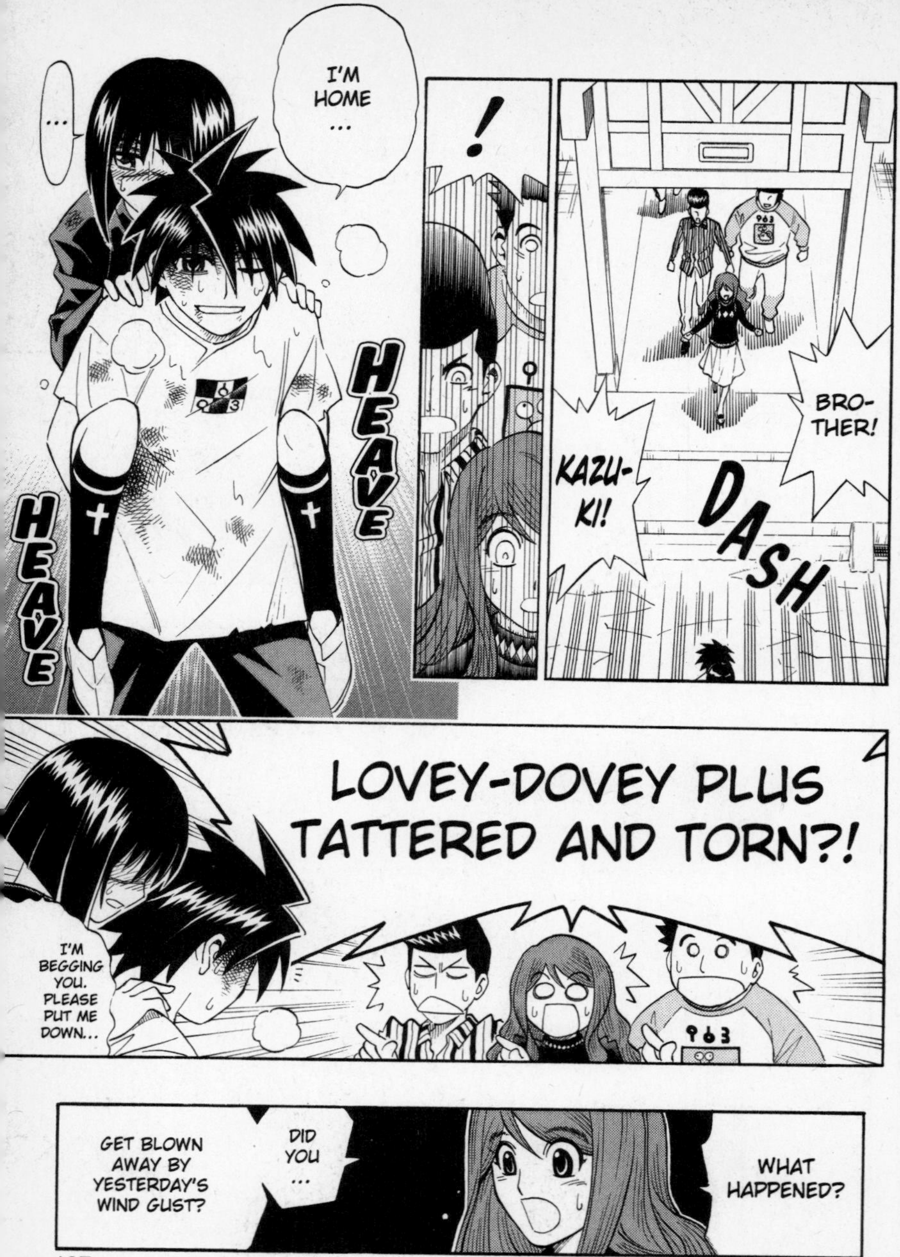
BRO-THER!
KAZU-KI!
DASH
!
I'M HOME ...
...
HEAVE
HEAVE
LOVEY-DOVEY PLUS TATTERED AND TORN?!
I'M BEGGING YOU. PLEASE PUT ME DOWN...
WHAT HAPPENED?
DID YOU ...
GET BLOWN AWAY BY YESTERDAY'S WIND GUST?

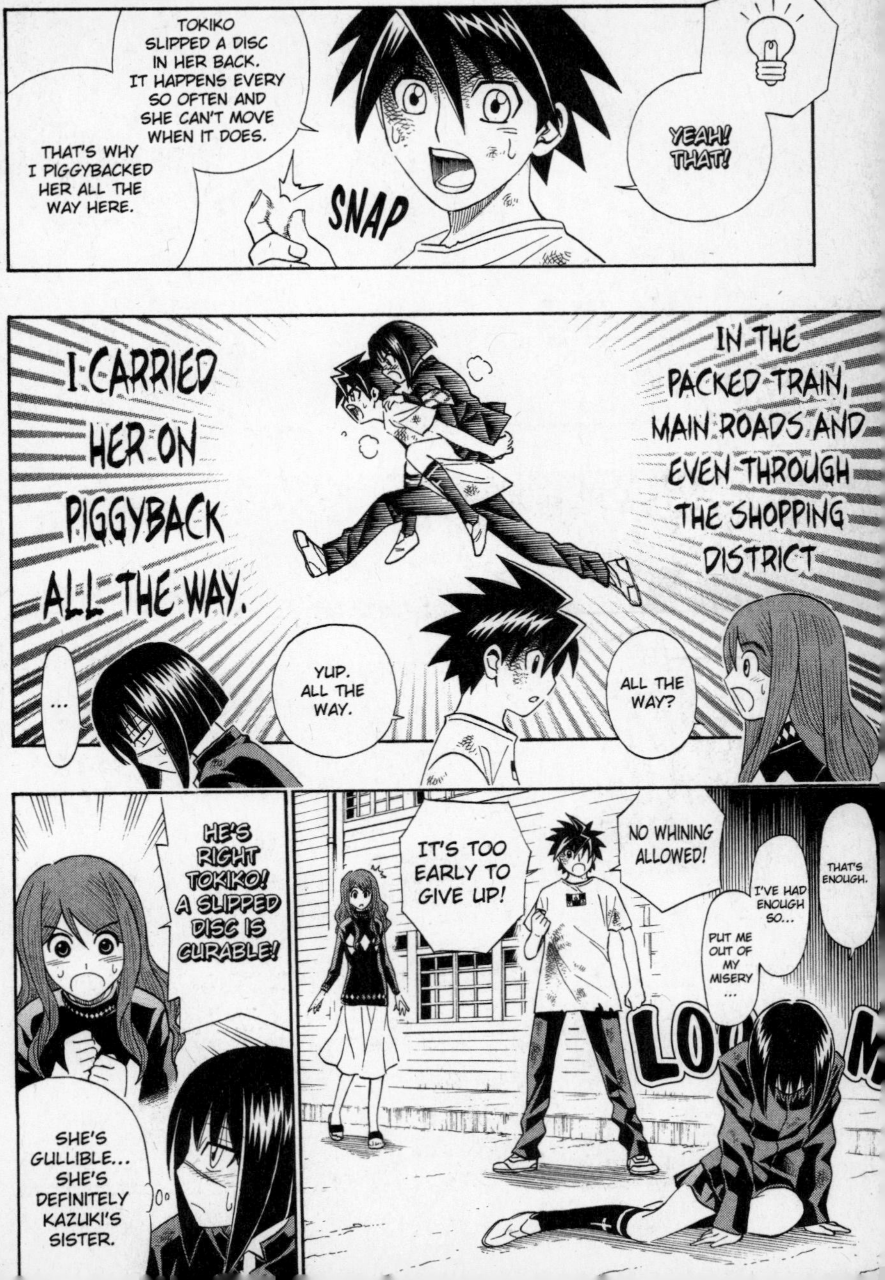

YEAH! THAT!
SNAP
TOKIKO SLIPPED A DISC IN HER BACK. IT HAPPENS EVERY SO OFTEN AND SHE CAN'T MOVE WHEN IT DOES.
THAT'S WHY I PIGGYBACKED HER ALL THE WAY HERE.
IN THE PACKED TRAIN, MAIN ROADS AND EVEN THROUGH THE SHOPPING DISTRICT
I CARRIED HER ON PIGGYBACK ALL THE WAY.
ALL THE WAY?
YUP. ALL THE WAY.
...
THAT'S ENOUGH.
I'VE HAD ENOUGH SO...
PUT ME OUT OF MY MISERY...
NO WHINING ALLOWED!
IT'S TOO EARLY TO GIVE UP!
HE'S RIGHT TOKIKO! A SLIPPED DISC IS CURABLE!
SHE'S GULLIBLE... SHE'S DEFINITELY KAZUKI'S SISTER.

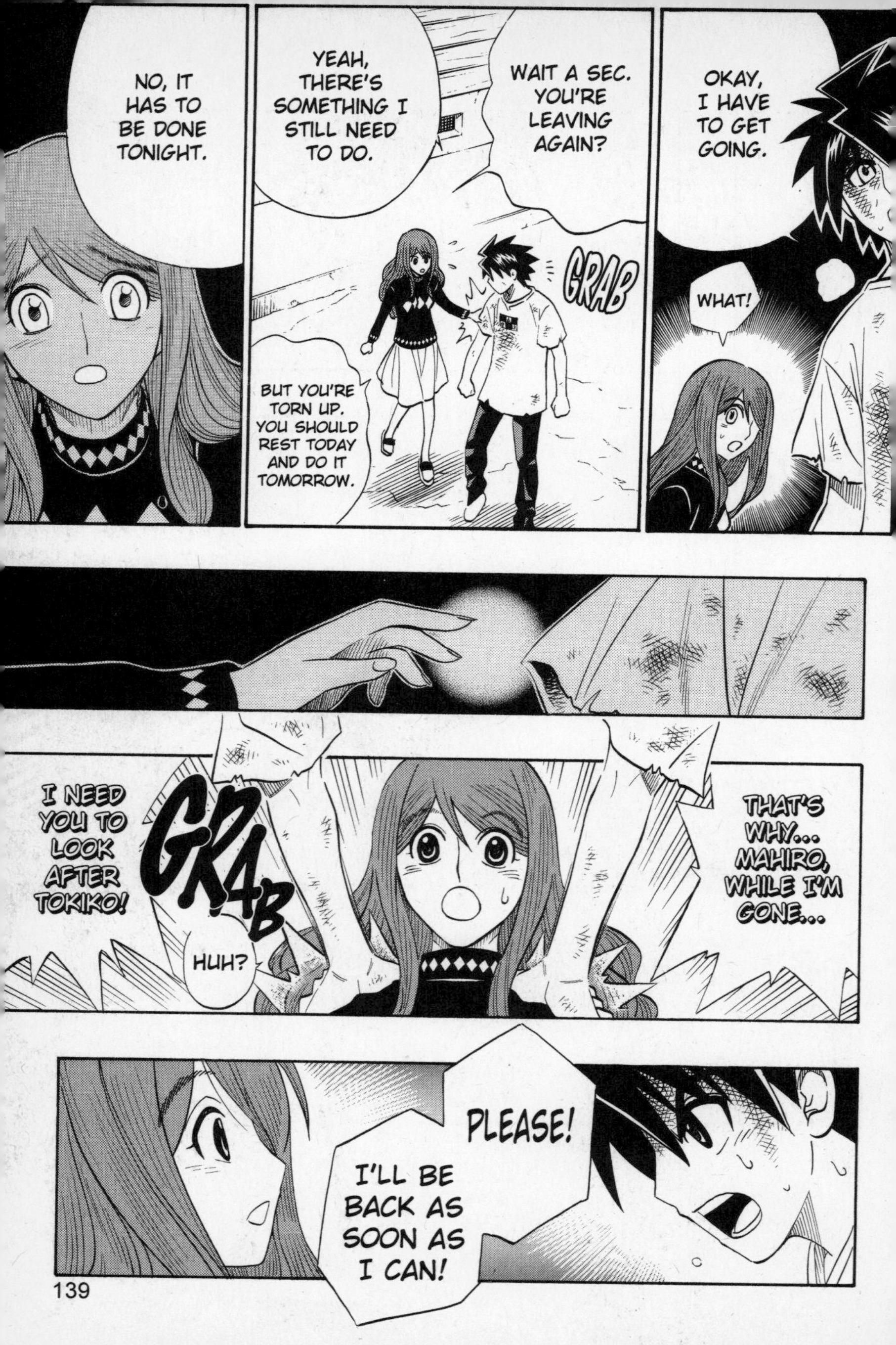
OKAY, I HAVE TO GET GOING.
WHAT!
WAIT A SEC. YOU'RE LEAVING AGAIN?
YEAH, THERE'S SOMETHING I STILL NEED TO DO.
GRAB
BUT YOU'RE TORN UP. YOU SHOULD REST TODAY AND DO IT TOMORROW.
NO, IT HAS TO BE DONE TONIGHT.
THAT'S WHY... MAHIRO, WHILE I'M GONE...
GRAB
HUH?
I NEED YOU TO LOOK AFTER TOKIKO!
PLEASE!
I'LL BE BACK AS SOON AS I CAN!

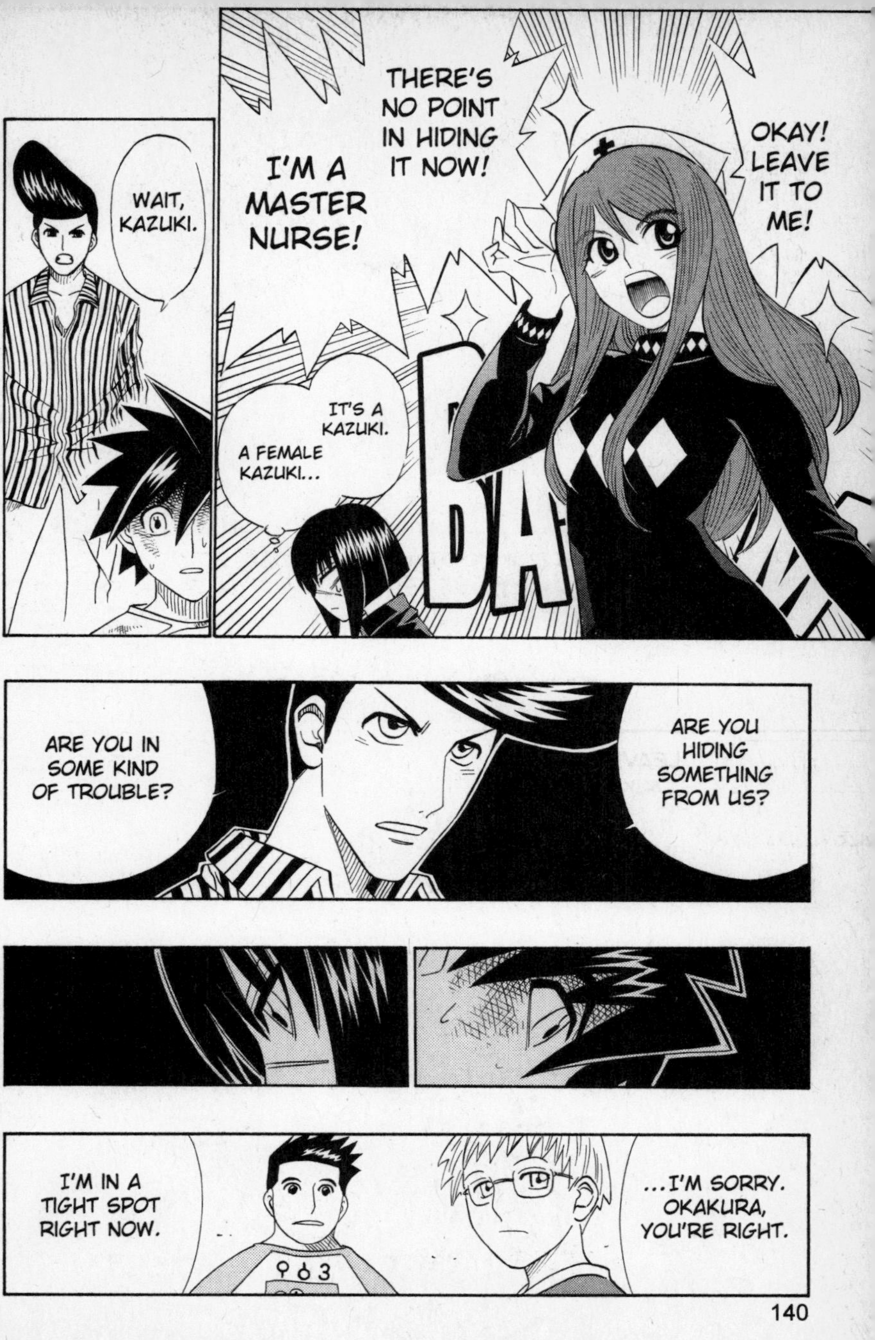
OKAY! LEAVE IT TO ME!
THERE'S NO POINT IN HIDING IT NOW!
I'M A MASTER NURSE!
BA
IT'S A KAZUKI.
A FEMALE KAZUKI...
WAIT, KAZUKI.
ARE YOU HIDING SOMETHING FROM US?
ARE YOU IN SOME KIND OF TROUBLE?
...I'M SORRY. OKAKURA, YOU'RE RIGHT.
I'M IN A TIGHT SPOT RIGHT NOW.

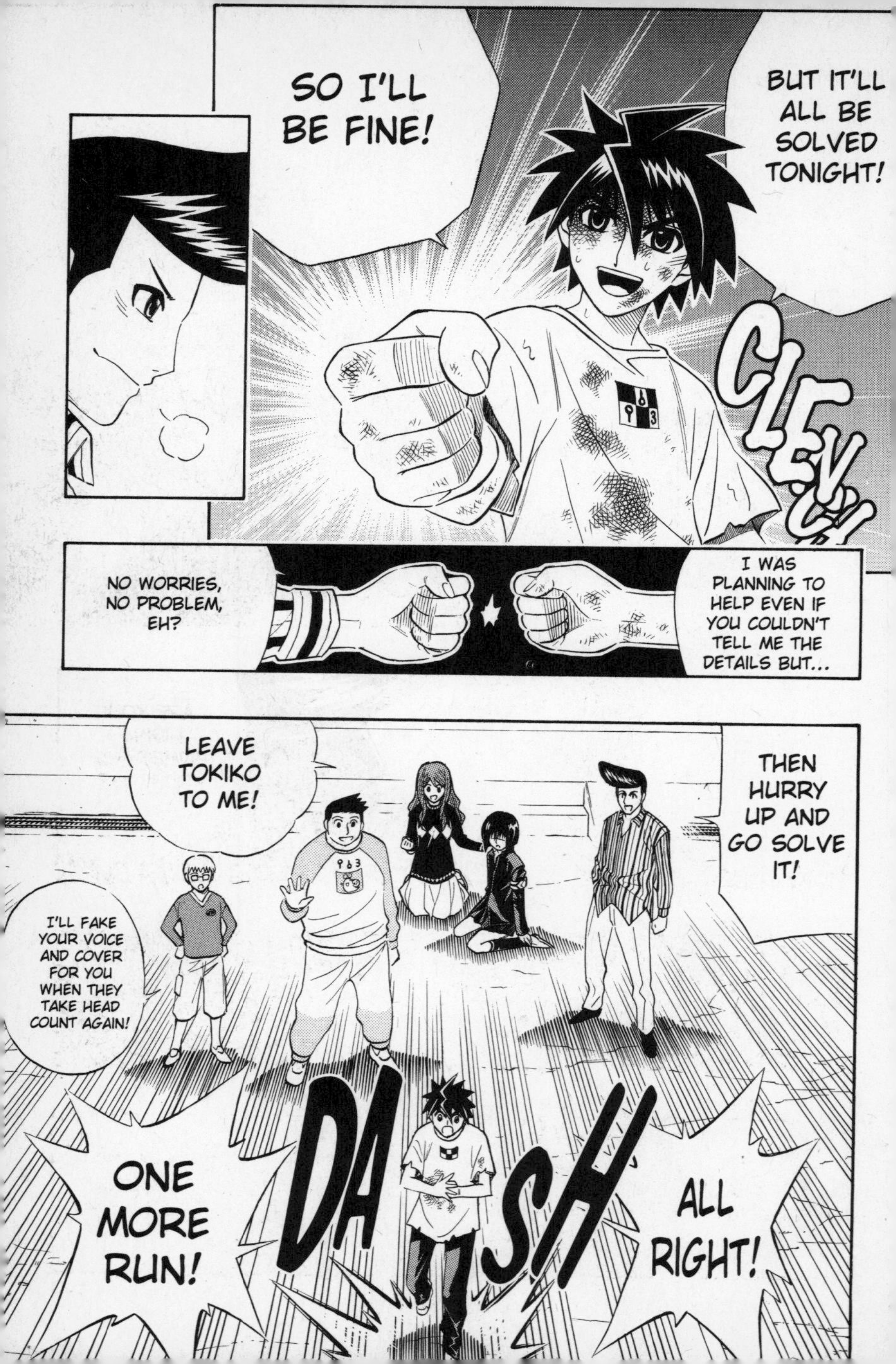
BUT IT'LL ALL BE SOLVED TONIGHT!
SO I'LL BE FINE!
I WAS PLANNING TO HELP EVEN IF YOU COULDN'T TELL ME THE DETAILS BUT...
NO WORRIES, NO PROBLEM, EH?
THEN HURRY UP AND GO SOLVE IT!
LEAVE TOKIKO TO ME!
I'LL FAKE YOUR VOICE AND COVER FOR YOU WHEN THEY TAKE HEAD COUNT AGAIN!
ALL RIGHT!
DASH
ONE MORE RUN!

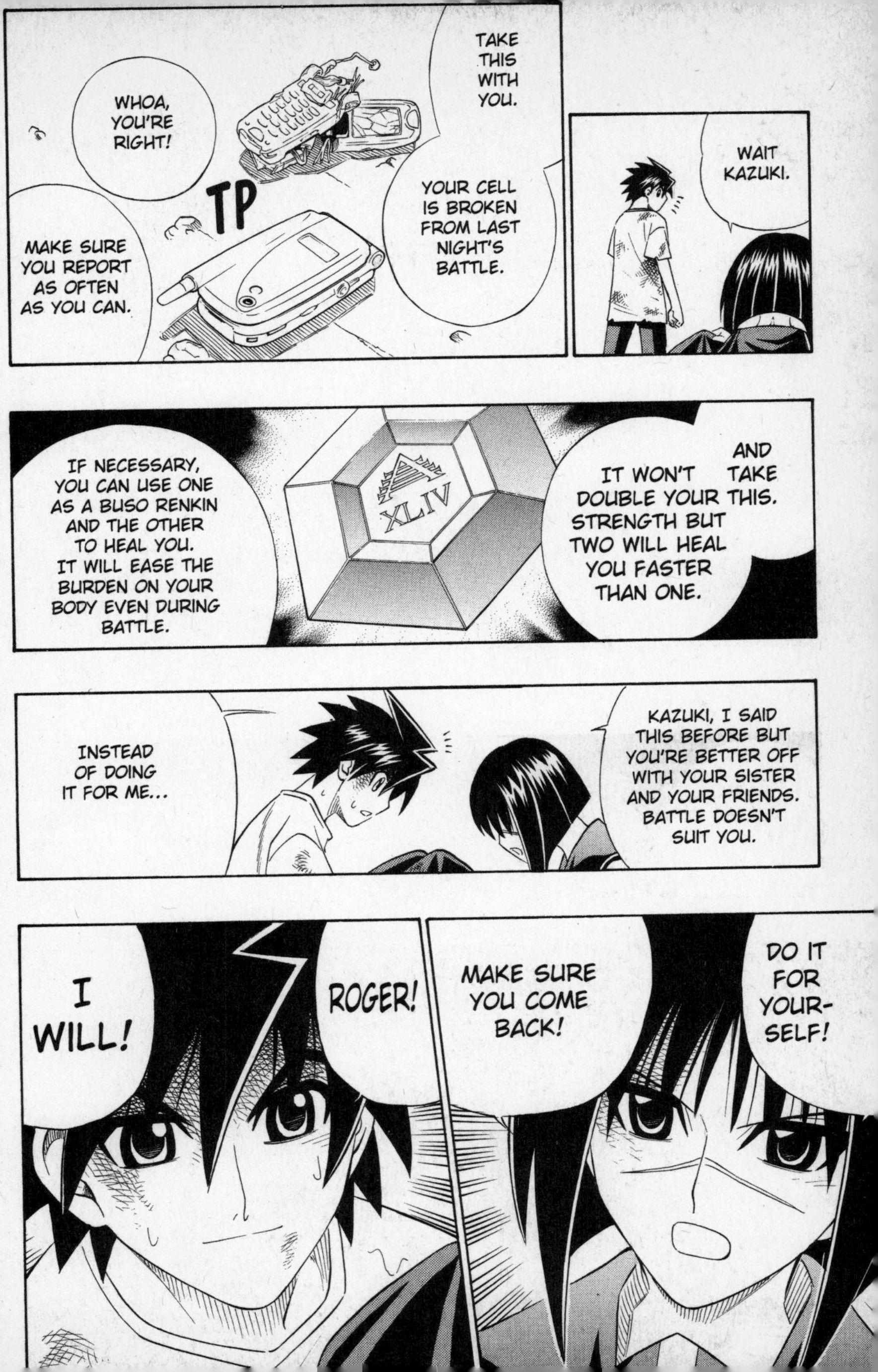
WAIT KAZUKI.
TAKE THIS WITH YOU.
YOUR CELL IS BROKEN FROM LAST NIGHT'S BATTLE.
WHOA, YOU'RE RIGHT!
TP
MAKE SURE YOU REPORT AS OFTEN AS YOU CAN.
AND TAKE THIS.
IT WON'T DOUBLE YOUR STRENGTH BUT TWO WILL HEAL YOU FASTER THAN ONE.
XLIV
IF NECESSARY, YOU CAN USE ONE AS A BUSO RENKIN AND THE OTHER TO HEAL YOU. IT WILL EASE THE BURDEN ON YOUR BODY EVEN DURING BATTLE.
KAZUKI, I SAID THIS BEFORE BUT YOU'RE BETTER OFF WITH YOUR SISTER AND YOUR FRIENDS. BATTLE DOESN'T SUIT YOU.
INSTEAD OF DOING IT FOR ME...
DO IT FOR YOURSELF!
MAKE SURE YOU COME BACK!
ROGER!
I WILL!

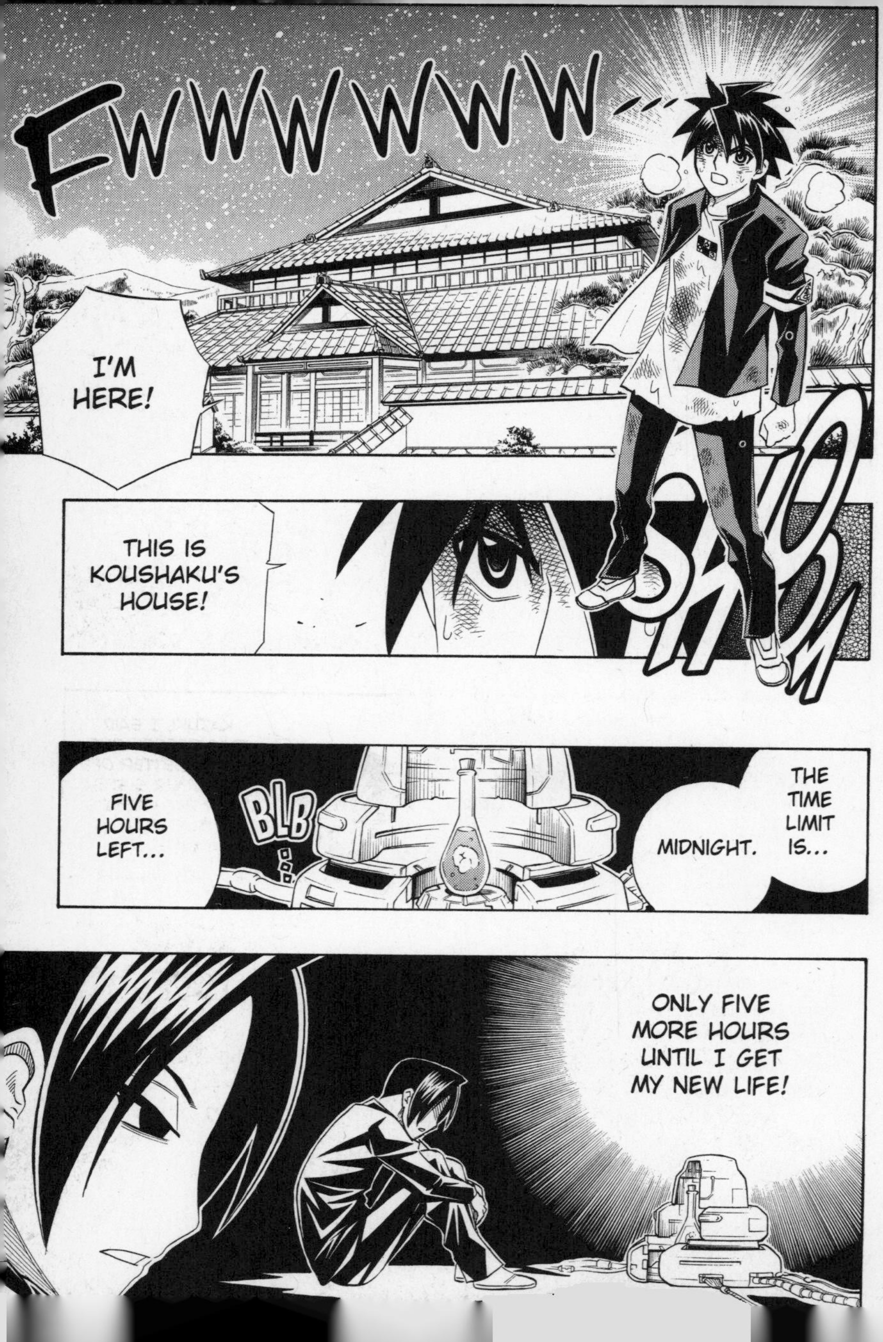
FWWWWWW
I'M HERE!
SHOOM
THIS IS KOUSHAKU'S HOUSE!
THE TIME LIMIT IS...
MIDNIGHT.
BLB
FIVE HOURS LEFT...
ONLY FIVE MORE HOURS UNTIL I GET MY NEW LIFE!

Chapter 15: Dark, Hot and Sweet

· Nurse Mahiro and Shishio Tokiko... I'm sorry. It's not the characters that are going out of control. It's me.

· I got the idea of the transformation scene in his underwear from *Devilman's* transformation scene and Santana from Part 2 in *Jojo's Bizarre Adventure.* No need to accessorize excessively! If you're Super Human show off that body! ...is what I thought but thinking I might have gone overboard I spoke to Kurosaki Sensei for advice. He said, "If you think it's interesting do it!" Those were very encouraging words. It's an understatement to stay the Papillon character was finalized from those words.

· Koushaku's lines describing human flesh came from Talleyrand, a French foreign minister. That's what he said when he described good coffee. I'd like to have some of the coffee he was having.

Chapter 16: Butterfly of Black Death

· This was the most cumbersome chapter of this volume. Seems like a lot of people were confused not knowing whether this chapter was serious or comedic. To be honest, I really don't know myself. I just know I had a lot of fun drawing it. I felt the "rush" a lot in this chapter. It's that feeling you get only in sequential manga. This is why I can't give up manga.

· I had thought of the Double Buso Renkin before the series started. Power-Ups are a part of the thrill of Shonen Manga but I thought it would be weird if he suddenly got stronger. I also didn't want him to get stronger with me unconvinced. That's why he ended up defeating Koushaku by borrowing Tokiko's power but it was all Kazuki.

· I got the second lance's design motif from *Getter Robo.* I LOVE *GETTER.*

Chapter 17: Fade to Black

· The four action pages. I learned from my mistake from the VS. Washio chapters. I omitted everything unnecessary and drew it to convey a sense of speed. It might look like a one shot drawing using ink but actually a lot of effort was put into drawing these pages.

· The scene where Kazuki says he's "sorry" and the part where Koushaku says, "don't apologize" is my favorite scene in the entire volume. It's very difficult to really sense the various emotions going through them with just words but these scenes are the most fulfilling to draw.

· The Warrior Chief entrance. I've saved the details for the next volume but he's a character that's challenging to draw in his own way.

· Tokiko's leg pillow was Kazuki's reward for working so hard. Woo-Hoo!

Hence… →   To be continued.

CHAPTER 15: DARK, HOT AND SWEET

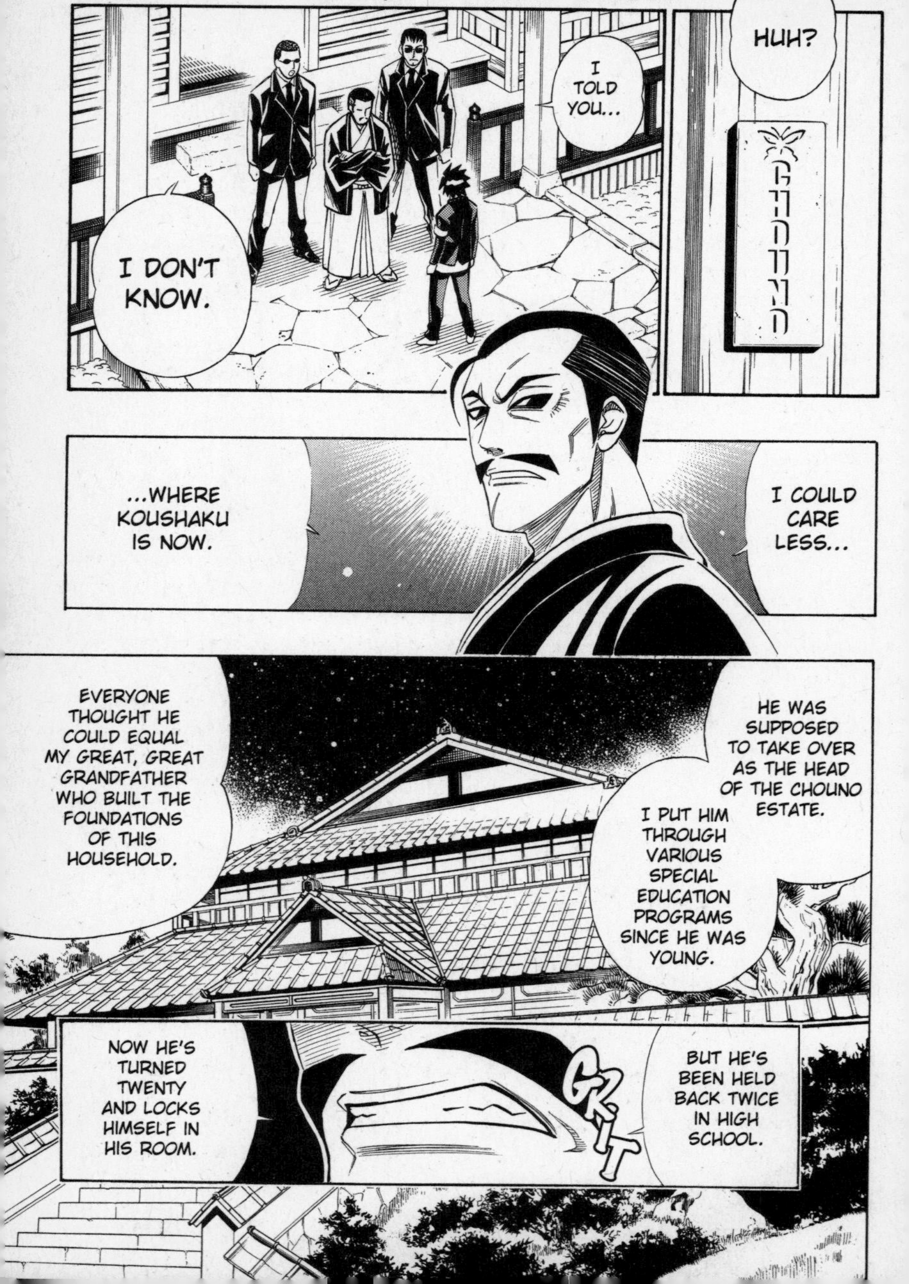
HUH?
I TOLD YOU...
I DON'T KNOW.
I COULD CARE LESS...
...WHERE KOUSHAKU IS NOW.
HE WAS SUPPOSED TO TAKE OVER AS THE HEAD OF THE CHOUNO ESTATE.
I PUT HIM THROUGH VARIOUS SPECIAL EDUCATION PROGRAMS SINCE HE WAS YOUNG.
EVERYONE THOUGHT HE COULD EQUAL MY GREAT, GREAT GRANDFATHER WHO BUILT THE FOUNDATIONS OF THIS HOUSEHOLD.
BUT HE'S BEEN HELD BACK TWICE IN HIGH SCHOOL.
GRIT
NOW HE'S TURNED TWENTY AND LOCKS HIMSELF IN HIS ROOM.

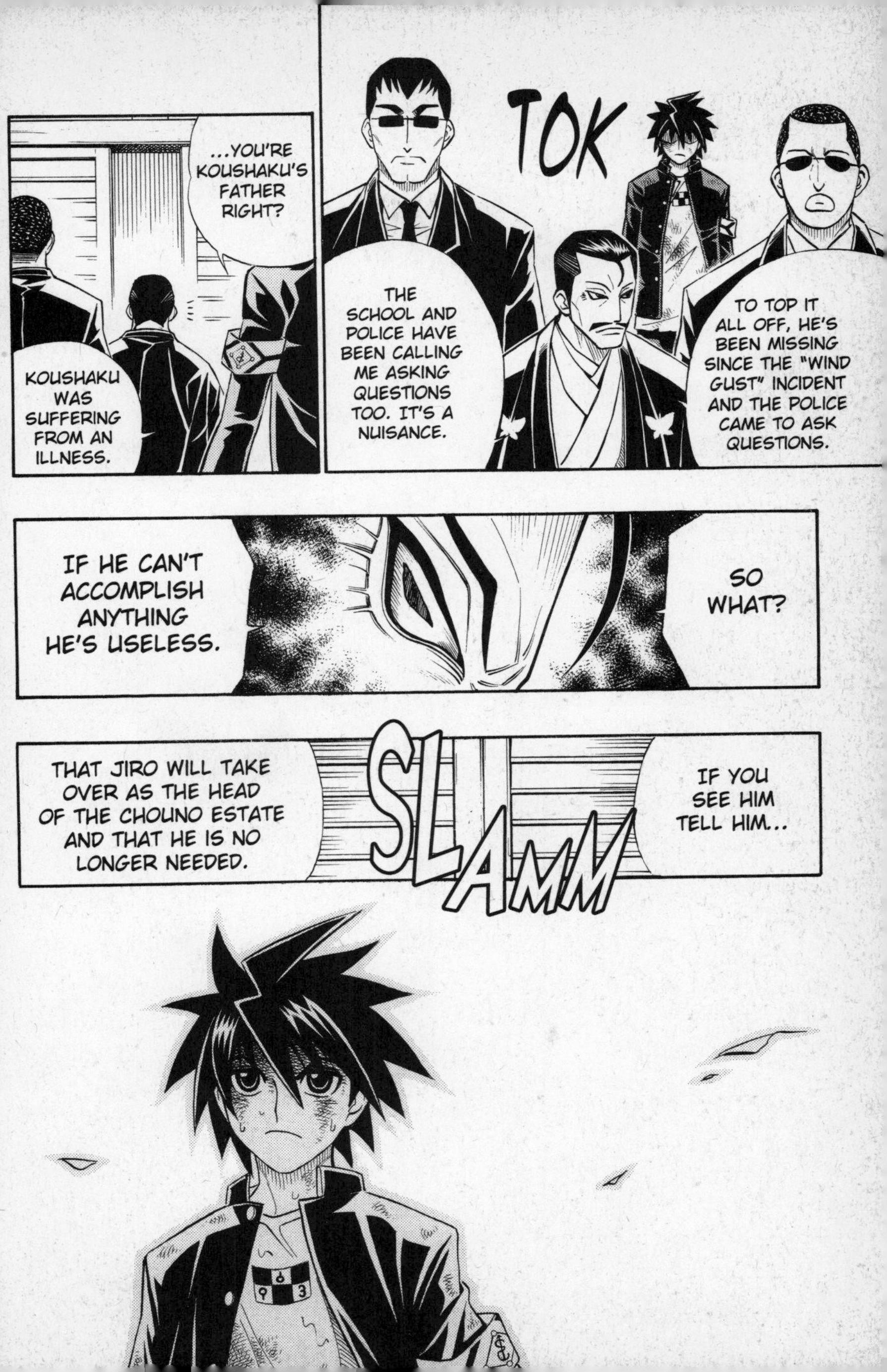
TOK
TO TOP IT ALL OFF, HE'S BEEN MISSING SINCE THE "WIND GUST" INCIDENT AND THE POLICE CAME TO ASK QUESTIONS.
THE SCHOOL AND POLICE HAVE BEEN CALLING ME ASKING QUESTIONS TOO. IT'S A NUISANCE.
...YOU'RE KOUSHAKU'S FATHER RIGHT?
KOUSHAKU WAS SUFFERING FROM AN ILLNESS.
SO WHAT?
IF HE CAN'T ACCOMPLISH ANYTHING HE'S USELESS.
IF YOU SEE HIM TELL HIM...
SLAMM
THAT JIRO WILL TAKE OVER AS THE HEAD OF THE CHOUNO ESTATE AND THAT HE IS NO LONGER NEEDED.

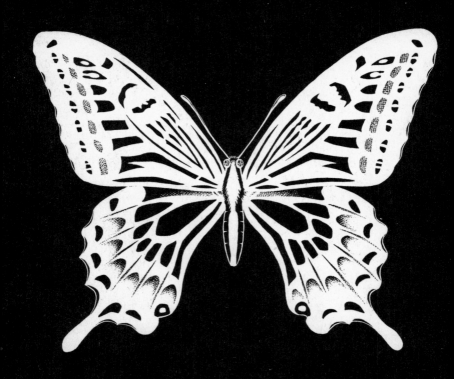

CHAPTER 15:
DARK, HOT AND SWEET

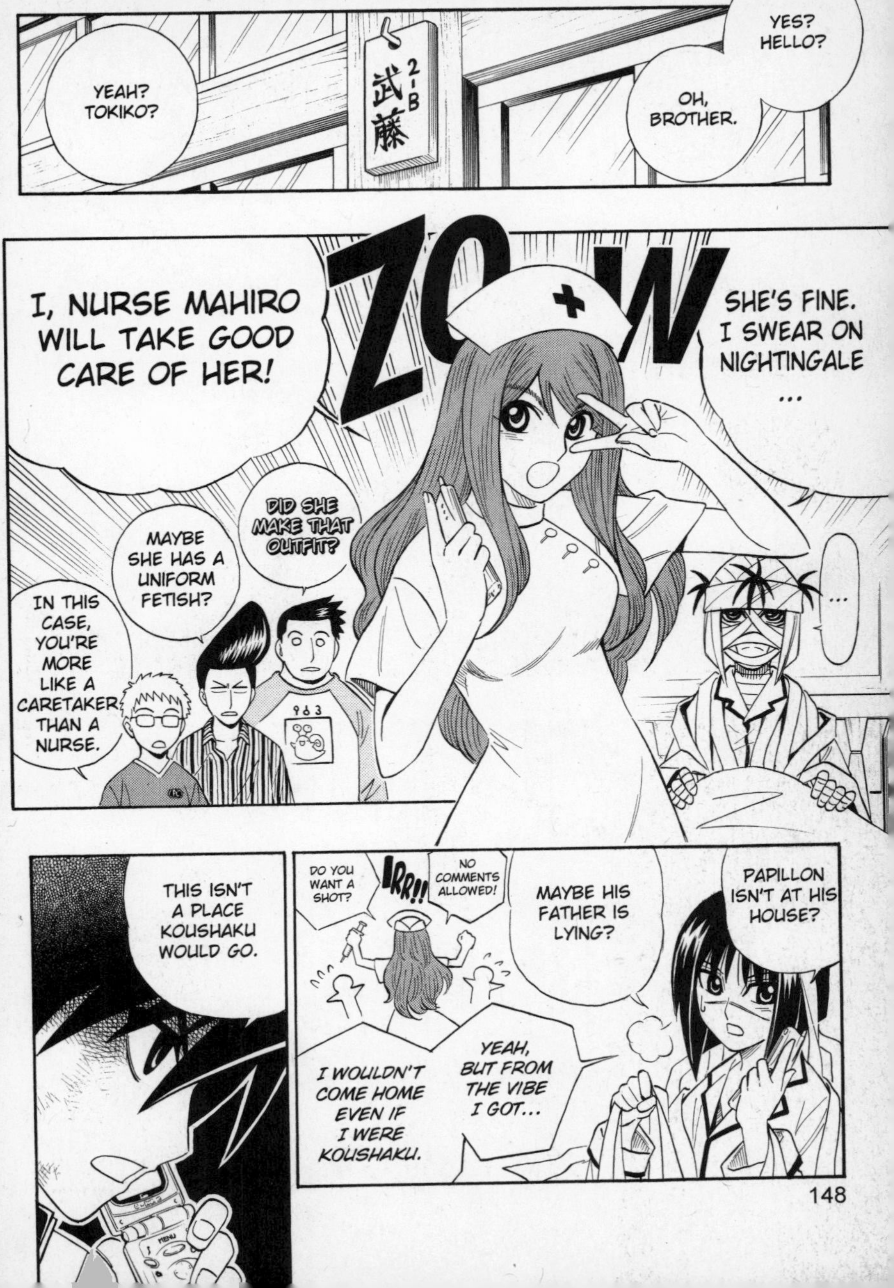
YES? HELLO?
OH, BROTHER.
2-B 武藤
YEAH? TOKIKO?
SHE'S FINE. I SWEAR ON NIGHTINGALE ...
I, NURSE MAHIRO WILL TAKE GOOD CARE OF HER!
ZOW
...
DID SHE MAKE THAT OUTFIT?
MAYBE SHE HAS A UNIFORM FETISH?
IN THIS CASE, YOU'RE MORE LIKE A CARETAKER THAN A NURSE.
PAPILLON ISN'T AT HIS HOUSE?
MAYBE HIS FATHER IS LYING?
NO COMMENTS ALLOWED!
IRR!!
DO YOU WANT A SHOT?
YEAH, BUT FROM THE VIBE I GOT...
I WOULDN'T COME HOME EVEN IF I WERE KOUSHAKU.
THIS ISN'T A PLACE KOUSHAKU WOULD GO.

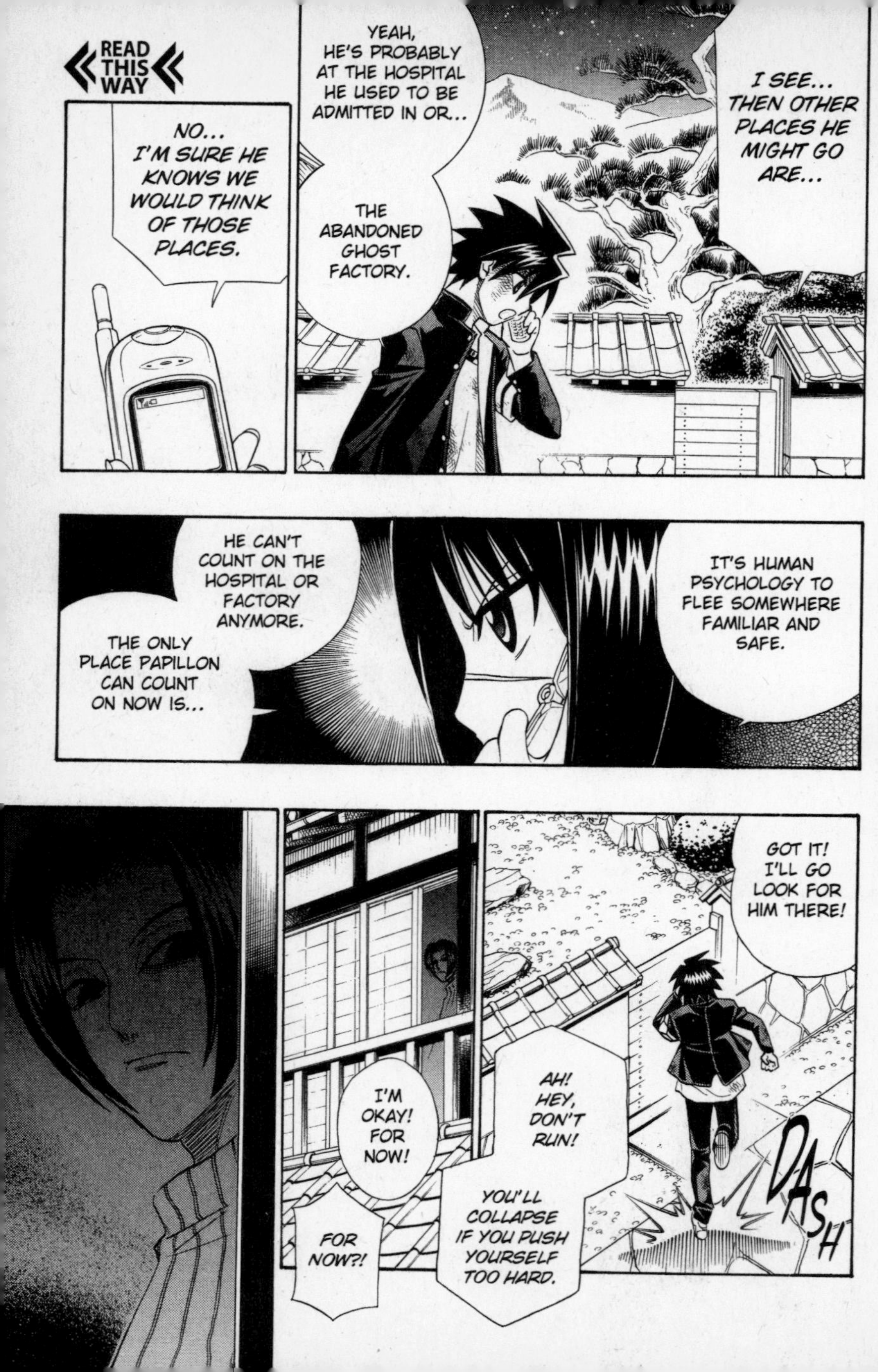
READ THIS WAY
I SEE... THEN OTHER PLACES HE MIGHT GO ARE...
YEAH, HE'S PROBABLY AT THE HOSPITAL HE USED TO BE ADMITTED IN OR...
THE ABANDONED GHOST FACTORY.
NO... I'M SURE HE KNOWS WE WOULD THINK OF THOSE PLACES.
IT'S HUMAN PSYCHOLOGY TO FLEE SOMEWHERE FAMILIAR AND SAFE.
HE CAN'T COUNT ON THE HOSPITAL OR FACTORY ANYMORE.
THE ONLY PLACE PAPILLON CAN COUNT ON NOW IS...
GOT IT! I'LL GO LOOK FOR HIM THERE!
DASH
AH! HEY, DON'T RUN!
YOU'LL COLLAPSE IF YOU PUSH YOURSELF TOO HARD.
I'M OKAY! FOR NOW!
FOR NOW?!

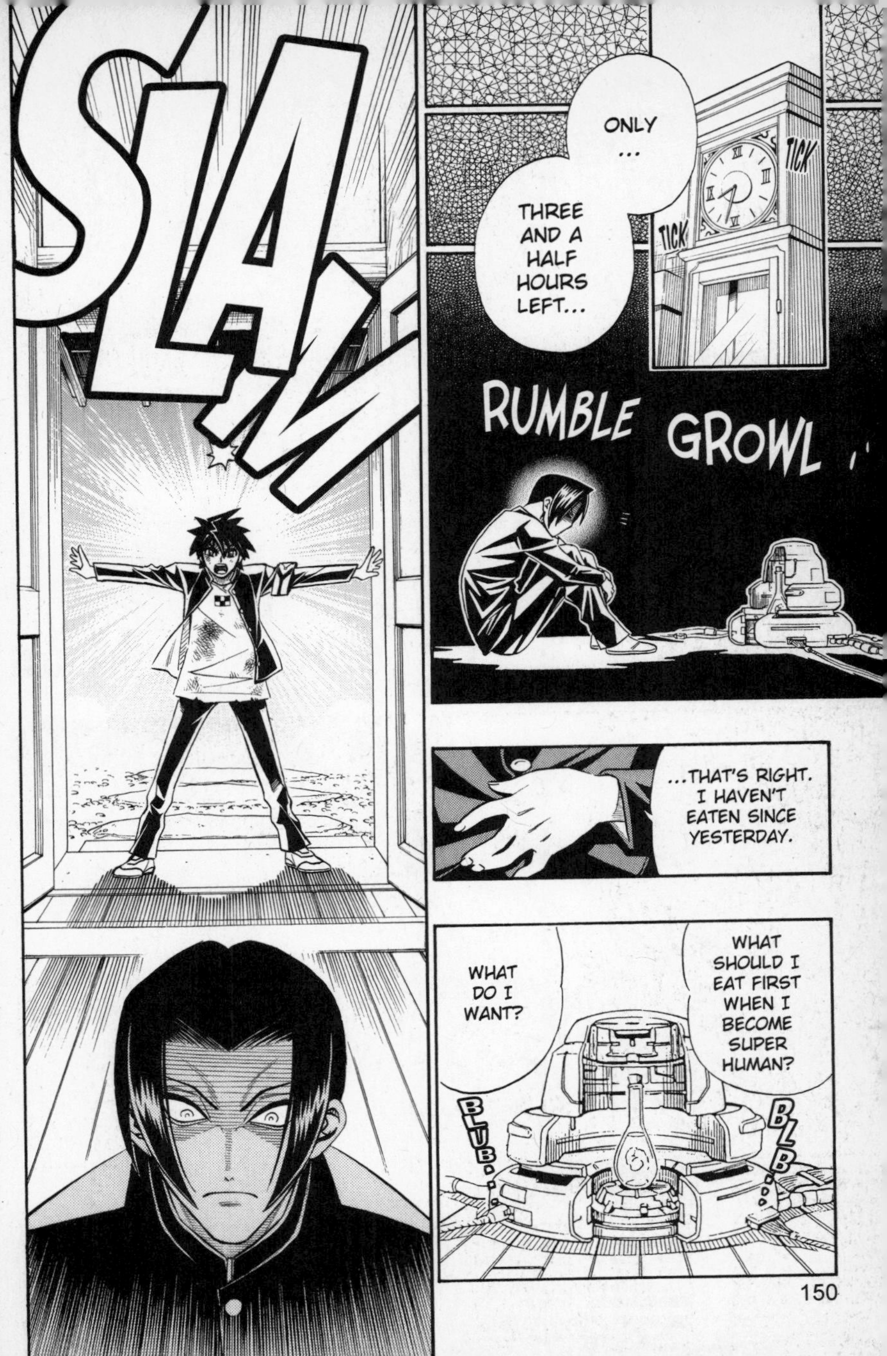
ONLY ... THREE AND A HALF HOURS LEFT...
TICK
TICK
RUMBLE GROWL
...THAT'S RIGHT. I HAVEN'T EATEN SINCE YESTERDAY.
WHAT SHOULD I EAT FIRST WHEN I BECOME SUPER HUMAN?
WHAT DO I WANT?
BLB
BLUB
SLAM

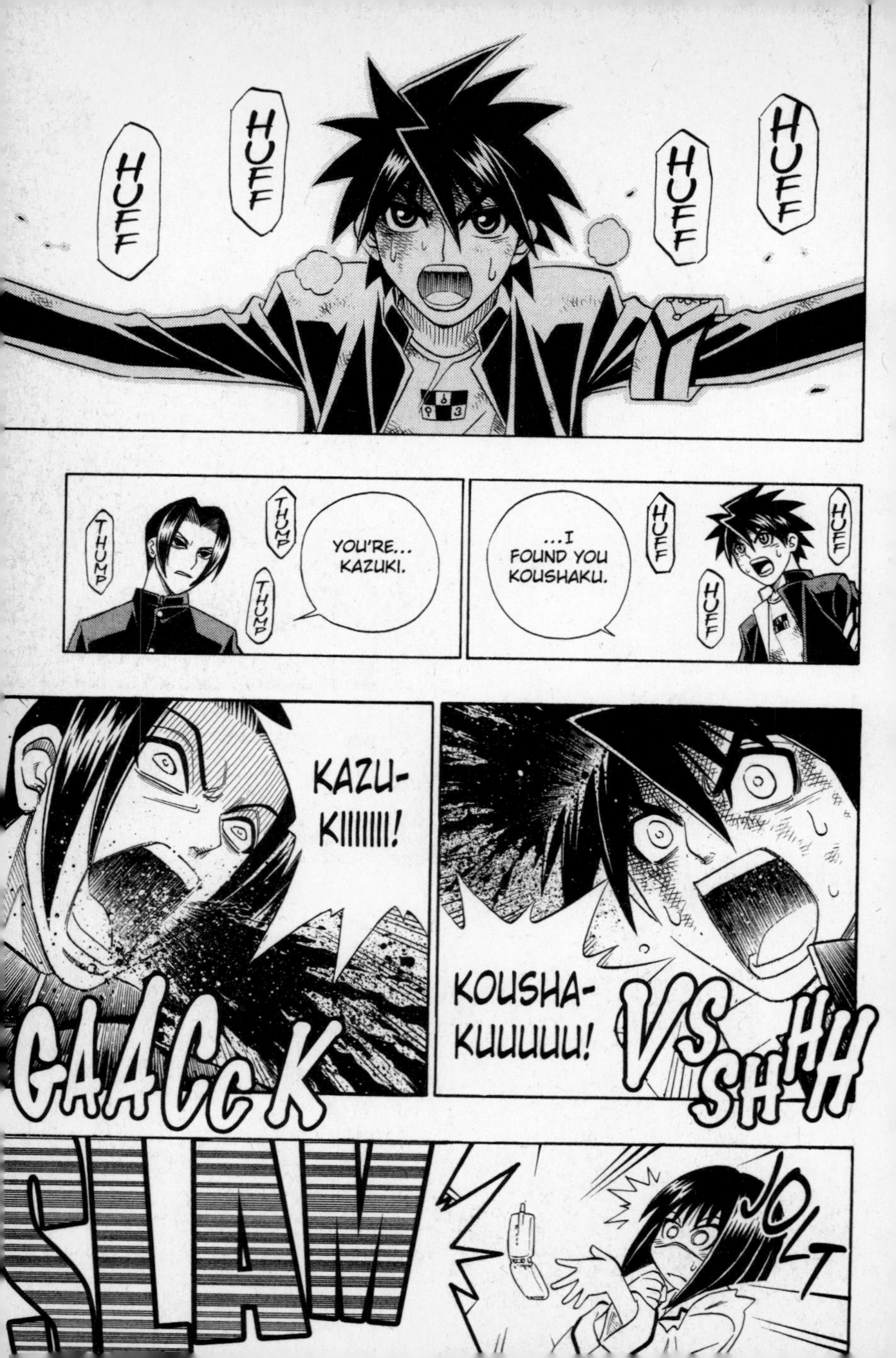
HUFF
HUFF
HUFF
HUFF
HUFF
HUFF
...I FOUND YOU KOUSHAKU.
HUFF
THUMP
THUMP
YOU'RE... KAZUKI.
THUMP
KOUSHA-KUUUUUU!
VSHHH
KAZU-KIIIIIII!
GAACcK
JOLT
SLAM

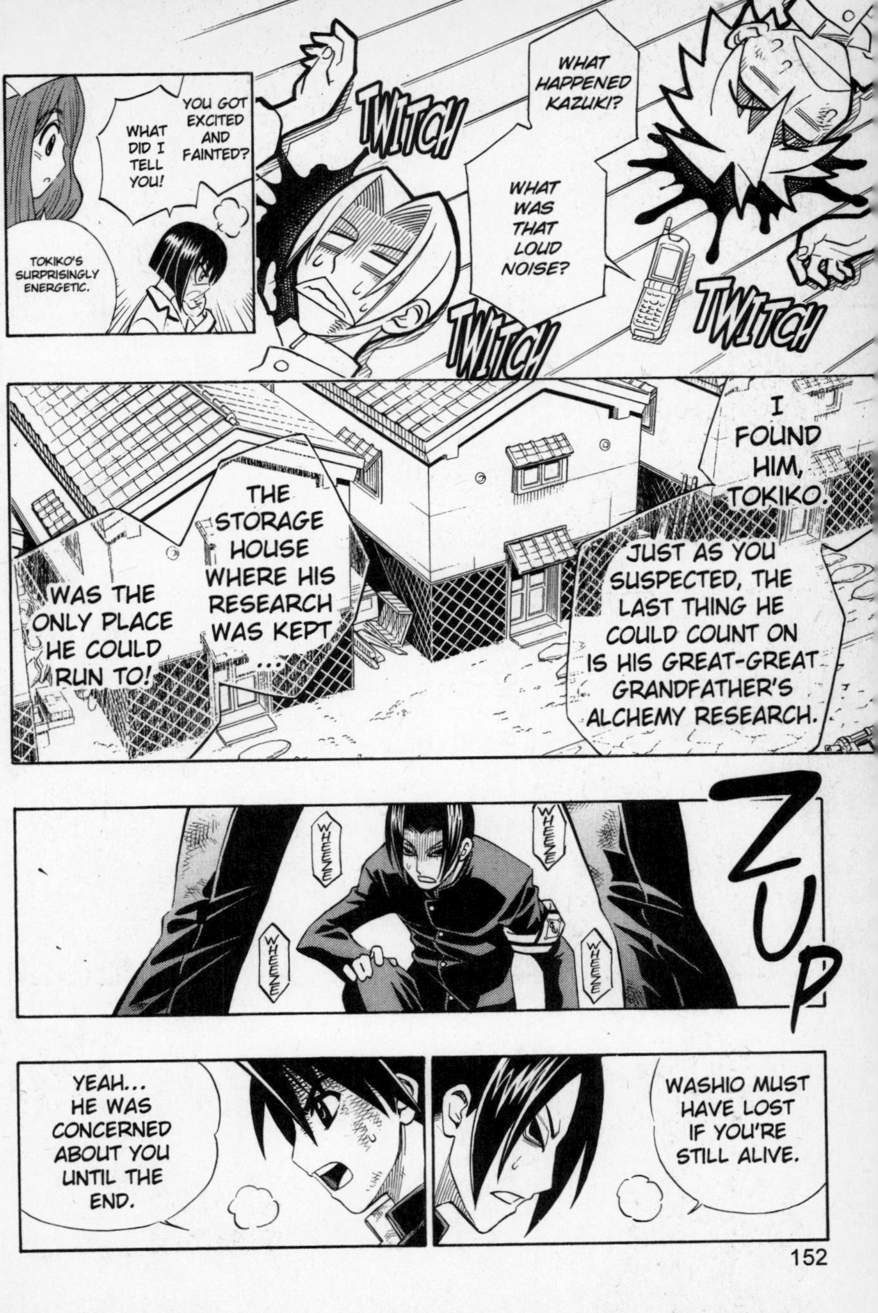
TWITCH
WHAT HAPPENED KAZUKI?
WHAT WAS THAT LOUD NOISE?
TWITCH
TWITCH
YOU GOT EXCITED AND FAINTED?
WHAT DID I TELL YOU!
TOKIKO'S SURPRISINGLY ENERGETIC.
I FOUND HIM, TOKIKO.
JUST AS YOU SUSPECTED, THE LAST THING HE COULD COUNT ON IS HIS GREAT-GREAT GRANDFATHER'S ALCHEMY RESEARCH.
THE STORAGE HOUSE WHERE HIS RESEARCH WAS KEPT...
WAS THE ONLY PLACE HE COULD RUN TO!
ZUP
WHEEZE
WHEEZE
WHEEZE
WHEEZE
WASHIO MUST HAVE LOST IF YOU'RE STILL ALIVE.
YEAH... HE WAS CONCERNED ABOUT YOU UNTIL THE END.

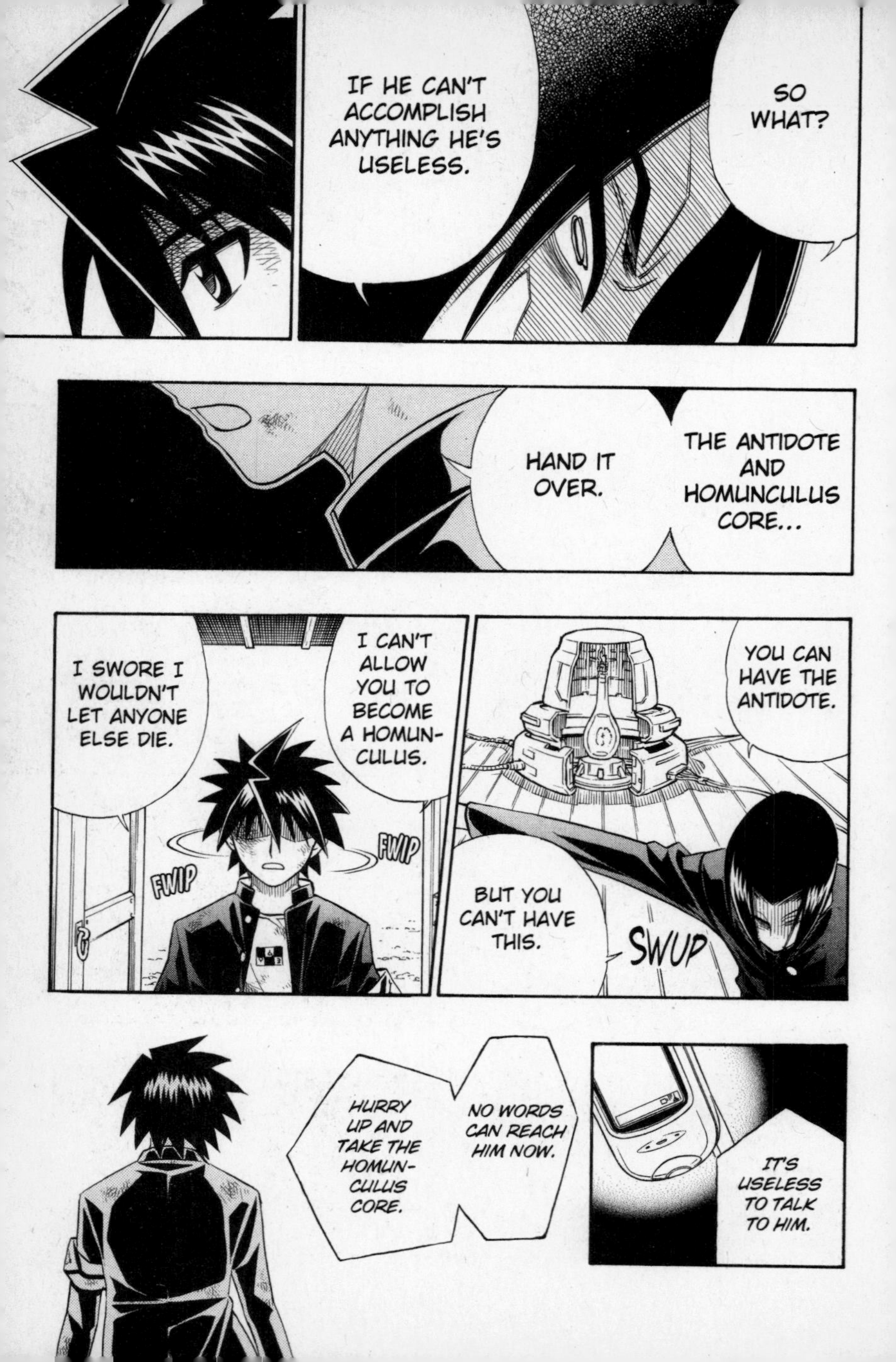
SO WHAT?
IF HE CAN'T ACCOMPLISH ANYTHING HE'S USELESS.
THE ANTIDOTE AND HOMUNCULUS CORE...
HAND IT OVER.
YOU CAN HAVE THE ANTIDOTE.
SWUP
BUT YOU CAN'T HAVE THIS.
I CAN'T ALLOW YOU TO BECOME A HOMUN-CULUS.
I SWORE I WOULDN'T LET ANYONE ELSE DIE.
FWIP
FWIP
IT'S USELESS TO TALK TO HIM.
NO WORDS CAN REACH HIM NOW.
HURRY UP AND TAKE THE HOMUN-CULUS CORE.

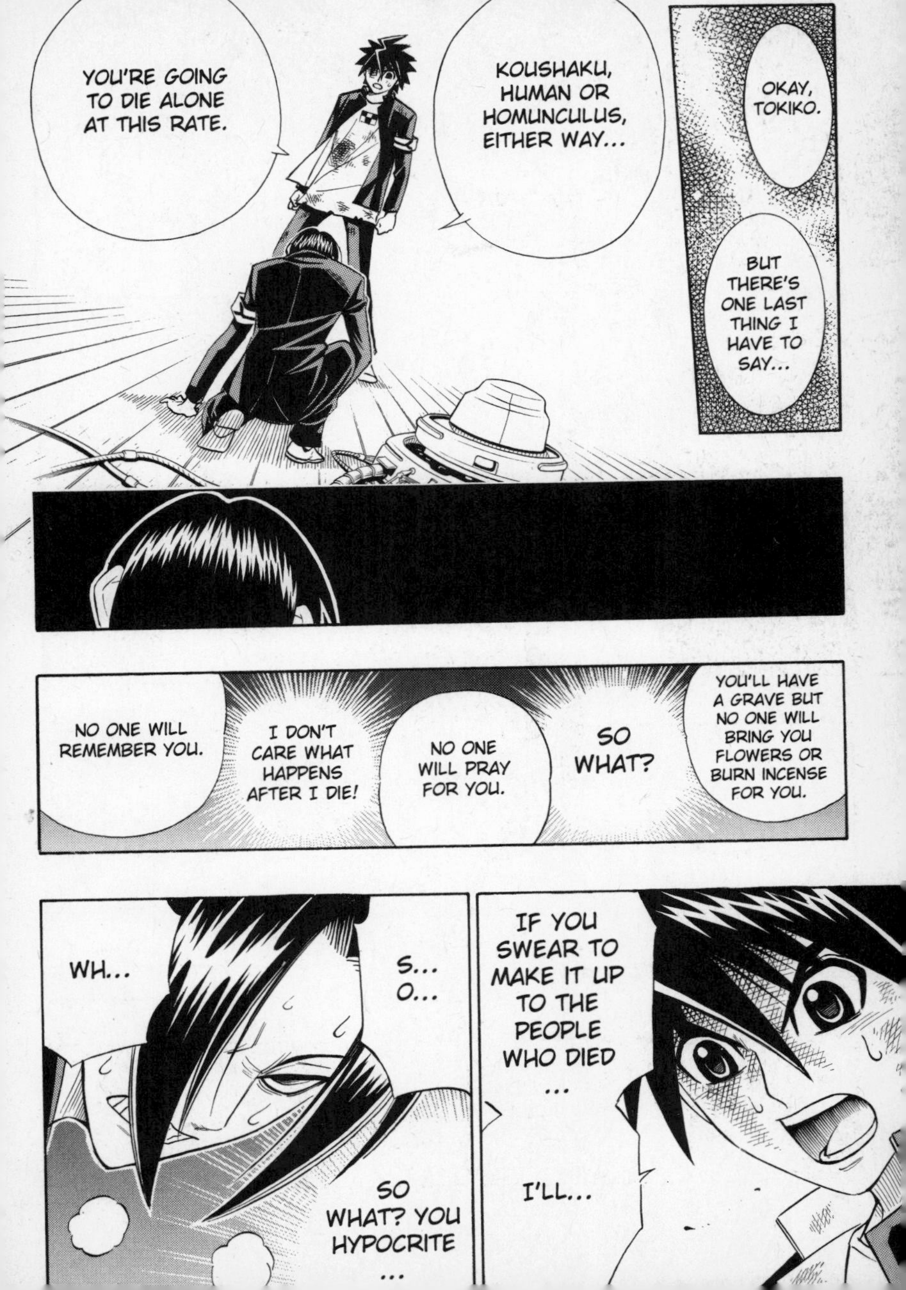

OKAY, TOKIKO.
BUT THERE'S ONE LAST THING I HAVE TO SAY...
KOUSHAKU, HUMAN OR HOMUNCULUS, EITHER WAY...
YOU'RE GOING TO DIE ALONE AT THIS RATE.
YOU'LL HAVE A GRAVE BUT NO ONE WILL BRING YOU FLOWERS OR BURN INCENSE FOR YOU.
SO WHAT?
NO ONE WILL PRAY FOR YOU.
I DON'T CARE WHAT HAPPENS AFTER I DIE!
NO ONE WILL REMEMBER YOU.
IF YOU SWEAR TO MAKE IT UP TO THE PEOPLE WHO DIED...
I'LL...
S... O...
WH...
SO WHAT? YOU HYPOCRITE...

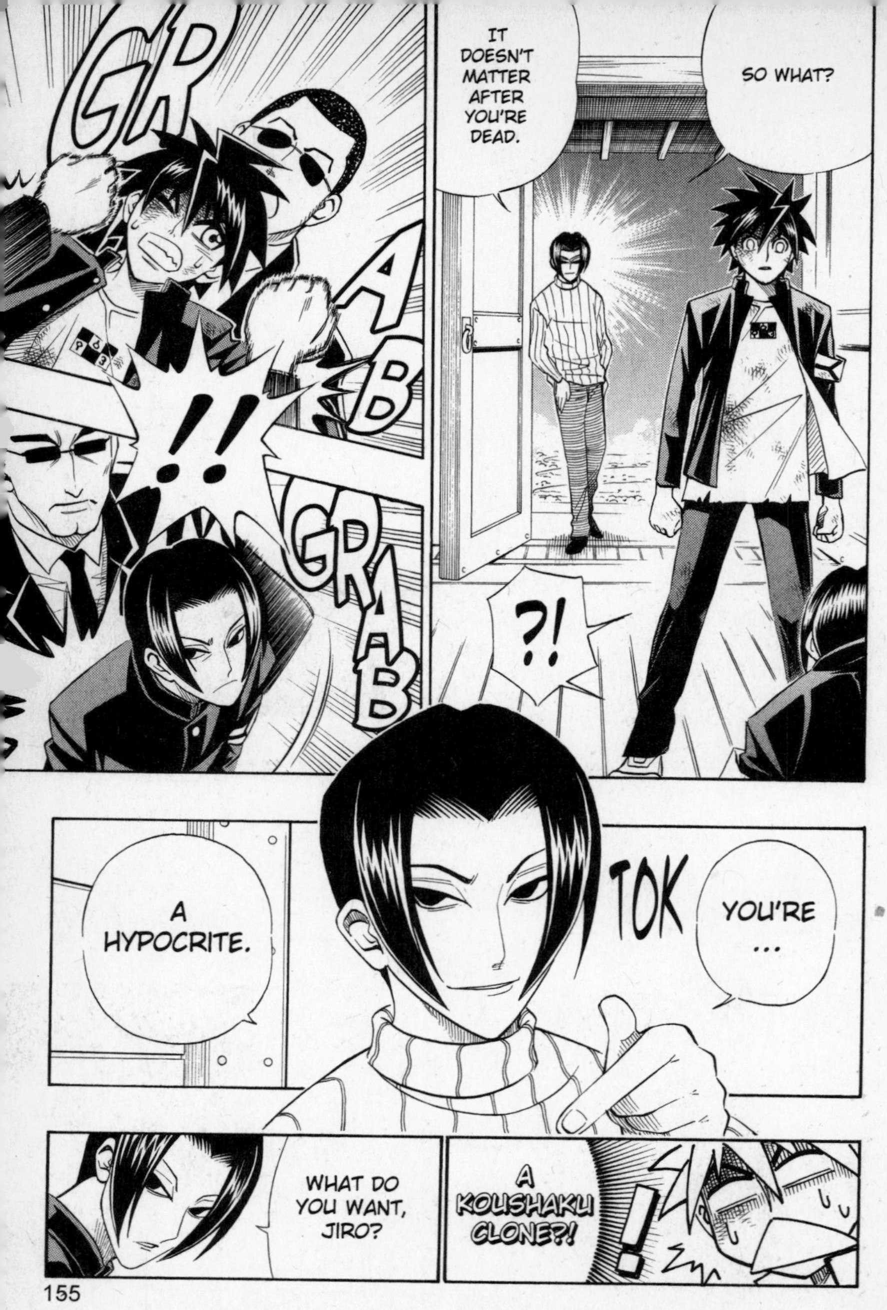
SO WHAT?
IT DOESN'T MATTER AFTER YOU'RE DEAD.
?!
GRAB
!!
GRAB
YOU'RE ...
TOK
A HYPOCRITE.
A KOUSHAKU CLONE?!
!
WHAT DO YOU WANT, JIRO?

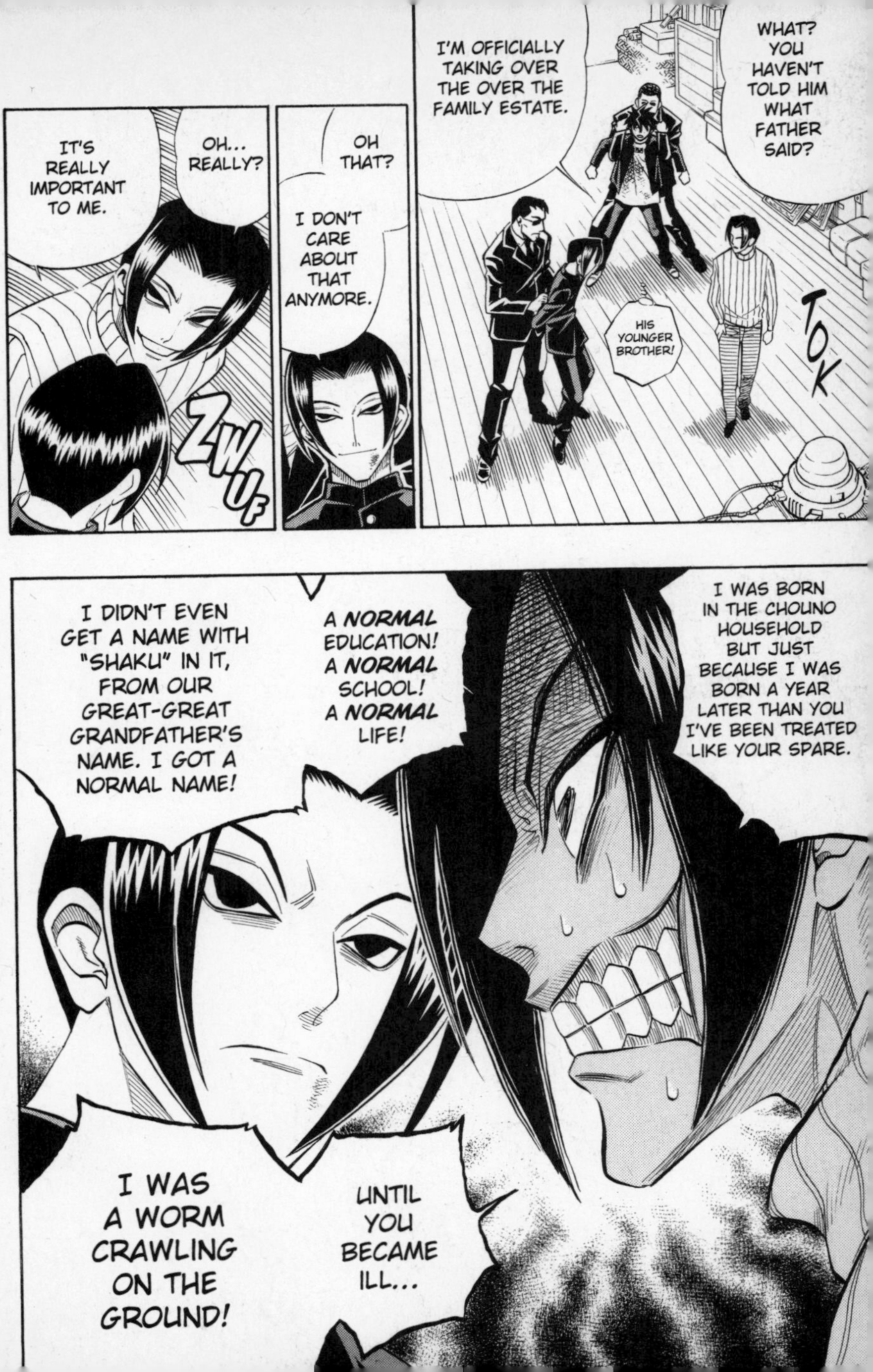
WHAT? YOU HAVEN'T TOLD HIM WHAT FATHER SAID?
I'M OFFICIALLY TAKING OVER THE OVER THE FAMILY ESTATE.
HIS YOUNGER BROTHER!
TOK
OH THAT?
I DON'T CARE ABOUT THAT ANYMORE.
OH... REALLY?
IT'S REALLY IMPORTANT TO ME.
ZWUF
I WAS BORN IN THE CHOUNO HOUSEHOLD BUT JUST BECAUSE I WAS BORN A YEAR LATER THAN YOU I'VE BEEN TREATED LIKE YOUR SPARE.
A NORMAL EDUCATION! A NORMAL SCHOOL! A NORMAL LIFE!
I DIDN'T EVEN GET A NAME WITH "SHAKU" IN IT, FROM OUR GREAT-GREAT GRANDFATHER'S NAME. I GOT A NORMAL NAME!
UNTIL YOU BECAME ILL...
I WAS A WORM CRAWLING ON THE GROUND!

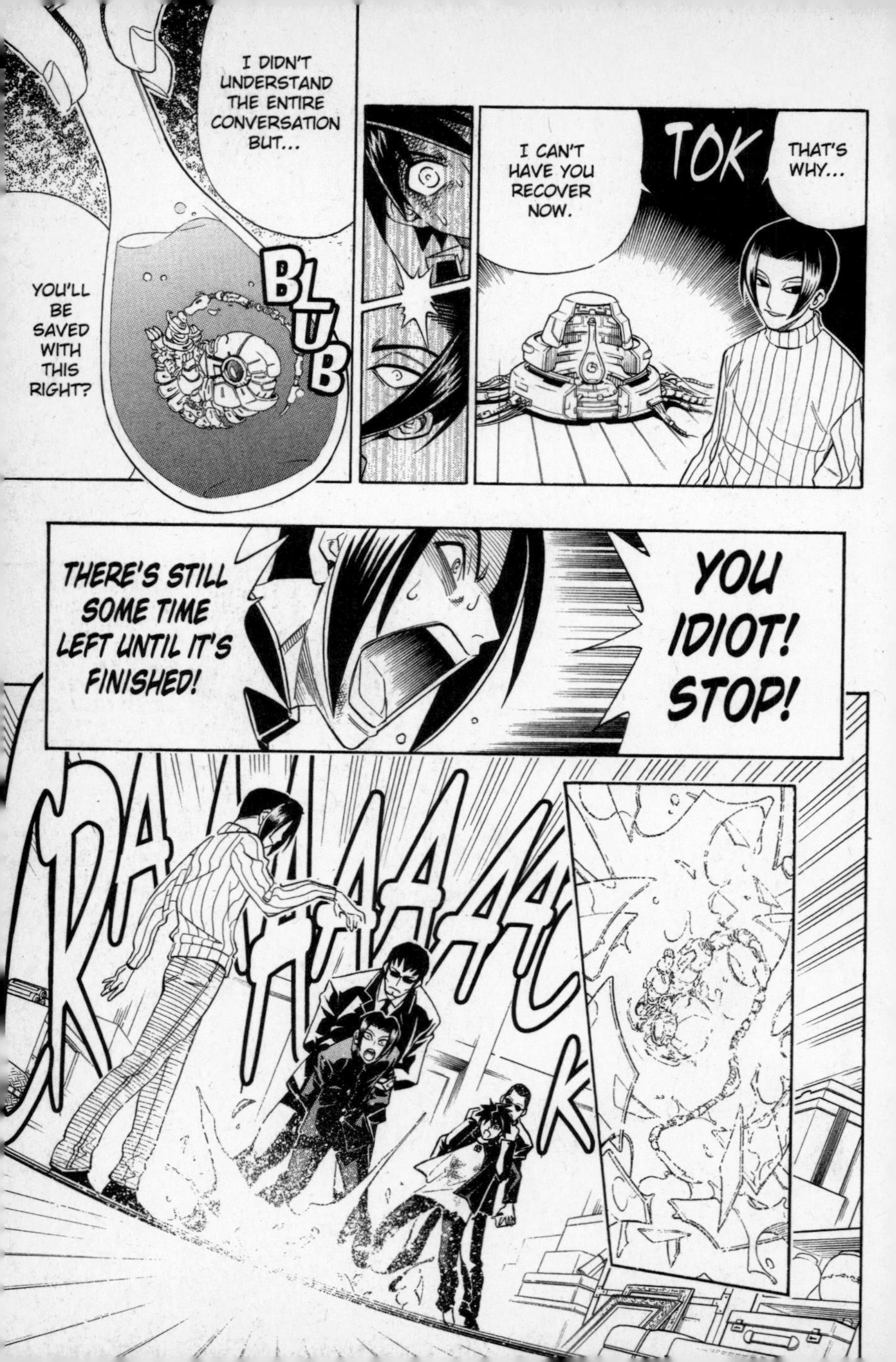
THAT'S WHY...
TOK
I CAN'T HAVE YOU RECOVER NOW.
I DIDN'T UNDERSTAND THE ENTIRE CONVERSATION BUT...
BLUB
YOU'LL BE SAVED WITH THIS RIGHT?
YOU IDIOT! STOP!
THERE'S STILL SOME TIME LEFT UNTIL IT'S FINISHED!
CRAAAAACK

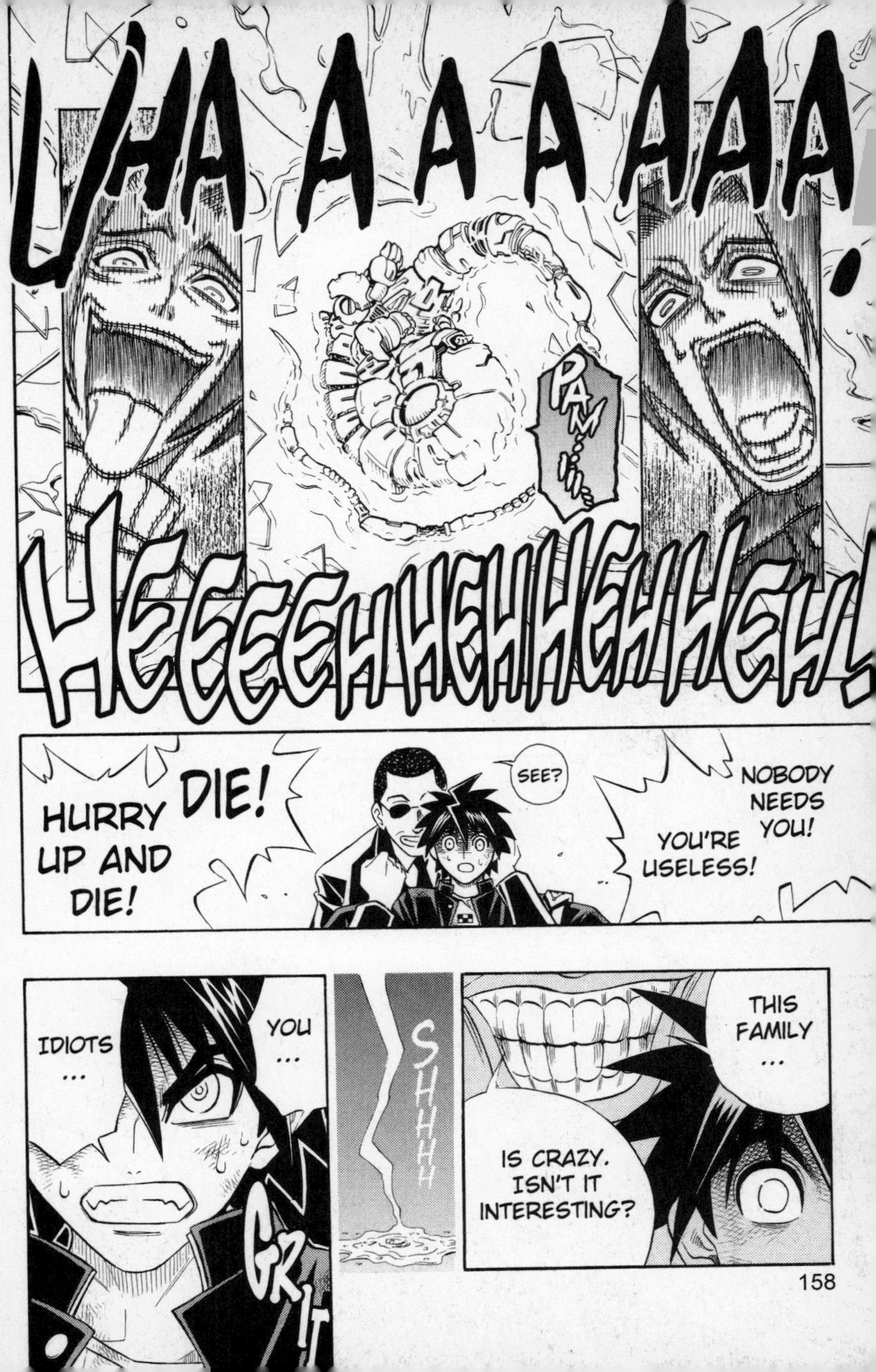

UHAAAAAAA!
PAM...
HEEEEHHEHHEHHEH!
NOBODY NEEDS YOU!
YOU'RE USELESS!
SEE?
DIE!
HURRY UP AND DIE!
THIS FAMILY ...
IS CRAZY. ISN'T IT INTERESTING?
SHHHH
YOU ...
IDIOTS ...
GRIT

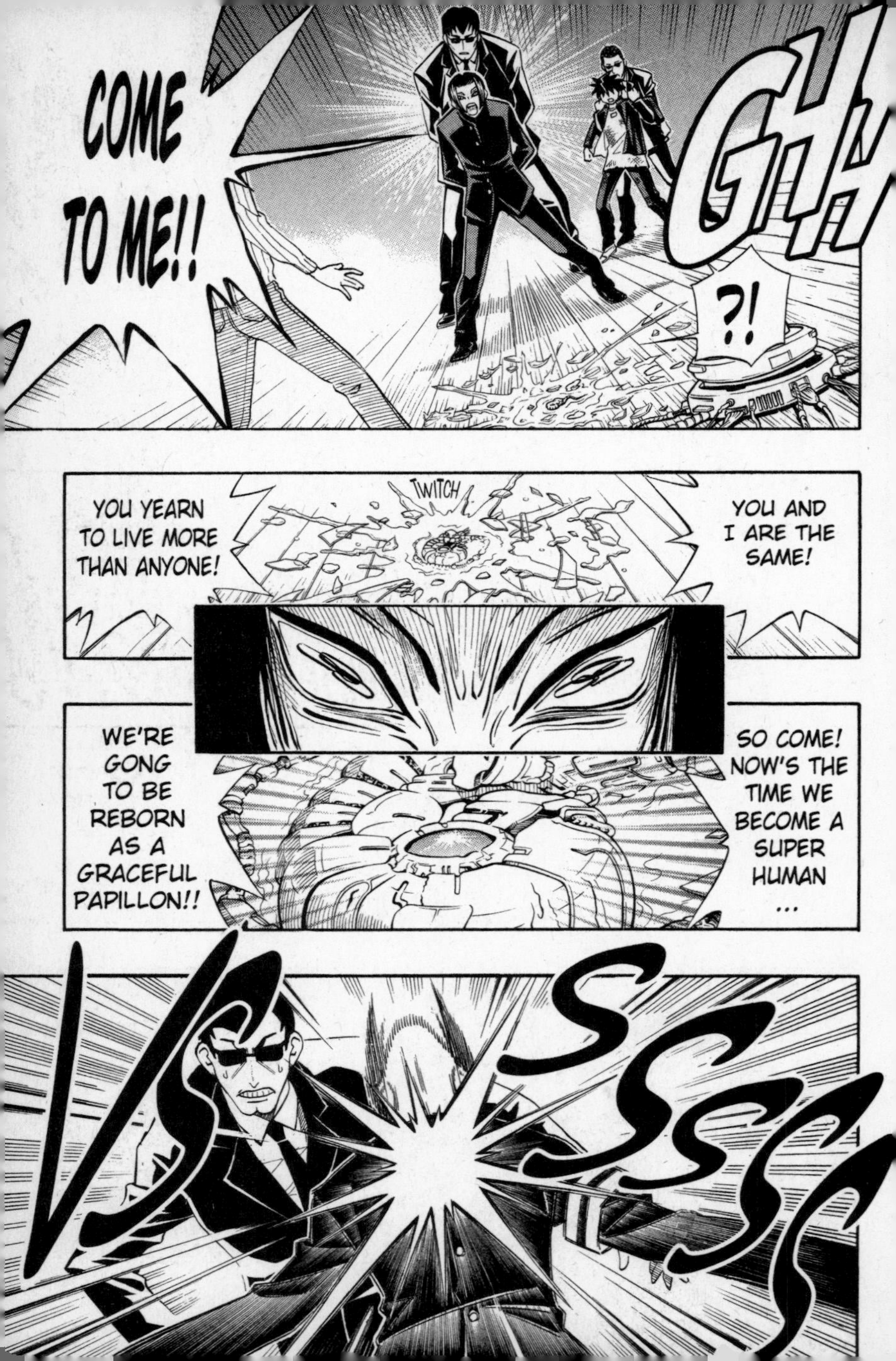

GH
?!
COME TO ME!!
YOU AND I ARE THE SAME!
TWITCH
YOU YEARN TO LIVE MORE THAN ANYONE!
SO COME! NOW'S THE TIME WE BECOME A SUPER HUMAN ...
WE'RE GONG TO BE REBORN AS A GRACEFUL PAPILLON!!

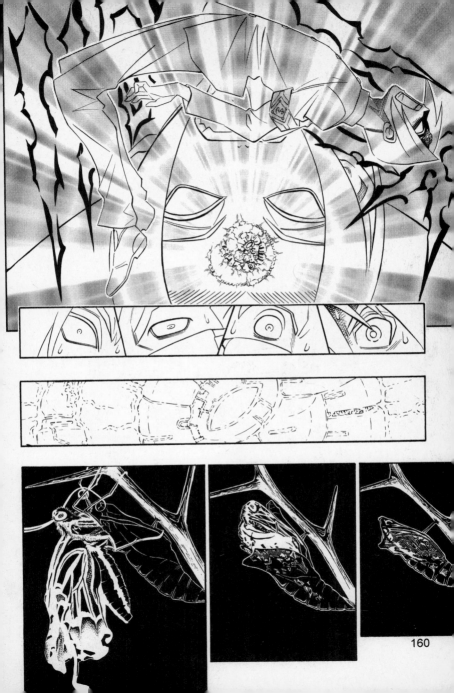

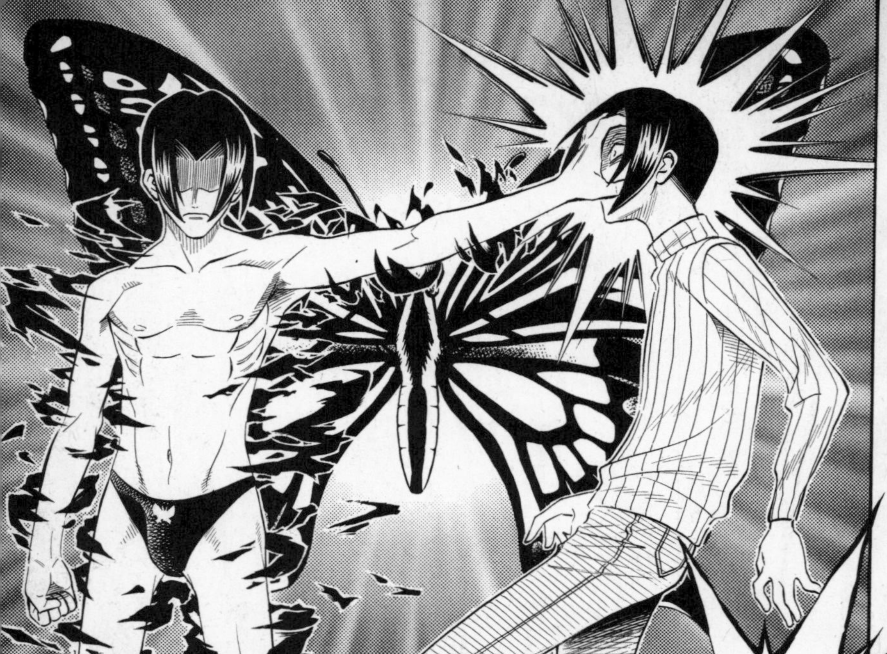
?!?
CRAAB

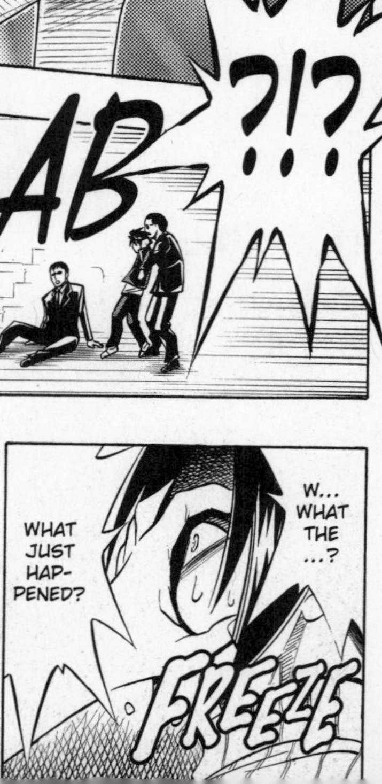
W... WHAT THE ...?
WHAT JUST HAP-PENED?
FREEZE

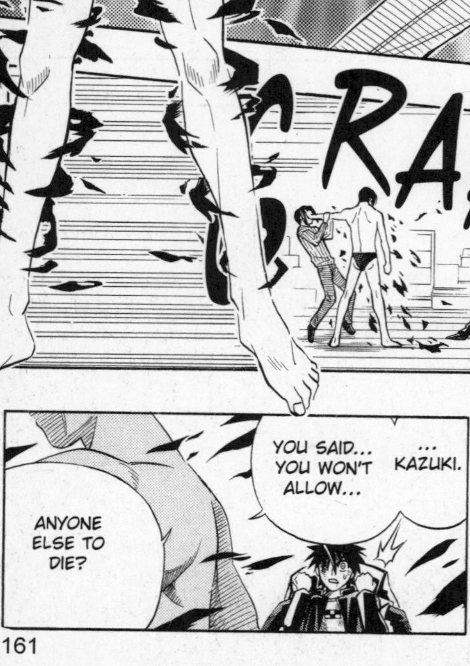
... KAZUKI.
YOU SAID... YOU WON'T ALLOW...
ANYONE ELSE TO DIE?

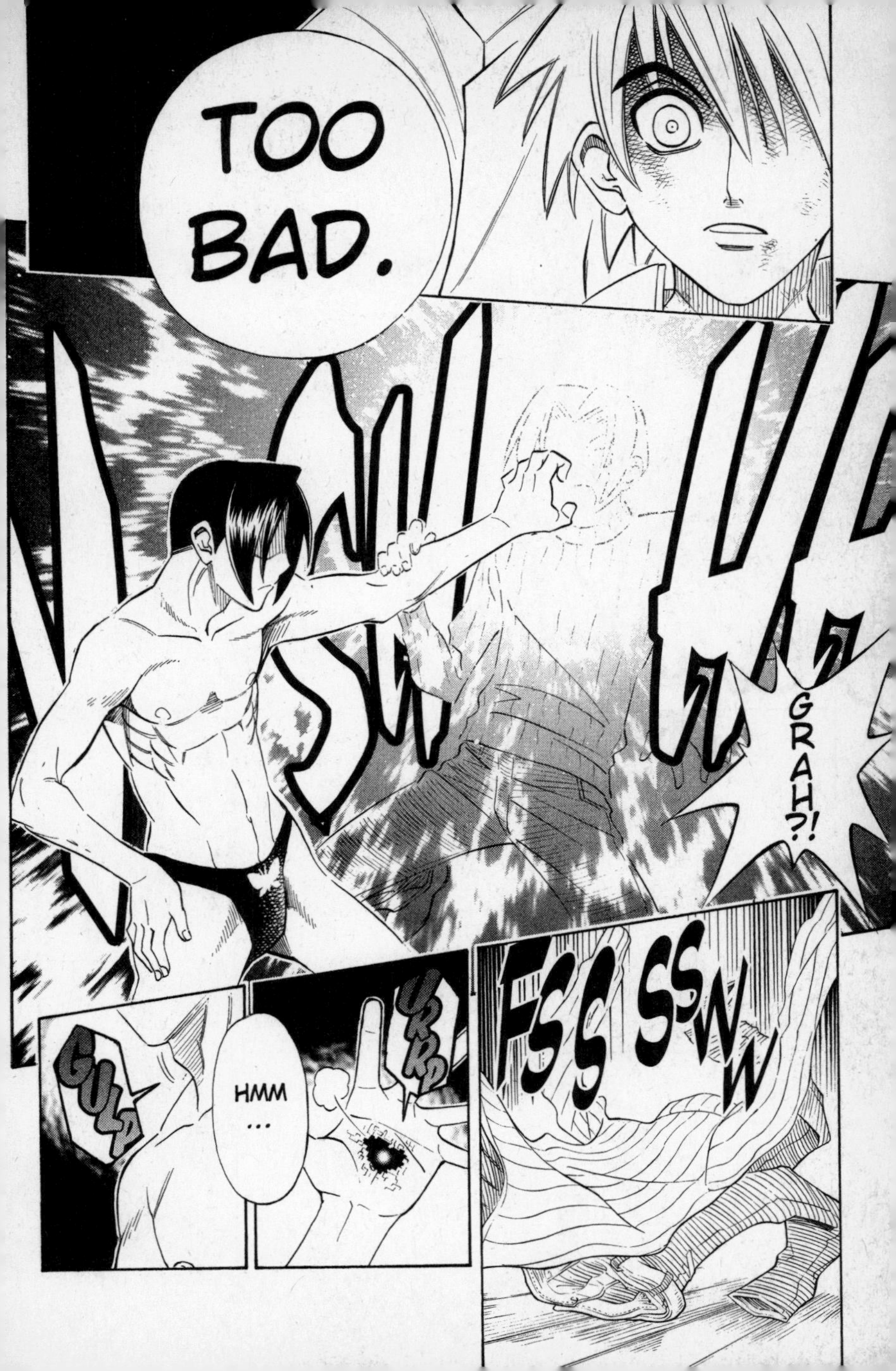
TOO BAD.
GRAH?!
FSSSSSWW
URKP
HMM ...
GULP

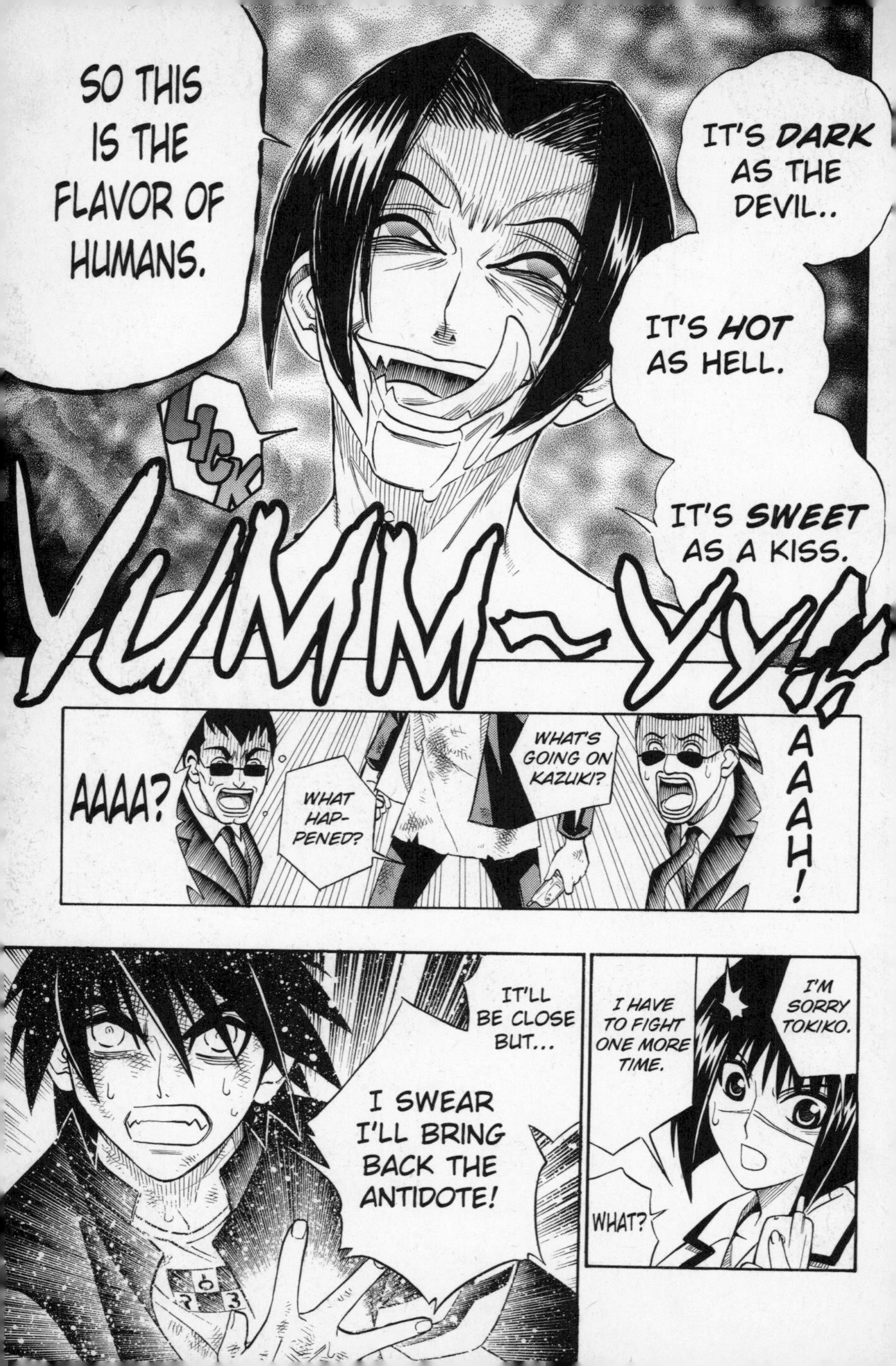
IT'S DARK AS THE DEVIL..
IT'S HOT AS HELL.
IT'S SWEET AS A KISS.
SO THIS IS THE FLAVOR OF HUMANS.
LICK
YUMM~YY!!
AAAAH!
WHAT'S GOING ON KAZUKI?
WHAT HAP-PENED?
AAAA?
I'M SORRY TOKIKO.
I HAVE TO FIGHT ONE MORE TIME.
WHAT?
IT'LL BE CLOSE BUT...
I SWEAR I'LL BRING BACK THE ANTIDOTE!

Character File No.12

Koushaku Chouno

- Height: 180 cm; Weight: 64kg
- Born: June 26th; Cancer; Blood Type cisAB; 19 years old
- Favorites: Himself, butterflies, to make the impossible possible.
- Dislikes: Everything other than himself and butterflies. People who don't even try to make the impossible possible.
- Hobbies: Collecting insects, alchemy research
- Things he's good at: Coughing blood
- Affiliation: Private Ginsei Academy 3rd Year High School Student Class Room C (held back twice), Dorm resident

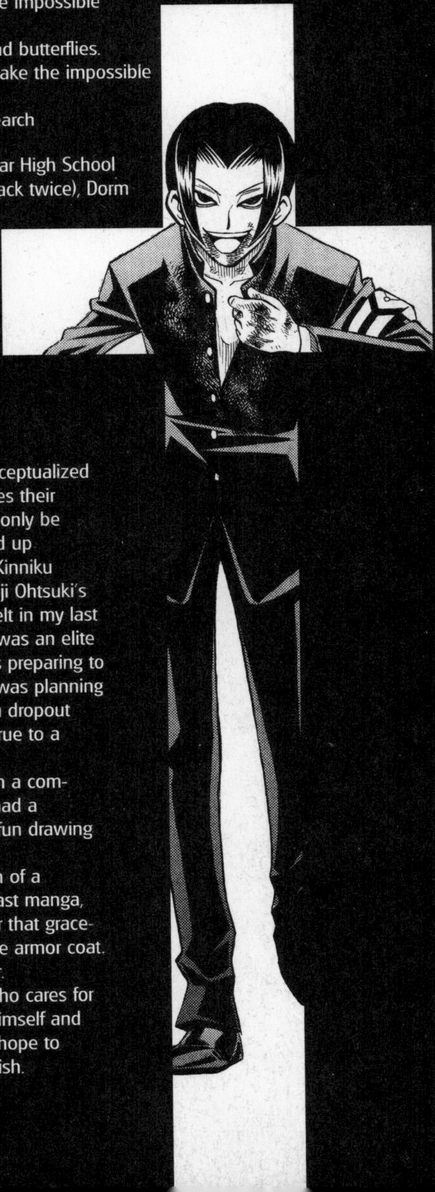

Author's Notes

- An outcast, every class has one. I conceptualized him from the type of person who hides their feeling and negative energy, and can only be described as magma and slime mixed up together. He was created combining Kinniku Shojotai song lyrics, characters in Kenji Ohtsuki's novels and the feeling of isolation I felt in my last year of high school. (My high school was an elite school and everyone in my class was preparing to take college entrance exams while I was planning to become a manga artist. I felt like a dropout more or less. Well, I guess that was true to a certain extent.)
- But somehow his character headed in a completely different direction. I've never had a character like this so it's sooo much fun drawing him.
- I got his design by altering the design of a character I didn't get to draw in my last manga, "Gun Blaze West." He was a matador that gracefully repelled bullets using his reactive armor coat. He was quite the ridiculous character.
- He is the polar opposite of Kazuki, who cares for others. Koushaku only cares about himself and continues to become more selfish. I hope to illustrate how he becomes more selfish.

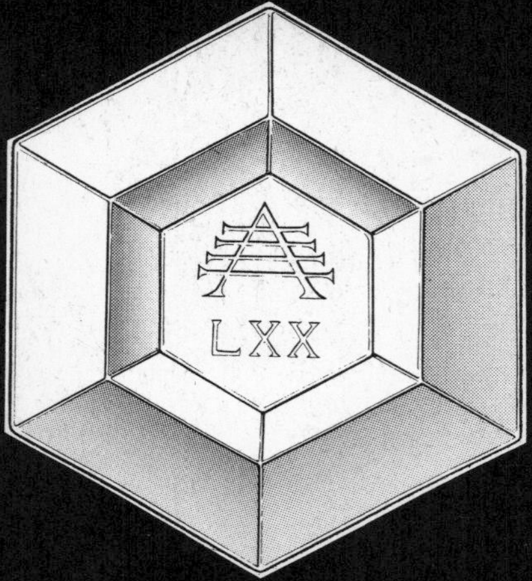
LXX

CHAPTER 16:
BUTTERFLY OF BLACK DEATH

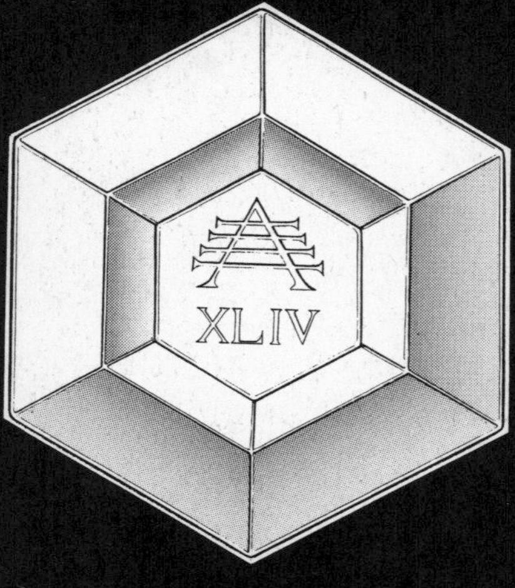
XLIV

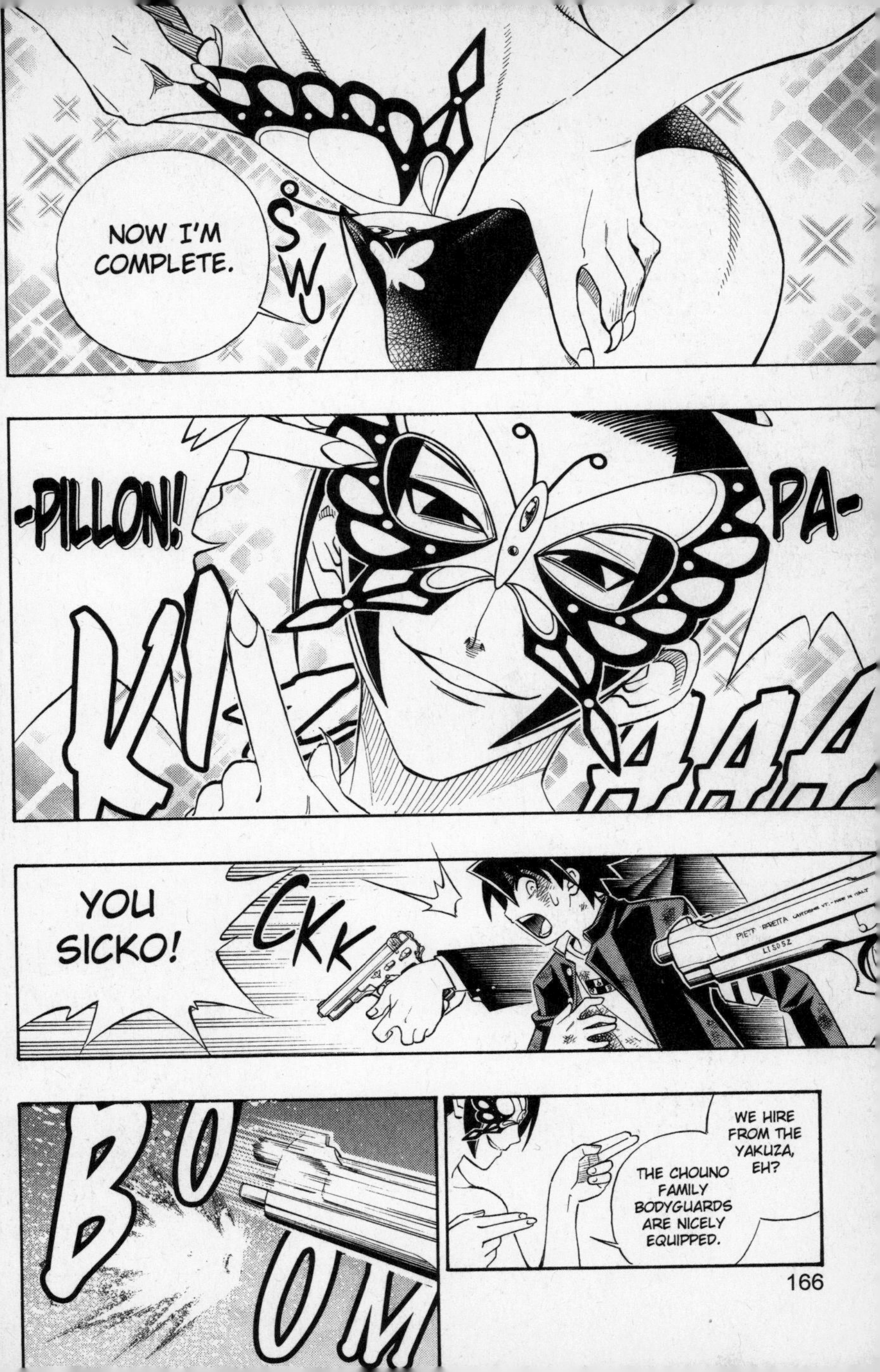
NOW I'M COMPLETE.
SWU
PA-
-PILLON!
CKK
YOU SICKO!
WE HIRE FROM THE YAKUZA, EH?
THE CHOUNO FAMILY BODYGUARDS ARE NICELY EQUIPPED.
BOOM

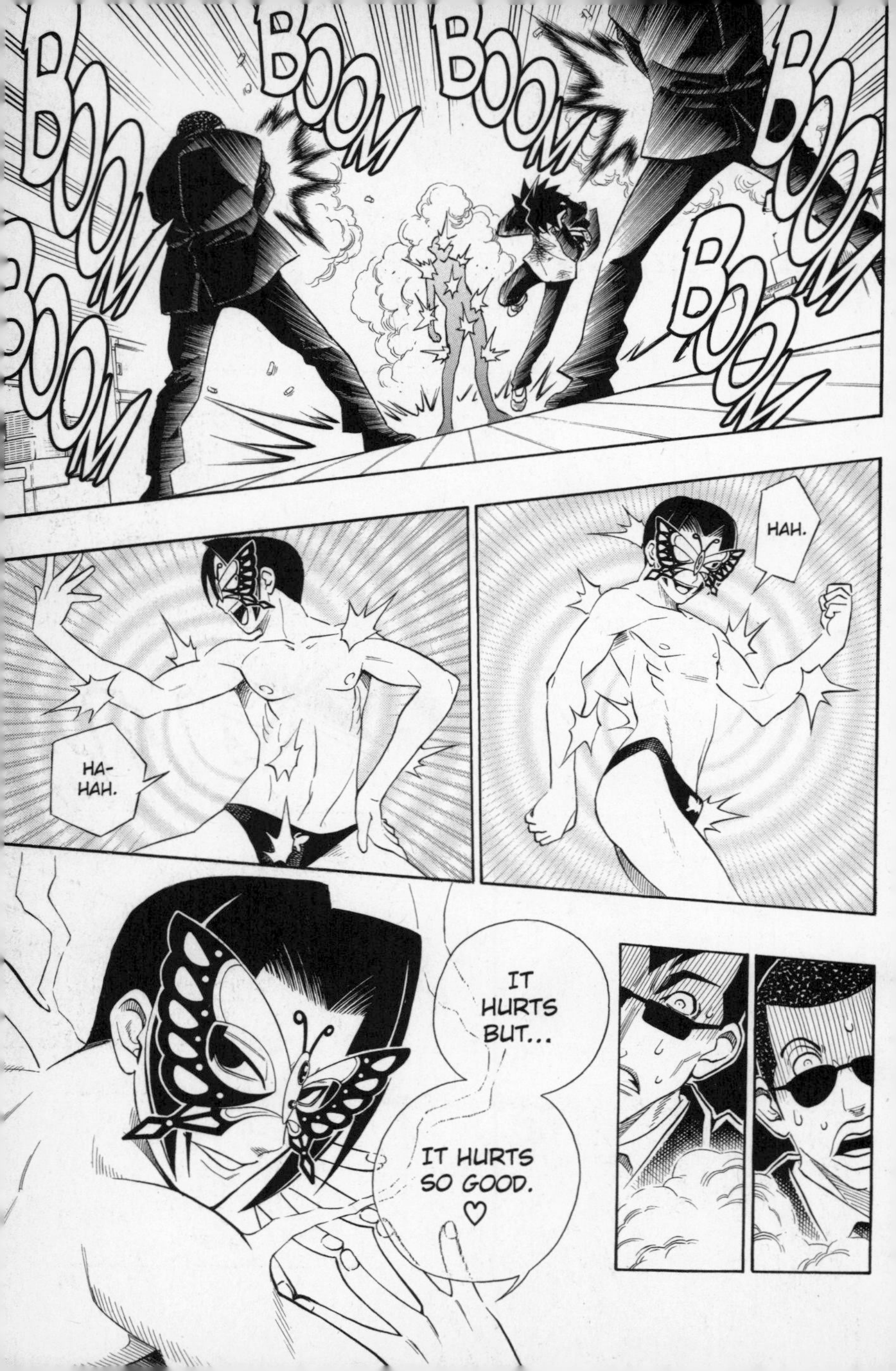
BOOM
BOOM
BOOM
BOOM
BOOM
BOOM
HAH.
HA-HAH.
IT HURTS BUT...
IT HURTS SO GOOD. ♡

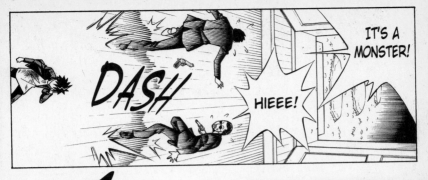

IT'S A
MONSTER!

DASH

HIEEE!

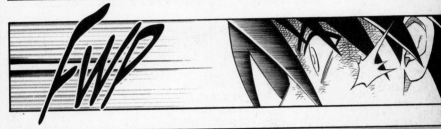

FWP

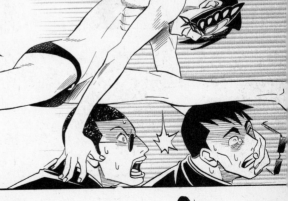

I'M NOT
A MONSTER.
I'M A SUPER
HUMAN.

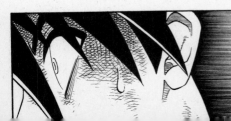

GYAAAAAA

VSHH

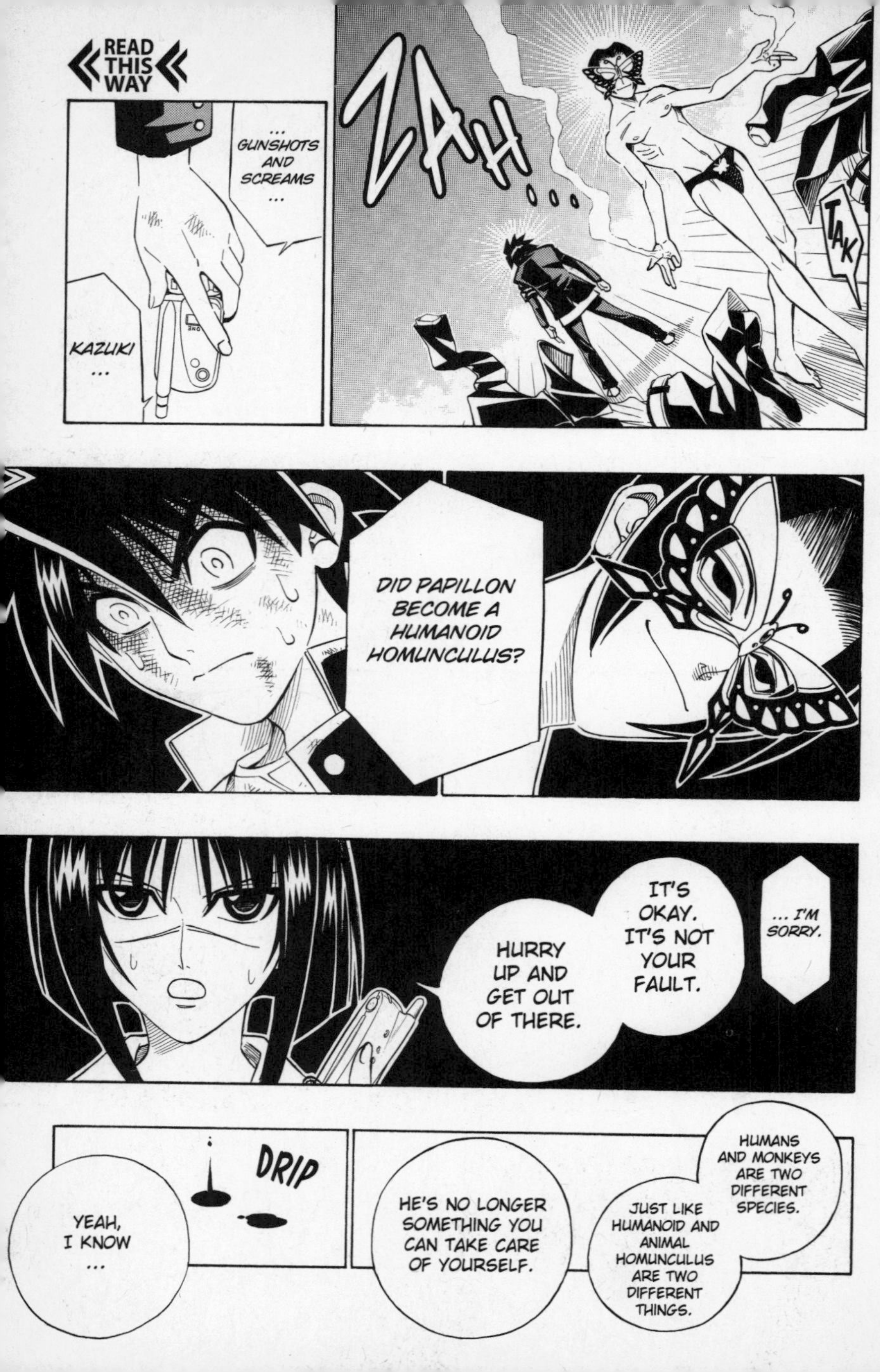
READ THIS WAY
ZAH...
TAK
... GUNSHOTS AND SCREAMS ...
KAZUKI ...
DID PAPILLON BECOME A HUMANOID HOMUNCULUS?
... I'M SORRY.
IT'S OKAY. IT'S NOT YOUR FAULT.
HURRY UP AND GET OUT OF THERE.
HUMANS AND MONKEYS ARE TWO DIFFERENT SPECIES.
JUST LIKE HUMANOID AND ANIMAL HOMUNCULUS ARE TWO DIFFERENT THINGS.
HE'S NO LONGER SOMETHING YOU CAN TAKE CARE OF YOURSELF.
DRIP
YEAH, I KNOW ...

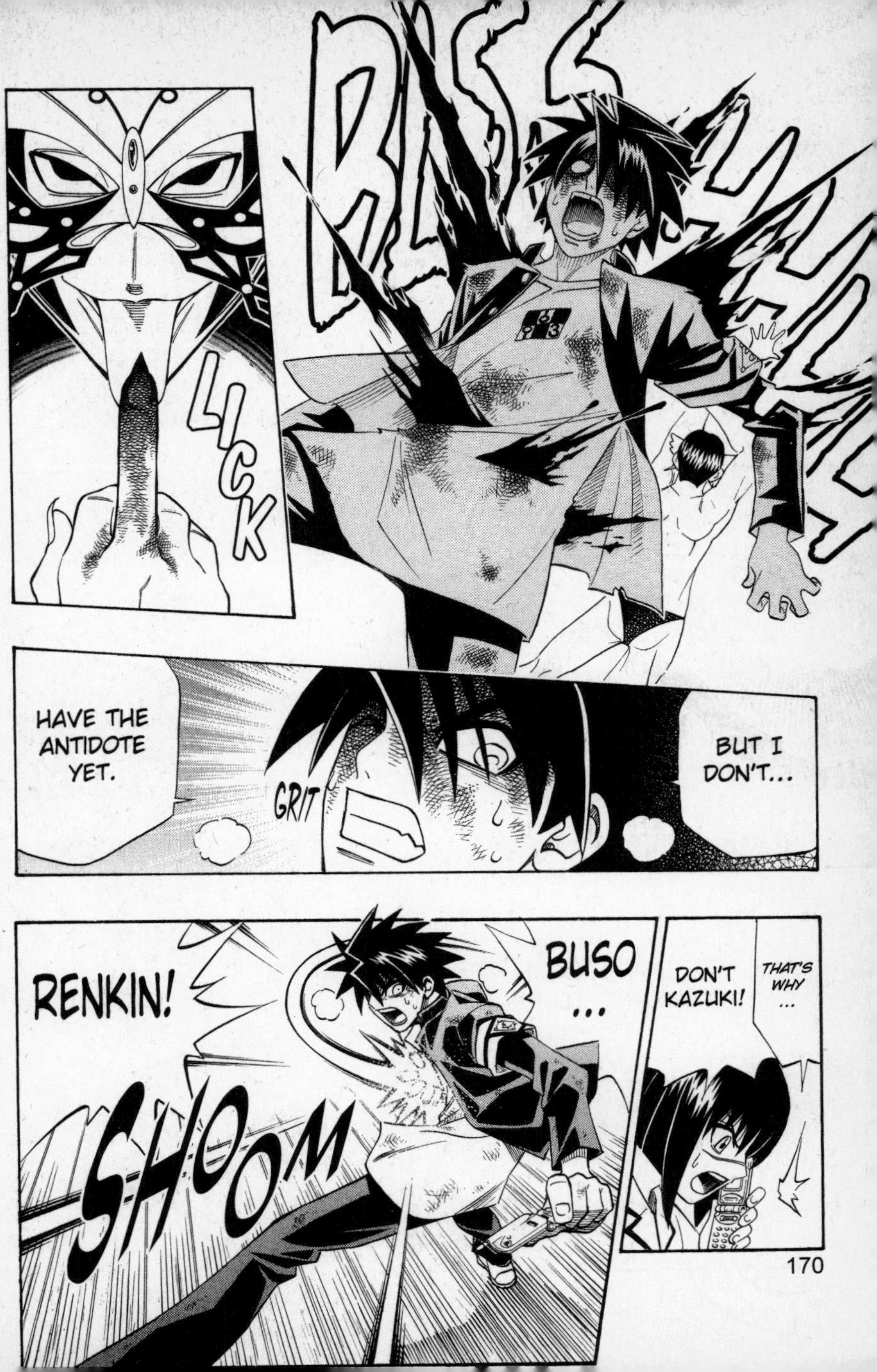
LICK
BUT I DON'T...
GRIT
HAVE THE ANTIDOTE YET.
THAT'S WHY ...
DON'T KAZUKI!
BUSO ...
RENKIN!
SHOOM

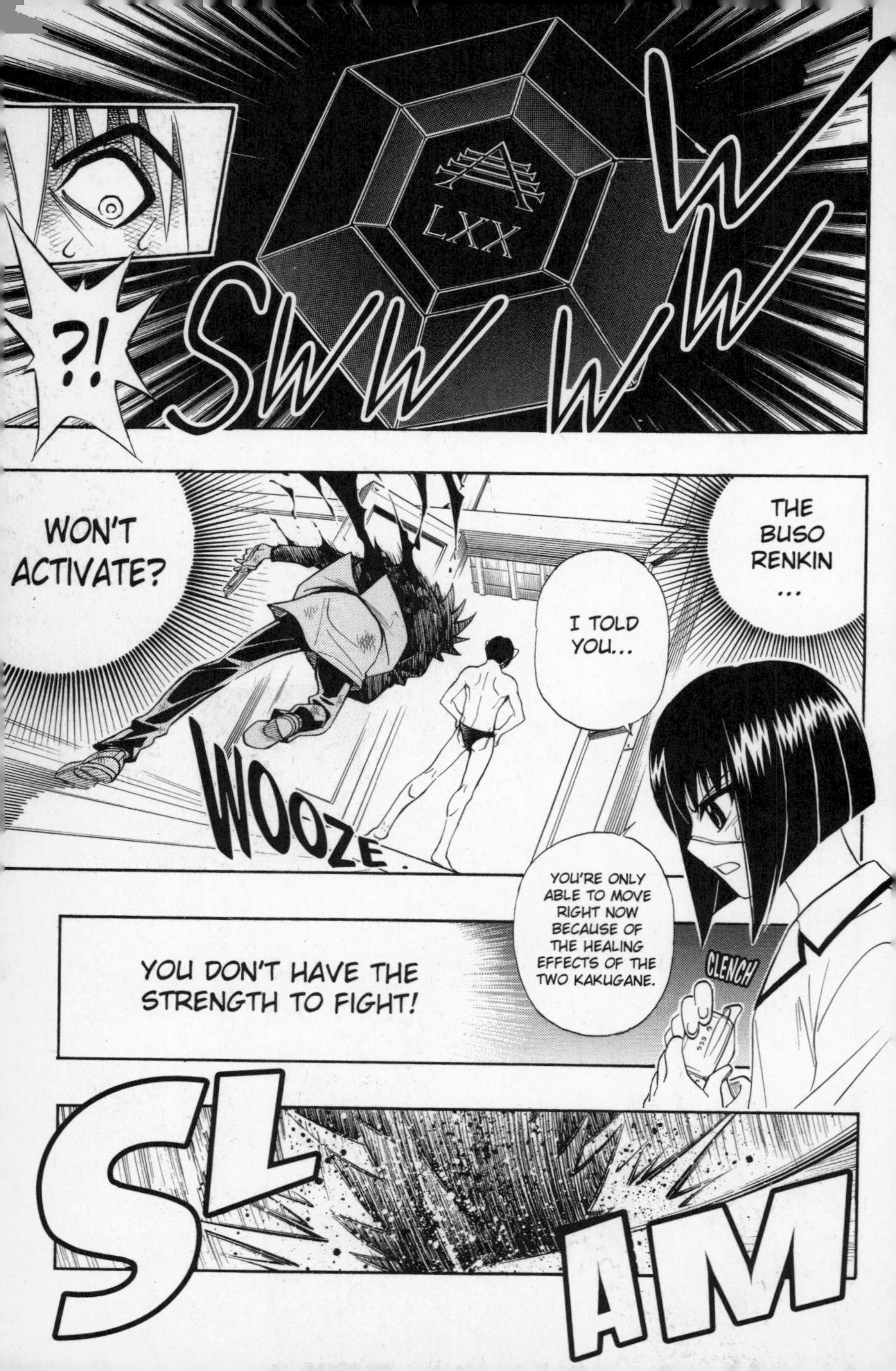

SWWWWW
?!
THE BUSO RENKIN ...
I TOLD YOU...
WON'T ACTIVATE?
WOOZE
YOU'RE ONLY ABLE TO MOVE RIGHT NOW BECAUSE OF THE HEALING EFFECTS OF THE TWO KAKUGANE.
CLENCH
YOU DON'T HAVE THE STRENGTH TO FIGHT!
SLAM

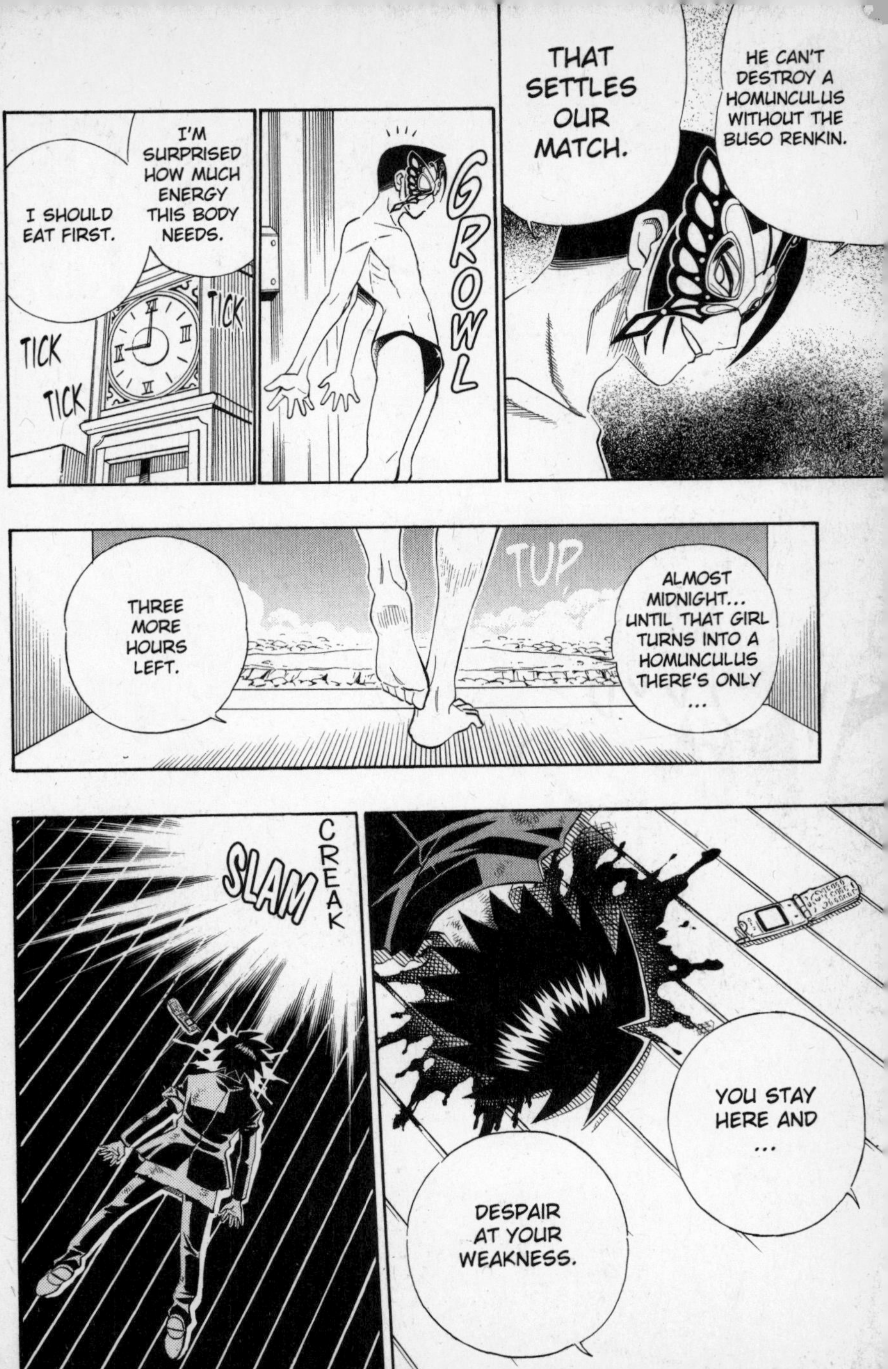
HE CAN'T DESTROY A HOMUNCULUS WITHOUT THE BUSO RENKIN.
THAT SETTLES OUR MATCH.
GROWL
I'M SURPRISED HOW MUCH ENERGY THIS BODY NEEDS.
I SHOULD EAT FIRST.
TICK
TICK
TICK
TUP
ALMOST MIDNIGHT... UNTIL THAT GIRL TURNS INTO A HOMUNCULUS THERE'S ONLY ...
THREE MORE HOURS LEFT.
YOU STAY HERE AND ...
DESPAIR AT YOUR WEAKNESS.
CREAK
SLAM

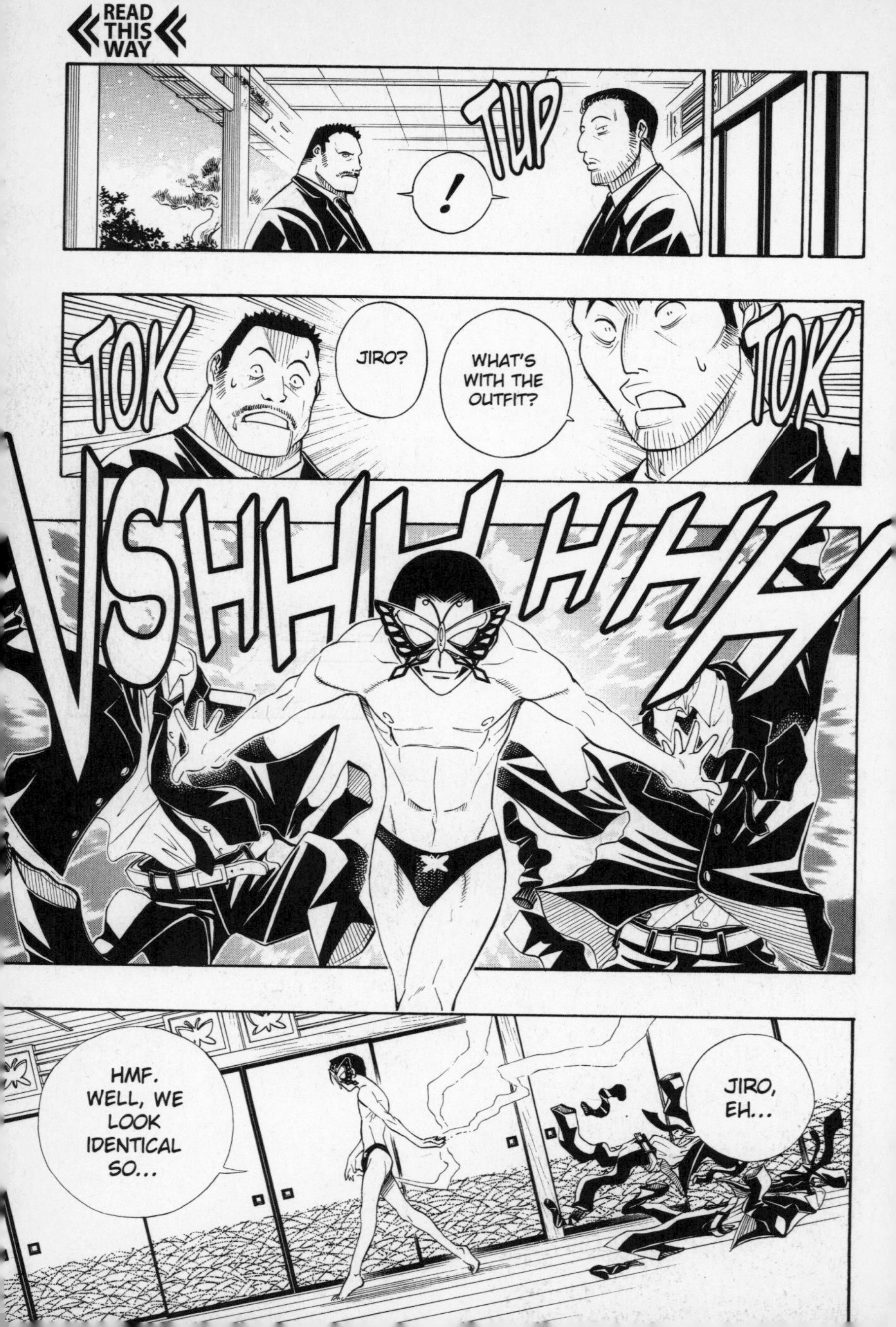
READ THIS WAY
TUP
!
TOK
WHAT'S WITH THE OUTFIT?
JIRO?
TOK
VSHHHHHH
JIRO, EH...
HMF. WELL, WE LOOK IDENTICAL SO...

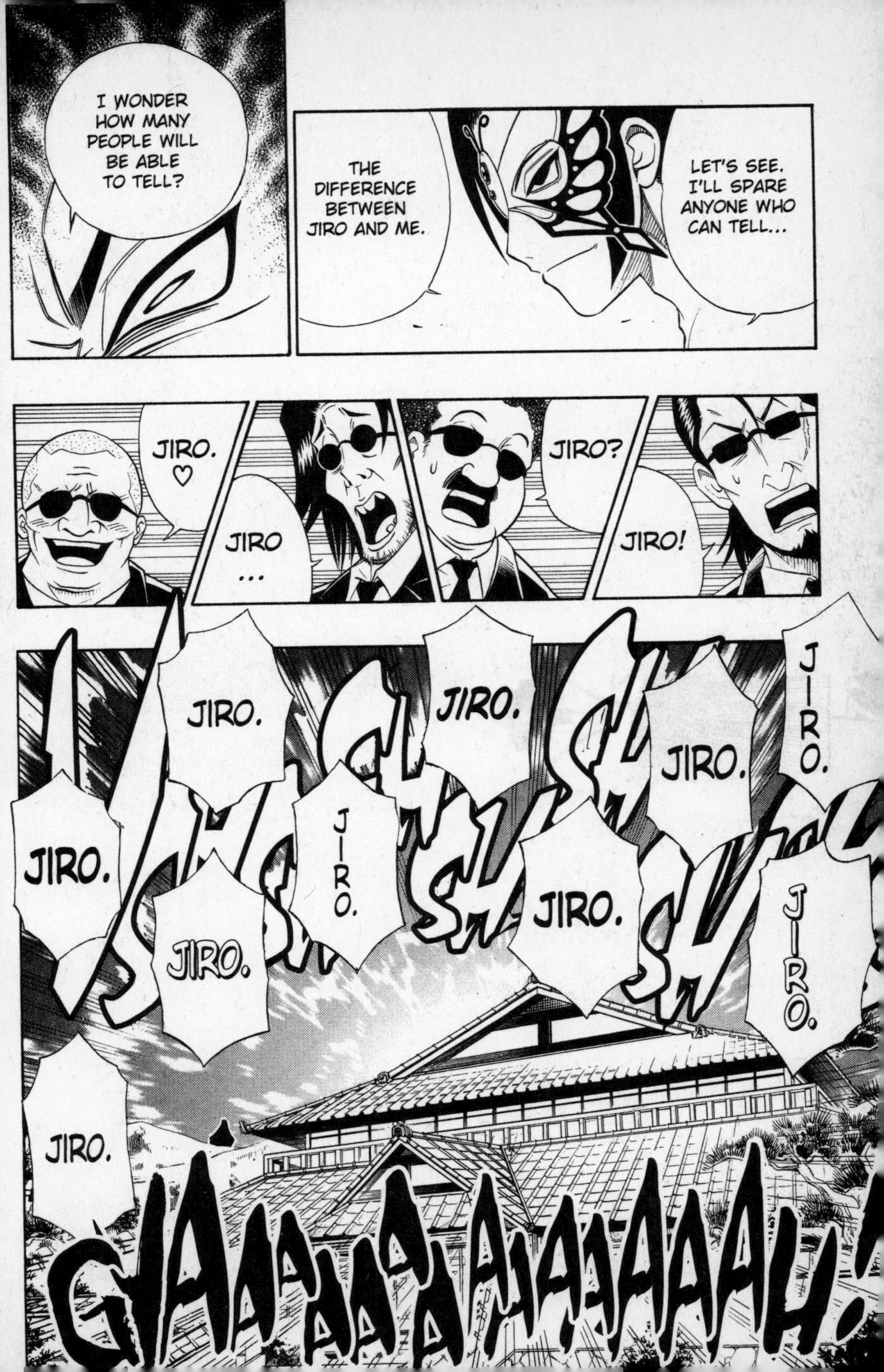
LET'S SEE. I'LL SPARE ANYONE WHO CAN TELL...
THE DIFFERENCE BETWEEN JIRO AND ME.
I WONDER HOW MANY PEOPLE WILL BE ABLE TO TELL?
JIRO!
JIRO?
JIRO ...
JIRO. ♥
JIRO.
JIRO.
JIRO.
JIRO.
JIRO.
JIRO.
JIRO.
JIRO.
JIRO.
JIRO.
GYAAAAAAAAAAAAH!

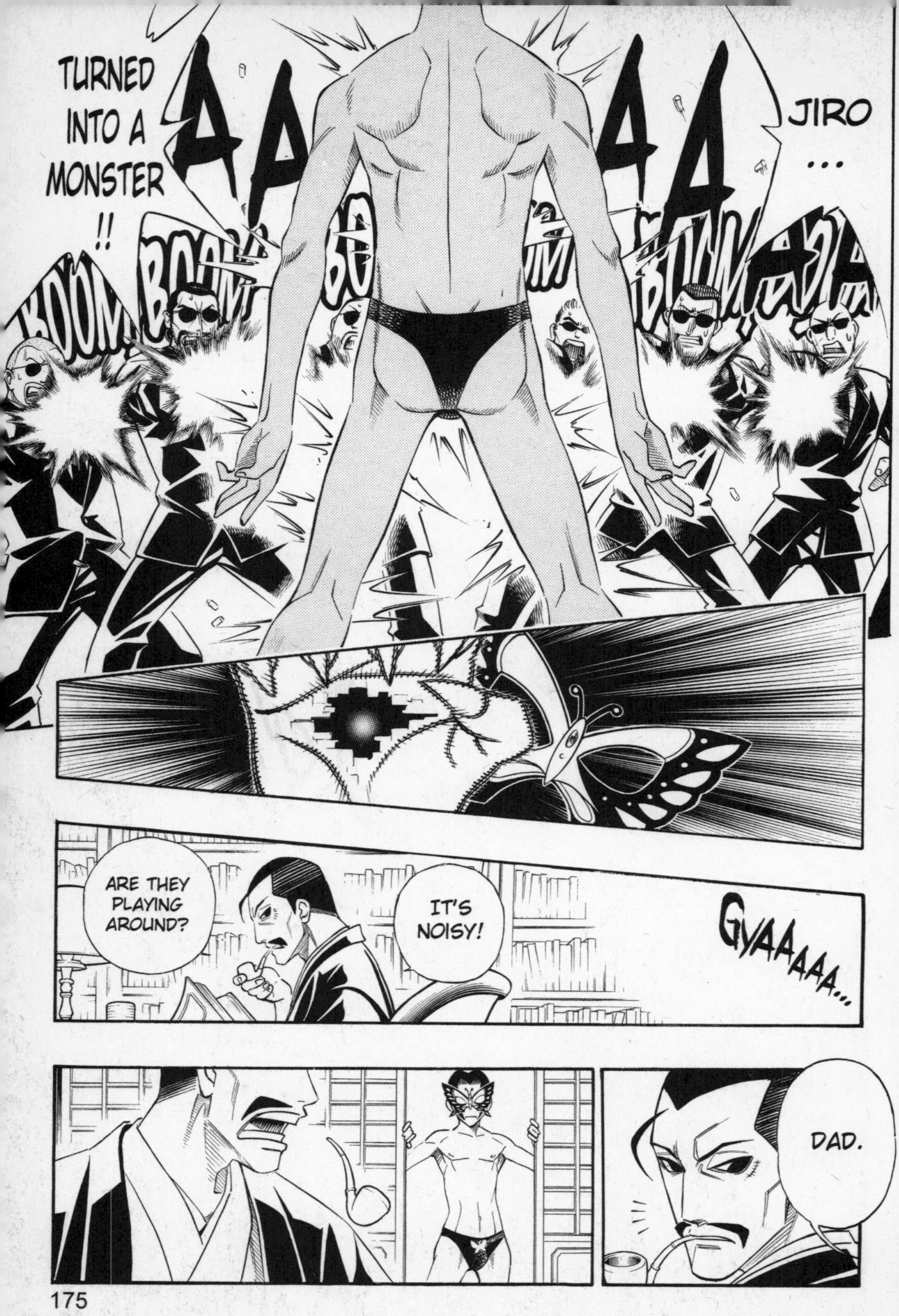

JIRO ...
TURNED INTO A MONSTER !!
GYAAAAAA...
IT'S NOISY!
ARE THEY PLAYING AROUND?
DAD.

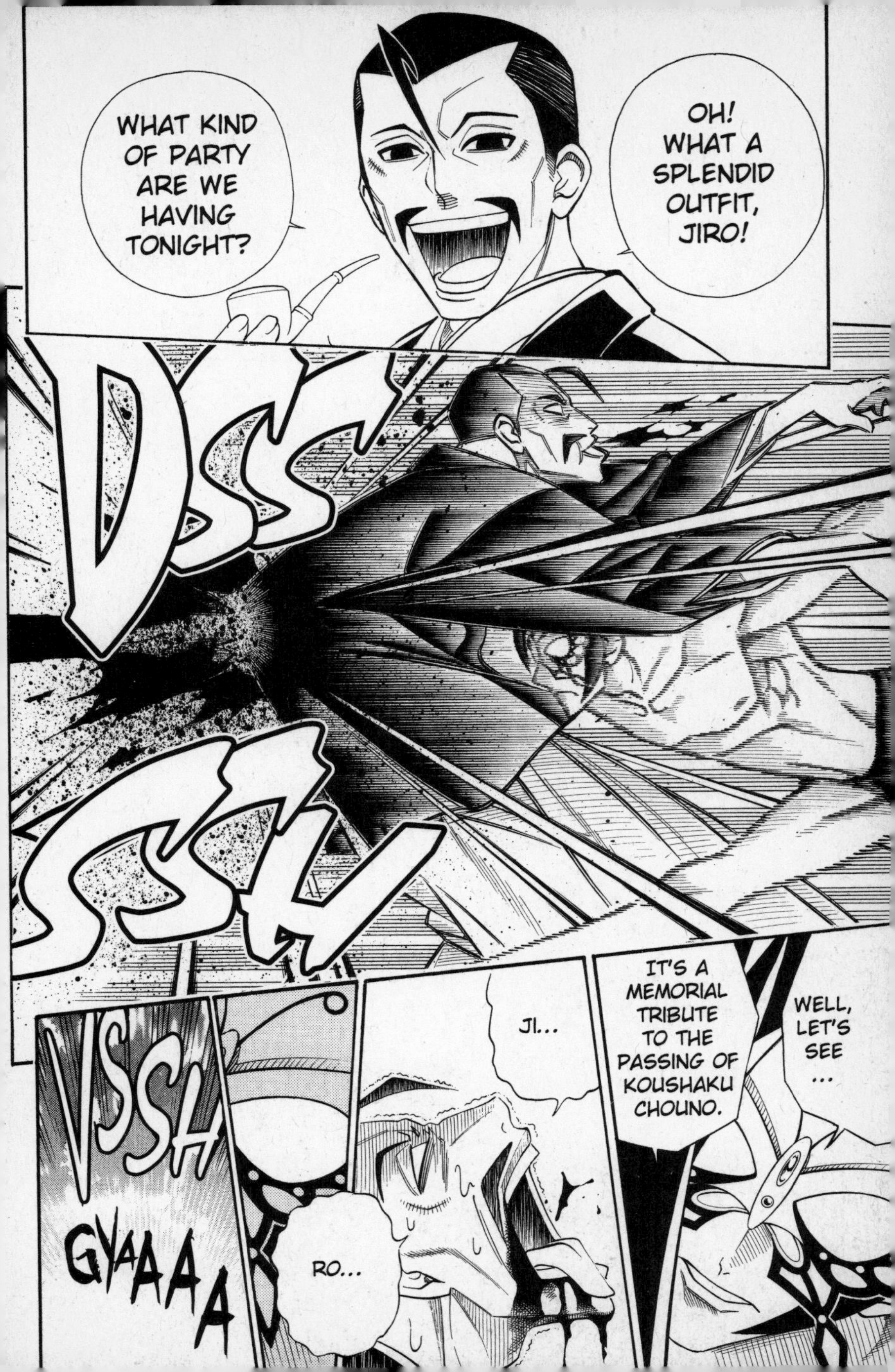
OH! WHAT A SPLENDID OUTFIT, JIRO!
WHAT KIND OF PARTY ARE WE HAVING TONIGHT?
DSS
SSH
WELL, LET'S SEE ...
IT'S A MEMORIAL TRIBUTE TO THE PASSING OF KOUSHAKU CHOUNO.
JI...
RO...
VSSH
GYAAAAA

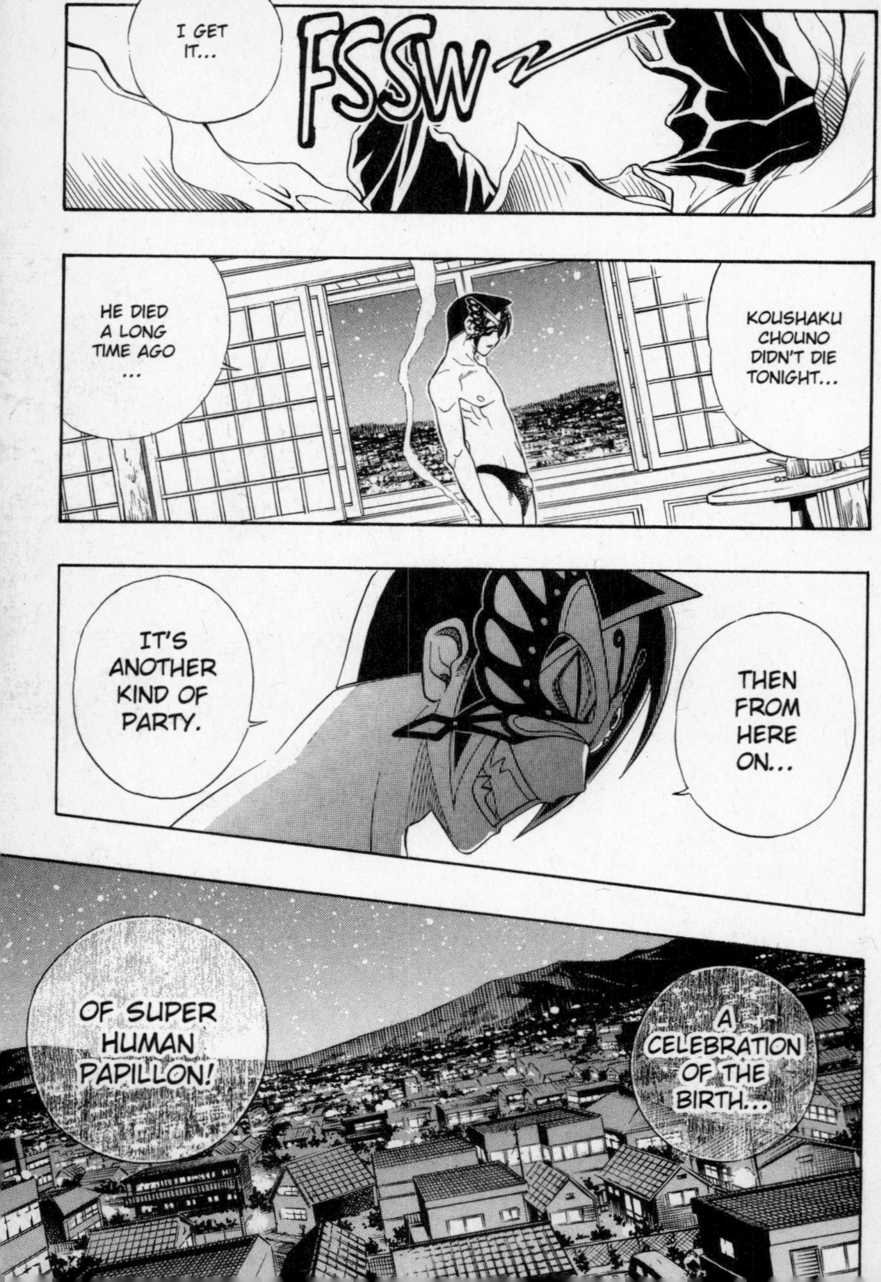
FSSW
I GET IT...
KOUSHAKU CHOUNO DIDN'T DIE TONIGHT...
HE DIED A LONG TIME AGO...
THEN FROM HERE ON...
IT'S ANOTHER KIND OF PARTY.
A CELEBRATION OF THE BIRTH...
OF SUPER HUMAN PAPILLON!

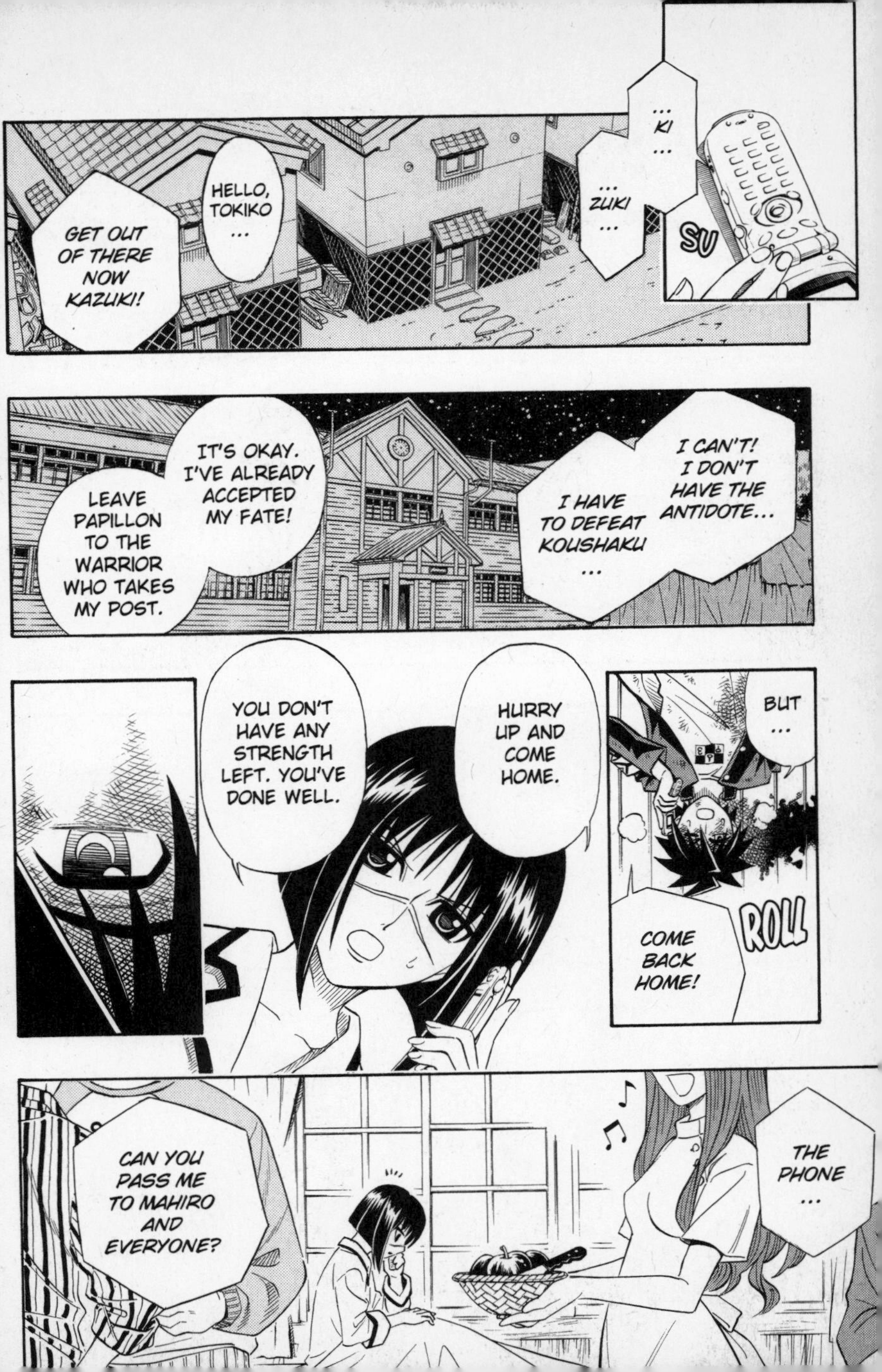

...KI...
...ZUKI...
SU
HELLO, TOKIKO...
GET OUT OF THERE NOW KAZUKI!
I CAN'T! I DON'T HAVE THE ANTIDOTE...
I HAVE TO DEFEAT KOUSHAKU...
IT'S OKAY. I'VE ALREADY ACCEPTED MY FATE!
LEAVE PAPILLON TO THE WARRIOR WHO TAKES MY POST.
BUT...
ROLL
COME BACK HOME!
HURRY UP AND COME HOME.
YOU DON'T HAVE ANY STRENGTH LEFT. YOU'VE DONE WELL.
THE PHONE...
CAN YOU PASS ME TO MAHIRO AND EVERYONE?

READ THIS WAY

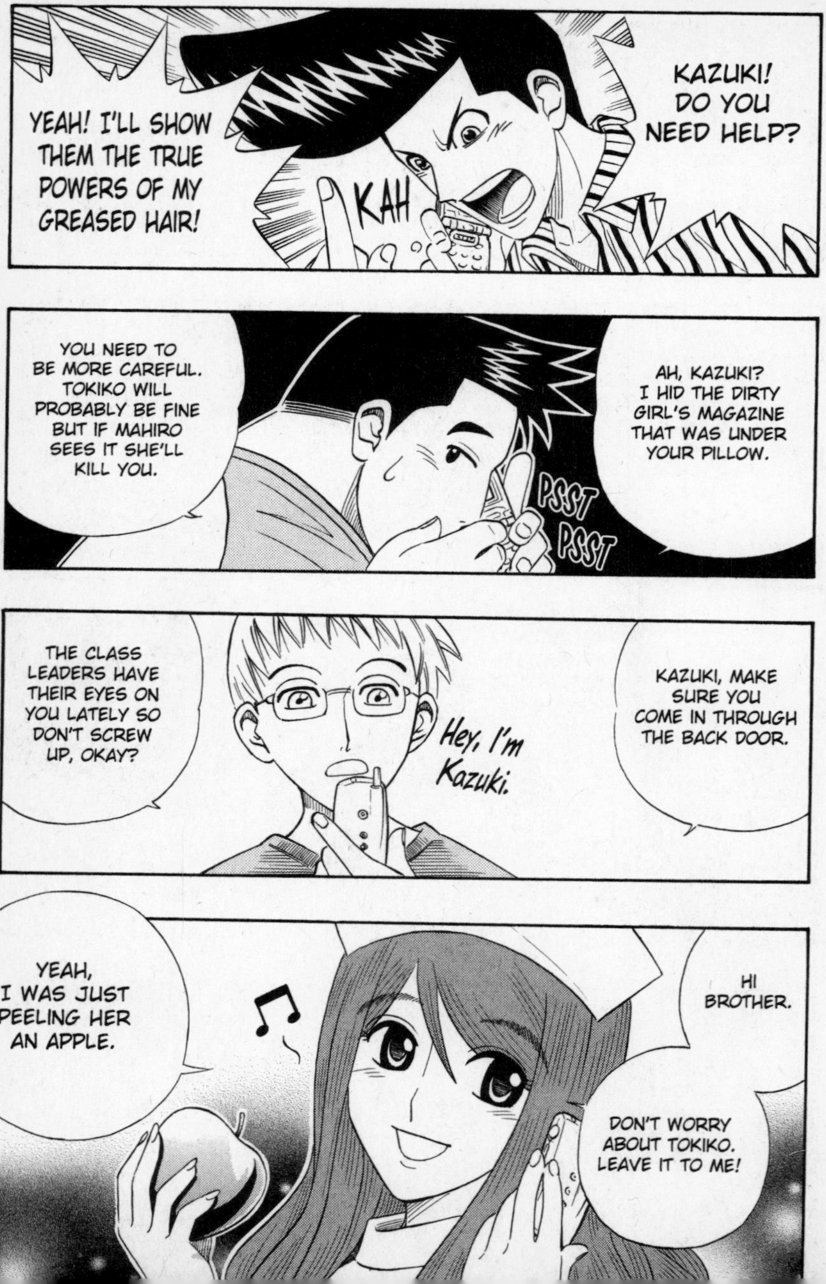
KAZUKI! DO YOU NEED HELP?
KAH
YEAH! I'LL SHOW THEM THE TRUE POWERS OF MY GREASED HAIR!
AH, KAZUKI? I HID THE DIRTY GIRL'S MAGAZINE THAT WAS UNDER YOUR PILLOW.
PSSST PSSST
YOU NEED TO BE MORE CAREFUL. TOKIKO WILL PROBABLY BE FINE BUT IF MAHIRO SEES IT SHE'LL KILL YOU.
KAZUKI, MAKE SURE YOU COME IN THROUGH THE BACK DOOR.
Hey, I'm Kazuki.
THE CLASS LEADERS HAVE THEIR EYES ON YOU LATELY SO DON'T SCREW UP, OKAY?
HI BROTHER.
YEAH, I WAS JUST PEELING HER AN APPLE.
DON'T WORRY ABOUT TOKIKO. LEAVE IT TO ME!

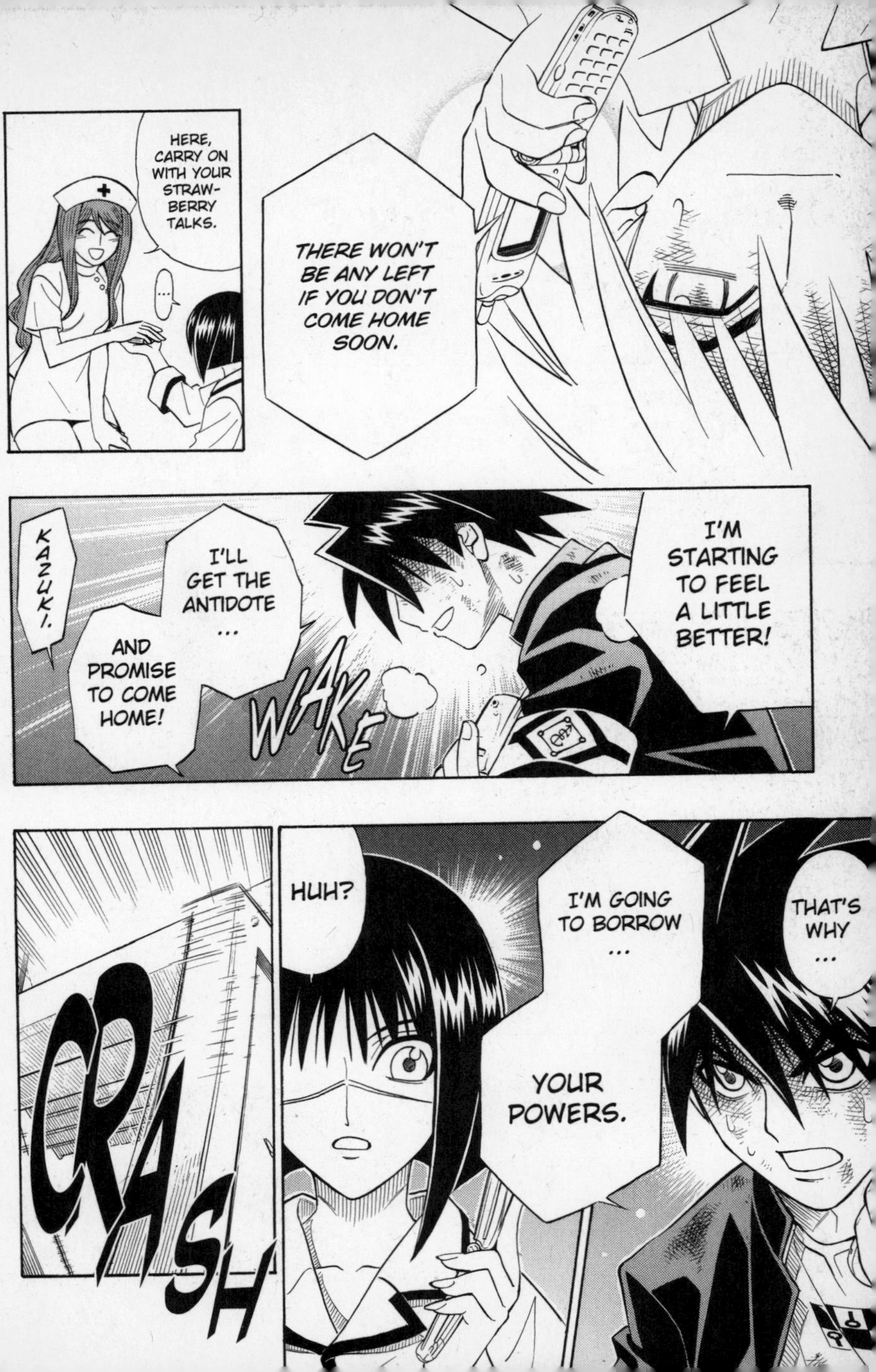
THERE WON'T BE ANY LEFT IF YOU DON'T COME HOME SOON.
HERE, CARRY ON WITH YOUR STRAW-BERRY TALKS.
...
I'M STARTING TO FEEL A LITTLE BETTER!
WAKE
I'LL GET THE ANTIDOTE ...
AND PROMISE TO COME HOME!
KAZUKI.
THAT'S WHY ...
I'M GOING TO BORROW ...
YOUR POWERS.
HUH?
CRASH

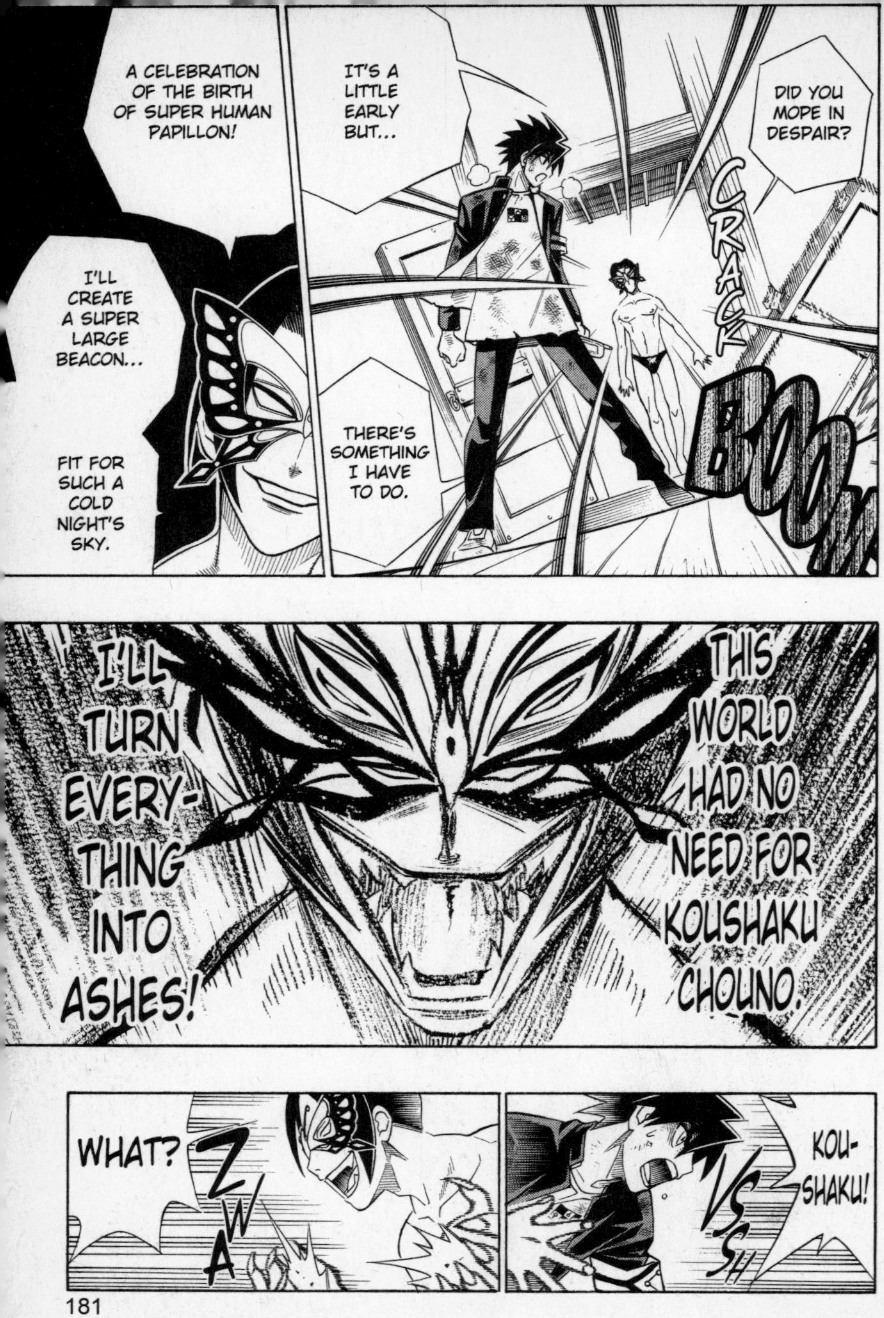
DID YOU MOPE IN DESPAIR?
CRACK
IT'S A LITTLE EARLY BUT...
THERE'S SOMETHING I HAVE TO DO.
A CELEBRATION OF THE BIRTH OF SUPER HUMAN PAPILLON!
I'LL CREATE A SUPER LARGE BEACON...
FIT FOR SUCH A COLD NIGHT'S SKY.
THIS WORLD HAD NO NEED FOR KOUSHAKU CHOUNO.
I'LL TURN EVERY-THING INTO ASHES!
KOU-SHAKU!
VSSH
WHAT?
ZWA

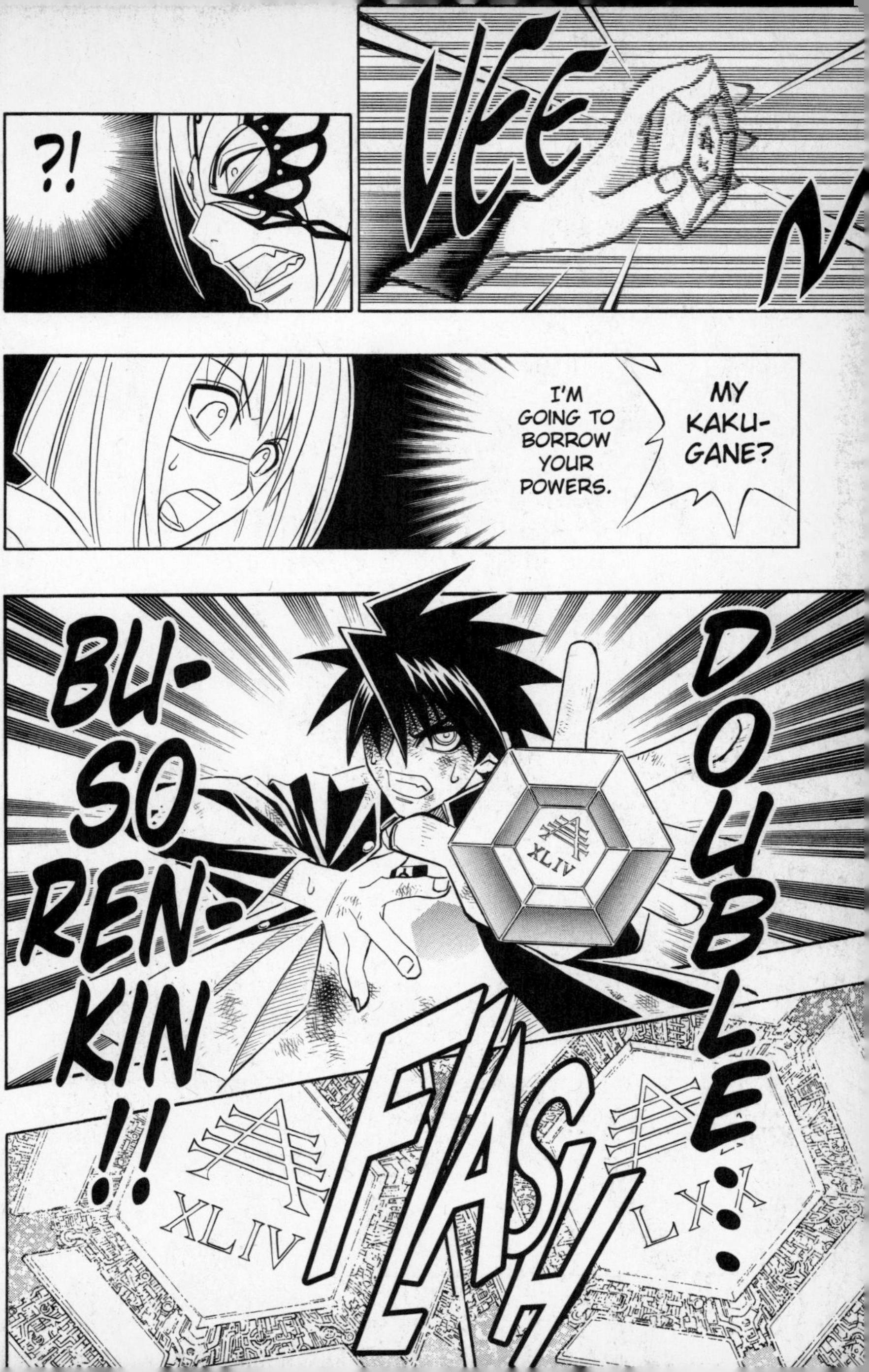
VEEN
?!
MY KAKU-GANE?
I'M GOING TO BORROW YOUR POWERS.
BU-SO REN-KIN!!
DOUBLE...
XLIV
FLASH
XLIV
LXX

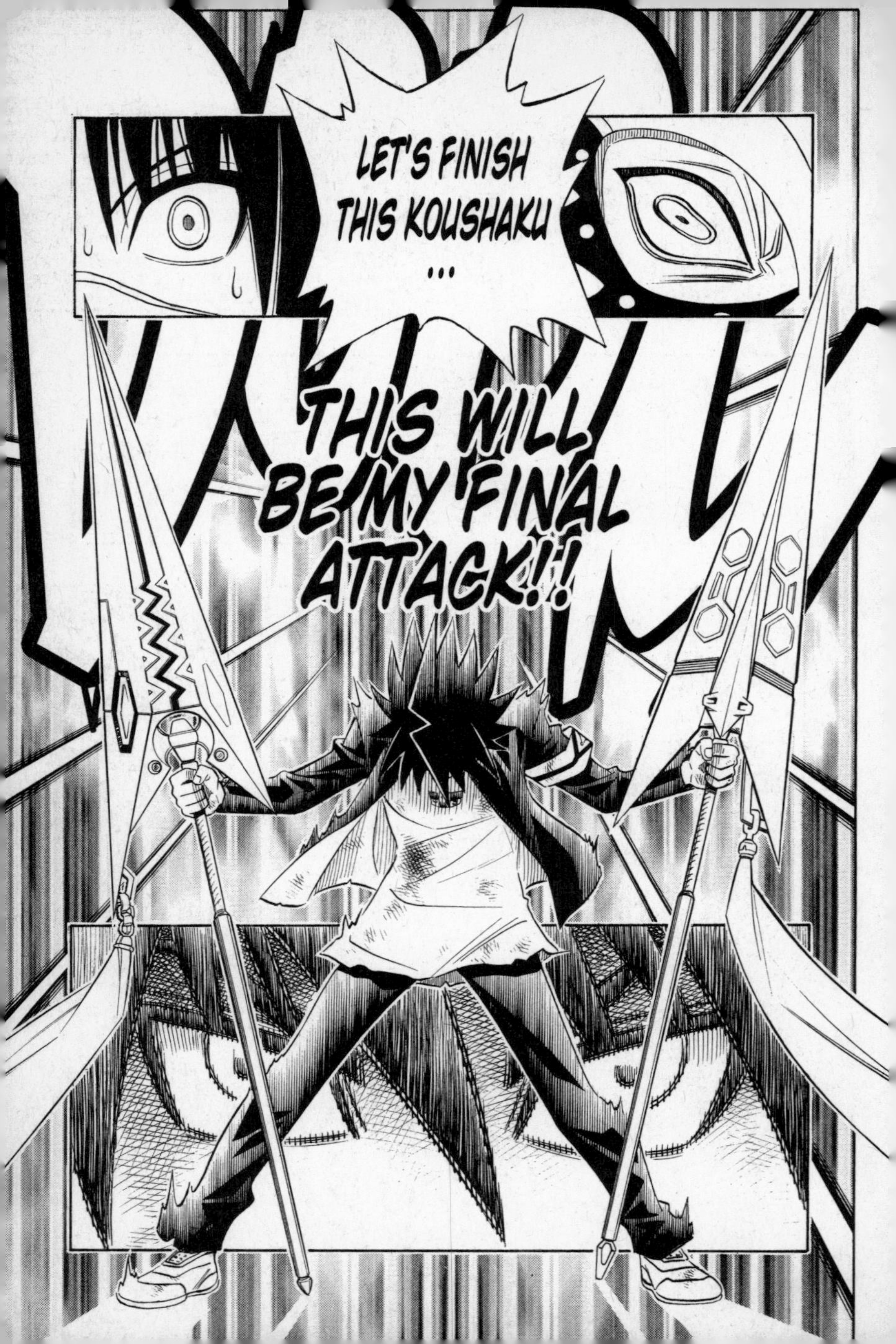
LET'S FINISH THIS KOUSHAKU ...
THIS WILL BE MY FINAL ATTACK!!

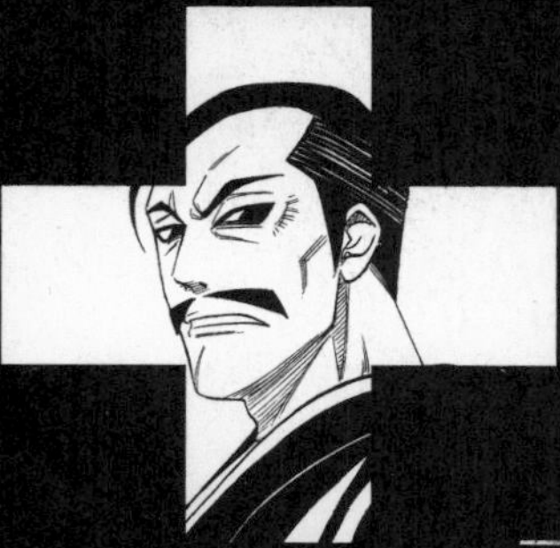

· Koushaku's father. He only sees worth in geniuses and likes to categorize people as either necessary or unnecessary. His love for his sons runs deep but his convictions run deeper.
· He's separated with his wife and is currently in the middle of a divorce.

Author's Notes

· To illustrate where Koushaku got his twisted personality I introduced his family. "A son strives to surpass his father," so I decided he kills his father.
· Koushaku's weird fashion taste runs in the family.

Shishaku Chouno

Character File No.13

The People of the Chouno Family

· Koushaku's younger brother. He is talented and gifted but as the second son he is named Jiro. His brother is his biggest enemy.

Author's Notes

· To emphasize that Jiro does not get acknowledged by anyone, I made him look exactly the same as Koushaku. It also symbolizes Jiro as the mirror image of Koushaku. I had a lot of fun drawing his twisted smile.
· It wasn't his fault. I felt sorry for him. (Praying)

Jiro Chouno

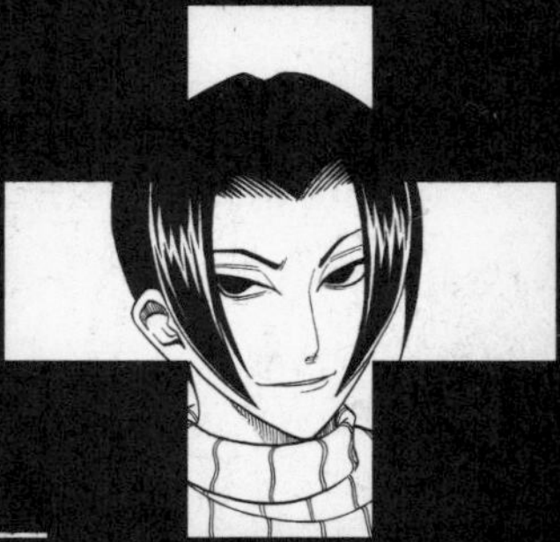

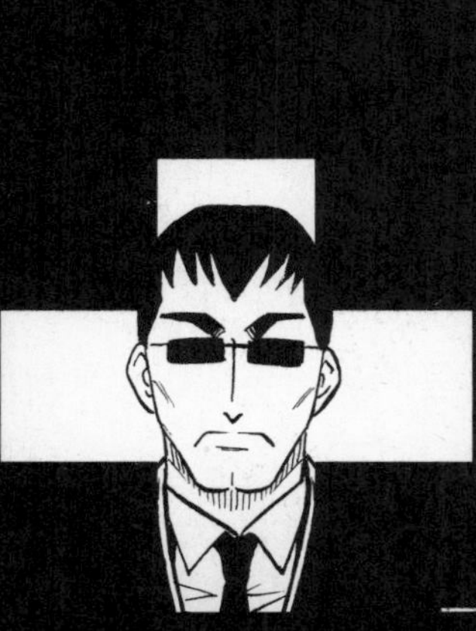

· A Yakuza group on good terms with the Chouno family sent them as bodyguards. They oversee the security of the estate and "fix" any kind of problems that may arise.
· They are pretty strong.
· One of them is gay.

Author's Notes

· If humans were going to get eaten I thought I'd go all out instead of making it seem gruesome so I needed a lot of people. I treated them as throwaway soldiers.
· I thought drawing guys in black suits and sunglasses might be lame but once I started drawing, I realized they were easy to draw and surprisingly I was able to give them a lot of character.
· They are "Men in Black."

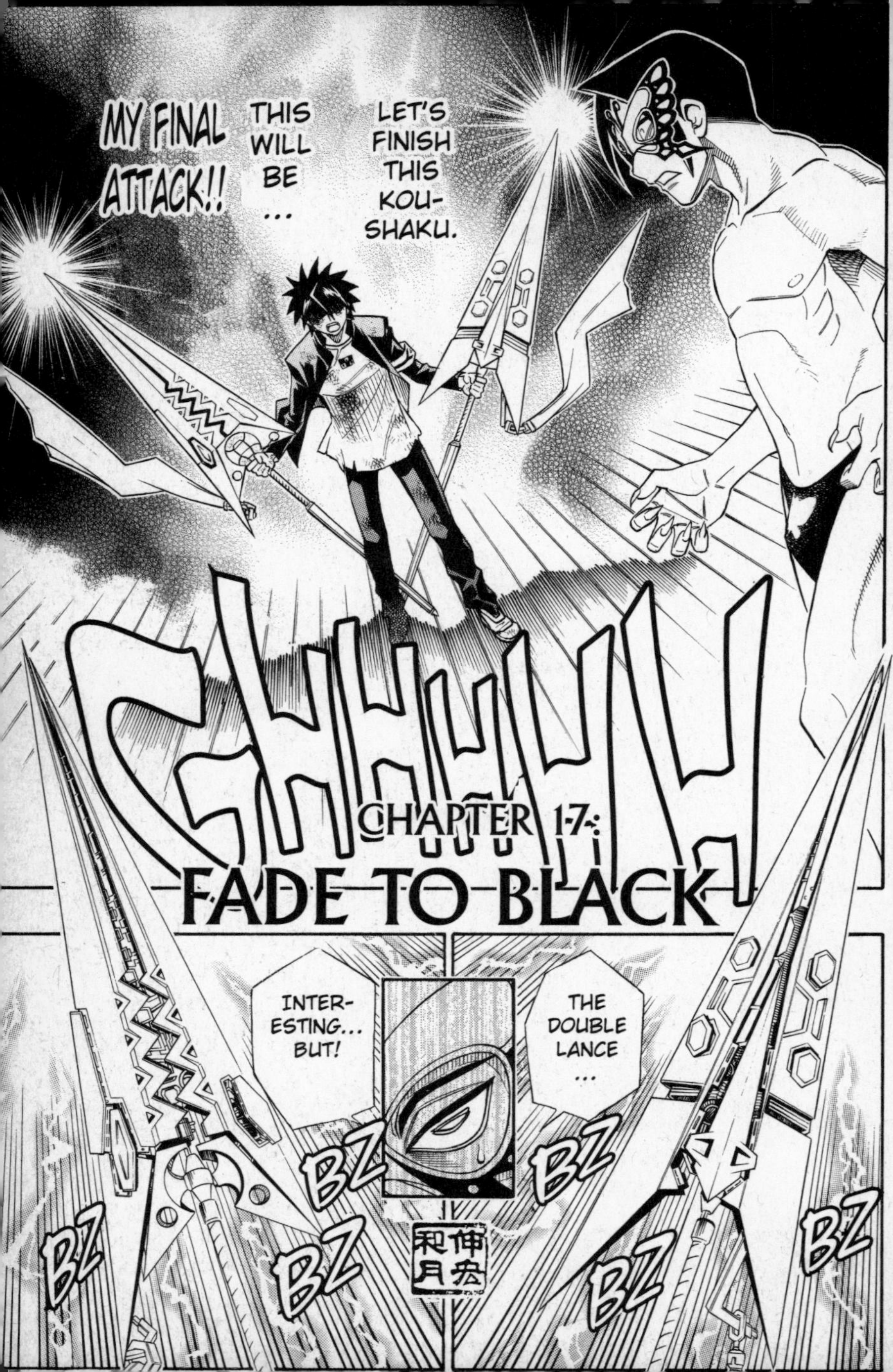
LET'S FINISH THIS KOU-SHAKU.
THIS WILL BE ...
MY FINAL ATTACK!!
CHAPTER 17:
FADE TO BLACK
THE DOUBLE LANCE ...
INTER-ESTING... BUT!
BZ
BZ
BZ
BZ
BZ
BZ
BZ
BZ
伸宏
和月

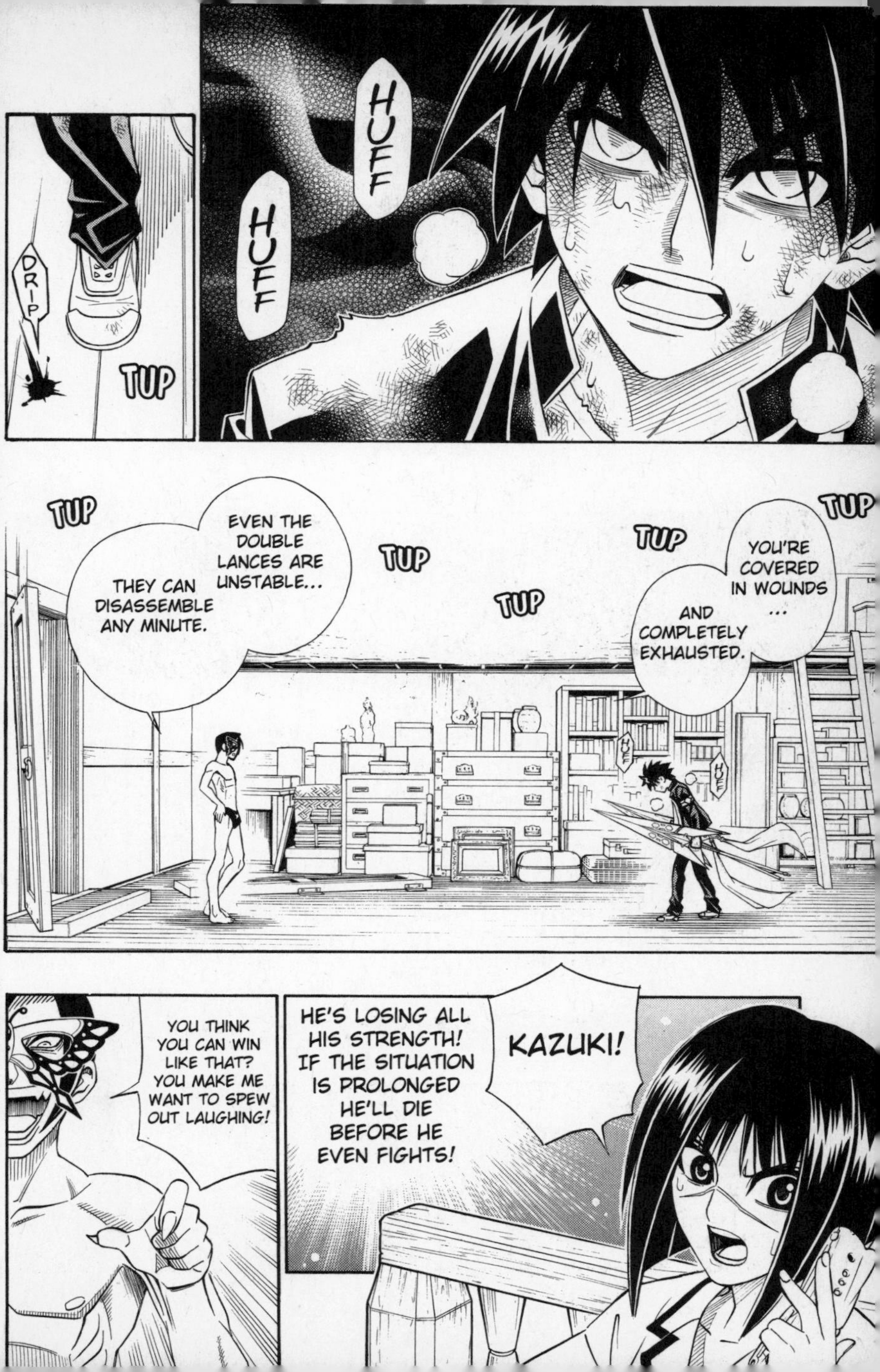
HUFF
HUFF
DRIP
TUP
TUP
YOU'RE COVERED IN WOUNDS...
AND COMPLETELY EXHAUSTED.
TUP
HUFF
HUFF
TUP
TUP
EVEN THE DOUBLE LANCES ARE UNSTABLE...
THEY CAN DISASSEMBLE ANY MINUTE.
TUP
KAZUKI!
HE'S LOSING ALL HIS STRENGTH! IF THE SITUATION IS PROLONGED HE'LL DIE BEFORE HE EVEN FIGHTS!
YOU THINK YOU CAN WIN LIKE THAT? YOU MAKE ME WANT TO SPEW OUT LAUGHING!

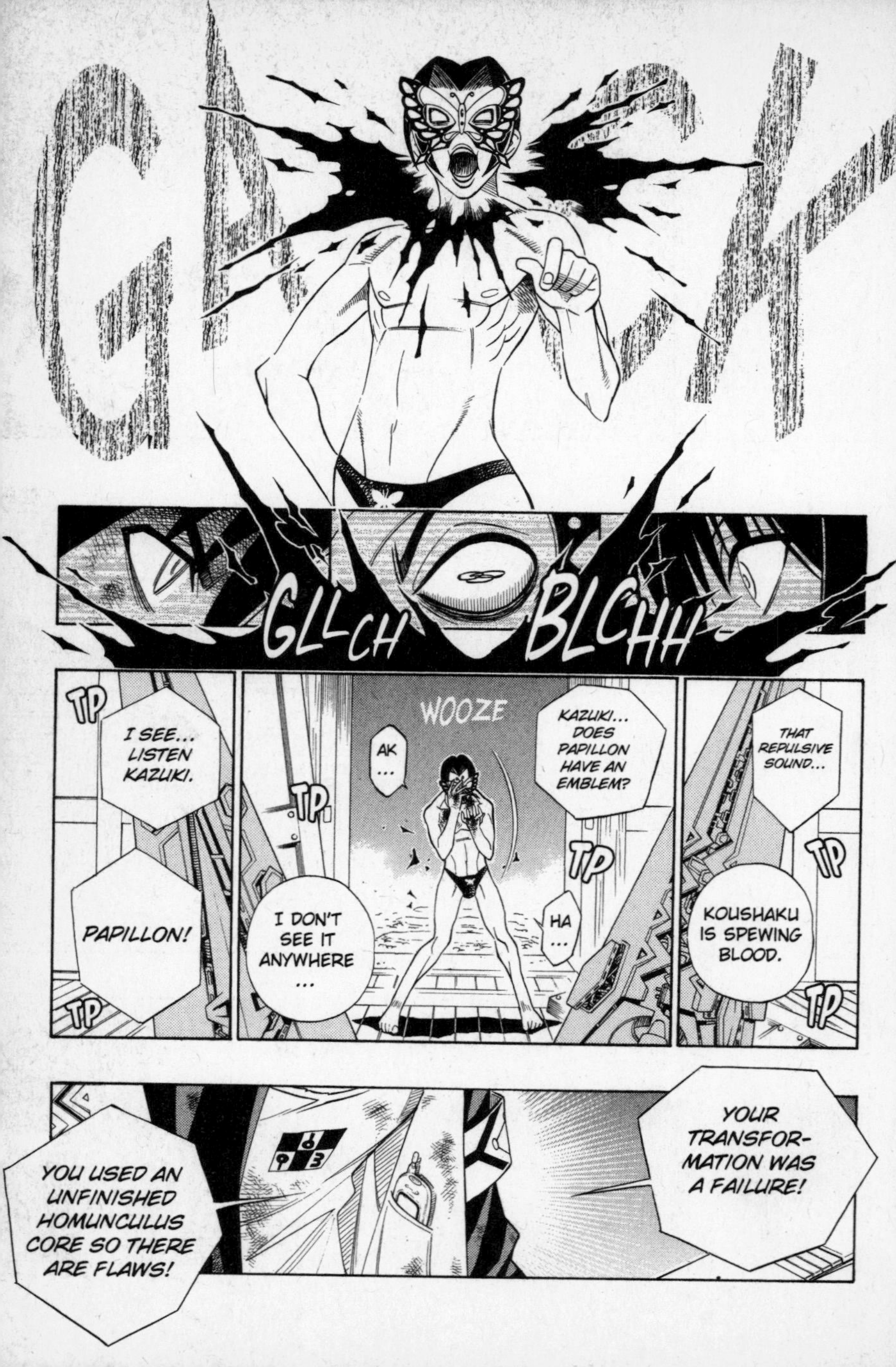
BLCHH
GLLCH
THAT REPULSIVE SOUND...
TP
KOUSHAKU IS SPEWING BLOOD.
TP
KAZUKI... DOES PAPILLON HAVE AN EMBLEM?
WOOZE
TP
HA ...
AK ...
TP
I DON'T SEE IT ANYWHERE ...
TP
I SEE... LISTEN KAZUKI.
PAPILLON!
TP
YOUR TRANSFOR-MATION WAS A FAILURE!
YOU USED AN UNFINISHED HOMUNCULUS CORE SO THERE ARE FLAWS!

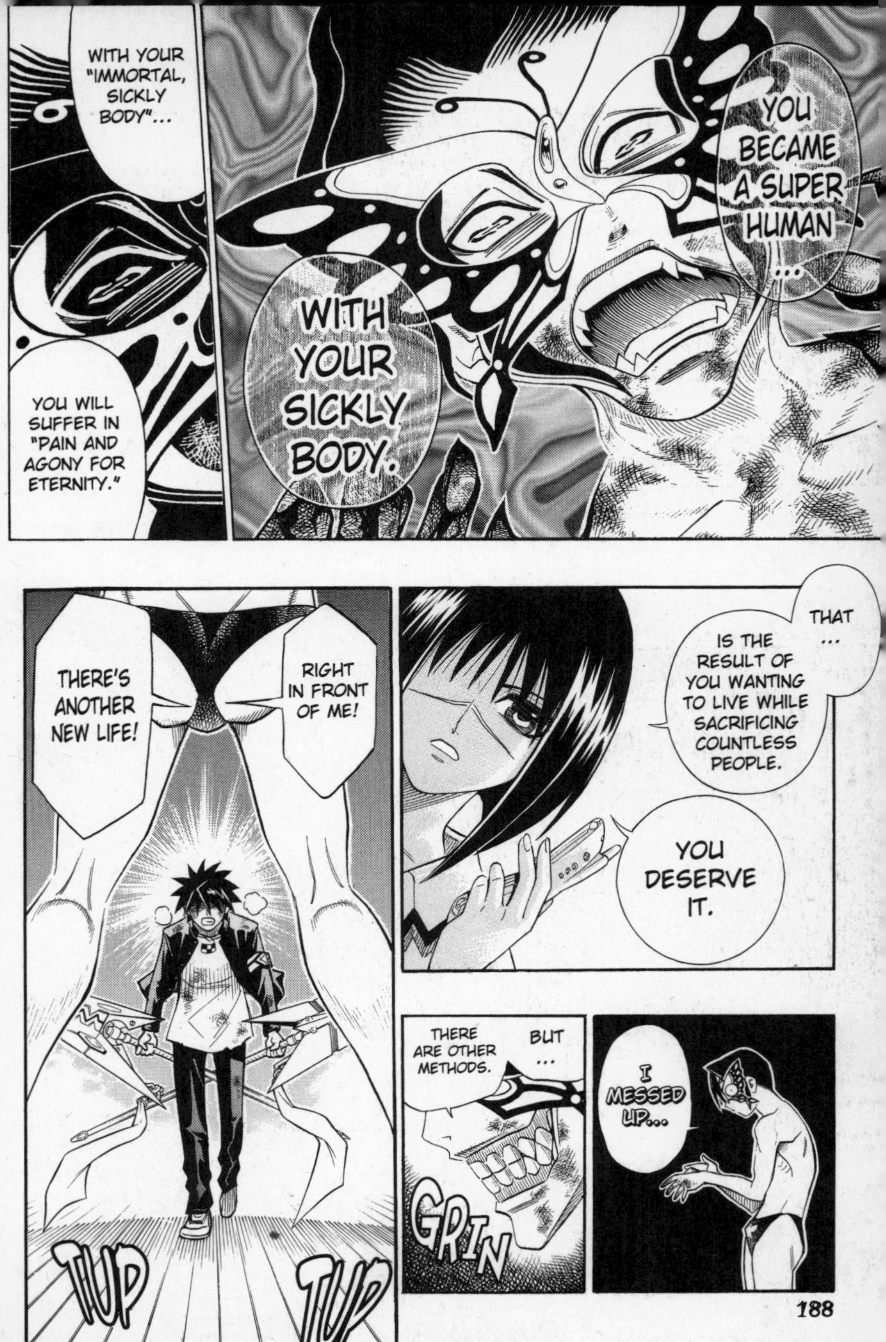
YOU BECAME A SUPER HUMAN...
WITH YOUR SICKLY BODY.
WITH YOUR "IMMORTAL, SICKLY BODY"...
YOU WILL SUFFER IN "PAIN AND AGONY FOR ETERNITY."
THAT...
IS THE RESULT OF YOU WANTING TO LIVE WHILE SACRIFICING COUNTLESS PEOPLE.
YOU DESERVE IT.
I MESSED UP...
BUT...
THERE ARE OTHER METHODS.
GRIN
RIGHT IN FRONT OF ME!
THERE'S ANOTHER NEW LIFE!
TUP
TUP

READ THIS WAY

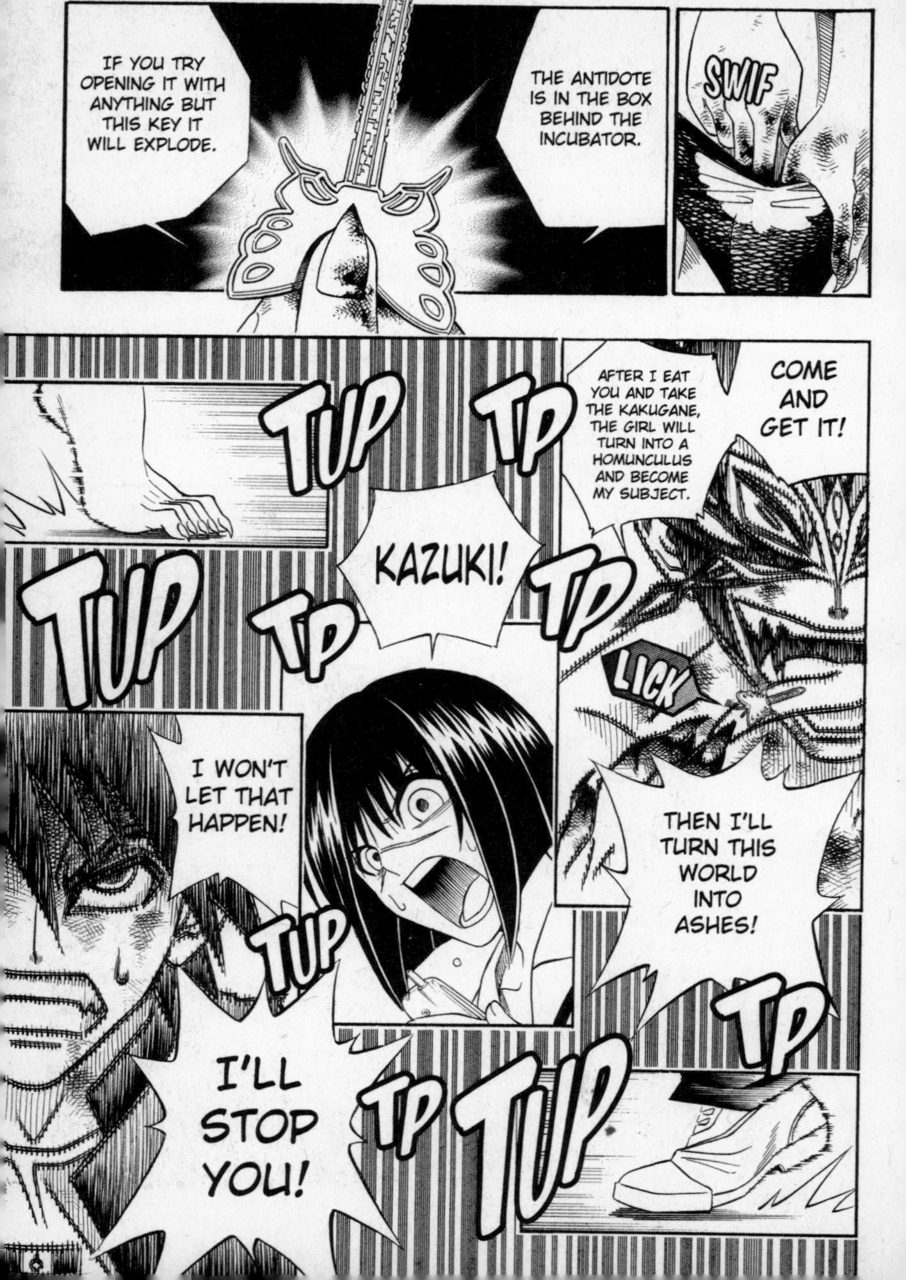
SWIF
THE ANTIDOTE IS IN THE BOX BEHIND THE INCUBATOR.
IF YOU TRY OPENING IT WITH ANYTHING BUT THIS KEY IT WILL EXPLODE.
COME AND GET IT!
AFTER I EAT YOU AND TAKE THE KAKUGANE, THE GIRL WILL TURN INTO A HOMUNCULUS AND BECOME MY SUBJECT.
LICK
THEN I'LL TURN THIS WORLD INTO ASHES!
TP
TUP
KAZUKI!
TP
TP
TUP
TUP
I WON'T LET THAT HAPPEN!
TP
TUP
TP
I'LL STOP YOU!

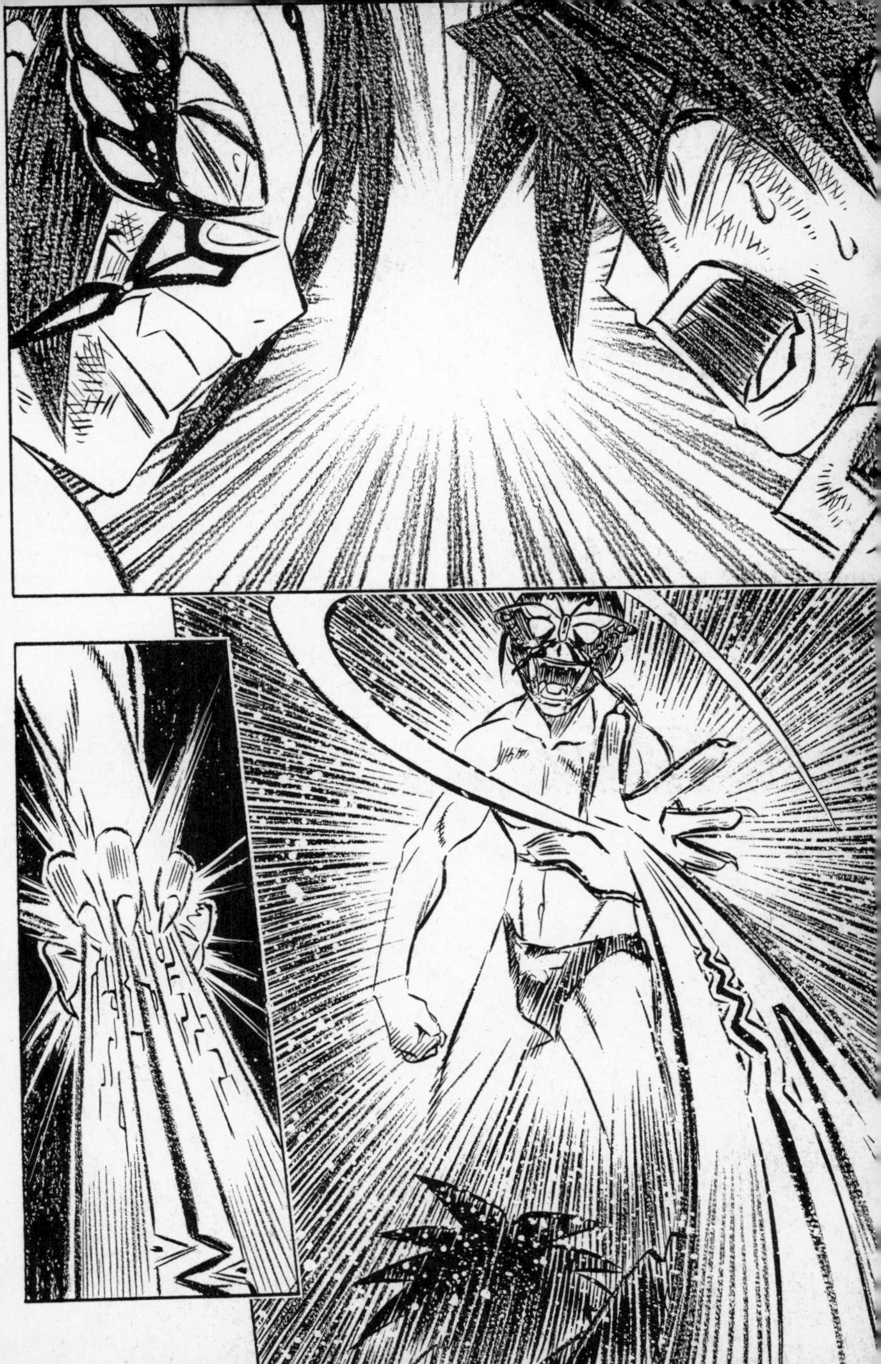

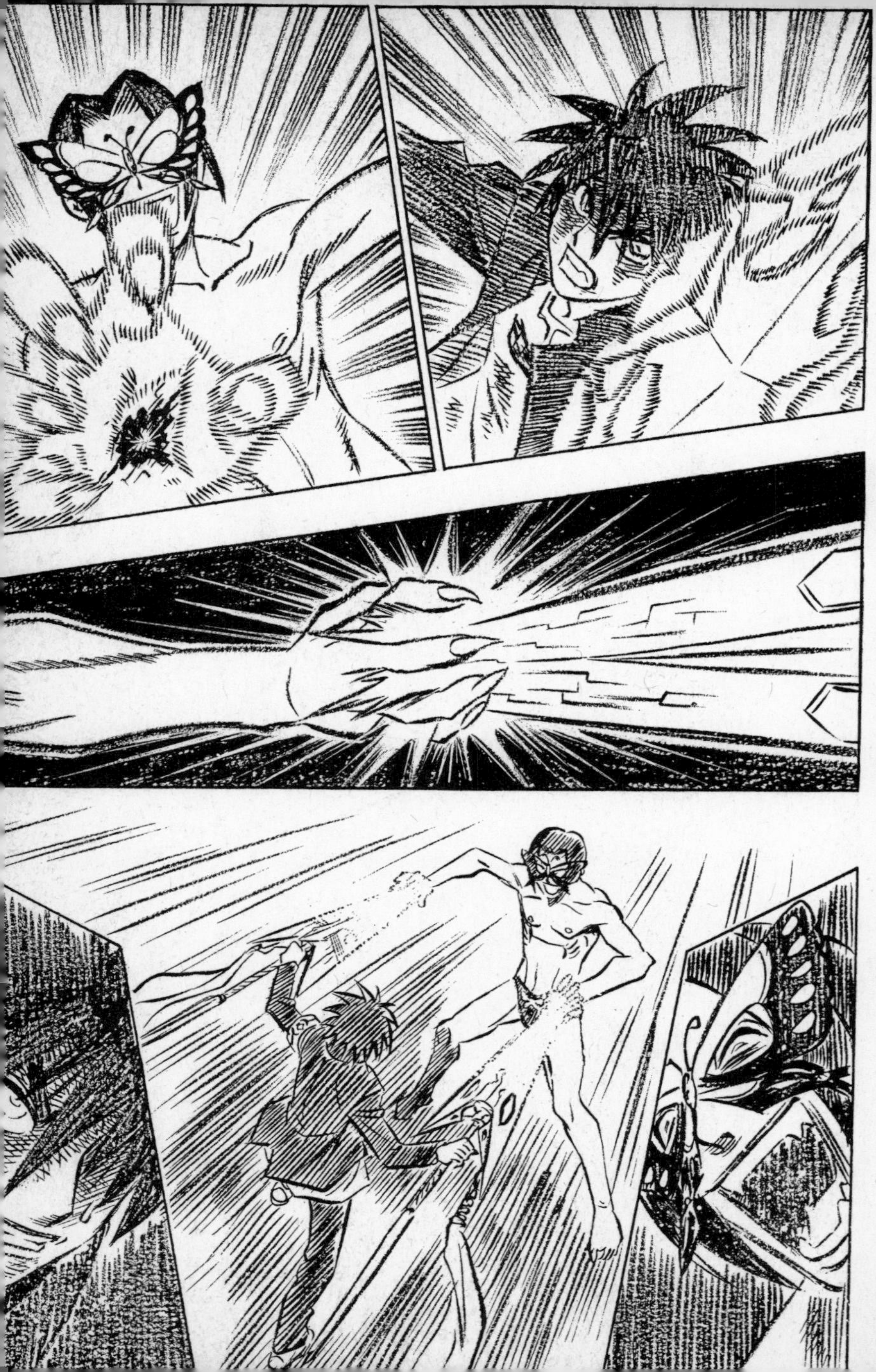

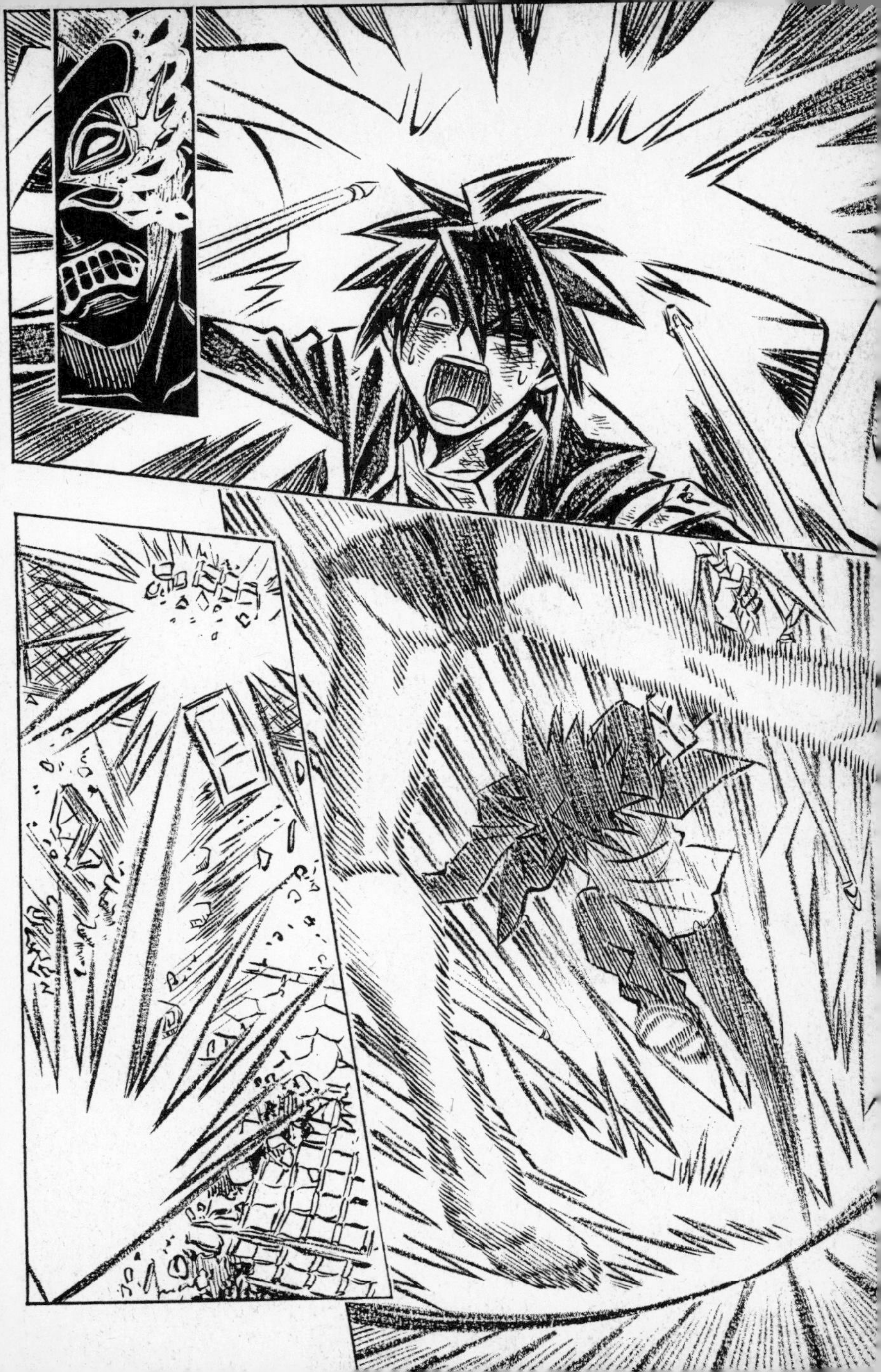

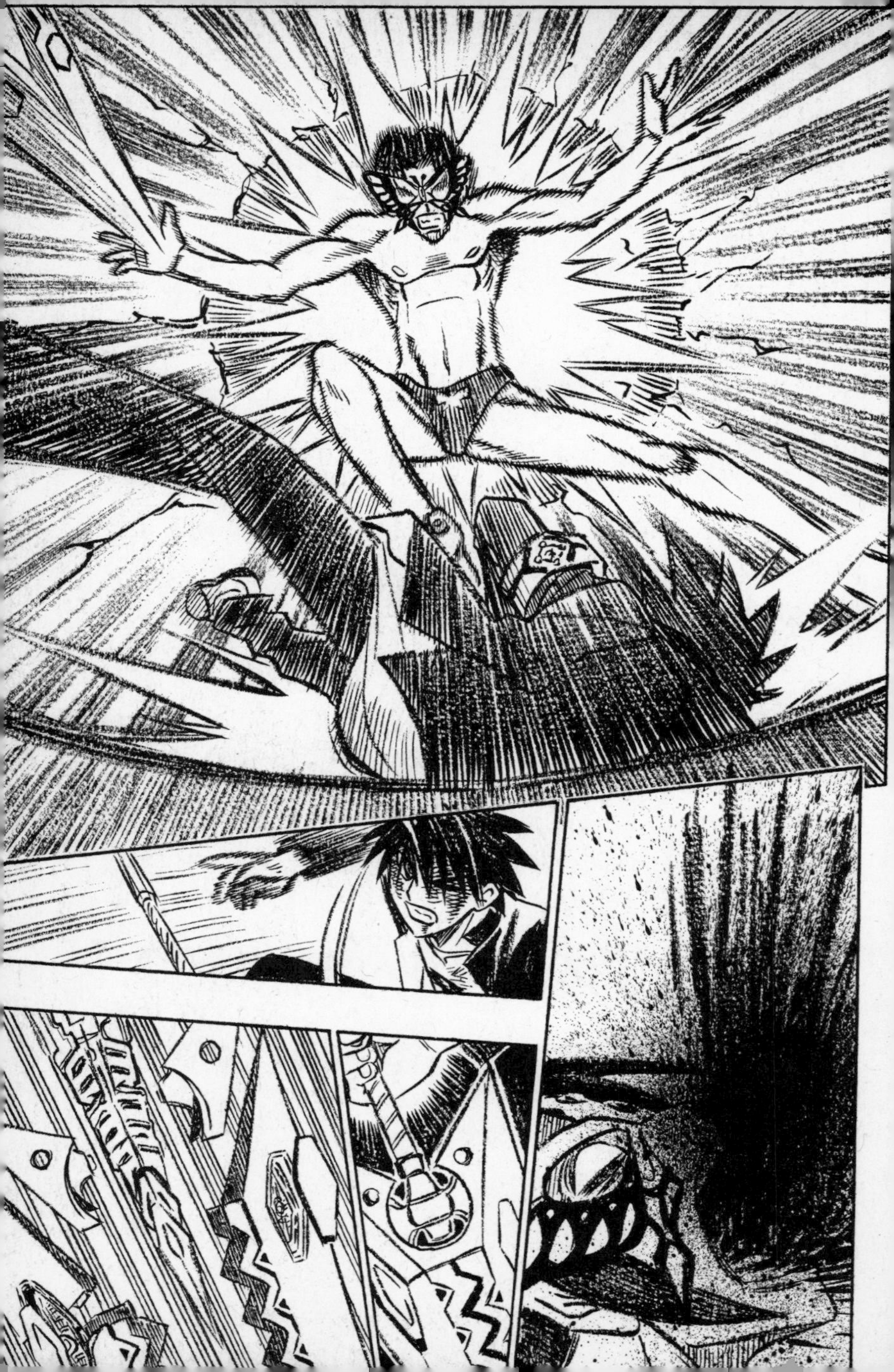

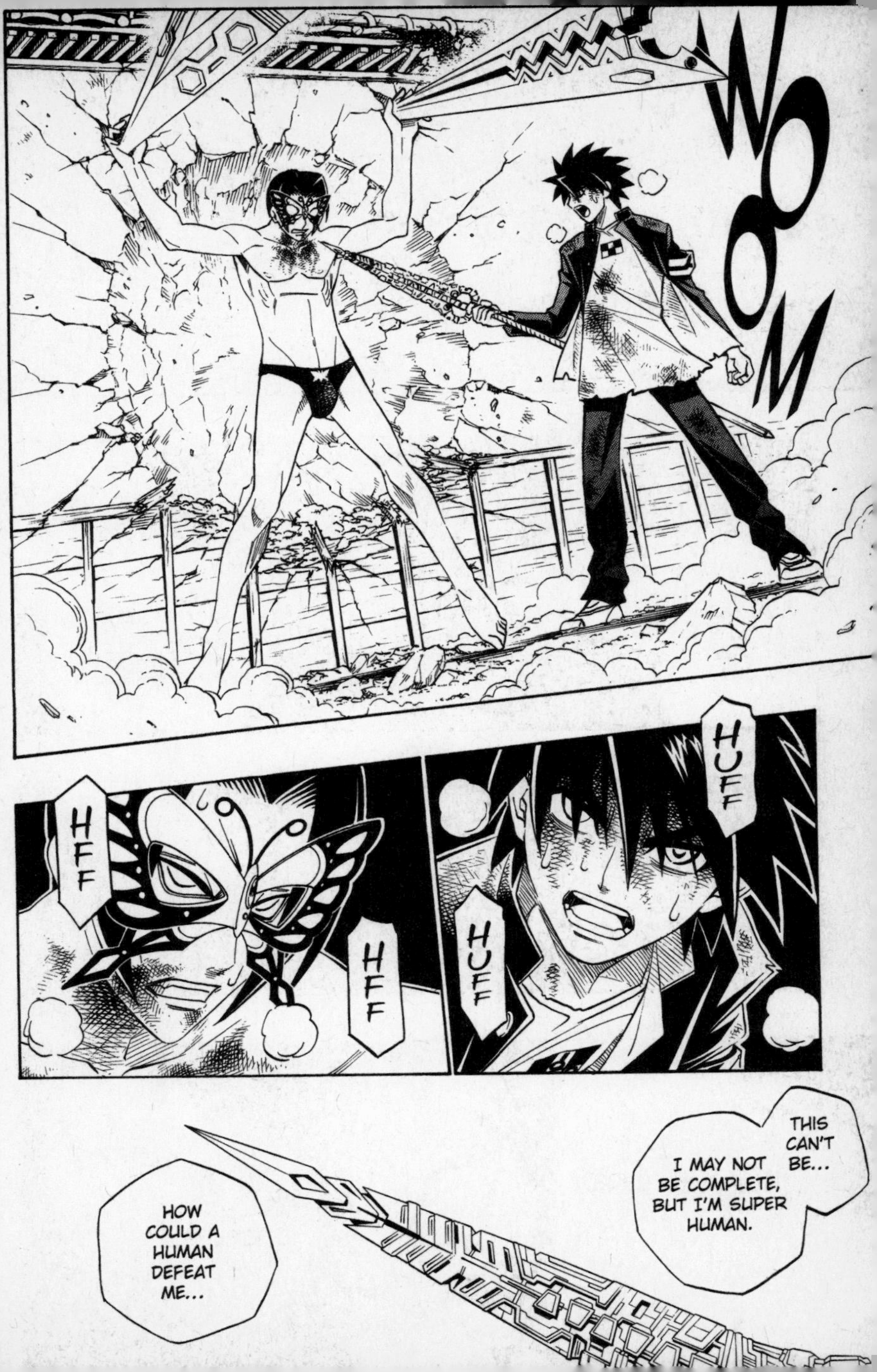
WOOM
HUFF
HUFF
HFF
HFF
THIS CAN'T BE...
I MAY NOT BE COMPLETE, BUT I'M SUPER HUMAN.
HOW COULD A HUMAN DEFEAT ME...

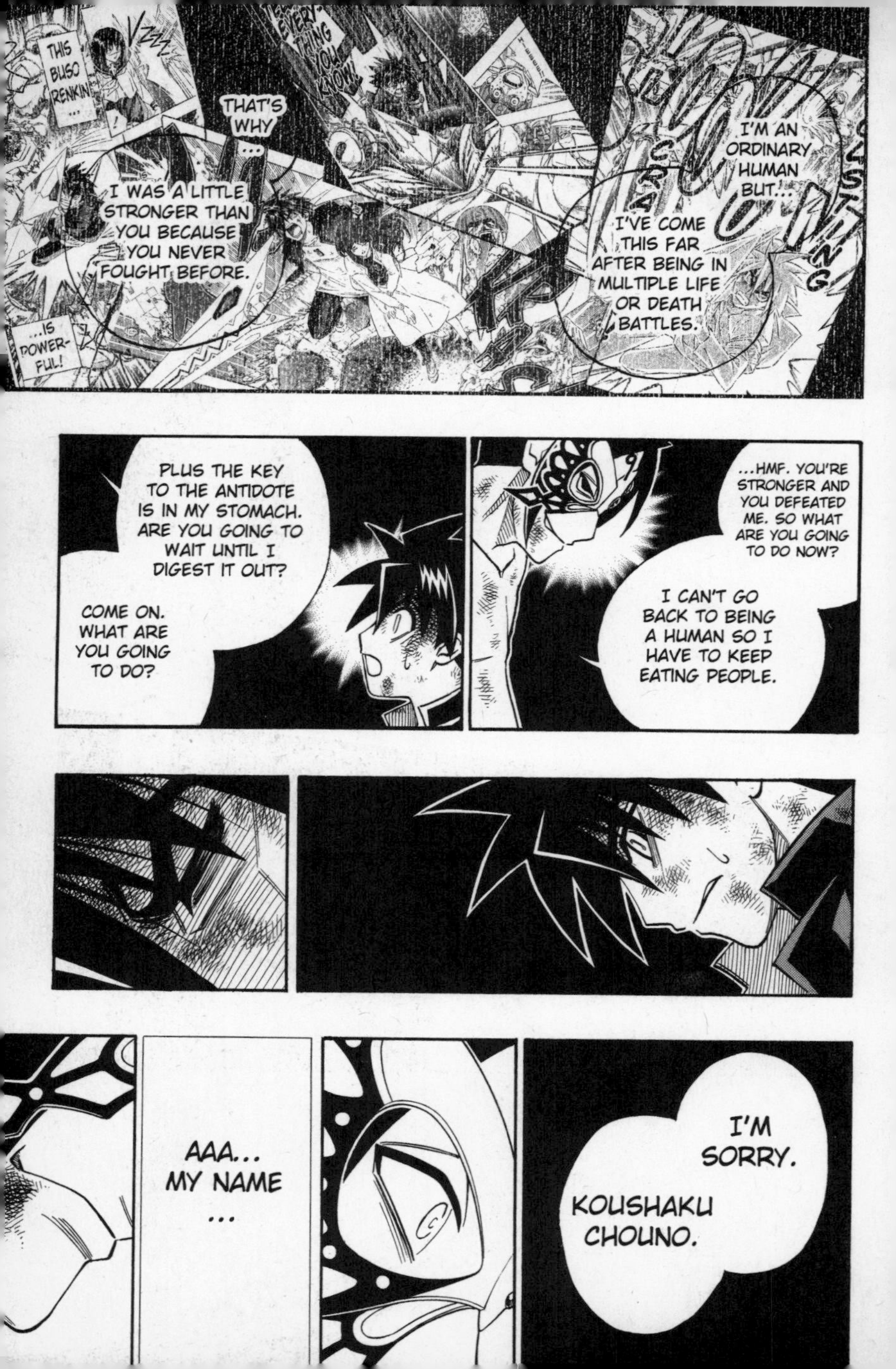

I'M AN ORDINARY HUMAN BUT...
I'VE COME THIS FAR AFTER BEING IN MULTIPLE LIFE OR DEATH BATTLES.
EVERY-THING YOU KNOW!
THAT'S WHY...
I WAS A LITTLE STRONGER THAN YOU BECAUSE YOU NEVER FOUGHT BEFORE.
THIS BUSO RENKIN...
...IS POWER-FUL!
...HMF. YOU'RE STRONGER AND YOU DEFEATED ME. SO WHAT ARE YOU GOING TO DO NOW?
I CAN'T GO BACK TO BEING A HUMAN SO I HAVE TO KEEP EATING PEOPLE.
PLUS THE KEY TO THE ANTIDOTE IS IN MY STOMACH. ARE YOU GOING TO WAIT UNTIL I DIGEST IT OUT?
COME ON. WHAT ARE YOU GOING TO DO?
I'M SORRY.
KOUSHAKU CHOUNO.
AAA... MY NAME ...

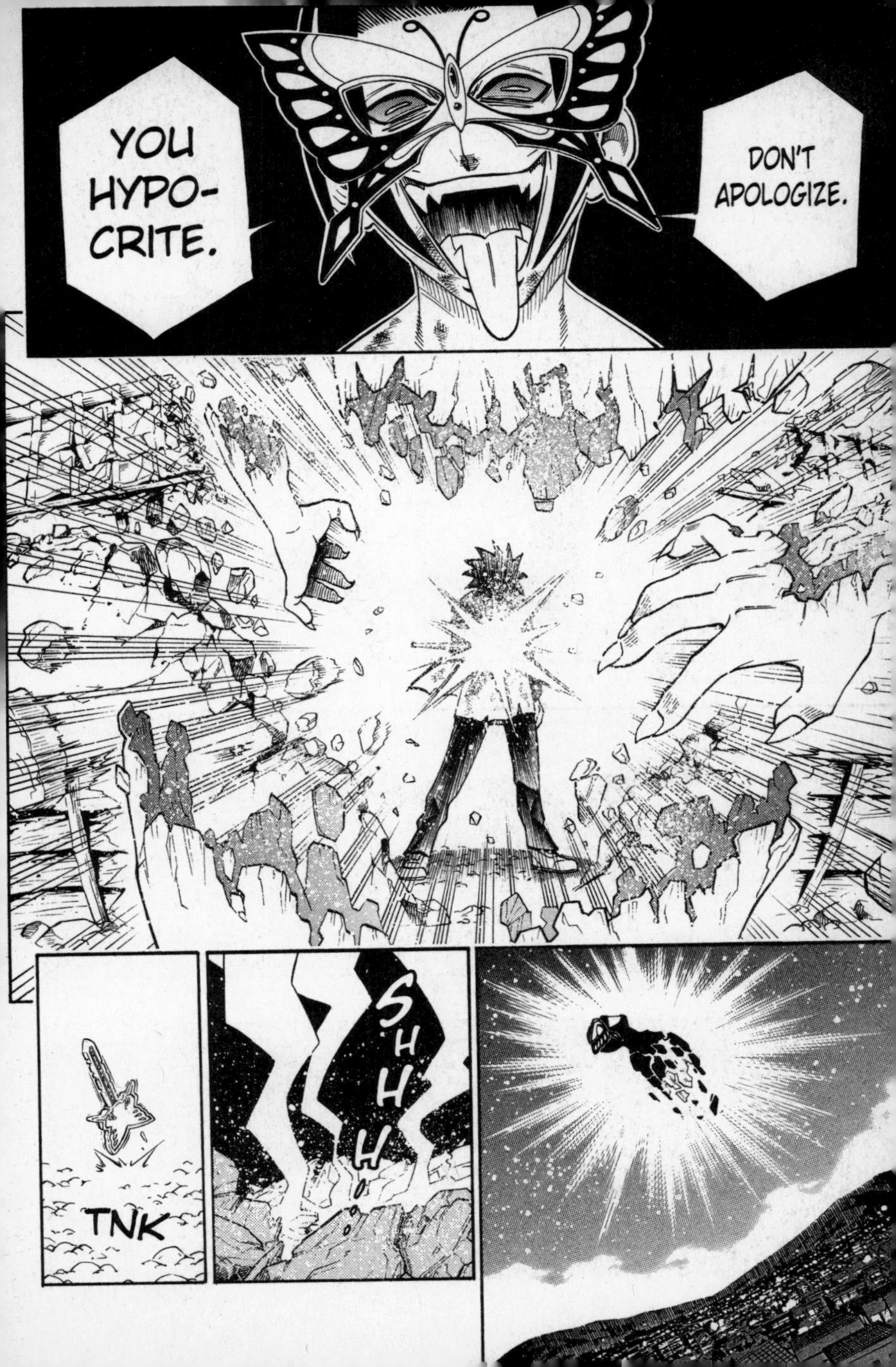
DON'T APOLOGIZE.
YOU HYPOCRITE.
SHHH
TNK

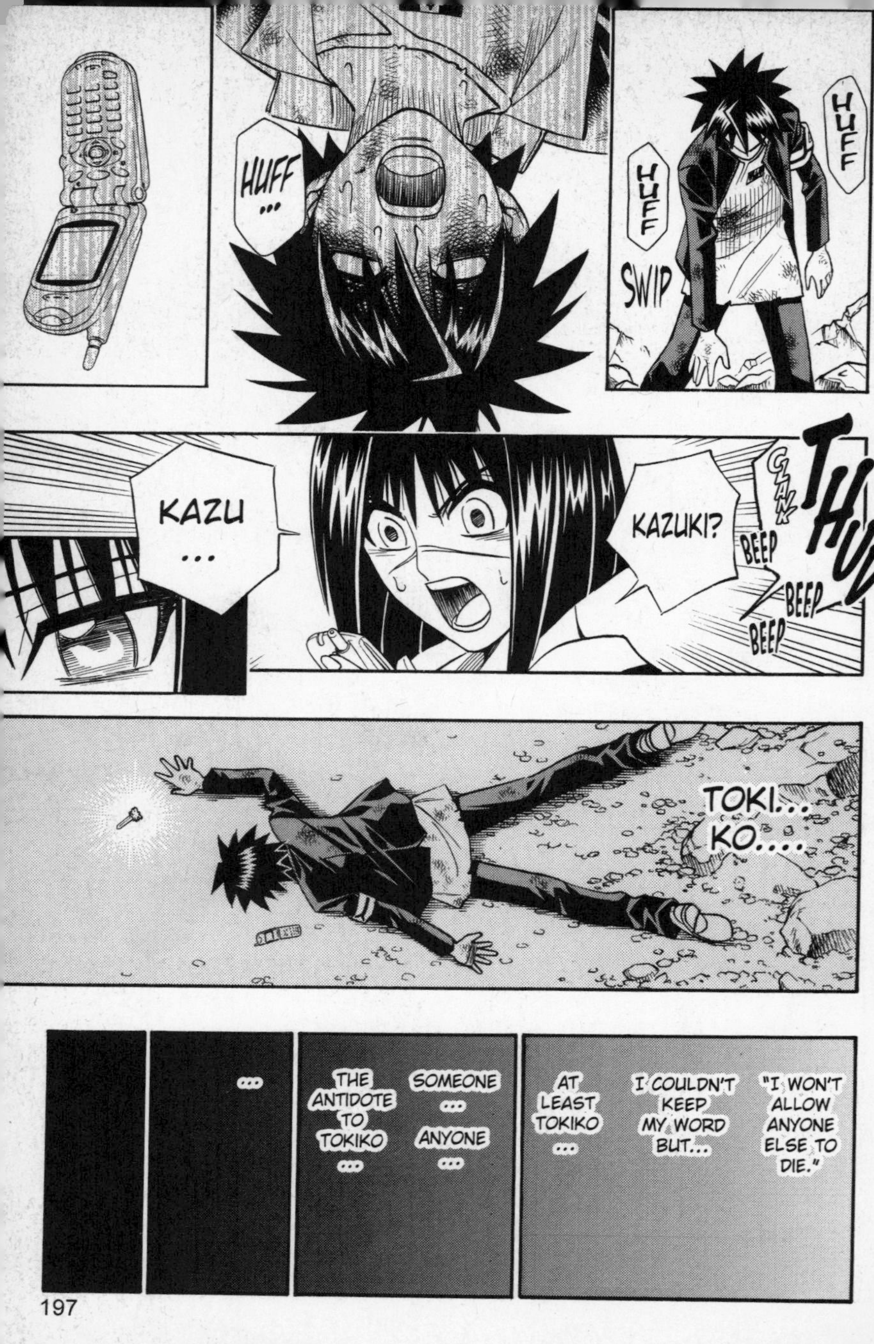
HUFF
HUFF
SWIP
HUFF...
THUD
CLANK
BEEP
BEEP
BEEP
KAZUKI?
KAZU...
TOKI... KO....
"I WON'T ALLOW ANYONE ELSE TO DIE."
I COULDN'T KEEP MY WORD BUT...
AT LEAST TOKIKO...
SOMEONE... ANYONE...
THE ANTIDOTE TO TOKIKO...
...

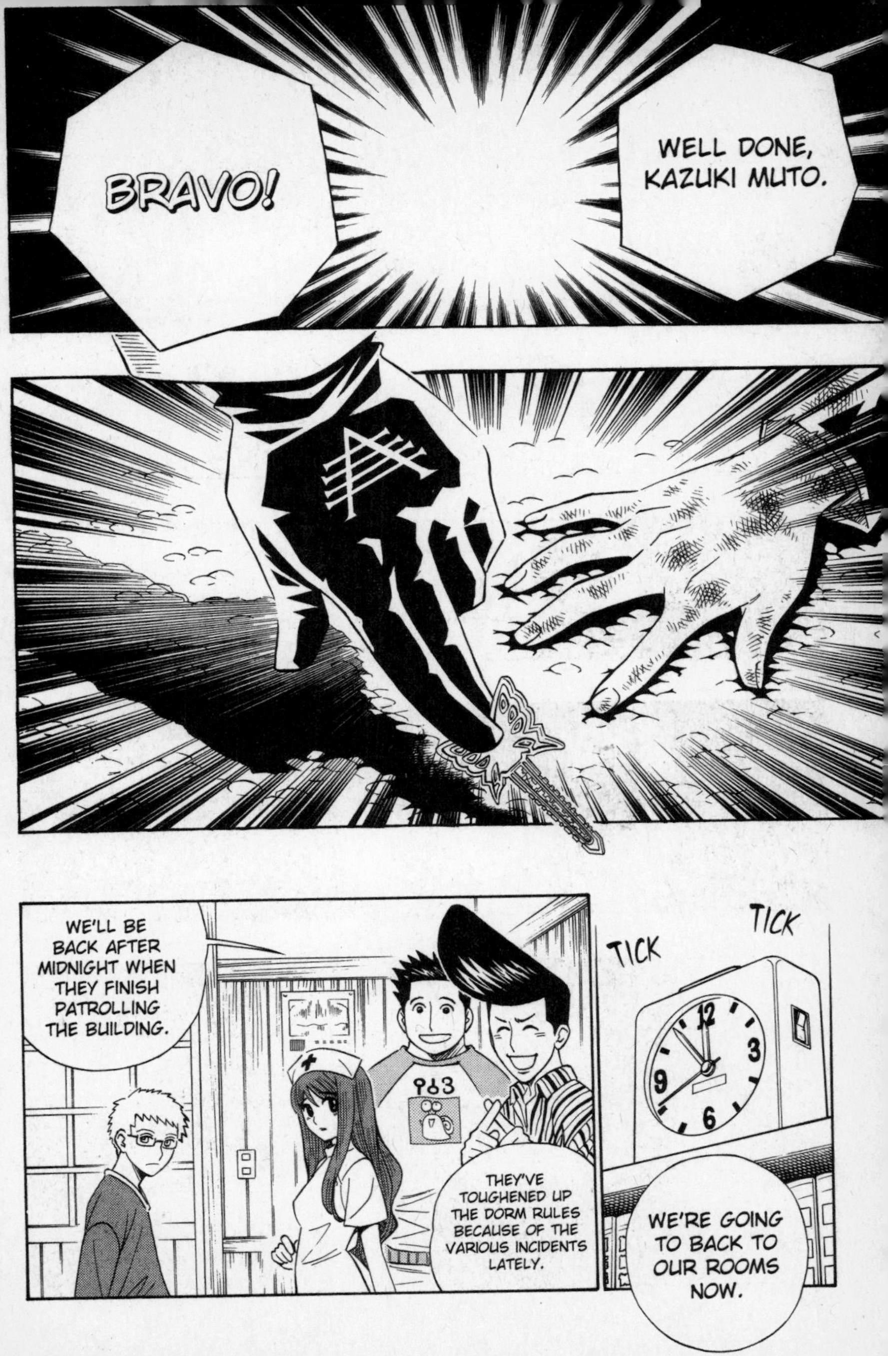
WELL DONE, KAZUKI MUTO.
BRAVO!
TICK
TICK
WE'RE GOING TO BACK TO OUR ROOMS NOW.
WE'LL BE BACK AFTER MIDNIGHT WHEN THEY FINISH PATROLLING THE BUILDING.
THEY'VE TOUGHENED UP THE DORM RULES BECAUSE OF THE VARIOUS INCIDENTS LATELY.

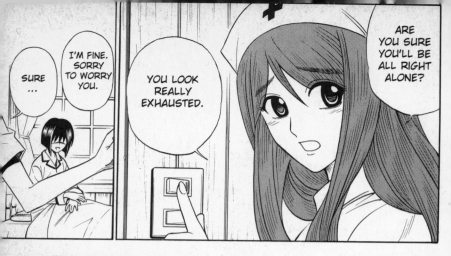

ARE YOU SURE YOU'LL BE ALL RIGHT ALONE?

YOU LOOK REALLY EXHAUSTED.

I'M FINE. SORRY TO WORRY YOU.

SURE ...

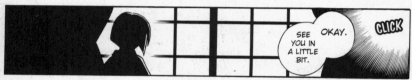

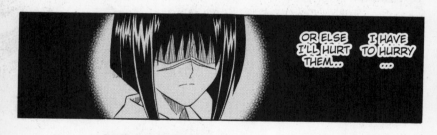

OKAY.

SEE YOU IN A LITTLE BIT.

CLICK

I HAVE TO HURRY ...

OR ELSE I'LL HURT THEM...

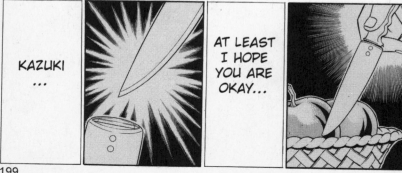

KAZUKI ...

AT LEAST I HOPE YOU ARE OKAY...

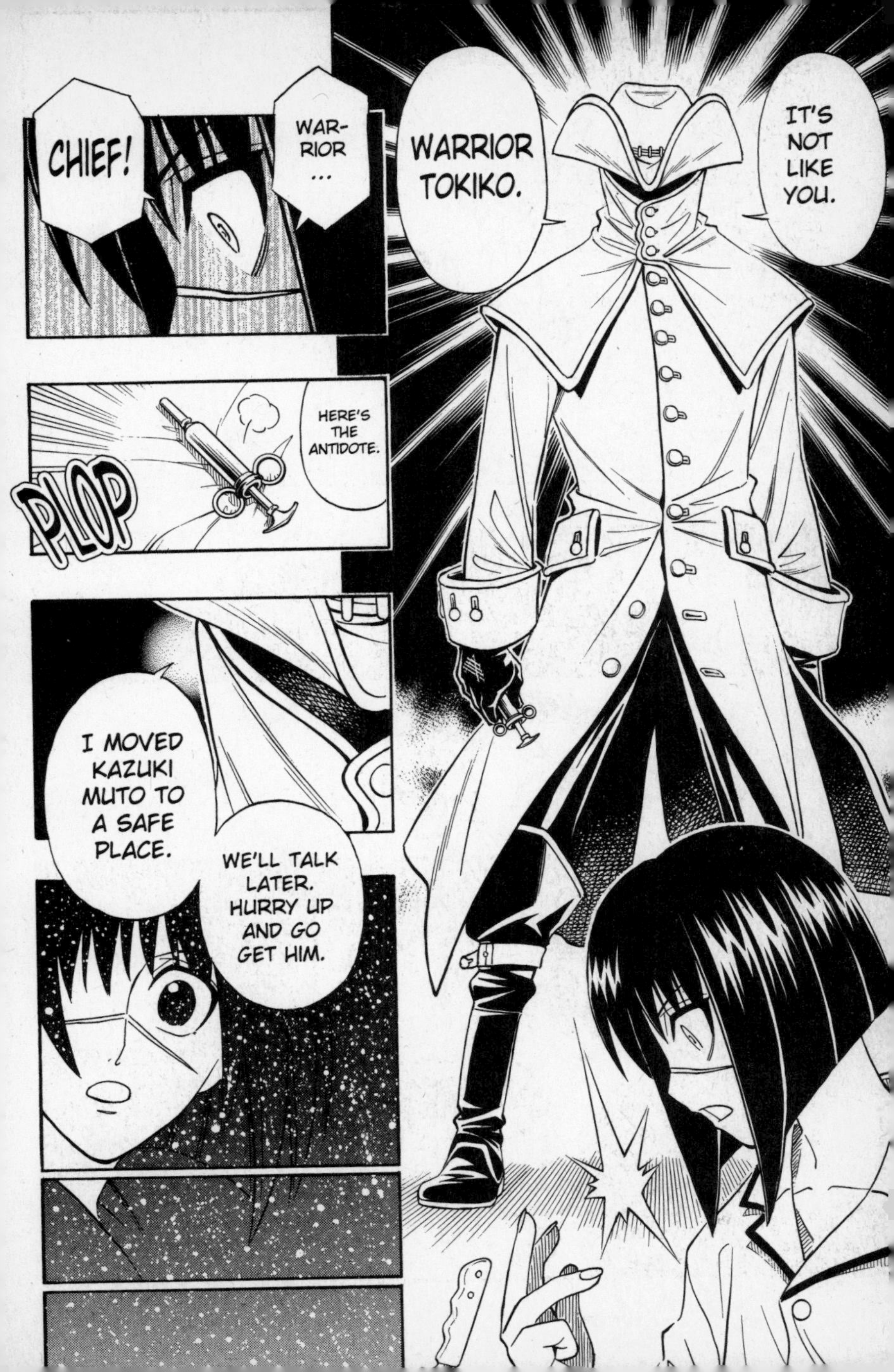
WARRIOR TOKIKO.
IT'S NOT LIKE YOU.
WAR-RIOR ...
CHIEF!
HERE'S THE ANTIDOTE.
PLOP
I MOVED KAZUKI MUTO TO A SAFE PLACE.
WE'LL TALK LATER. HURRY UP AND GO GET HIM.

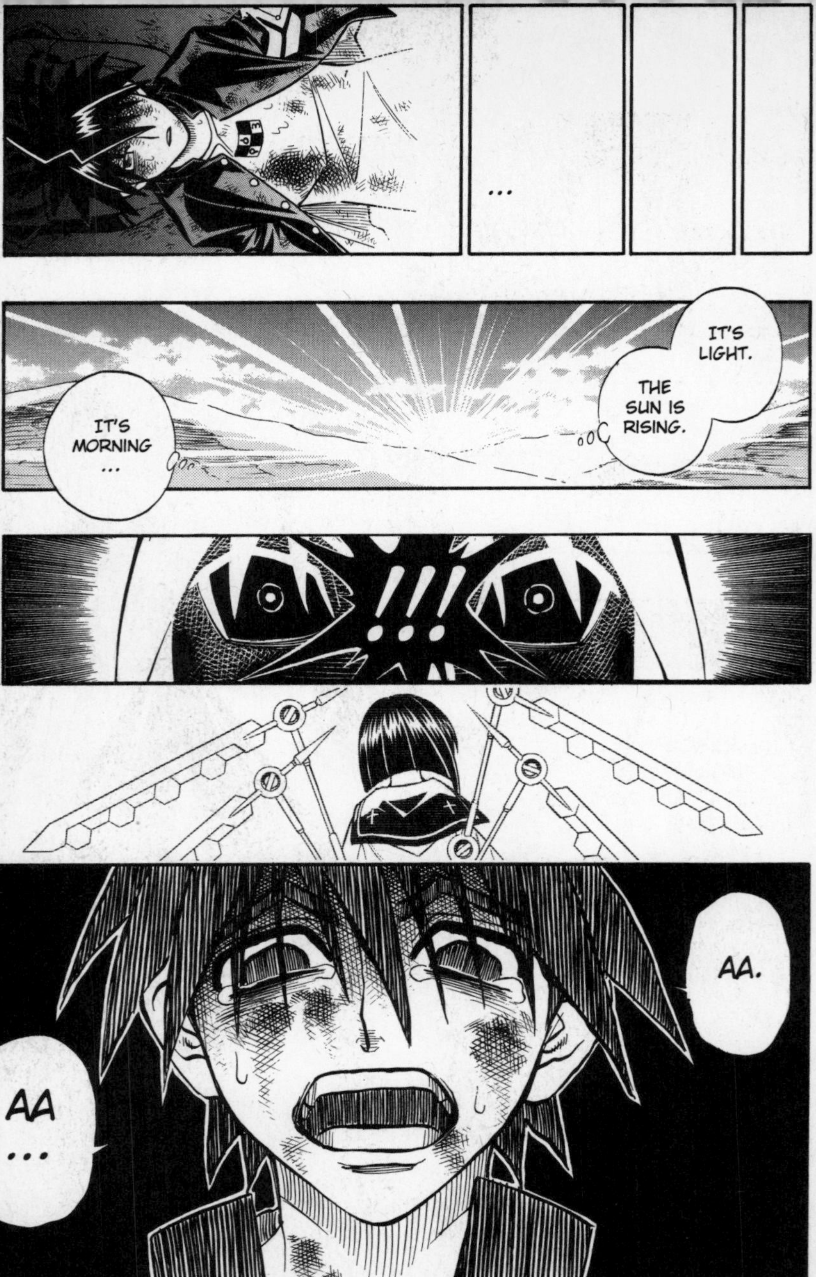
...
IT'S LIGHT.
THE SUN IS RISING.
IT'S MORNING ...
!!!
AA.
AA ...

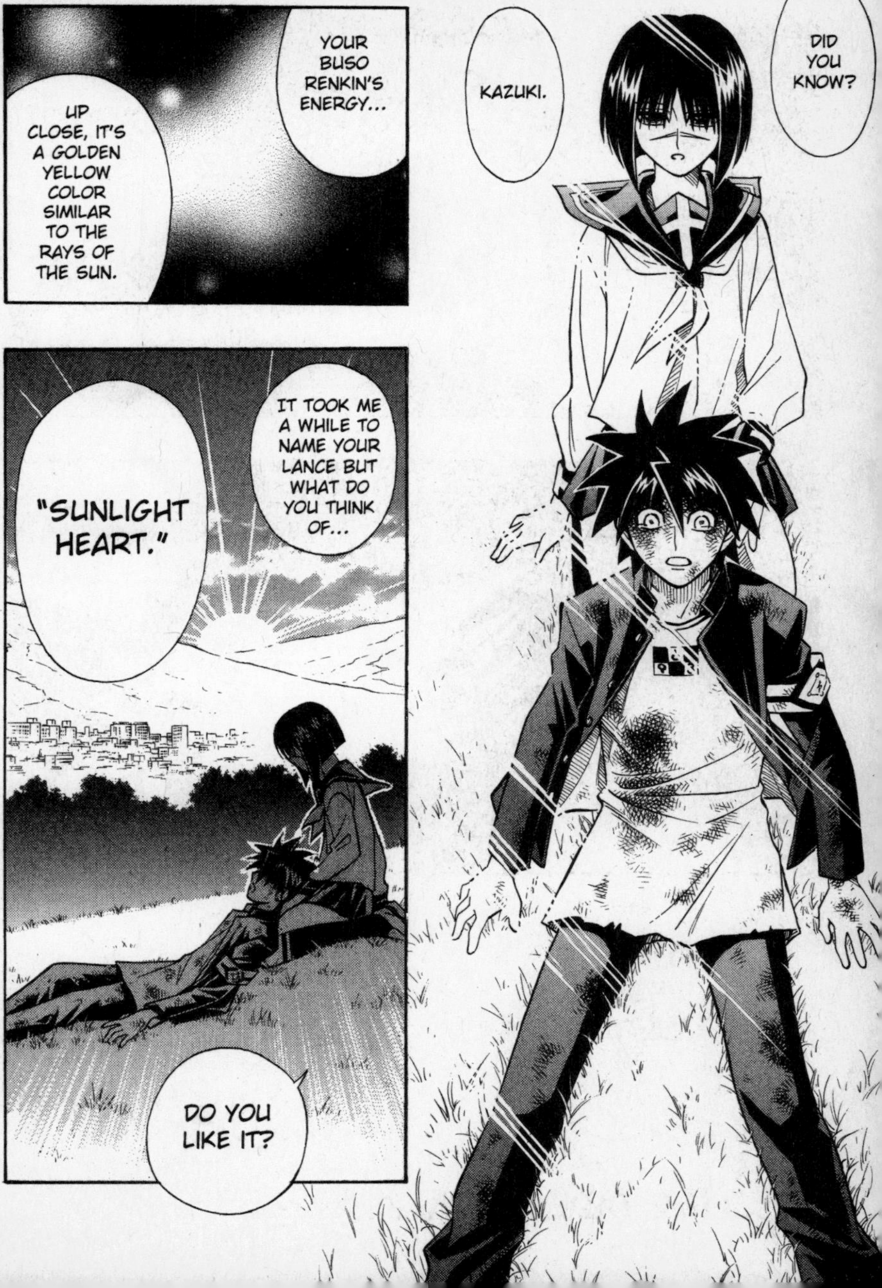
DID YOU KNOW?
KAZUKI.
YOUR BUSO RENKIN'S ENERGY...
UP CLOSE, IT'S A GOLDEN YELLOW COLOR SIMILAR TO THE RAYS OF THE SUN.
IT TOOK ME A WHILE TO NAME YOUR LANCE BUT WHAT DO YOU THINK OF...
"SUNLIGHT HEART."
DO YOU LIKE IT?

READ THIS WAY

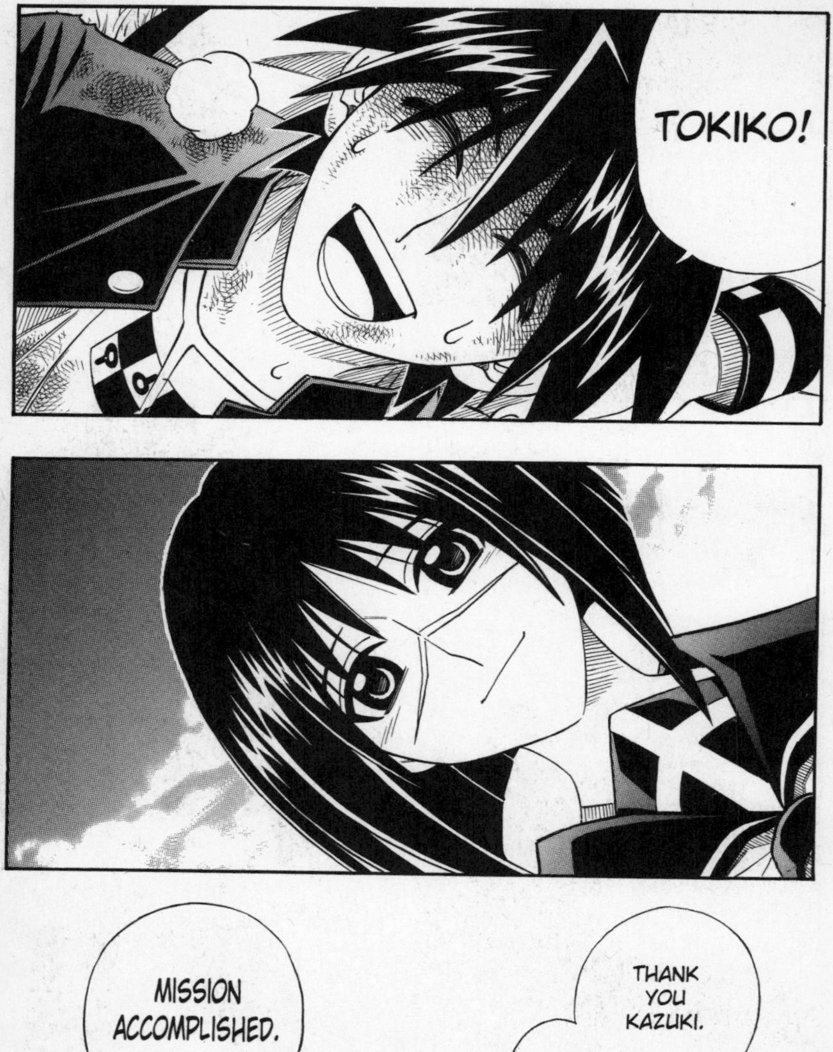
TOKIKO!
THANK YOU KAZUKI.
IT'S ...
MISSION ACCOMPLISHED.

VOLUME 2: FADE TO BLACK (THE END)

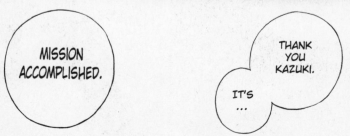

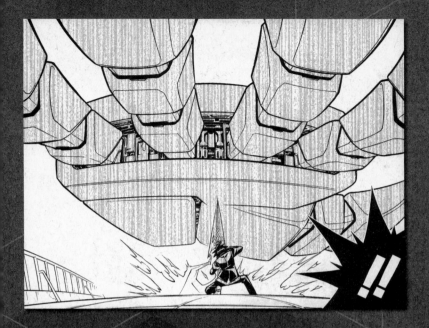

Coming Next Volume

An old enemy with a slight butterfly fetish once thought to be destroyed makes a surprising comeback! Impressed with Kazuki's progress in such a short time, Captain Bravo recruits him as a full-fledged Alchemist Warrior! And he orders Tokiko to enlist in the same school as Kazuki! All this, plus the appearance of a new Homuculus that has the power to use a Buso Renkin!

Available in December 2006!

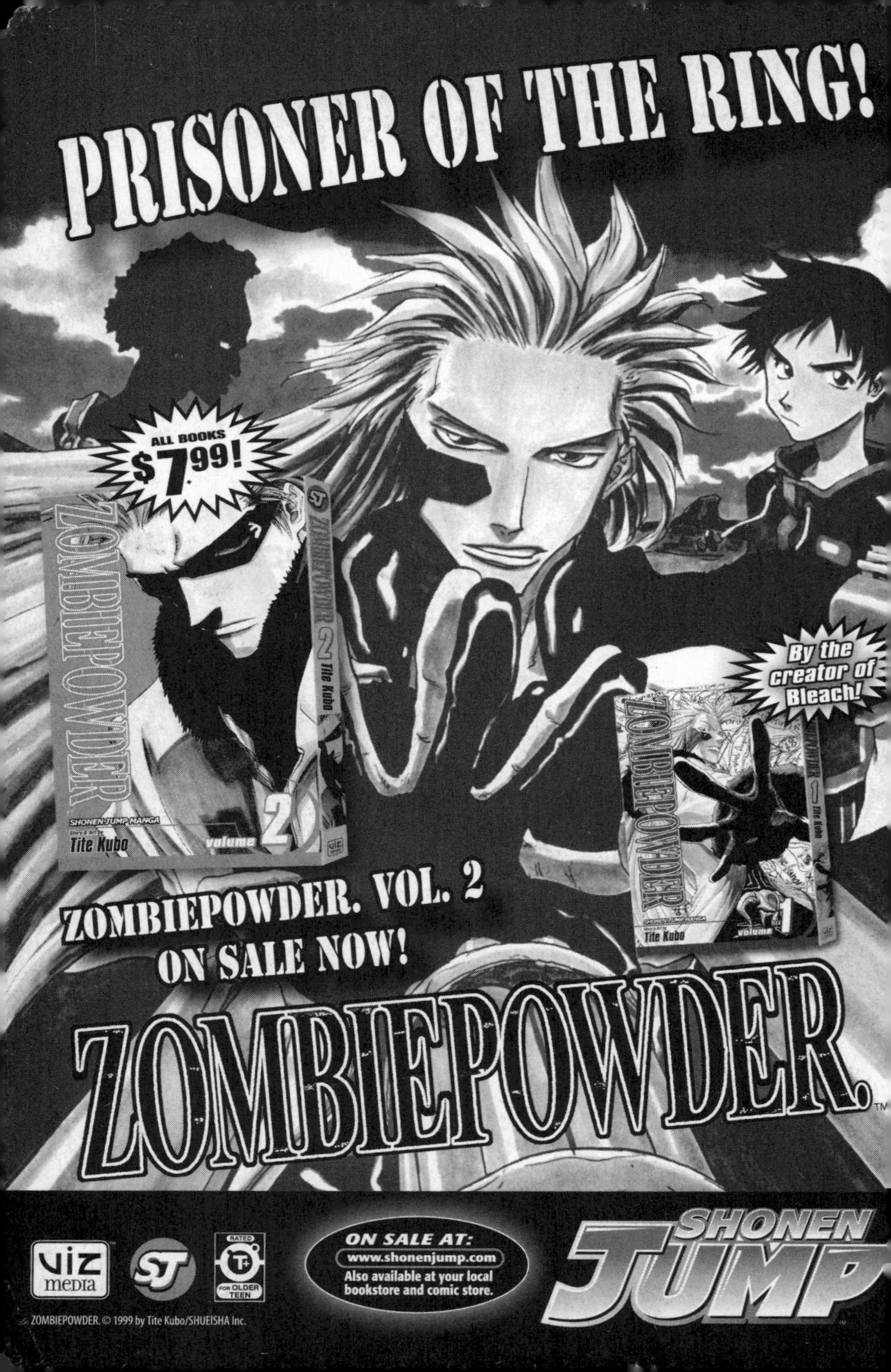
PRISONER OF THE RING!
ALL BOOKS $7.99!
ZOMBIEPOWDER 2 Tite Kubo
SHONEN JUMP MANGA
Story & Art by Tite Kubo
volume 2
By the creator of Bleach!
ZOMBIEPOWDER 1 Tite Kubo
volume 1
ZOMBIEPOWDER. VOL. 2
ON SALE NOW!
ZOMBIEPOWDER.™
viz media
SJ
RATED T+ FOR OLDER TEEN
ON SALE AT:
www.shonenjump.com
Also available at your local bookstore and comic store.
SHONEN JUMP
ZOMBIEPOWDER. © 1999 by Tite Kubo/SHUEISHA Inc.

Tell us what y...
SHONEN JUMP manga!

Our survey is now available online.
Go to: www.SHONENJUMP.com/mangasurvey

Help us make our product
offering better!

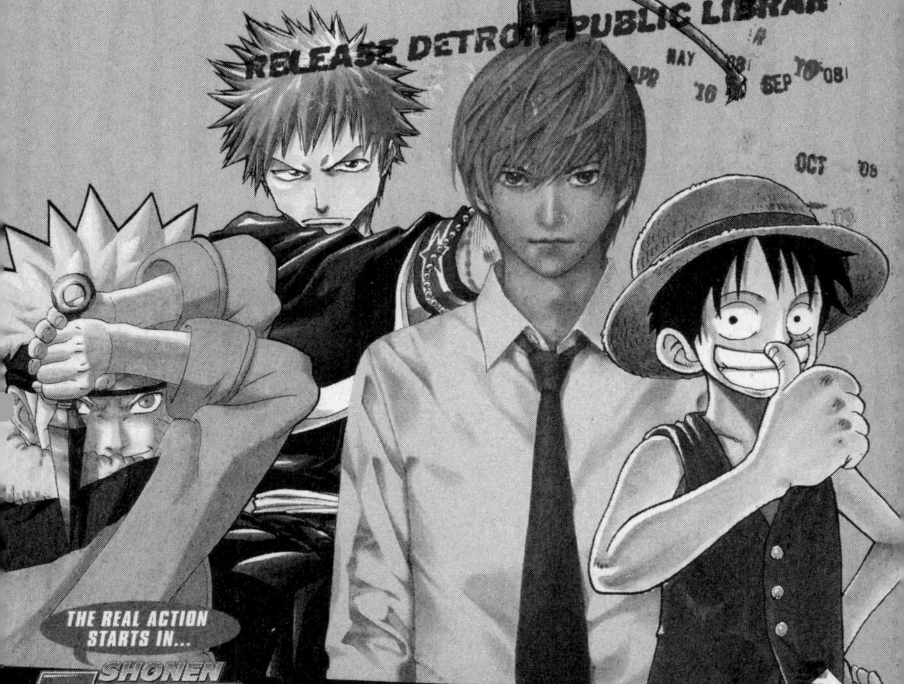

THE REAL ACTION STARTS IN...

SHONEN JUMP
THE WORLD'S MOST POPULAR MANGA
www.shonenjump.com

ST ADVANCED

ST